International Management

BRIDGWATER COLLEGE LRC

This book must be returned on or before the latest date shown below. It may be renewed for a further period provided it is not reserved by another reader. Renewals may also be made by telephone on 01278 441223.

DATE DUE	DATE DUE
- 2 FEB 2011	
2 3 FEB 2011	
2 3 MAR 2011	
2 7 FEB 2012	
1 7 JUN 2014	
1 5 OCT 2014	
- 7 JAN 2015	

FOURTH EDITION

International Management

CULTURE AND BEYOND

Richard Mead and Tim G Andrews

A John Wiley and Sons, Ltd., Publication

Published in 2009 by   John Wiley & Sons Ltd, The Atrium, Southern Gate, Chichester,
                              West Sussex PO19 8SQ, England
                              Telephone (+44) 1243 779777

Email (for orders and customer service enquiries): cs-books@wiley.co.uk

Visit our Home Page on www.wiley.com

Other Wiley Editorial Offices

John Wiley & Sons Inc., 111 River Street, Hoboken, NJ 07030, USA

Jossey-Bass, 989 Market Street, San Francisco, CA 94103-1741, USA

Wiley-VCH Verlag GmbH, Boschstr. 12, D-69469 Weinheim, Germany

John Wiley & Sons Australia Ltd, 42 McDougall Street, Milton, Queensland 4064, Australia

John Wiley & Sons (Asia) Pte Ltd, 2 Clementi Loop #02-01, Jin Xing Distripark, Singapore 129809

John Wiley & Sons Canada Ltd, 6045 Freemont Blvd. Mississauga, Ontario, L5R 4J3 Canada

Wiley also publishes its books in a variety of electronic formats. Some content that appears in print may not be available in electronic books.

Library of Congress Cataloging-in-Publication Data

Mead, Richard.
  International management: culture and beyond / Richard Mead and Tim G. Andrews.
    p. cm.
  Include bibliographical references and index.
  ISBN 978-1-4051-7399-5 (pbk. : acid-free paper)   1. International business enterprises–Management–Social aspects.   2. Corporate culture.   3. Intercultural communication.   I. Andrews, Tim G., 1968–   II. Title.
  HD62.4.M4 2009
  658′.049–dc22   2009011961

British Library Cataloguing in Publication Data

A catalogue record for this book is available from the British Library

ISBN 978-1-4051-7399-5(P/B)

Typeset in 10/12.5 Rotis Serif by Aptara Inc., New Delhi, India
Printed and bound in Great Britain by CPI Antony Rowe, Ch

CONTENTS

PREFACE

In response to a survey of Fortune 1000 companies enquiring about "the biggest barrier in doing business in the world market", cultural differences ranked at the top of the list (*The Guardian*, September 20, 2007). The report suggested that the failure to recognize these differences was the most common cause of failure for cross-national enterprises. (Other barriers ranked were the concerns of law, price competition, information, languages, delivery, foreign currencies, and time differences.)

Members of different cultures express different values and priorities when they make and implement decisions. These values influence work relationships, whether between superior and subordinate, peers, international joint venture partners, managers in head-quarters and subsidiaries, and others.

How do international managers recognize the opportunities and threats that cultural difference presents? And how do they respond?

The answers do not lie simply in learning more culture. The influence of culture is never stable and its effect on behavior can never be precisely predicted. Further, a range of other factors may intervene. These include the social and business environments, industry and organizational interests, and the personalities of the people concerned. The problem for the manager is deciding which have priority in any given situation.

Culture is SOMETIMES very significant; and on other occasions it is not, and the other factors are more so. The manager needs the skills to recognize WHEN culture is significant, to weigh its influence against that of the other factors, and then respond appropriately. This book aims to equip managers with these skills.

A: Who is the Book for?

Students and managers can find the study of cross-cultural management frustrating unless it is related to some other aspect of the management syllabus. The book is recommended for those majoring in international management. It is also aimed at those with interests in:

- International human resource management;
- Strategic planning;
- Cross-cultural communication.

The globalization of business means that new managers are almost certain to work and interact with members of other cultures during their careers. They are increasingly likely to cooperate in global and virtual teams. This is true in headquarters as much as in the subsidiary or international joint venture.

Whether or not all cultures are converging to the point at which the differences are so slight that they can be safely ignored is a matter of opinion, and arguments can be found on both sides. The practical answer for today is that any final convergence is still a long way in the future. Today's manager cannot afford to ignore the obvious differences. These are real, and vitally affect the workplace.

B: What Makes the Book Different?

In addition to the core topics discussed in most textbooks on international management, this book includes others that are not normally discussed in this context. They include:

- The influence of culture on family companies;
- Informal patronage, *Guanxi* and *Wasda*;
- The tension between globalization and localization;
- E-communication;
- Convergence and divergence in subsidiary cultures;
- The relevance of Western human resource management to other cultures;
- Corporate brand control – the lynchpin of the relationship between contemporary headquarters and the subsidiary.

Many MBA and other management students have to write a dissertation or report as part of the assessment exercise. This book includes an Appendix on planning the dissertation.

C: What's New About the Fourth Edition?

This edition is co-written. In order to give the book wider scope and new insights, Richard Mead has been joined by Tim Andrews.

All topics have been revised and updated. The increasing importance of China and the Middle East in international business is recognized.

Some of the topics covered in single chapters in the Third Edition are now given two. These include cultural analysis (now in Chapters 2 and 3, and updated) and the planning and implementation of strategy (now Chapters 14 and 15).

All chapters are considerably shorter than in previous editions, but retain their core messages.

This edition consists of 24 chapters, as opposed to 18 in the Third Edition. The entirely new chapters are:

Chapter 16: E-Communication
Chapter 19: Managing Human Resources
Chapter 22: The Expatriate Brand Manager
Chapter 23: The Culture of the Subsidiary: Convergence and Divergence

There are also new sections on growth strategies, mergers and acquisitions, and corporate social responsibility.

Almost all the Introductions, Exercises and Cases are new. The Bibliography is radically revised and updated.

D: How are the Chapters Organized?

The material is organized in four parts. Part One consists of an introductory first chapter. In Part Two, Chapters 2–12 focus on cross-cultural management, and examine how far culture influences behavior in the workplace and the internal systems of the company. In Part Three, Chapters 13–22 focus on global and strategic issues in international business, and emphasize the influence of non-cultural factors on decision-making and implementation. Part Four consists of two concluding chapters, 23 on cultural convergence and divergence in the subsidiary, and 24 on ethics. These two chapters rework many of the themes introduced earlier. Short case studies follow each part.

Finally, there is an Appendix on planning a management dissertation.

The *Instructors' Manual* that accompanies this book suggests alternative arrangements by which the instructor can structure teaching courses based on it.

ACKNOWLEDGMENTS

The four editions of this book were written in a range of countries – the USA, Thailand, England, Scotland, Germany, Spain and Portugal.

In particular, we benefited from the support and services offered by:

- Middlesex Business School, Middlesex University, London, UK
- The Kellogg School, Northwestern University, Illinois, USA
- SasinGIBA, Bangkok, Thailand
- The School of Oriental and African Studies, University of London, UK
- Strathclyde Business School, Strathclyde University, Glasgow, UK

Teachers and students have contributed useful comments on previous editions, for which we are grateful. We are indebted to Colin McClune for permission to use the case for Chapter 24.

This book is for our families; Kullada and Paron, Air and Mae.

Dr Richard Mead
Centre of Finance and Management Studies, School of Oriental and African Studies, University of London, UK E-mail: rm14@soas.ac.uk

Dr Tim Andrews
Department of Management, Strathclyde Business School, University of Strathclyde, UK E-mail: Tim.andrews@strath.ac.uk

School of Oriental and African Studies, University of London

PART ONE

Introduction

CHAPTER ONE
International Management and Culture

1.1   Introduction

The book deals with international management, and has four parts. This part consists of a single chapter and is introductory. In Part Two, Chapters 2–12 deal with cross-cultural management topics, and focus on the influence that national culture has on arrangements within the organization. In Part Three, Chapters 13–22 deal with international management topics, and focus on the tensions between the organization and its international and global environment. To conclude, Part Four deals with cultural convergence and divergence in the subsidiary in Chapter 23, and ethics in Chapter 24.

1.1.1   When is national culture important, and when not?

Some management scholars claim that national culture is the predominant force driving ALL decisions made in human organizations. But others dispute the notion that culture has any relevance to management at all.

This book rejects both extremes as oversimplistic. It takes the point made by Francis Fukuyama in a newspaper article (our italics) most economists do not accept that culture can explain economic growth, and treat culture as:

> a residual category in which lazy social scientists take refuge when they can't develop a more rigorous theory. There is indeed reason to be cautious about using culture to explain economic and political outcomes. *Culture is only one of many factors that determine the success of a society.* [1]

We argue that culture is always LIKELY to be an influence on how an organization responds to its environment and structures, roles and relationships, and how its members make decisions, communicate, and respond to organizational structures. But in any particular event, culture may not be a factor, and even when it is, may not be the ONLY significant factor. Other possible influences include factors internal and external to the organization. Those internal include the organizational strategy and the personality of the chief executive officer (CEO); those external to (other than) national culture include economic conditions, markets, technologies, the activities of competitors, and so on. (Section 1.2 gives a more complete list, and shows how internal factors are moderated by the external.)

The problem for the international manager is to decide *under what circumstances is culture likely to be a significant factor and when not?* In any particular event, he/she needs to answer particular questions:

- How much weight should be given to culture as against other factors when explaining or predicting behavior?
- How much weight should be given to culture when seeking to respond to, or cause, behavior?

The book aims to develop skills of identifying when national culture is significant, and has to be taken into account in making and implementing plans, and when it can be ignored.

An understanding of culture and its influences does not guarantee successful decision-making; but it does reduce the possibilities of failure.

The book is principally aimed at decision-making in the private sector. But it also deals with topics relevant to managers employed by state sectors and international not-for-profit organizations. These include organizations with an extra-national identity (the United Nations, World Health Organization, the World Bank); national organizations such as embassies and cultural organizations (the British Council, Alliance Française, Goethe Institute); and non-governmental organizations (Amnesty International, OXFAM, Medicins Sans Frontières)

1.2   Factors that Influence Decision-making

Here is a list of SOME of the internal factors that influence decision-making within the organization:

- The CEO's psychological make-up;
- The organizational strategy;

- Resources (financial, plant, staff, technology) already secured;
- Organizational history;
- Policies and systems;
- ORGANIZATIONAL CULTURE.

The EXTERNAL factors include

- decisions made by competitors;
- decisions made by suppliers;
- decisions made by customers;
- labor markets;
- technology;
- the national, regional and world economies;
- financial markets;
- local, national, regional, and international politics;
- laws and regulations;
- infrastructure factors (transport, power, etc.);
- trade unions;
- consumer groups;
- ethical and religious systems;
- factors in the green environment;
- industry norms;
- national culture.

It might seem that the internal and external influences can be easily distinguished – as in Figure 1.1. However, this model provides only a broad generalization. The internal F1 factors are themselves influenced by the wider environment. For example, the formulation and implementation of strategy is influenced by analysis of market factors, the activities of competitors, and the economic environment. The organizational culture is influenced by the national culture; staff resources by the cost and availability of labor available in external markets; and so on. In practice, the boundary between the internal and external factors influencing decision-making in the organization is porous, as is shown in Figure 1.2.   F2

When the company is dealing with a subsidiary or joint venture partner operating in another country, decision-making is influenced by its own environment *and* the environment of this second player. This second environment may be very different. Decision-makers

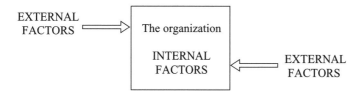

Figure 1.1   The organization in its environment (1)

Figure 1.2   The organization in its environment (2)

at the headquarters/first parent not only need to understand the internal structures and organizational culture of the subsidiary/second company but also need to understand factors of the environment within which it operates, and how these influence its interpretation of the headquarters/first parent's interests and strategy. These environmental factors include

- the other country's laws and regulations;
- its economic profile;
- its market conditions and competition from local companies;
- the other national culture.

The company is continually interpreting its external environment, and reinterpreting its own history, present capacities and possible futures, in terms of how best it can respond to this external environment. The company collects and analyses information about its external and internal environments, and in this sense it functions as a system for making interpretations. Then plans are made and implemented on the basis of the interpretations made.

This means that the importance given to culture, and the descriptive categories used, depend largely on the needs and interests of the person making the interpretation. This person may be a manager, consultant, or scholar. Their needs, and therefore their interpretations, may vary widely.

Here is an example. A communications professor saw the study of culture as vitally important in understanding what happens within the firm and how the firm communicates with its business environment. She was married to a macro-economist, who was employed to analyze and predict trade cycles, and notions of culture were irrelevant to this work. In fact, he dismissed the study of culture as a waste of time. Given their different professional interests and needs, this disagreement on the importance of culture was not surprising. And hence, it is to be expected that scholarly descriptions vary – depending on the interests and objectives of the person making the description. The next chapter gives examples.

1.3   Using Culture

Here we focus on one of the environmental factors listed above, NATIONAL CULTURE – and references below to "culture" are to national culture. Organizational culture is dealt with as a separate phenomenon, in Chapter 5. As we shall see, these two phenomena differ in important aspects, and they should not be confused.

Values in the culture influence the behavior of members of this national community. This means that when members are working together in an organization, their shared culture means that they are likely to respond similarly to events in the world and decisions taken by management.

On the basis of cultural analysis, the manager can assume a degree of uniformity in the values held by group members, and hopes to be able to make generalizations about their behavior. These generalizations give a basis for predicting their future behavior in routine situations.

For example, your understanding of Culture X gives you a basis on which to predict how Culture X negotiators might respond to your offers, concessions, and refusals. It gives you an indication of how Culture X managers might respond to more or less centralized control. It suggests how the Culture X workforce might respond to a new incentive scheme, to group-based activities or an individually based activity, to competition between work groups, to pay-scales based on individual achievement or group achievement.

1.3.1   Personal factors

National culture is not the only factor influencing values and behavior. The individual's personality is molded by such factors as

- PSYCHOLOGICAL characteristics;
- GENETIC profile;
- GENDER stereotypes;
- AGE;
- SOCIAL constraints, including those imposed by family and social class.

Ideally, the manager needs to understand the personality of each one of those individuals for whom he/she is responsible, to realize their potential and to help resolve their problems. However, it is often not practical that decisions are based on the different needs of individuals. The manager who needs to motivate a unit of 10 employees can only afford to invest the necessary resources (of time, labor, research and so on) into tailoring 10 individual schemes if each individual is of extraordinary value to the success of the company, and if each individual has to have his/her needs correctly catered for. So, given the economic constraints on applying personality analysis to a small unit, is it possible for the manager to design an individual scheme for each of, say, 100? Or 1,000? More probably, the manager treats the 100, or 1,000, as a group with some shared identity. This means generalizing about their values and needs, testing this generalization by observation and experience, and acting on this basis. This explains why managers find it useful to apply CULTURAL ANALYSES as a support for (or substitute for) personality analyses.

1.3.2   *Predictability is limited*

However, the predictive worth of cultural analysis is limited. First, the manager can never precisely calculate the influence of culture against that of other factors in the environment listed in Section 1.2 – for example, economic factors. Second, in extraordinary and non-routine situations – say, a takeover, an unexpected bankruptcy, a natural disaster – individuals may respond in unexpected ways. They feel an overriding need to safeguard their own interests, and not to conform to group norms. In these cases, cultural predictions lose their validity. Organizations hate the non-routine, and in general fail to plan for drastic change – including their own demise. Third, every society produces persons whose psychological make-up makes them atypical, and persons who are inept at understanding their culture and accepting its norms. Every society produces social outsiders, criminals, and lunatics.

In sum, models of cultural analysis give the manager invaluable instruments that are applied in work of interpreting and predicting the behavior of the workforce. But, as we see throughout this book, these models are never 100 percent reliable.

1.3.3   *Defining national culture*

Scholars have produced hundreds of definitions of "culture". Hofstede's (1984) definition is still the best known to management scholars and is used here:

> Culture is the collective programming of the mind which distinguishes the members of one human group from another. . . . Culture, in this sense, includes systems of values; and values are among the building blocks of culture.   *(p. 21)*

This implies that

- a culture is particular to one human group and not others;
- it is learned, and is not innate. It is passed down from one generation to the next;
- culture includes systems of values.

Sections 1.3.4–1.3.7 examine the implications of this definition. Sections 1.3.8–1.3.13 deal with aspects of culture that the definition does not cover.

1.3.4   *Culture and the group*

The first point raised above is that a culture is particular to one human group and not others. This means that

- different human groups have different cultures;
- different human groups may respond to similar situations in different ways.

For example, the staff of an American organization were asked to contribute to a medical charity. In New York, each person made his/her decision about how much to contribute on an individual basis, and did not consult with any other person either before or after the collection was made. A few weeks later, it was suggested that the Panamanian subsidiary subscribe to the same charity. Members of the subsidiary were unsure about how much each should give, and consulted in groups and with their local superiors to decide on a figure. Each person at each level of the company hierarchy contributed the same sum, but higher levels contributed more, and the local CEO most.

This shows different national groups responding to the same situation in very different ways – by deciding on the basis of individual interests, or by deciding on the basis of collective and hierarchical interests.

The notion of national culture assumes that the cultures of, say, the Japanese, Americans and Portuguese have their particular characteristics shared by members, and are distinct. This generalization is useful if you have to compare the three countries. Assume, for example, that you are trying to decide where to situate a new plant, and you need to take into account the likely behaviors of the workforces.

In much cross-cultural management, the national group is taken as the unit of analysis. This has certain advantages over the alternatives. The limits of subcultural groups below this level may be difficult to identify, and reliable data scarce. On the other hand, larger groups – which lack the shared historical and economic experiences that bind a nation – may permit only very loose predictions to be made.

For example, journalists and politicians like to distinguish between "Eastern culture" (or "Asian culture") and "Western culture". But this level of generality oversimplifies, and is potentially damaging because it blinds us to real differences within each region.

Japan, India, Iraq, and Hong Kong might be vaguely grouped in the Asian sphere, but the manager who expects the behavior of his/her Iraqi employees to correspond with that of Japanese employees may be making a serious mistake. Poland, the USA, Spain, and Finland all belong in the Western sphere, but their national cultures differ markedly. Similarly, the national cultures of the countries comprising the European Union differ enormously, and even its most fervent advocates of this rickety political structure are unable to identify any common value system.

The point was made in the UK by a Hindu correspondent writing to a newspaper after the September 11, 2001 attack on the World Trade Center:

> Sir – Once again, I see that you are writing articles on Muslims and then suddenly referring to Asians [article reference . . .]. If you continue to use the term "Asian" then please refer to the citizens of this country as Europeans, as this will have the same validity.[2]

The same point applies in the case of the West – and always has. Gray (2000) writes:

> The pot-pourri sometimes called Western civilization has always contained conflicting values. Greek, Roman, Christian and Jewish traditions each contain distinctive goods and virtues that cannot be translated fully into the ethical life of the others. The notion of a "western tradition" in which these irreconcilable elements were once fused cannot withstand philosophical – or historical – scrutiny. There was never a coherent synthesis of these values, nor could there have been. *(p. 12)*

1.3.5   National territory and the national group

On the other hand, it is not always safe to assume a correspondence between national territory and the culture group. That is, homogeneity within the national culture cannot always be taken for granted. According to Barber (2001):

> . . . less than 10 percent (about twenty) of the modern world's states are truly homogeneous and thus, like Denmark or The Netherlands, can't get smaller unless they fracture into tribes or clans. In only half is there a single ethnic group that comprises even 75 percent of the population.   *(p. 9)*

This means that predictions of behavior are more reliable when made of populations that are relatively homogeneous; Japan is one, although even here important subcultural differences can be found between, say, mainstream Japanese, Korean Japanese, and the people of Okinawa, for whom home rule is an issue. Other populations are much more heterogeneous – in particular, in those countries that have welcomed large numbers of immigrants; the USA, Brazil and Canada, for example.

Barber (2001) comments that in the USA, multiculturalism is the rule and homogeneity the exception. Cuban Americans, Irish Americans, Chinese Americans, Black Americans and Jewish Americans share many mainstream "Anglo-Saxon" beliefs, in particular those associated with national symbols such as the Presidency and the Constitution. But their subcultures differ significantly. If you have to choose whether to site your new factory in Boston or Miami you cannot assume that the values of these different workforces will correspond. The influence of Irish culture is still strong in Boston, and in Miami, where many of your employees have Spanish as a first language, you might need to refer to models of Cuban culture.

The lack of precise correspondence between national territory and national culture is developed in Chapter 2, where we examine the problems arising in making comparative analysis.

1.3.6   Culture is learned

The second implication of Hofstede's definition is that your culture is not programmed into your genetic structure. You learn it. In the case of a national culture, you learn most intensively in the early years of life. By the age of five you were already an expert in using your language. You had learned how to communicate different language functions appropriately; for example, how to

- interact with other members of your family;
- elicit rewards and avoiding punishments;
- negotiate for what you wanted;
- cause, avoid, and resolve conflict.

Your behavior as a small baby was at first indistinguishable from that of babies in any other society. But very quickly you learned to mold your behavior to the particular constraints of your culture group, and to recognize the meaning of messages communicated by other members of the group.

Here is an example. Koreans learn in their childhood to be cautious of claiming "my" relationships; rather than "my mother" and "my house", the well-behaved child soon learns to refer to "our mother", "our house". A Korean explained:

> We try to avoid saying the word "my" something. And when we have to, we use a very polite form. When we are introducing something [as a topic] we use "our" – "our parents", "our book". "My" sounds very selfish.

When Koreans visit English-speaking countries, they compensate:

> When Koreans come to England, they often say "parents" [rather than either "my parents" or "our parents"]. They know that "our parents" is wrong in English but they don't like to say "my parents". So they miss [the possessive adjective] out.

The Korean preference for the plural possessive adjective ("our" rather than "my") reflects the collectivist values of the culture; Koreans are brought up to believe that they are united by common ancestry and descent from the same two original parents. Second, this shows Koreans aware of differences between their own and Anglo cultures.[3]

Who does the child learn from? In childhood, cultural values are passed on to you first by parents and family. Then friends and school mates influence learning. The American psychologist Harris (2007) claims that the biggest environmental influences on children occur outside the home, and the need to survive at school and mix with friends has a more significant impact on a child's behavior than lessons learned in the home. Is the importance of peer values equally significant in all cultures? In Japan, the mother is mainly responsible for early rearing, while in Scandinavian countries the parents play more equal roles. In many Islamic societies the mosque plays a great part in educating the young than might the church in many Christian societies. In some areas of China, it is still common for small children to be brought up by grandparents, leaving parents free to join the labor force.

Much of the child's learning is unconscious. When you began learning your mother language you were not aware of being inducted into the group culture. And so these values become second nature, and massively influence your behavior in later life. Because your cultural values are acquired so early and without conscious application, they are extremely deep-rooted.

1.3.7   *Values*

We saw in Section 1.3.3 that Hofstede's definition of culture includes systems of values. Values are defined here as assumptions that members of a culture group about how they should behave and do behave. The person may never articulate these assumptions, or even think of them; we have seen that persons start learning their cultural values in early childhood, at a preconscious level. As such, these values are engrained and are slow to change. Because they are taken for granted as the right way to behave, values strongly influence what behavior occurs.

Here is an example. In an Indonesian business school, students were separated into small tutorial groups for the last class of the morning. After this class, students waited in the reception area for all members of their friendship circle coming out of other tutorial groups before they went off to lunch together. A group of Americans were studying in the school at the same time. They noticed the Indonesian behavior and challenged it in class. Didn't this waste time? The Indonesians answered that paying respect to other members of their friendship group was how they "ought to behave", and they took this expression of loyalty for granted. An individual overlooked by his friends would feel betrayed, and this would have negative effects on them all. Then they challenged the Americans; how long do you wait for your friends after class? Two minutes at the most. To the Indonesians, this showed coldness and unfriendliness.

But there is one practical problem with focusing on this definition of culture. Most people are not good at describing their deepest values, and these are not easily accessible. The analyst cannot expect to learn much by asking direct questions such as "what are your values?"

Members' deep cultural values can be observed in their behavior, which provides a direct reflection. In this case, the Indonesians' relatively high collectivism was reflected in how they organized their lunch-hours, and influences a wide range of other work-place activities, it is evident in all their social and work priorities, loyalties, and relationships between groups. Whereas Indonesians hoped to achieve their goals through membership of, and loyalty to, a powerful group, the Americans expressed theirs in a drive to succeed on an individual basis. But until the two groups began to analyse each other's behavior, neither had thought to examine their own fundamental values.

1.3.8   What other factors influence behavior?

Hofstede says that culture INCLUDES values, which raises the question of what else is included. Here are some of the other factors, discussed in the sections below:

* BELIEFS;
* POLITICAL SYSTEMS;
* RELIGION;
* TECHNOLOGY;
* ARTISTIC CULTURE.

1.3.9   Beliefs

Individuals express their ideas about how the world is, or how it ought to be, by articulating their beliefs and attitudes. Unfortunately, even when a great number of people share and articulate the same belief, it may be only weakly predictive of how they will behave.

This is because people often do not behave according to their beliefs. The great majority of us everywhere profess some religious belief, and all religions condemn killing and theft.

But murders occur in all countries, and most of us have committed some form of theft at some time or another. Here is an example from the workplace. Most managers agree that communication initiated by subordinates is useful and important, and many may claim that "my office door is always open, and you can come and discuss your problems at any time". Often, they believe this. But how many managers do you know for whom this is true? What often happens is that

- he/she is too busy and asks you to come back at some other time; OR
- he/she tells you that your problem is trivial and that you are wasting time; OR
- he/she hears what you say, but is thinking of something else; OR
- he/she listens, and promises to help, but forgets.

In these cases, behavior does not correspond with conscious belief. This suggests that you cannot reliably predict how people will behave in particular situations from their stated attitudes.

A survey conducted in Singapore found wide differences between public attitudes – which were "progressive" – and "traditional" domestic attitudes. Although 97 percent of the respondents believed that men and women should be treated equally:

> 78 per cent of men and 77 per cent of women agreed that husbands must always be the household head. In 83 per cent of households surveyed, the wife cooks, 77 per cent wash toilets, 80 per cent wash dishes and laundry 78 per cent do the ironing.[4]

To sum up; although culture includes beliefs (and attitudes, opinions, etc.), these are less reliable than values in predicting behavior. For this reason, the book focuses on values.

1.3.10   *Political systems*

A mature political system succeeds because it reflects values in the national culture. The gladiatorial party politics of the Anglo countries have evolved over 400 years, and express relatively high tolerances of conflict and uncertainty, and the relatively low power distances. The one-party Communist system developed in the People's Republic of China gives the senior members of the ruling party centralized political powers that are not very different from those exercised by imperial courts before the Communist revolution.

However, the specific characteristics of political arrangements at any one time are also influenced by immediate considerations; for example, economic conditions, the country's recent history, relations with its neighbors, and the ambitions and personalities of its leaders. Changes made in response to these problems and opportunities may be frequent but, although they can seem radical at the time, their effects are often short-lived. In practice, the policies followed by the government of the day may bear little relationship to the deep culture of the people. That is, a revolution in the political structures does not necessarily reflect a change in the underlying value system. Adedaji (1995) made this point in the context of the official "transition to democracy" in Nigeria (1992):

> Democracy cannot be decreed. Unlike instant coffee, there is no instant democracy. You cannot move from totalitarianism to democratic practice from one day to another. Democracy is more than just the ballot boxes, the political parties and all the institutional trappings. It is a way of life, a culture and a lifestyle at all levels of society and in all spheres of human endeavour.
>
> *(p. 95)*

Adediji is arguing that political models that suit, say, the USA or the UK, may not be appropriate elsewhere in different cultural settings. The same applies now; some American or other Anglo policy makers seem surprised that their concept of democracy has not been immediately welcomed in Iraq. And the point can be applied to management practice; what works well in headquarters may be inappropriate in the country of the subsidiary.

1.3.11   Religion

Most of the major religions are shared by a number of national cultures:

- CHRISTIANITY is the most widely practiced. The majority live in Europe and the Americas, and numbers are growing rapidly in Africa. Protestant Christianity emphasizes the individual's responsibility for his/her own actions, and in the Anglo cultures has had a major effect on business values associated with individualism and independent thinking.
- ISLAM is practiced mainly in Africa, the Arab countries, in parts of South East Asia, Afghanistan and in some countries and regions comprising the former Soviet Union – for example, in Chechnya.
- HINDUISM is most common in India. Beliefs emphasize the spiritual progression of each person's soul rather than hard work and wealth creation.
- BUDDHISM has adherents in Central and South East Asia, China, Korea, and Japan. Like Hinduism, it stresses spiritual achievement, although the rapid economic development of these regions shows that this does not necessarily impede economic activity.
- CONFUCIANISM has adherents mainly in China, Korea and Japan. The emphases on loyalty and reciprocal obligation between superiors and subordinates, and honesty in dealing with others, have influenced the development of family companies in these regions.

Even when the same religious forms are shared by a range of cultures, this does not guarantee common values expressed outside religious practice. Catholicism is practiced in Peru and Poland, and Islam in Indonesia and Libya, but the manager cannot predict the workplace behavior of Peruvians and Poles to correspond, or the workplace behavior of Indonesians and Libyans.

Robertson et al. (2001) examined the differences between beliefs and values in Saudi Arabia, Kuwait, and Oman. They found the same belief system operating in these countries, and that is deeply rooted in the common religion, Islam.

> But values differ significantly; Saudis tend to have a stronger work ethic than Kuwaitis do, and are more independently motivated in the workplace.   *(p. 236)*

> Saudi Arabia may have a stronger emphasis on individuality in the workplace.   *(p. 240)*

Religion expresses the culture and also influences it. That means that in some respects national cultural values may overlie the influence of religion. The implication is that Buddhists and Christians in Thailand may share common values associated with being Thai. Buddhism teaches moderation and the importance of seeking a middle way between extremes. But here is an educated Thai noting the contradiction between the behavior and religious beliefs of his townspeople:

> Characteristically, the Muang Petch people are suited to be *nak-leng* (patrons). Killing and revenge is the name of the game, not necessarily based on any particular principle except for defending one's honour in the old way. We're quite extreme people which is strange considering that the people are mostly devout Buddhists.[5]

The implication is that the religion practiced by the group expresses a system of ethical belief, and is essentially idealistic. This means it may not be descriptive of how they actually behave. The international manager needs a basic understanding of the religious beliefs of the people whom he/she is managing, and to look for instances when behavior does express these beliefs, and when it does not.

1.3.12   Technology

Modern technologies are used across all cultures and this fact is sometimes used as evidence to argue that all cultures are converging. But this ignores the important differences that occur in how technologies are used in different cultures. For example, some information technologies are used on a group basis in the more collectivist cultures, but on an individual basis in the more individualist cultures. When the international manager finds the same technology used in different cultures, he/she asks, for each culture:

- Who SELECTS the technology?
- Who USES it?
- Who DIRECTS use?
- What STATUS is given to those who use and direct use?
- What other ACTIVITIES co-occur with use?
- WHEN is it used?
- WHERE is it used?
- What is the use of this technology intended to achieve? WHY is it used?

When different cultures typically provide different answers to these questions about the same technology, cultural analysis is needed to explain the differences.

1.3.13   *Artistic culture*

A common-sense of the term "culture" relates to artistic production, but this has little relevance to the needs of the manager in other industries. Arts and crafts immediately reflect the producers' individual psychologies. And although they give some indication of the values held by the culture group within which they belong, the relationship between the art item and the values shared by the members of the culture group may be obscure, even to a skilled sociologist or art critic. In general, the international manager is not expected to have skills of predicting workplace values from artistic culture.

1.4   Cross-cultural and International Management

In different circumstances, managers perform a range of different roles. These include leading, acting as figurehead, communicating information, negotiating, allocating resources, handling disturbances, planning, overseeing implementation of plans, and evaluating. Factors that influence which of these roles a PARTICULAR manager exercises, and how much emphasis he/she gives to them, include

- his/her personal psychology;
- his/her functional responsibilities;
- the organizational culture and history of the company;
- industry factors. Banks have relatively greater needs for hierarchical structures and controls than do advertising agencies. Advertising agencies need structures that facilitate rapid creativity;
- NATIONAL CULTURE. For example, in some cultures the manager is expected to emphasize control and direction elsewhere, to facilitate and participate.

The national culture of the workforce influences how they respond to the structures and systems planned and implemented by management. This means that a workforce in one culture may respond differently to a workforce in another. That is, in different cultural and industrial contexts, different management roles are emphasized. The international manager must be prepared for these different responses, and he/she adapts to the different contexts.

CROSS-CULTURAL MANAGEMENT is defined here as development and application of knowledge about cultures in the practice of international management, when the people involved have different cultural identities. These people may or may not belong to the same business unit.

Gooderham and Nordhaug (2004) define INTERNATIONAL MANAGEMENT as the generation and transfer of knowledge across settings and organizations (p. 1). O'Connell (1998) defines the notion as the planning, staffing, and control of international business activities (p. 320). These activities occur between business units that are located in different countries, whether joint venture partners, headquarters and subsidiary, principal and agent, supplier and customer. Both emphases – international management as a knowledge-based activity and as a function-based activity – are applied at different points in this book.

The two terms do not correspond entirely. Some international managers in senior positions may have no face-to-face interactions with the other-culture workforce; many home-based managers deal with immigrant groups assimilated into a workforce that serves domestic markets.

1.4.1   Cross-cultural management skills

A SKILL is defined as the ability to demonstrate a sequence of behaviors that are related to attaining a performance goal. The manager needs cross-cultural skills to manage a single-culture group when he/she is a member of some other culture. This situation occurs typically when the manager is expatriate, managing his/her company's subsidiary or other investment abroad. It may occur in headquarters when managing a group consisting entirely of immigrants.

The core assumption of cross-cultural skills learning is that the manager cannot expect to force-fit members of another culture into his/her own cultural norms. They cannot easily be made to accept his/her perceptions of reality as superior to values in their own culture. This is not an ethical matter so much as practical. The organization that attempts to impose its behavioral norms upon unwilling employees from another culture faces an uphill battle.

The manager also needs cross-cultural skills when managing diverse groups, including members from a range of cultures.

1.5   Implications for the Manager

How can the material covered in Section 1.4.1 above be applied to your organization? Answer for your company or business school:

1 In what departments/classes are a range of cultures represented? What cultures are represented?
2 How far can the typical behaviors of these cultures be distinguished? What cultural values are reflected in these different behaviors?
3 Can you distinguish the effectiveness of culturally diverse groups from the single-culture groups? How?
4 If cultural diversity is managed:
   (a)   What tasks are allocated to the diverse groups?
   (b)   What benefits arise from diversity?
   (c)   What problems arise?
   (d)   How could the diversity be better managed?

1.6 SUMMARY

This introductory chapter has focused on the importance of understanding culture. Section 1.2 examined FACTORS THAT INFLUENCE DECISION-MAKING in the business environment. The relationship between internal and external factors is complex, and problems of responding to external factors are further complicated when the company is making international investments and is operating in more than one national environment. National culture is only one of the factors involved, and the manager needs skills of distinguishing when it is, and is not, significant. Section 1.3 saw that models of CULTURE are useful because they give the manager bases for predicting behavior within the culture group. A definition, commonly applied by managers, was discussed and its implications discussed. A culture is specific to a group, and is learned by its members. A culture includes systems of values, and values were defined. Section 1.4 examined the scope of CROSS-CULTURAL AND INTERNATIONAL MANAGEMENT.

1.7 EXERCISE

Cultural values that are thought desirable and normal in one culture might be undesirable and deviant elsewhere.

1 Rank each of the values below in terms of how far you think most members of YOUR culture group would agree. Rank on a 6-point continuum, from A ("strongly agree") to F ("strongly disagree"):

(a) Men should be competitive
A (strongly agree): B (agree): C, D, E (disagree): F (strongly disagree)

(b) Women should be competitive
A (strongly agree): B (agree): C, D, E (disagree): F (strongly disagree)

(c) Managers should participate with their subordinates
A (strongly agree): B (agree): C, D, E (disagree): F (strongly disagree)

(d) Good work relationships are more important than task efficiency
A (strongly agree): B (agree): C, D, E (disagree): F (strongly disagree)

(e) Powerful people should have privileges
A (strongly agree): B (agree): C, D, E (disagree): F (strongly disagree)

(f) The manager should have all the answers to subordinates' questions
A (strongly agree): B (agree): C, D, E (disagree): F (strongly disagree)

2 Compare your answers to those given by some other student, from another culture.

3 Explain any differences.

Notes

1 Francis Fukuyama. The Calvinist manifesto in today's globalized world. *New York Times* (reprinted in *Daily Telegraph*, March 17, 2005).

2 Letters to the Editor. *Daily Telegraph*, November 8, 2002.

3 In this book, the expression "Anglo cultures" refers to the mainstream cultures of Australia, Canada (outside Quebec), New Zealand, the UK and the USA.

4 Associated Press. Singaporeans don't practice what they preach on equality. *The Nation* (Bangkok), December 25, 1994.

5 Piya Angkinand. Of fear and honour. *Bangkok Post*, January 25, 1991.

CHAPTER ONE **International Management and Culture**

CASE SLICING THE MEAT

A Norwegian–American MBA student was studying culture, and began to think about how cultural values influenced her own behavior. She remembered that she had been taught always to slice a joint of meat into two pieces before baking it in the oven.

She phoned her mother and asked, "Mum, why do we Norwegians always bake meat in two halves?"

"I don't know," her mother said. "But we have to, we always do." Then she thought about it, and said, "I'll ask your grandmother."

So she phoned her own mother and asked, "Mother, why do we Norwegians always bake meat in two halves?"

"I don't know," the grandmother said, "but that's what my mother told me. I'll ask her."

The next day the grandmother visited the student's great-grandmother and reminded her of the slicing. "That's what you said we must do. But why?"

The old lady still had a good memory and answered immediately. "Because when you were a little girl, we lived in a house in Norway which only had a very small oven. And you had many brothers and sisters. So the only way I could bake enough meat for all of us was to bake it in two halves."

QUESTIONS

1 Was this slicing of the meat into two:
   - A matter of national culture?
   - A matter of personal preference?
   - A matter of family tradition?
2 What mistake did the younger women make?
3 Which (if any) of these do you agree with? Too often, people:
   - Don't forget what they're told to do.
   - Make unwarranted assumptions about their culture.
   - Don't question what they're told to do.

DECISION

4. *You are visiting your foreign subsidiary. This is your first time in the country. You notice that on Fridays, all employees go home an hour early. You ask why, and are told "That's what we always do." What question do you ask next?*

PART TWO
Cross-cultural Management

CHAPTER SIX   **Culture and Communication**
Your message is most effective when it reflects the shared values of the context. If it does not reflect these values other people may not understand you. The chapter focuses on the factors that influence communication style. These include national culture. The communication systems reflect and generate needs for company structure.

CHAPTER SEVEN   **Motivation**
The workforce are most productive when they are motivated to achieve company goals. The most effective incentives offer employees the opportunity to satisfy their needs – which assumes that management have made a realistic assessment of these needs. The chapter discusses a range of both monetary and non-monetary incentives. Culture plays a part in deciding why a particular incentive is (or is not) motivating.

CHAPTER EIGHT   **Dispute Resolution**
Disputes arise from a range of factors including argument, competition for scarce resources, and misunderstandings. Tolerances of conflict vary across cultures, and behavior that causes conflict in one culture may be acceptable in some other. Participants negotiate as a means of both resolving conflict and sharing resources.

CHAPTER NINE   **Formal Structures**
Formal structures determine roles and relationships within the company, and determine what communication options are more or less acceptable. A structure is influenced by factors that include the work being done, the national culture and needs for organizational culture. Formal structures tend to be bureaucratic and impersonal.

CHAPTER TEN   **Informal Systems**
Informal systems may have a greater influence than do formal systems in deciding how management decisions are made and implemented. Patron and client are bound by long-standing ties of loyalty and obligation. Patronage networks reinforce in-groups and exclude outsiders. Cultural variations include (*guanx*i) in Chinese cultures and (*wasda*) in Arab cultures.

CHAPTER ELEVEN   **The Culture and Politics of Planning Change**
Planning to make change has a political dimension in the sense that it needs the commitment of other people. If they are persuaded that the proposed change lies in their interests, the plan may be accepted and implemented. Otherwise, the plan is unlikely to achieve its goals. Some planning models demand heavy investments of time and information, and under some business conditions long-term planning may be impossible.

CHAPTER TWELVE **When Does Culture Matter? The Case of Small/Medium Sized Enterprises**

All the Chapters in this part show that national culture is sometimes very significant; and on other occasions not. The manager needs the skills to recognize when culture is significant, and to respond appropriately. The final chapter in this part reiterates the point by examining the importance of culture and other factors in starting up and managing a small or medium sized company in different national cultures.

CHAPTER TWO
Analyzing Cultures: Making Comparisons

CHAPTER OUTLINE

Introduction	**Applying Hofstede's Model**
Comparative Analysis	**Implications for the Manager**
Kluckhohn and Strodtbeck (1961)	**Summary**
Hall (1976)	**Exercise**
Hofstede's Model	**Notes**

2.1   Introduction

A Thai mother and English father lived with their only son in Bangkok. At the age of four the boy was sent to a school in Bangkok. Eighteen months later, the family returned to the UK for a year and he joined a local school.

A few weeks into the school year, the teacher told the children that they would go for a walk in the neighboring park, and should stand in a straight line and stop talking. When the children took no notice and continued to run around making a noise, the boy took it on himself to remind them that teacher had said they should stand in a straight line and stop talking. The other children threatened to beat him.

When the year was up, the family returned to Bangkok, and the boy went back into a Thai school. Two weeks later his parents received a letter from the teacher saying he was a pleasant boy and obviously intelligent. So when he was told, why couldn't he stand in a line and stop talking?

This story opens up questions about notions of authority and how values are taught in different cultures. Cultural differences may be identified through comparison, and this and the next chapter see how useful comparisons can be made.

These chapters do NOT deal with organizational (or corporate) culture, which in crucial aspects differs from national culture and is discussed in Chapter 5. Nor do they deal with behavioral norms in different industries.

2.2   Comparative Analysis

A model of culture gives parameters within which patterns of group behavior can be described and analyzed. The model is applied to members of a culture group.

The theories and models discussed in this chapter are descriptive and NOT concerned with prescriptive models, which rule how members ought to behave.

International managers need research into culture because they need to be able to predict what behavior is typical in routine situations and how members of the culture group will behave in such situations. A single-culture model is used to examine one culture in depth. It makes a discrete analysis in the sense that it describes and analyzes the culture in terms of its own features without necessarily making reference to other cultures. Anthropologists tend to use analysis of this type.

But increasingly in our globalized world, international managers need to be able to predict relationships between different cultures; that is, they need cross-cultural research. Boyacigiller et al. (2003) differentiate three different streams in cross-cultural research, and examine how the theoretical contexts within each has evolved, the methods employed and the insights gleaned. They discuss models that

- compare cultures;
- examine interactions between persons from different cultures;
- examine multiple-culture groupings, as for example those experienced by a global company. This approach introduces the notion that individuals acquire multi-cultural identities from their context.

These three streams provide reference points for the discussion in this and the next chapters. This chapter examines comparative approaches up to and including Hofstede's work in the early 1980s. Chapter 3 deals with developments since, and the swing in emphasis towards the second and third of the streams, interactions and groupings.

2.2.1   *The comparative approach*

A COMPARATIVE model measures one culture against another, and enables the manager or consultant to compare the behavior of one culture group with another. That is, the model has general applicability, and is not limited to only one culture. It makes statements comparing the values of, say, Cultures A, B and C; "members of Culture A are more individualist than those of Culture B, but Culture B is less individualist than Culture C".

A comparative model cannot describe one culture alone. It cannot be used to say that "the model shows that Finland has an individualist culture" because the question will always arise, individualist compared to what other culture?

Comparative models are useful when they help the manager compare the characteristics of different cultures and reach a decision:

- Where do I invest in a new factory? In Poland? Or in China?
- How far can I adapt my Japanese incentive system to use with my workforce in Thailand?
- Should I expect a matrix structure designed for a Swedish workforce to function effectively in Mexico? And if not, why not?

At the initial stages of learning about a new culture managers may prefer comparative analysis because it helps them decide about a culture that they don't know in relation to one that they do – perhaps their own. The controversies underlying all comparative analyses are:

- How far any one culture can be realistically measured against any other?
- How useful is simple bi-lateral analysis in multinational corporations (MNCs) where members of not two but a number of cultures may be interacting?
- How far do members of culture groups adapt their value systems when interacting with members of other culture groups?

In this chapter, examples are provided from these comparative models. Hofstede's model (Section 2.5) is pre-eminent but can only be understood in the light of earlier models. The two chosen for discussion are models by:

- Kluckhohn and Strodtbeck (1961);
- Hall (1976).

2.3   Kluckhohn and Strodtbeck (1961)

Kluckhohn proposed in a 1952 article that there should be universal categories by which cultures could be described. He developed this insight in a book with Strodtbeck. Kluck-hohn and Strodtbeck (1961) claim that members of a group exhibit constant "orientations" towards the world and other people. They identified five orientations set out in Table 2.1, and later research added a sixth, the conception of space. Cultures are mapped onto a range of variations proposed for each, and are distinguished in terms of dominant variations.

These categories are still influential – for instance, distinctions between lineal, col-lateral, and individualist relationships – and have been developed in a range of models

Table 2.1   The Kluckham and Strodtbeck (1961) model

Orientations	*Range of variations*
1. What is the nature of people?	- Good (changeable/unchangeable) - Evil (changeable/unchangeable) - A mixture of good and evil
2. What is the person's relationship to nature?	- Dominant - In harmony - Subjugation
3. What is the person's relationship to other people?	- Lineal (hierarchical) - Collateral (collectivist) - Individualist
4. What is the modality of human activity?	- Doing - Being - Containing
5. What is the temporal focus of human activity?	- Future - Present - Past
6. What is the conception of space?	- Private - Public - Mixed

since. Scarborough (1998) compared Western and Chinese cultural differences and finds in Western culture "an aggressive, active approach to nature, technology and progress" and "reliance on reason and the scientific method"; and in Chinese culture "passive, fatalistic submission" and "reliance on precedent, intuition, and wisdom" – reflecting orientations of the person's relationship to nature, and of the temporal focus of human activity. In 1998 a conference of users of the model attracted over 400 delegates; see Russo (2000). It was not designed specifically to contrast the influence of culture on management, and managers may wish to gloss it to meet this end. Table 2.2 gives a gloss on the first variation.

2.4   Hall (1976)

Hall (1976) came to the field of cross-cultural analysis from the discipline of anthropology. He argued that all peoples interpret and create messages in reference to shared information. This information includes values in the culture, which link members of the culture group and influence how they refer to their contexts when maintaining relationships. That is, members' experiences of context will influence how they communicate. And different culture groups respond to their contexts differently. This principle of applying shared cultural experience is crucial in Hall's model.

The model distinguished between high-context and low-context cultures. Members of HIGH-CONTEXT cultures depend heavily on their shared experience and interpretation

Table 2.2 Implications for management

Orientations	Variations	Implications for management
1 What is the nature of people?	GOOD	Optimistic about other people's motivations and capacities; Theory Y; participation encouraged; trust; direct communication valued
	EVIL	Pessimistic; Theory X; suspicion of peers and subordinates, and of negotiation partners; secretive
	MIXED	Use of middlemen and consultants; a discrepancy between optimistic attitudes and behavior – for instance, the values of open communication are proclaimed – but the message may be vetted by a lawyer *Example*: Mainstream United States culture is optimistic insofar as any achievement is thought possible if worked for, and humanity is ultimately perfectible – as the millions of self-help books and videos marketed every year demonstrate. But the dependence upon legal remedies to resolve conflict indicates pessimism
2 What is the person's relationship to nature?	DOMINANT	Control and planning (particularly when also "optimistic" – above); imposing one's will on the natural environment, and on the business environment; working to mold the organizational culture *Example*: In cultures with this orientation, the need to dominate natural forces is expressed by attempts to plan and mold the organizational culture and employees' experience of the work environment
	HARMONY	Coexistence; search for common ground; aversion to open conflict within the workplace; respect for different others
	SUBJUGATION	Fatalism; ready acceptance of external control; aversion to independent planning; pessimism about changing the organizational culture
3 What is the person's relationship to other people?	LINEAL (hierarchical)	Respect for authority, and for seniority as determined by age, family, gender; tall organizations; communication on a hierarchical basis
	COLLATERAL (collectivist)	Relationships within the group influence attitudes towards work, superiors, other groups. Members of other groups are treated with suspicion. Structures and systems that remove the individual from the group, and that break down group boundaries, are disliked
	INDIVIDUALIST	People primarily perceive themselves as individuals rather than as members of a group. A need for systems that maximize opportunities for personal achievement and status. Interesting work is more likely to be valued. Competition is encouraged. Egalitarian self-images; informal *Example*: In mainstream United States culture, self-identification is achieved through action and performance. Because other persons must be able to recognize this achievement, it has to be visible and measurable. In business, a financial statement provides one measure of success

(Continued)

Table 2.2 (*Continued*)

Orientations	Variations	Implications for management
4 What is the modality of human activity?	DOING	Performance valued, and hence financial and other measures of performance are valued. Work is central to the individual's life; practical orientation. Ambiguities frustrating performance cause anxiety *Example*: In the United States, the failure over several weeks to decide on a winner of the 2000 presidential election caused tension, and a rush of people needing psychiatric help. One psychiatrist commented "The election is causing ambiguity. We are used to there being a winner and loser."
	BEING	Status is derived by birth, age, sex, family connections more than by achievement. Feelings are valued. Planning is often short term; spontaneity is valued *Example*: Buddhist cultures believe in reincarnation, which means that the individual is born into his/her present status and circumstances by virtue of actions performed in a previous life, and that struggle is pointless. By avoiding sinful acts and maintaining harmony, you help your chances of being born into a higher position in your next reincarnation
	CONTAINING	Focus on self-control; striving for balance between feeling and doing; self-inquiring
5 What is the temporal focus of human activity?	FUTURE	Future planning is prioritized; past performance is less important; the concept of change valued. Career planning and training are valued
	PRESENT	Immediate realities are prioritized, and used as the basis of planning; long-term plans are liable to modification; an emphasis on contemporary impact and style
	PAST	The past is used as the model when planning for the future; respect for precedence; need for continuity; respect paid to age *Example*: A Japanese–American manager suggests "If you're having any trouble with a government department in Japan, take along someone who is really old. Japanese bureaucrats respect old people. When I had a problem, I took along a pensioner who used to work for my company and he explained my situation."
6 What is the conception of space?	PRIVATE	Respect for personal ownership; what is private is valued; private meetings are valued. Strangers are kept at a distance
	PUBLIC	Activities conducted in secret are held in suspicion. Social proximity is taken for granted; public meetings are valued *Example*: The introductory case in Section 2.1 shows differing perceptions of private and public space
	MIXED	Private and public activities are distinguished

of their cultural environment in creating and interpreting communications. Members of the culture group learn from birth to interpret the covert clues given in these contexts when they communicate, and so much meaning is conveyed indirectly. In languages such as Arabic, Chinese, and Japanese indirect styles of communication and the capacity to interpret non-verbal signals and indirect illusions are prized. But in LOW-CONTEXT cultures, the environment is less important, and non-verbal behavior is often ignored, and so communicators have to provide more explicit information. Samovar and Porter (1995) distinguish thus:

> A high context communication or message is one in which most of the information is already in the person, while very little is in the coded, explicitly transmitted part of the message. A low context communication is just the opposite; i.e. the mass of the information is vested in the explicit code. *(p. 101)*

HIGH-CONTEXT cultures have the following characteristics:

- RELATIONSHIPS (both positive and negative) are relatively LONG LASTING, and individuals feel deep personal involvement with each other.
- Because so much is communicated by SHARED CODE, communication is economical, fast, and efficient – in a routine situation. High-context cultures fully exploit the communicative context:

> The Japanese talk around the point. [They] think intelligent human beings should be able to discover the point of discourse from the context, which they are careful to provide. *(Hall, 1983, p. 63)*

- Communication in high-context cultures employs a far wider range of expression than is usual in Anglo cultures. The Japanese can communicate widely using non-verbal signaling, and non-language utterances known as *haragei* or "belly language". Where there is doubt, they interpret the meaning of this belly language by examining the person's face:

> Non-word sounds, such as hissing, grunting, growling, and sighing, are just one more way that Japanese communicate without using actual words. *(Kopp, 2001, p. 30)*

Such gestures are important everywhere; see 6.4. But they have been systematized in some cultures far more than in others.
- People in AUTHORITY are PERSONALLY RESPONSIBLE for the actions of subordinates. Loyalties between superiors and subordinates are reciprocal. A Thai employee related:

> When I was working in a commercial bank in Bangkok there was one mistake in a transaction that I dealt with. My direct boss then solved the problem even though she did not deal with the transaction directly before. It is quite usual for a direct boss to take responsibility for a subordinate's action in Thailand. I think it is reasonable for a subordinate to have high loyalty to such a boss.

- AGREEMENTS (between members) tend to be SPOKEN rather than written. This can mean that a written contract is only "best guess".
- INSIDERS and OUTSIDERS are closely DISTINGUISHED; insiders include first, members of the family, then clan, organization. Foreigners are usually treated as outsiders.
- CULTURAL PATTERNS are INGRAINED, and slow to change.

LOW-CONTEXT cultures have the opposite characteristics:

- RELATIONSHIPS between individuals are relatively SHORTER in duration, and deep personal involvement with others is valued less.
- MESSAGES must be made EXPLICIT, and the sender can depend less on the receiver inferring the message from the context. Members depend less on using non-verbal communications codes.
- AUTHORITY is DIFFUSED throughout the bureaucratic system and personal responsibility is difficult to pin down.
- AGREEMENTS tend to be WRITTEN rather than spoken. Low-context cultures treat contracts as final and legally binding and are less willing to renegotiate. The obsession with precision may bewilder members of high-context cultures. A Chinese negotiator commented:

   > The Americans spend much effort on one word or one sentence in the contract. Sometimes, they even argue non-serious items for a whole week. Then they have to ask approval from their lawyers. Their lawyers are picky and like to find bones in eggs.

- INSIDERS and OUTSIDERS are LESS CLOSELY DISTINGUISHED. This means that foreigners find it relatively easier to adjust.
- CULTURAL PATTERNS are faster to CHANGE.

Cultures with higher contexts include Japan, China, Korea, Vietnam and other Asian countries, countries around the Mediterranean and in the Middle East. Cultures with lower contexts include the USA, Scandinavian countries, and Germany. But no country exists exclusively at one end of the scale or the other, and all countries show high-context cultural behavior and low-context cultural behavior at different points. The low-context Anglo countries include associations with restricted membership such as Rotary and the Masons which are higher context organizations than is their surrounding culture. These offer members the opportunity to build long-term power and influence both in the association and more generally in society.

   France exemplifies a country whose culture is a mix of high- and low-context situations. Insiders and outsiders are distinguished and great importance is associated with speaking the language correctly. But the impersonality of bureaucratic organizations is more typical of low-context cultures.

   The model is useful in understanding WHY different cultures might communicate differently, for example in developing business relationships, negotiating with insiders and outsiders, and implementing contracts. For example, it helps to explain why family companies in high-context Southeast Asian cultures differ so widely from their equivalents in low-context Anglo cultures.

2.5   Hofstede's Model

Hofstede's research shows that

- work-related values are NOT universal;
- when a multinational headquarters tries to impose the same norms on all its foreign interests, their local values are likely to persist;
- local values determine how headquarters regulations are interpreted;
- by implication, a multinational that insists on organizational uniformity across its foreign investments is in danger of creating morale problems and inefficiencies.

Hofstede first introduced his model in 1980, and developed it thereafter. His research compared work-related values across employees in branches and affiliates of IBM. These values are expressed in behavior, and may not be consciously articulated.

The full model presented gave data for 50 countries and three regions (East Africa comprising Ethiopia, Kenya, Tanzania and Zambia; West Africa comprising Ghana, Nigeria, and Sierra Leone; and Arab countries comprising Egypt, Iraq, Kuwait, Lebanon and Saudi Arabia). Table 2.3 gives the key to the countries and regions.

The model has a quantitative basis. Comparisons between the different national cultures were plotted across at first four, later five, dimensions, and each culture was ranked. The dimensions are briefly explained and illustrated:

(a) *Power distance*; the distance between individuals at different levels of a hierarchy (see 2.5.1);
(b) *Uncertainty avoidance*; more or less need to avoid uncertainty in life (2.5.2);
(c) *Individualism* vs. *collectivism*; the relations between the individual and his/her fellows (2.5.3);
(d) *Masculinity* vs. *Femininity*; the division of roles and values in society (2.5.4).
(e) *Long-* vs. *short-term orientation*; temporal orientation towards life. This dimension was developed in 1987, later than the four core dimensions, and was tested in only 23 countries (see 2.5.5).

2.5.1   Power distance

This dimension measures how different national cultures cope with inequalities in society and their effects on the workplace. No country is entirely free from hierarchies, which may arise from physical and mental differences, social status, legal rights, wealth, power, and education.

Table 2.3 Key to the countries and regions

Abbreviation	Country or region	Abbreviation	Country or region
ARA	Arab-speaking countries (Egypt, Iraq, Kuwait, Lebanon, Libya, Saudi Arabia, United Arab Emirates)	ISR	Israel
		ITA	Italy
		JAM	Jamaica
ARG	Argentina	JPN	Japan
AUL	Australia	KOR	South Korea
AUT	Austria	MAL	Malaysia
BEL	Belgium	MEX	Mexico
BRA	Brazil	NET	Netherlands
CAN	Canada	NOR	Norway
CHL	Chile	NZL	New Zealand
COL	Colombia	PAK	Pakistan
COS	Costa Rica	PAN	Panama
DEN	Denmark	PER	Peru
EAF	East Africa (Ethiopia, Kenya, Tanzania, Zambia)	PHI	Philippines
		POR	Portugal
EQA	Equador	SAF	South Africa
FIN	Finland	SAL	Salvador
FRA	France	SIN	Singapore
GBR	Great Britain	SPA	Spain
GER	Germany F.R.	SWE	Sweden
GRE	Greece	SWI	Switzerland
GUA	Guatemala	TAI	Taiwan
HOK	Hong Kong	THA	Thailand
IDO	Indonesia	TUR	Turkey
IND	India	URU	Uruguay
IRA	Iran	USA	United States
IRE	Ireland (Republic of)	VEN	Venezuela
		WAF	West Africa (Ghana, Nigeria, Sierra Leone)
		YUG	Yugoslavia

Source: from Hofstede (1991, p. 35).

Figure 2.1 gives Hofstede's findings for this dimension. The power distances for the countries and regions are plotted on the horizontal axis; hence power distances are narrowest in Austria, then Israel; and broadest in Malaysia. The vertical axis plots the findings for uncertainty avoidance.

Cultures with relatively *narrow power distances* try to reduce them, for example by taxing the rich at higher rates than the poor and giving all the same access to social services. Hierarchies are seen as convenience arrangements rather than as having existential justification.

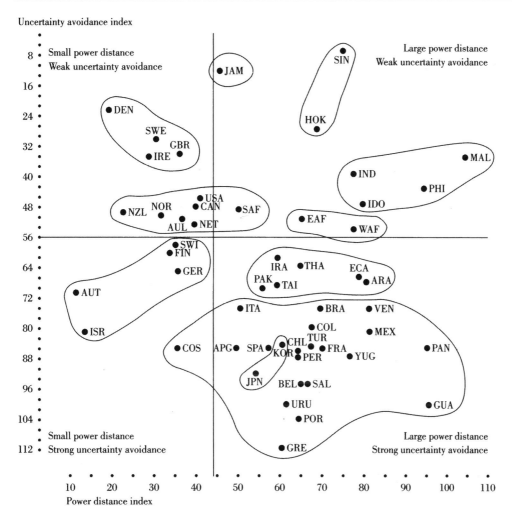

Figure 2.1 Uncertainty avoidance × power distance
Source: from Hofstede (2001, p. 152).

Managers see themselves as practical and systematic and admit the need for support. Subordinates expect to be consulted when important decisions are made, and prefer a participative superior with whom they can disagree without feeling at risk. They dislike close supervision. They find it easier to cooperate with each other, and interdependence is stressed. In the wealthier lower power distance cultures, technical education is used to acquire expert power rather than to signal social status.

All human societies show some people exercising power over others, and no societies are entirely without power distances. In cultures where distances appear to be least, informal perceptions of who has what power may be extremely subtle and not necessarily corresponding to formal structure. In the UK in 2005, Tony Blair led his New Labour party to a third successive general election victory with a majority of 67 seats in Parliament. His success was unparalleled in modern British politics and he should have been free to exercise his power with few constraints. However, he was perceived to be losing power, both because the New Labour majority had fallen from 161 (before the election), and because a powerful party rival, Gordon Brown, was preparing a challenge for the leadership. In cultures where power distances are narrow, members grow very sensitive to differences between elites

Hofstede finds that one connotation of narrow power distances is that close supervision is resented. Managers are expected to work hard for their rewards, but those who do not deserve their salaries may be censored. A 2003 MORI poll conducted in the UK found that

> 78 per cent of Britons think that company directors are overpaid and 80 per cent think that they cannot be trusted. Ordinary people are outraged by what they see as excessive executive rewards that seem to bear no relation to performance.[1]

In cultures with *wider power distances,* members accept the hierarchical ordering and may even encourage the differences, for example by giving their elites privileged access to political power, good medical services and university education, and low taxation. Children treat parents with respect.

Managers are expected to make decisions autocratically and paternalistically. Less powerful people feel themselves dependent on the more powerful. Employees manage their work according to what the manager wants – or they intuit what he wants. Managers like to see themselves as benevolent decision-makers. Employees find it easier to cooperate with superiors than with peers, unless under the direction of a powerful superior respected by all. Coercive and referent powers are stressed over reward, expert and legitimate powers.

In China, differences in power are signalled by when people come to a meeting. The junior person may arrive up to 30 minutes or more before the agreed time. This early arrival indicates respect. An arrival after the senior person has entered would be interpreted as disrespect.

Anglos may find this social inequality hard to accept; the Chinese do not.

Behavior reflecting wide power distances both underlines the superior status of the senior person, and can also provide a model to other members of the group in a similar relationship with this superior person. In this case, they have to be demonstrated publicly. In the Cameroons in 2002, African Nations Cup soccer players were late returning to their European clubs because they were made to return to their capital

> to meet the country's president, who, unfortunately, was busy and could not see the squad until later in the week. The players' passports were taken away, ensuring that they could not leave until the presidential handshake had been received.[2]

Hofstede argued that where power distances are wide, managers are more likely to dictate how their subordinates should behave and less likely to consult. Kaynak (1986) illustrates this point with respect to the Middle East. Managers believe subordinates to be incompetent, so they don't consult, and they defend centralization of authority.

2.5.2   Uncertainty avoidance

Everywhere, life is uncertain. No one can be entirely certain of the future, or about relationships with others. This dimension measures how far cultures socialize their members into tolerating uncertainty about the future and ambiguous situations.

In cultures where *needs to avoid uncertainty are higher,* members appear anxiety-prone. Ambiguities are feared. In Kuwait, a politician warned that

> since the countdown for elections has started ... rumours will fill the arena, along with contradictions and irresponsible statements which will not benefit Kuwait.[3]

Members devote more energy to "beating the future" and long-term stability is valued. Kwok and Tadesse (2006) found that in cultures with relatively higher needs to avoid uncertainty – in continental Europe and Japan – financial systems are predominantly bank based. But in cultures with relatively low needs (such as the US and the UK) financial systems are dominated by the stock markets on which investments may be highly speculative.

Where needs to avoid uncertainty are higher, the effects of conflict and competition in society and in organizations are more feared. Expert managers are preferred to facilitators, and clear rules and precise job descriptions are expected. Subordinates are given little opportunity to take their own initiatives. Individuals are relatively less entrepreneurial. Job security, career patterning and detailed retirement plans are expected.

Members of cultures where *needs to avoid uncertainty are lower* experience lower levels of anxiety and job stress. They may be more willing to take risks, and be less resistant to change. While teaching in Chicago, one of the authors met a student who had worked as a brand manager in a cookie factory. On her first day at work, she and another woman discovered that they had been given precisely the same job with the same responsibilities. Management had decided that whichever of the two performed most successfully over two months would be hired on a permanent basis; the loser could expect immediate dismissal. The two women accepted the condition as reasonable.

Managers are of lower average age in higher level jobs. Little virtue is attached to loyalty to the boss. Managers may be generalists and build their careers on facilitating skills. The manager breaks formal rules and by-passes hierarchical structures if necessary. Foreigners are accepted as managers with relative ease. Competition and even some forms of conflict may be accepted as healthy and desirable.

Figure 2.1 shows that needs to avoid uncertainty are highest in Greece and Portugal, and Japan is seventh. Needs are lowest in Singapore; third lowest in Denmark; seventh lowest in the UK.

2.5.3   *Individualism vs. collectivism*

Everywhere, questions arise about how much a person has to depend on his/her own resources in order to achieve a good life, and how much he/she has to depend on a group. Figure 2.2 gives Hofstede's findings for this dimension plotted on the horizontal axis, and for masculinity/femininity plotted on the vertical axis.

The *more individualist* (and less collectivist) cultures stress individual identity. The person is expected to achieve for him/herself, and to satisfy his/her own needs. Individual achievements and rights are respected. Individual decisions are valued above group decisions, and the individual has a right to thoughts and opinions which differ from those held by the majority. Social philosophies tend to reflect universalistic concerns with society, rather than the needs of a particular group or family. In practice, individualism CANNOT be equated with greed - which arises in any cultural context.

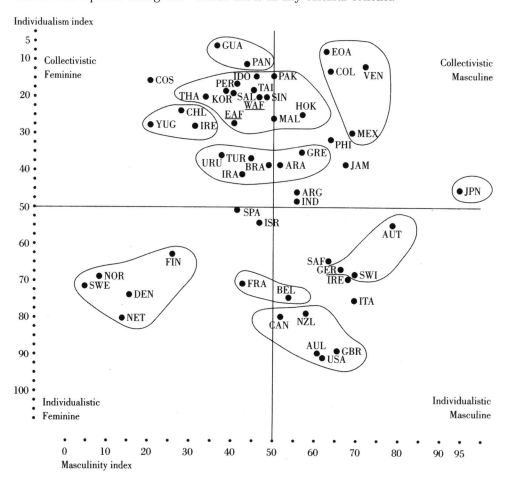

Figure 2.2   Individualism/collectivism × masculinity/femininity
Source: Hofstede (2001, p. 294).

Individualism may be expressed by rebellion against conformity, even when the rebellion is symbolic and superficial. A television commercial advertised "Hugo. The fragrance from Hugo Bros. Don't imitate, innovate."[4] Most advertising attempts to create a response from thousands or millions of consumers, and this sets out to attract customers by suggesting that by buying the product each becomes an individualist leader.

The manager aims for variety rather than conformity in work and does not have strong emotional connections with the company. He/she is loyal for as long as this suits his/her interests; that is, loyalty is calculative. Competition is more likely to be tolerated, even between members of the same group.

In the *more collectivist* (and less individualist) cultures, the opposite conditions apply. Group interests prevail over individual interests, and the individual derives his/her social identity from the groups of which he/she is a member – including family, school class, work unit. A premium is placed on loyalty to other members of the group, and this loyalty may be considered more important than efficiency. However, links between groups may be very loose; within a company the different functional groups may have very limited interaction.

The manager rewards conformity within the group and loyalty to the organization, and the inefficient but loyal employee may be more valued than the efficient but apparently disloyal. Andrews and Chompusri (2001) comment:

> The collectivist nature of Thai business culture is . . . expressed in the manner "insiders" and "outsiders are tightly distinguished in organizational sub-culture. Loyalty is expected between group members – as within a family – because they are considered to share the same world-views, and communicate more efficiently in routine situations.   (p. 81)

In Thai culture the distinction between insiders and outsiders was voiced by a Thai ex-prime minister after the crisis of 1997:

> "Those in a position of responsibility for the Kingdom's administration should offer only constructive criticism," [General Prem Tinsulanonda] said . . . "If foreigners think that people in this country are not united, then trade and investment which are essential to our economic recovery will not take place."[5]

The greater the loyalty to the group, the greater may be competition with other groups. Our observer finds that, in Vietnam, rivalry between institutions is endemic

> whether it is between party and government, between the centre and city, or between every conceivable combination of offices within the city itself. . . . At the root of this rivalry is a struggle to maintain control over regulatory, inspection and licensing responsibilities and to head off encroachments by rival offices.[6]

Figure 2.2 shows that the most individualist culture is the USA, then Australia and the UK. The least individualist (and most collectivist) is Guatemala, then Equador and Panama.

2.5.4   Masculinity vs. femininity

Hofstede uses the terms "masculine" and "feminine" in technical senses, and the terms should not be interpreted simply in terms of gender prejudice or to mean less or more effeminate.

In the *more masculine* cultures sex roles are sharply differentiated. Some occupations are reserved for men, and some for women. For example, few men are primary school teachers and few women senior politicians. The social ideal is performance, and the maintenance of economic growth has top priority.

Employees may think that time spent on company business is more valuable than time spent in unrelated social pursuits or with the family. Men are expected to be competitive and assertive, and women tender and able to take care of relationships.

In Japan, masculinity is still expressed in a degree of job discrimination. Even though this is breaking down in newer industries, certain professional roles are far more likely to be performed by men than women. In traditional industries, few women reach the top levels of management, and they are normally expected to stay at home after marriage and bring up the children. A 1999 survey found that men with children under six years old spend 17 minutes a day caring for them, while women spend an average of 2 hours and 39 minutes.[7]

The culture of the UK is more masculine than most, and a report by the Equal Opportunities Commission in the UK ("Free to Choose", March 31, 2005) noted continuing "gender segregation" in British schools. Eight out of 10 girls and more than half of boys wanted the chance to learn a "non-traditional" job or at least try work normally done by the opposite sex before making a final job choice. Only 15 percent of the girls or boys surveyed received any information on work experience currently dominated by the opposite sex.

This bias seemed to be rooted in schools rather than in the workplace. Eight in 10 employers surveyed said a better gender mix would create a better range of skills and talents. However, this idealism is not expressed in remuneration paid. In 2005, British women who worked full-time were earning 18 percent less per hour than men who worked full-time and the gap had changed little since 1980. In 2007, the Chartered Management Institute discovered that the pay gap was actually widening. At director level, men earned 23 percent more, an increase over the decade of three percentage points. This was despite evidence that women were more motivated and productive.[8]

In the *more feminine* cultures, sex roles are less sharply distinguished, and men and women have more equal access to the same job at all levels. For example, both may be senior politicians, air pilots, nurses, primary school teachers. In a family, the better paid parent might go to work, whether male or female, and the parent with less earning power would stay at home to bring up the children. The company should not interfere in its employees' private lives. Achievement is measured in terms of human contacts rather than of power and property, and motivation is less. Members stress relating to others rather than competing. Individual brilliance is suspect and the outsider and anti-hero are regarded sympathetically.

Figure 2.2 shows that the most masculine culture is Japan, followed by Austria and Venezuela. The most feminine is Sweden, followed by Norway and The Netherlands.

2.5.5   Long- vs. short-term orientation

Hofstede's team producing the model and the questionnaire items were all Western, and this was held up by some as evidence of an inherent Western bias. At the same time, a group of researchers from nine Asian and Pacific countries administered a version of an alternative instrument to small groups of students in 10 national or ethnic groups, posing questions that reflected Asian cultures. Michael Bond re-analyzed these findings and found a close correlation with most of the Hofstede findings, but less so with uncertainty avoidance. He designed a new questionnaire, the Chinese value survey (CVS), and Hofstede and Bond (1988) presented a new dimension termed the "Confucian dimension", tested with students of 23 countries. This discriminated between values associated with long- and short-term orientations. It indicated a distinction between Western concerns with truth and the eastern search for virtue.

Hofstede's (1991) theory of Confucianism was that

*   the stability of society is based upon unequal relationships between people;
*   the family is the prototype of all social organizations;
*   virtuous behavior towards others consists of not treating others as one would not like to be treated oneself;
*   virtue with regard to one's task in life consists of trying to acquire skills and education, working hard, not spending more than necessary, being patient and persevering (p. 165).

Of the 23 countries surveyed the most Confucian culture was China, followed by Hong Kong and Taiwan. The least was Pakistan followed by Nigeria and the Philippines.

2.6   Applying Hofstede's Model

This section reviews some of the opportunities and problems in applying Hofstede's model, and deals generally with the implications for comparative analysis. This discussion is continued in the next chapter.

2.6.1   Applying the model

Hofstede's model has strengths, which have to be taken into account:

*   Perhaps no other model has gone so far in controlling its INFORMANT POPULATION across so wide a number of cultures. All informants are employees of the same company, IBM. This control means that comparisons can be made, despite questions that might arise over generalizing to other occupational groups within the same national culture.

- The DIMENSIONS tap into deep cultural values and make significant comparisons between national cultures.
- The connotations of each dimension have RELEVANCE to management.
- The comparisons that can be made are of immediate interest to the international manager concerned with establishing and implementing management structures and systems.

No other study compares so many other national cultures with comparable rigor. Despite its limitations, this is still the best formal model there is.

The model is most useful when its limitations are respected. It cannot be applied to describing individual psychology or organizational culture. It does not examine values that might be shared by regions – other than Confucianism, particular to the Chinese world. It does not make absolute statements about any particular culture, but offers sets of comparisons.

The findings indicate which orientation *most* members of a culture group are likely to adopt in routine situations. They may have to be modified to the *specific* situation and needs. The manager who needs to understand a particular setting is wise to supplement comparative findings by the single-culture research conducted by anthropologists. In addition, he or she is likely to be concerned with making decisions for a specific industry and organization, and for this needs an understanding of industry standards and the organizational culture.

It is not the case that Hofstede profiles describe only the values accepted by the power elite. In practice, the majority endorse their shared culture, even though an outsider might perceive that they are its victims. (In times of crisis, this consensus can break down, and when this happens the culture starts to shift – see Chapter 4.) The implication is that members' cultural values must be inferred from their behavior in routine circumstances and not be their ideals of how they think they should behave and their attitudes, or by the outsider's values and attitudes.

Finally, the manager needs to take into account how far the target situation equates to Hofstede's informant pool – IBM. Members of an organization participating in the same industry are likely to share many of the same characteristics, and the manager might feel more inclined to take the IBM findings on trust. On the other hand, the model might be more questionable when applied to, say, a food producer based in a rural area of the country.

2.6.2   Limitations of the model

First, Hofstede's unit of analysis is the NATION STATE, which imposes artificial limits on the notion of the culture group. This criticism is commonly made against all models in the comparative tradition, and is dealt with in greater length in 3.2.7.

Second, the model implies that dimensions have the SAME MEANING in all cultures; for example, that the phenomenon of "individualism" has the same connotations in both Culture A and Culture B, and differs only in degree – that Culture A is the more individualist. This also is a problem in all comparative analysis, and is developed in 3.3.2.

Third, Hofstede's informants worked within a SINGLE INDUSTRY (the computer industry) and a single multinational. This raises the question of how far each IBM unit can be considered culturally typical of the country in which it is based (see McSweeney, 2002, p. 101). It can be argued that the values of IBM employees are common only to a small group (educated, generally middle class, city dwelling); other social groups (for instance, unskilled manual workers, public sector employees, family entrepreneurs, etc.) are more or less unrepresented.

Fourth, doubts arise in respect of BIAS IN THE QUESTIONNAIRE RESPONSES. McSweeney (2002) argues that the

> ... administration of the survey and the ownership of its results were IBM's; some of the questionnaires were completed within groups and not individually. *(p. 103)*

And he claims that some respondents had foreknowledge that their managers might develop new policies on the bases of the survey results.

Many of the criticisms made of Hofstede's model apply far wider, to the notion of any cross-cultural comparison. Questions of relevance arise in applying a bi-lateral model to a global organization in which a number of cultures are interacting and possibly influencing each other. These questions are addressed in the next chapter.

2.7   Implications for the Manager

Compare an organization that you know well in YOUR OWN CULTURE and an organization in the same industry but in SOME OTHER CULTURE.

1   In which organization:
   (a)   Is the manager more likely to participate with his/her subordinates as an equal?
   (b)   Is competition for jobs, resources, and benefits more likely to be tolerated?
   (c)   Are hirings and promotions more likely to be decided by membership of social groups outside the organization?
   (d)   Are male and female jobs distinguished?
   (e)   Is conflict between departments considered normal?
   (f)   Are staff willing to work outside office hours – possibly without pay?
   (g)   Are staff willing to accept micro-supervision?
2   How far do these factors explain your answers?
   (a)   Differences in organizational cultures (see Chapter 5);
   (b)   Differences in size;
   (c)   Differences in the personalities of the CEOs;
   (d)   Differences in national cultures.

In instances where you think national culture is the main differentiating factor, how far do your answers reflect Hofstede's comparisons of the two cultures.

2.8 SUMMARY

This chapter has introduced the notion that national cultures can be effectively analyzed on a comparative basis, and has examined three models that reflect this approach. Section 2.2 discussed the implications of COMPARATIVE ANALYSIS. The KLUCKHOHN AND STRODTBECK model was presented in 2.3, the HALL model in 2.4, and the HOFSTEDE model in 2.5. Section 2.6 dealt with questions of APPLYING the HOFSTEDE's MODEL. General problems in using comparative analysis are dealt with in the next chapter.

2.9   EXERCISE

Decide whether the behavior described in the last sentence of each of the following might be TYPICAL or UNTYPICAL in the cultural context. Apply Hofstede's model.

1 Explain your answers.
2 Think of circumstances under which your first answer might NOT apply – for example, in a particular industry, in extraordinary competitive or economic circumstances.
   (a) In the UK, you discover that a junior employee is the daughter of a powerful politician, and so you promote her to a senior job. She is a poor communicator and unqualified. Nevertheless, this promotion is happily accepted by (almost) all other employees.
   (b) At company headquarters, you form a mixed-culture work team consisting of Japanese men and Swedish women, and chaired by a woman. These persons have been temporarily borrowed from your subsidiaries in Tokyo and Stockholm. The team is neither compatible nor productive.
   (c) In Australia, the great majority of your employees opt to take relatively low salaries in return for guarantees of life-time employment.
   (d) In Sweden, your subsidiary is losing money. You decide to introduce new technology, which means scrapping the previous technology and retraining many of the workforce. The outcomes of making the change are uncertain; the technology might be a great success, but if it fails, all will suffer. The workforce quickly accept your proposals.

(e) In Thailand, you appoint a new local top manager who has a reputation for "micro-managing". Khun Samet is very good at telling subordinates how to perform the details of their jobs, what they are doing right and what they are doing wrong. He expects to be consulted about every decision. A visiting American consultant has advised you that "he's too fussy. Employees don't like that. And they expect power to be delegated. There's going to be trouble." But your Thai employees don't agree. They welcome this close supervision.

Notes

1 Tom Lloyd. Personal view. *Daily Telegraph*, July 14, 2003.

2 Christopher Davies. Arsenal counting on Campbell to stand tall. *Daily Telegraph*, February 19, 2002.

3 No cancellation of power, water bills. *Kuwait Times*, February 11, 1996.

4 Commercial for Hugo Bros. *Music TV*, aired in December 1998.

5 Time to button our lips. *The Nation* (Bangkok), December 20, 2001.

6 Martin Gainsborough. The Ho Chi Minh city elite. *The Vietnam Business Journal*, November 23, 2000.

7 Juliet Hindell. New age for Japan's fathers. *Sunday Telegraph*, May 2, 1999.

8 Gordon Rayner. Pay gap is growing between men and women. *Daily Telegraph*, September 5, 2007.

CHAPTER THREE

Analyzing Cultures: After Hofstede

CHAPTER OUTLINE

Introduction	Implications for the Manager
Comparative Analysis since Hofstede	Summary
	Exercise
New Approaches	

3.1 Introduction

Mr Park was a Korean manufacturer of computer parts. He planned to open a subsidiary in the USA, and asked an American friend where he might find a good workforce and build his plant:

> "Some of my friends say Boston, but my family want Florida. Except that Florida is hot; does it matter?"
>
> "It matters a great deal," said his consultant. "Boston still has an Irish culture. And in Florida, many of the people are Hispanic. Many speak Spanish better than English."
>
> "They're both in America," objected Mr Park. "They can't be very different."
>
> "They are," his friend asserted. And then he asked, "Have you thought about California? There are large Korean minorities on the coast."
>
> "Yes," Mr Park agreed. "But in America . . . are they still Korean?"

The problems that faced Mr Park was that he could neither make assumptions about cultural homogeneity within a single country, nor about how far immigrant groups had modified their original values. This chapter examines why these uncertainties cause problems in making bi-lateral comparisons of culture. By "bi-lateral" we mean comparisons

between two cultures as systems, without taking into account how individuals representing the cultures might influence each other's behavior in their interactions.

The previous chapter introduced the notion of cross-cultural management research,
and suggested its importance to the international manager. It embarked from Boyacigiller
et al.'s (2003) distinction between three streams of research, those that

- compare cultures;
- examine interactions between persons from different cultures;
- examine multiple-culture groupings, for example in a global company in which members of many different cultures may interact.

Chapter 2 focused on models that make comparisons and in particular on the most
influential of all, that offered by Hofstede. Here we examine work conducted since Hofstede's model was introduced, and ask how far cross-cultural research is being progressively influenced by the second and third streams.

3.2   Comparative Analysis since Hofstede

In the nearly 30 years since Hofstede first published *Culture's Consequences* (1980) the
model has been widely utilized in a large body of theoretical and empirical work. It
has attracted a range of endorsements, many of which have confirmed his findings: see
Sondergaard (1994); Smith (1994); Smith, Dugan and Trompenaars (1996) Merritt (1999).
A useful review of 180 studies was contributed by Kirkman et al. (2006), which discussed
limitations in the Hofstede-inspired research and made recommendations for its application. On the other hand, the model has also attracted criticism, and many scholars have
called for radically different approaches to the problem of doing cross-cultural analysis.

This section discusses five models that post-date *Culture's Consequences* and still retain
its fundamental principle of making bi-lateral comparisons. They are

- Laurent (1983) – see 3.2.1;
- Trompenaars (1993) – see 3.2.2;
- Schwartz (1994) – see 3.2.3;
- Schwartz (1999) – see 3.2.4;
- House et al. (various authors and dates) – see 3.2.5.

They indicate how far comparative analysis still follows Hofstede's model.

3.2.1   *Laurent (1983)*

Laurent (1983) examined attitudes to power and relationships. He analyzed the values of
managers in nine European countries (Switzerland, Germany, Denmark, Sweden, the UK,
The Netherlands, Belgium, Italy, France) and the USA. Adler, Campbell and Laurent (1989)
collected additional data from the People's Republic of China, Indonesia and Japan.

This work differs from the other comparative studies examined here in that it focuses on how managers in different cultures resolve problems, and only distinguishes the cultures by influence. It treats management as a process by which managers express their values. It examines perceptions of the organization as a political system, an authority system, a role formulation system, and a hierarchical relationship system. Three illustrations are used here:

(a) how far the manager carries his/her status into the wider context outside the work-place;
(b) the manager's capacity to bypass levels in the hierarchy;
(c) the manager as expert in contrast to the manager as facilitator.

(a) Managerial status in the wider context   In response to the statement "through their professional activity, managers play an important role in society", the percentages IN AGREEMENT were as follows (fragment only):

Denmark   32%
UK   40%
The Netherlands   45%
Germany   46%
Sweden   54%
USA   52%
Switzerland   65%
Italy   74%
France   76%
(Laurent, 1983, p. 80).

In France and Italy the manager carries his status into activities outside the workplace. But in Denmark and the UK, rank in the workplace does not carry automatic seniority in other spheres. In a recent English Football Association cup match, the referee was a police sergeant, and his subordinate official on the touchline a police inspector.

(b) Bypassing the hierarchy   In response to the statement "In order to have efficient work relationships, it is often necessary to bypass the hierarchical line", the national groups responded thus in DISAGREEMENT (fragment only):

Sweden   22%
UK   31%
USA   32%
Denmark   37%
The Netherlands 39%
Switzerland   41%
Belgium   42%
France   42%
Germany   46%

Italy   75%
(Laurent, 1983, p. 86).
People's Republic of China 66%
(Adler et al., 1989, p. 64).

These figures mean, for instance, that Swedish employees bypass hierarchical lines when direct contact with knowledge sources located elsewhere in the company promises to produce greater efficiency and speed. Swedes are relatively happy working in matrix structures, in which the subordinate reports to two managers on the same hierarchical level. But suppose that they are working in an Italian company; their Italian boss perceives this lack of respect for the hierarchy as insubordinate and threatening. And Italians are less likely to accept a matrix structure.

(c) The manager as expert vs. the manager as facilitator Adler et al. (1989) asked managers from 13 countries to respond to the statement, "It is important for a manager to have at hand precise answers to most of the questions that his subordinates may raise about their work". Percentages in AGREEMENT were (fragment only):

Sweden   10%
The Netherlands   17%
USA   18%
Denmark   23%
UK   27%
Switzerland   38%
Belgium   44%
Germany   46%
France   53%
Italy   66%
Indonesia   73%
People's Republic of China 74%
Japan   78%
(Adler et al., 1989, p. 69).

In Sweden, it is more important that the manager should be able to tap sources of expert power, perhaps elsewhere in the company, than give all the technical answers him/herself. The Swede is less inhibited about approaching an outsider for advice.

At the opposite extreme, the manager in a traditional Japanese company should be able to provide specialist answers to technical questions. Because subordinates cannot easily challenge his/her advice, they tend to value it above suggestions given by peers, whatever its quality. The Japanese manager who cannot answer questions associated with his/her function loses status. Because the unity of the group depends on their superior's maintaining status, any loss would endanger the security of the entire group, and so also the interests of its individual members. So it is in their interests to maintain their superior's status. This may mean that they restrict questions to topics on which they know that the superior is technically competent.

Lee (2003) argues a case that appears to contradict this. He claims that in negotiations Asian professionals focus on affiliation in their partner selection process, while Westerners emphasize personal expert knowledge. Perhaps a distinction needs to be drawn between values associated with the negotiator and the manager directing a group who may resist detailed supervision.

3.2.2   *Trompenaars (1993)*

Trompenaars was particularly concerned with the practicalities of managing, consulting, and doing business with members of other cultures. His model is based on questionnaire responses given by 15,000 informants, of whom about 75 percent were managers and 25 percent administrative staff, representing a range of companies and industries. The informants were drawn from 50 countries. Responses were given to short case questions used in training. The model had seven parameters:

1 Relationships and rules; *UNIVERSALISM* vs. *PARTICULARISM*. Cultures can be located between these two extremes. The universalist approach is to say that what is good and right applies everywhere; for instance, rules penalizing sales staff who do not fulfill their quotas apply whether or not the individual claims extenuating circumstances. The particularist emphasizes the obligation of relationships; a salesman failed to fill his quota because of his concern for a sick son, and so can be excused.
2 The group and the individual; *COLLECTIVISM* vs. *INDIVIDUALISM*. International management is seriously affected by collectivist or individualist preferences, particularly in the areas of negotiations, decision-making, and motivation. Collectivist cultures prefer plural representation in negotiations, and typically spend longer in decision-making because of the need to develop a consensus.
3 Feelings and relationships; *NEUTRAL* vs. *AFFECTIVE cultures*. Members of more neutral cultures keep their feelings carefully controlled and subdued, and typically try not to let emotions corrupt their reasoning processes when doing business. Members of affective cultures signal their emotions.
4 How far we get involved; *SPECIFIC* vs. *DIFFUSE cultures*. In more specific cultures, the manager separates his/her task relationship with a subordinate from other dealings he/she has with this person. Each aspect of their relationship is separated from all other aspects. In a diffuse culture, every aspect of their relationship influences all others.
5 How we accord *STATUS*. Some cultures accord status to people on the basis of their achievements; this is known as achieved status. Other cultures accord status on the basis of class, gender, family background, age. This is known as ascribed status.

6 How we manage *TIME*. Some cultures are more sequential in that time is treated as a series of events, and some are more synchronic, in which a number of events are juggled at the same time. Some cultures try to live entirely in the present; some believe in destiny that they must realize; and some focus on nostalgia.

7 How we relate to *NATURE*. Some cultures believe that we can and should control nature; these "inner-directed" cultures are prepared to fight against nature. "Outer-directed" cultures are prepared to go along with the laws, directions and forces of nature.

In 1997 Trompenaars produced a second edition of the book, this time in collaboration with Hampden-Turner. This departed significantly from the first edition and rejected much of its comparative underpinning, and is discussed in 3.3.

3.2.3   Schwartz (1994)

Schwartz developed his model over a number of stages. In 1994, he argued both that human values have an implicit universality, and can also be differentiated – that is, a particular configuration expresses a particular national culture. So in this respect Schwarz treats the national group as the unit of analysis – like Hofstede.

Schwartz differed from Hofstede in that he claimed values were articulated, and expressed desirable goals that served as guiding principles in the life of the person or group. That is, they express motivations.

In this model, 10 value types are differentiated. They are power, achievement, hedonism, stimulation, self-direction, universalism, benevolence, tradition, conformity, security. And each value type has exemplary values; in the case of power, these are social power, authority, and wealth; of achievement, successful, capable, and ambitious. In general the national culture is assumed to be a valid unit of analysis. Each national culture has its core emphasis, and national cultures fall into broad cultural groupings, and which are related by geographical proximity.

3.2.4   Schwartz (1999)

Schwartz (1999) reiterated Hofstede's point that the appropriate unit of analysis is the society or cultural group, not the individual (see also Schwartz and Sagiv, 1995). He asked how the meaning of work in the life of individuals is influenced by prevailing cultural value priorities.

These values influence the emphasis of institutions; for example: economic and legal systems tend to be more competitive in cultures where success by the individual is more highly valued. On the other hand, these systems tend to emphasize the well-being of the group where cooperation is more highly valued.

The model applies data collected from 49 nations around the world. Seven value types are identified, structured along three polar dimensions:

1 CONSERVATISM vs. INTELLECTUAL and AFFECTIVE AUTONOMY;
2 HIERARCHY vs. EGALITARIANISM;
3 MASTERY vs. HARMONY.

Associated with these value types are 45 values, for example: *Humble, Authority, Influential, Wealth, Social Power* are associated with HIERARCHY, and *Capable, Successful, Choosing own goals, Independent, Ambitious,* and *Daring* with MASTERY. Values are inferred from the informants' beliefs. These are derived from the choices they make between prepared sentences. For example, they might choose between "Every person in our society should be entitled to interesting and meaningful work" as against "A worker should value the work he or she does even if it is boring, dirty or unskilled."

Each culture has its core emphasis and this is expressed in work goals. The implication for the international manager is that work goals vary across cultures, and hence motivators tied to specific work goals are likely to have varying success in different cultures. And so in cultures where hierarchy and mastery are most valued, the open pursuit of power is more acceptable; for example in (Hierarchy) China, Korea, and (Mastery) USA, England, Israel.

Cultures fall into broad cultural groupings, and these groupings are related to geographical proximity. Like Hofstede, Schwartz found that the cultures of Sweden and its neighbor Denmark were almost identical. In terms of his seven value types, they share high EGALITARIANISM, INTELLECTUAL and AFFECTIVE AUTONOMY, moderately high HARMONY, moderately low MASTERY, very low HIERARCHY and CONSERVATISM. And cultures not in geographical proximity may also differ significantly. Schwartz points to China and Italy, which have virtually opposite profiles on all but CONSERVATISM and AFFECTIVE AUTONOMY.

This model has a quantitative basis. Informants valued the importance of 45 values as guiding principles in their lives. Evaluations were made on the basis of an eight point Likert scale. Hofstede attempted to standardize his research by drawing all his informants from one multinational; Schwarz drew most of his informants from one industry – school teaching. Teachers were presumed to be key carriers of their national cultures, and further testing suggested that teachers typified their culture in the values which they articulated and tried to pass on.

As for applications; Schwartz suggests that his model defines the centrality of work, societal norms about work, and work goals in different cultures. In addition it should be applied in predicting and interpreting national differences in

> ... risk-taking and innovation in work; managers' behaviour towards workers; decision-making styles of reliance on own judgment, rules, consultation with superiors or subordinates, etc.; penetration of work involvements into other areas of life. *(p. 45)*

The model is well grounded in the theory of comparative analysis, and introduces a number of categories not used elsewhere. It also achieves a level of complexity that may attract the scholar but deter the manager.

3.2.5 *House* et al. *(various authors and dates)*

House and his colleagues take the standard comparative to cultural analysis. Their massive Project GLOBE is summarized in a work of 848 pages (House et al., 2004); see also House et al. (1999), Littrell (2002), and the review in Petersen (2004).

The GLOBE team focused on the leadership traits thought desirable in different cultures. They described cultural variables and then predict their impact on organizational processes and leadership styles. Their model refined Hofstede's model and disentangled the five basic dimensions (including the Confucian dynamic), ending up with nine. The first five of their dimensions reflect Hofstede's pioneering model, including two types of collectivism. These usefully distinguish between the work-based focus of Japanese culture, and the family-based focus of Chinese culture:

1 UNCERTAINTY AVOIDANCE
2 POWER DISTANCE
3 COLLECTIVISM I: societal emphasis on collectivism
4 COLLECTIVISM 2: family collectivist practices
5 GENDER EGALITARIANISM
6 ASSERTIVENESS
7 FUTURE ORIENTATION
8 PERFORMANCE ORIENTATION
9 HUMANE ORIENTATION

3.2.6 *Problems in using comparative analysis*

The examples above show the continuing influence of comparative analysis based on the notion that values in one culture can be compared to those in some other culture, and that conducted on a bi-lateral basis. All adopt the nation state as the unit of analysis, and all use categories that in some cases can be traced at least back to Hofstede – and in the case of Trompenaars' (1993) use of nature, back to Kluckhohn and Strodtbeck. The most recent, that offered by House et al., is perhaps the most loyal to Hofstede's model, despite the authors maintaining a highly critical stance.

These problems commonly arise in using comparative analysis:

* the use of the national culture group as the unit of analysis – see 3.3.1;
* the points on which national cultures can be realistically compared – see 3.3.2;
* the different uses of qualitative and quantitative comparisons – see 3.3.3.

3.2.7   The unit of analysis: the nation state

The first criticism commonly made against all models in the comparative tradition is that the use of the nation state as the unit of analysis imposes artificial limits on the notion of the culture group. This is a convenient generalization, but gives rise to a range of problems.

First, it is assumed that the national territory and the limits of the culture correspond. This is misleading. Some cultures spread across national boundaries; for example, French language and culture is dominant in parts of Belgium and Switzerland. And some members have left the homeland to live elsewhere. How far should a model of Japanese culture take into account the values of those Japanese who prefer to work in the USA, or Europe?

Second, this assumes equivalent degrees of cultural homogeneity in all nations, or that varying degrees of heterogeneity may be overlooked. The concept of "national culture" is assumed to apply to the USA in the same respect that it applies to Japan. But it cannot distinguish differences between the mainstream culture and subcultures, and between subcultures.

In many situations this may not matter. But the Introduction made the point that in a heterogeneous society such as the USA, generalizations about the mainstream culture may have limited application in regions where the majority do not even speak the mainstream language of English. In several of the southern states, Hispanic cultures are at least as significant. That is, the model is not equipped to identify and evaluate differences between the mainstream culture and minorities (see Sivakumar and Nakata, 2001). Swiss territory is shared between French, German, Italian and Romansch groups.

Third, some nations are relatively more heterogeneous than others; the USA and Brazil, for instance. The massive land mass of China contains a number of subcultures that have their own dialects of Chinese and command economic power. Relations between mainstream cultures and subcultures vary, and variations may arise from political, economic, or historical factors. In his generally sympathetic discussion of Hofstede's work, Smith (2002) points out that

> It is very possible that societies differ in the degree to which they hang together in a unified
> manner.   *(p. 56)*

Comparative models are unable to show these variances, or their effects. And the models cannot distinguish the values of long-term members of the group from those that have newly joined. These newcomers may include immigrant groups still loyal to their native culture; perhaps they consciously reject aspects of the culture of their hosts, and perhaps only gradually assimilate their values.

3.2.8   Points of comparison

Comparative analysis means not only that the same qualities are observed in the cultures being compared, but that dimensions have the same meaning in all cultures. For example, it implies that the phenomenon of "individualism" means the same in both Culture A and

Culture B, and differs only in degree – that Culture A is the more individualist. But is this necessarily the case?

In American culture, individualism is generally seen in positive terms. But the Japanese sometimes equate it with selfishness. Brummelhuis (1984) explained the Thai concept in terms of avoidance and distrust of authority:

> The individual's preoccupation is not so much with self-realization and autonomy as with adaptation to the social or cosmological environment. *(pp. 44–5)*

In other words, he or she resorts to individual solutions as a reaction to social pressures and as a means of escaping them. This does not correspond to the American sense of the term.

The same problem arises in respect of the other dimensions. Many scholars applying notions of collectivism tend to classify both Japan and China as similarly collectivist (the model proposed by House et al. being exceptional). Yet, in practice, this is usually not the case other than trivially. For instance, in Japan loyalty is directed more towards the organization or workplace, and in China towards the family unit. That is, the bases of collectivism differ, and hence no precise comparison can be made.

Schwartz (1999) asserts that cross-cultural comparisons can only be made when values have "relatively equivalent meanings to respondents across cultures" (p. 30). This is fundamental, but whether there is equivalence in meanings is difficult to substantiate, particularly in studies that purport to make valid comparisons of values across different language groups. In practice, the international manager is asked to take equivalence on trust. This problem is not particular to Schwartz's model. It applies to Hofstede's model, and to all others that are based on questionnaire analysis.

3.2.9 The data

The models produced by Hall and Kluckhohn–Strodtbeck provide frameworks for the analyst to structure his observations and intuitions, and in themselves say little about specific cultures. Some applications have been made Kluckhohn–Strodtbeck, but in small-scale survey work (see Hills, 2002). The original model provided few measures for the proposed orientations. It is general rather than specific and can only be used to examine general trends in behavior, and not used to predict specific behaviors in any one situation. (Hills, 2002)

The user is made responsible for their applications to events in the real world.

Other models discussed here (Laurent, Trompenaars, Schwartz) are based on quantitative data. Trompenaars' database includes in excess of 15,000 participants, of whom 75 percent belong to management and 25 percent to general administration.

The quantitatively-based models might seem to give some precision and so to have greater predictive value. But as we have seen, this must depend in part on what is being measured, and whether the manager can be assured that the same values are being compared in the two cultures. In sum, a cultural dimension carries different associations when used to describe different cultures, and hence there can be no EXACT point of comparison.

Second, quantitative analysis is often based on written questionnaire surveys. In some cultures it is assumed that an objective relationship exits between survey and informants, and that the responses given by all informants are treated with equal objectivity. Questionnaires used in the Anglo cultures commonly carry a guarantee that answers given will be treated in confidence. But this relationship between research instrument and informant does not occur in all cultures. Elsewhere, it might be assumed that the researcher represents the hierarchy in the organization, and that top management will insist on access to the raw data. In such cases, the informants may feel that they are obliged to provide the "correct" answers that top management hopes to see, and therefore these "correct answers" have to be deduced.

The implication is that the communicative relationship between research instrument (reflecting the researcher) and informant varies. The Anglo researcher may be making a mistake if he assumes that quantitative data collected from different culture groups has equal validity as expressions of their values.

3.2.10   The strengths of comparative analysis

Comparative analysis enables the manager to make broad comparisons. It can make him sensitive to points at which differences between cultures might occur, and hence sensitive to possible points of conflict, for example. Many of these models focus on aspects of social life that are of relevance to the manager – for example, relations between members of groups, between superiors, subordinates, and peers.

If these models are interpreted as though carved in stone and not to be questioned, they contribute little. They must be used pragmatically, in response to the context. Depending on the identity of the group with which he is immediately concerned, the manager has to decide how much emphasis to lay on the findings provided by the model. For example, when working in Japan, in a traditional industry, in a company that has been relatively untouched by global influences, the manager might decide that Hall's model of high context is still very useful. But it might give weaker predictions of behavior in the Tokyo subsidiary of an American advertising agency. Finally, comparative analysis should usually be treated as a "first best guess"; the manager needing deeper understanding of the culture among which he is working may need to supplement it with single-culture studies and perhaps his own analysis.

3.2.11   The weaknesses of comparative analysis

In the time when the pioneers developed comparative analysis, cultural stability could be assumed as normal. Thirty years later, this is much less the case.

As our global business world becomes increasingly complex, scholars have become aware of the weaknesses in the early models. First and most important, the assumption of the national group as an appropriate unit of analysis is unreliable.

Second, common values are assumed among those identified as group members, and the values of fringe members cannot be easily taken into account. That is, points at which non-mainstream culture does not correspond to mainstream culture cannot be taken into account except as deviance.

Third, these models lack descriptive depth that an anthropologist might demand in respect of any one particular society. They may give useful indications of difference between any two or more cultures, but only shallow findings in respect of any one culture. Because they are essentially comparative, they cannot make definitive judgments about any one culture. Hence, statements such as "Italy has a high-context culture", and "Swedish culture is individualist", and so on, are always weak. These examples beg the questions "high-context compared to where?", "individualist compared to where?", and how are these characteristics expressed in each culture?

Fourth, they do not help the manager distinguish the influence of non-cultural factors – such as economic factors, or organizational culture – on a particular instance of behavior. They do not help the manager distinguish the effects of national culture, organizational culture, and industry norms.

Fifth, bi-lateral models are static in the senses that

- they do not help the manager predict change in the culture. This topic is investigated in Chapter 4;
- they do not explain why groups and individuals are led to modify their values through interaction with each other. The next section deals with attempts to overcome this problem.

3.3 New Approaches

The new approaches designed to resolve these problems can mean rethinking the notion of culture.

For example, Triandis et al. (1988) turned to three cases of in-group relationships in arguing that characterization of individualism and collectivism in opposition is inaccurate. Members of different collectivist cultures do not share the same characteristics, and some aspects of social interaction in a given collectivist culture may appear as typical of a given individualist culture. The status of different in-groups varies across cultures, and degrees of collectivism depend very much on which in-group is present and in what context.

Lenartowicz and Roth (1999) re-examined anthropological arguments that cultures are so complex that they cannot be measured but merely observed and described. They discussed the interrelationship of culture with a range of factors normally overlooked by comparative analysts; these include age, gender, education and location. They were particularly interested in how far regional affiliations made in childhood influence cultural identity, and proposed a framework by which cultural groupings function as the unit of analysis.

Comparative analysis implies a gap between cultures which is constant. This has given rise to the notion of cultural distance, which is widely applied both in planning expansion to foreign markets and deciding staffing needs. The notion holds that the wider the gap, the greater the needs for headquarters control and hence the greater the transaction costs. However, the Shenkar (2001) argued that the notion of a constant gap is without foundation. Even if cultural differences can be described, distances cannot be measured. And the construct says more about the ability – or failure – of individuals and organizations to adjust. In practice, differences are as likely to be synergetic as destructive. Shenkar suggested focusing less on the void between cultures and rather on the "friction" arising from the positive interface between them.

Lowe (2002) also examined the process of cultural change, and the integration and synthesis of values in practice. He argued that the structural-functionalist research tradition dominated by Hofstede reflects Western orthodoxies that may be far removed from the interparadigmatic approaches taken in the cultures under discussion.

Fang (2006) focused on the importance of understanding the dynamics of cultural change, and in particular

- intracultural variations within a national culture;
- the meaning of national culture from contextual and time points of view;
- the new identity of national cultures in the age of globalization.

Trompenaars and Hampden-Turner (1997) is the second edition of a book published by Trompenaars alone in 1993, but, as noted in 3.2.2, it differs in important respects. This critiques Hofstede's model and contributes a revised model on seven dimensions. Although this looks like a standard comparative model, the authors argue that we should move away from thinking in terms of national stereotypes and instead focus on understanding persons with different cultural roots and interactions between them, which are often expressed in a shared need to find harmony. The dimensions are

- Universalism vs. Particularism;
- Analyzing vs. Integrating;
- Individualism vs. Communitarianism;
- Inner-directed vs. Outer-directed;
- Time as sequence vs. Time as synchronization;
- Achieved status vs. Ascribed Status.
- Equality vs Hierarchy.

These dimensions build on the great tradition. Individualism vs. Communitarianism reflects distinctions made by Kluckhohn and Strodtbeck and Hofstede. The useful distinction made between Achieved as against Ascribed status carries us back to work by Laurent and his colleagues.

Bhawuk (2001) adopted a similarly practical approach to the problem of discovering cultural differences, through the development of teaching materials. The proposed cultural assimilators are designed to teach both theoretical and practical lessons, and to teach an awareness of the cultural differences in the relationship between the individual and how he/she relates to groups and interpersonal and intergroup relationships. Bhawak's work demonstrates the second and third approaches discussed by Boyacigiller et al. (2003).

3.4   Implications for the Manager

- The body of work described above indicates that the theoretical foundations of the comparative tradition are increasingly questioned. A range of novel approaches are being discussed and even the notion of "culture" is under scrutiny. See also the papers collected in Andrews and Mead (2008).
- But as yet, no analytical system has emerged that has the authority of that developed by Hofstede.
- In this part of the book, examples of difference are clarified by reference to Hofstede's model and by bi-lateral comparisons. But in later chapters we have moved towards a more fluid treatment of culture and on the extent to which relationships between different cultures influence individual behavior.
- The notion that culture is not a constant belongs to the individual, evolves in his/her experience, and introduces a temporal dimension to the discussion.
- The implication for the manager is, first, to look at how change in values and behavior as individuals and groups interact over time.
- Second, the manager needs to develop skills of predicting the effect of interactions in changing economic and business contexts.
- On the macro-cultural level, the effect of context on national culture is examined in the next chapter.

3.5   SUMMARY

The previous chapter introduced the notion of cross-cultural research and its applications in management. It focused on comparative analysis and on Hofstede's model. This chapter has discussed developments since the model was first presented, and has indicated possible future paths.

Section 3.2 discussed COMPARATIVE ANALYSIS SINCE HOFSTEDE and examined five models developed since 1980. All indicate critical rethinking, but all adhere to the fundamentals of the tradition and in particular to the notion of the nation state as the unit of analysis. However, it is increasingly apparent that this and other aspects of comparative analysis give rise to PROBLEMS, both in theory and practice, and these are examined in 3.3. Section 3.4 introduced a number of NEW APPROACHES being tried by scholars. The field of cross-cultural research is thriving.

3.6 EXERCISE

This exercise asks you to research how far the individual's behavior is influenced by interactions with members of other cultures. If you are studying in a business school, your class may include members of other cultures. If you are a LOCAL student, answer (1)–(4) below. If you are from SOME OTHER CULTURE, answer (5)–(7).

1 LOCAL STUDENTS: ask your colleagues who have previously studied in some other culture about their behavior when they joined the class. How has their behavior changed? In particular, ask about their present
   (a) attitude towards a teacher;
   (b) behavior when the teacher enters the room;
   (c) willingness to give a teacher information in class;
   (d) willingness to argue with a teacher;
   (e) willingness to follow rules for submitting assignments;
   (f) attitudes towards other students in class.

2 How far does their present behavior in each of the above differ to their behavior when studying at school or university in their previous culture?

3 How do they explain any changes in their behavior? How far is their present behavior explained by interactions with your culture or other cultures?

4 How far has your behavior changed? How do you explain this?

5 If you have previously studied in SOME OTHER CULTURE, decide how far your behavior has changed. Use the categories in (1). above as a framework for your answers.

6 How do you explain any changes in your behavior? How far is your present behavior explained by interactions with the local culture or other cultures?

7 What other factors may have influenced your changing?

Movement in the Culture

4.1   Introduction

A 2005 survey conducted in Japan seemed to indicate a significant movement in the culture. In the past, most Japanese – both male and female – had assumed that wives should not go out to work. But for the first time those who believed

> that wives should stay at home are in a minority for the first time, but the majority still want women to do most household chores.
>
>   The Cabinet Office survey on gender equality showed that 48.9 percent of respondents were against wives being home-bound, while 45.2 percent supported it.[1]

These facts can be read two ways; either as an indication that the practice of women at work is becoming increasingly accepted, or that traditional discrimination still applies. The ambiguity shows how difficult it is to map cultural movement, even in a technologically developed society. The problems of identifying movement shift and the factors that may cause it are discussed here.

4.2   Recognizing Significant Movement in the Culture

In all areas of life, including the workplace, people must adjust to transition. Today's manager has to develop skills of identifying those events that cause movement in the value system, and to predict how these cultural movements will influence the business environment.

Because changes in the business environment may directly the manager's company and its relations with markets, he/she needs to understand shifts in the culture. These shifts may lead to changes in

- service and product markets;
- technologies;
- industries. Old industries disappear, new industries are born;
- the labor market. Old skills fall out of demand, new skills are at a premium; new social groups seek employment. In many economies, increasing numbers of women are entering the managerial workforce;
- social needs of the workforce. Employees need different relations with superiors, peers, and subordinates. New structures and systems are needed to organize and motivate performance;
- relations with the green environment. New regulations are imposed in order to protect natural resources;
- social structures, which mean that new social agencies are developed and old agencies take on new responsibilities. Changes in work patterns and technologies force changes in the traditional extended family and a weakening of traditional family ties. Social breakdown means that governments and not-for-profit organizations have to invest more in family welfare, marriage counseling, and social problems among the young.

4.2.1   Stability and movement

Cultures need both stability and movement in order to develop. On the one hand, excessive stability removes the need for experiment and creativity; on the other, excessive change can lead to fragmentation and total breakdown – as the Introductory case demonstrates.

For centuries, scholars have tried to find the optimal balance between stability and change. Conflict theorists such as Marx, Mills, Dahrendorf and others perceived all social systems to be in continual conflict; and the point of conflict is reflected in the society's predominant values. Functionalists such as Parsons and Merton described change as an adjustment process and focus on the natural capacity of social systems to adapt to strains and stresses in order to find a new stability. Social systems are functional when all parts are related and integrated.

4.2.2   Why the manager needs to understand cultural movement

The manager seldom deals directly with abstractions of change in the value system. Rather, he/she responds to concrete factors such as new market developments, new labor supplies and demands, new efficiencies in the labor force. These changes may reflect shifts in the deep culture. The company that recognizes significant shifts in the deep culture, and also perceives how these impact upon the market, is well equipped to cope with strategic opportunities and threats.

Suppose that economic events have caused a narrowing of power distances throughout society and a need for greater informality. When the new values are expressed in a demand for more casual clothing, opportunities arise for a clothing manufacturer. These new values have less immediate impact on the business of an insurance company. However, the demand for insurance IS boosted by events that stimulate a sense of anxiety – such as rising crime and disease rates, and a perceived increase in natural disasters such as earthquakes and floods.

Shift in the national culture also affects the internal arrangements of companies located in that culture and employing members of the national cultural group. Again, assuming that power distances are narrower throughout society, employees might respond more positively to closer relationships between superiors and subordinates in flatter structures. Employees expect a greater degree of participation in decision-making. Authority is decentralized and information is shared.

The managements of flat companies rely heavily on linking suppliers, customers, designers and even competitors in shifting collaborations. These intercompany networks are set up to exploit specific market opportunities. They are less formal and permanent than traditional corporate alliances.[2]

However, this does not mean that flattening the organization brings the same advantages in all companies, in all industries, and in all national cultural context.

The company alienates its members when it continues to operate procedures and structures that reflect outmoded values, just as it loses customers when it goes on producing outmoded goods and services. On the other hand, it makes another expensive mistake if it overcommits in accommodating shifts that later prove short-lived.

4.2.3   *Problems in recognizing significant movement*

Problems arise in distinguishing significant and deep-rooted shifts from superficial movement. Media stories tend to portray all economic, social and technological change as important. Stories of change attract attention and sell newspapers, and stories of continuity do not. Journalists work under time constraints which mean that they do not usually have the time to analyze the long-term implications of the events they report. Journalism can lead the observer into mistaking the values of a subculture for shift in the mainstream culture, and to assuming that a shift in the subculture reflects a general movement.

Finally, appearances might suggest that Culture X has moved but if neighboring cultures have also moved in the same direction, the movement in Culture X may be less significant.

Four years after completing his original research, Hofstede (1983) repeated it, and concluded that in the 50 countries then under investigation, individualism had increased in all but one, Pakistan.

Hofstede (1997) commented that "the cultures shift, but they shift together, so that the differences between them remain intact" (p. 77). That is, Japan – for example – may appear to be growing more individualist; but if all the other cultures have also moved towards greater individualism, the comparative differences are the same. This underlines the fact that essentially the model is comparative. This means that although Thai culture, say, is growing more individualist, Thailand is not likely to approximate to the USA in the immediate culture – because American culture is also growing more individualist.

4.2.4   Movement and the manager's roles

A final reason why the manager needs to understand the relationship between change in the environment and cultural shift is that the process affects his/her own role as a manager.

The manager is no longer restricted to planning, organizing, coordinating and controlling – which is how the French industrialist Henri Fayol described managerial functions in 1916. Since then, the manager has to be more than expert and autocratic. He has had to respond to and control a range of new factors in the environment – new economic and market forces, new relations with customers and suppliers, new technologies, new relations with skilled workforces, new management experiments with different management styles and structures.

The environment has grown so complex that no manager can hope to control all sources of information. In this age of uncertainty and discontinuity the modern manager has had to acquire skills of facilitating other people to find and manage their own sources of information. This has long been the case in cultures where the manager is expected to be a facilitator rather than an expert. Describing American managers, Mintzberg (1975) identified the new roles of figurehead, leader, liaison, monitor, disseminator, spokesman, entrepreneur, disturbance handler, resource allocator, and negotiator. A quarter century later, Blumen (2002) stressed similar qualities; managers "negotiate, persuade and integrate" (p. 90).

The problems of dealing with new uncertainties are more severe in cultures that still give greater emphasis to the manager's qualities as an expert. A Taiwanese commented that if a manager does not know the answer to a technical question, he/she "must say nothing or find a way of not answering" – anything rather than admit ignorance. The problems of maintaining face are particularly severe in industries where developments in technology outpace the manager's capacities to keep his expertise up to date.

Role confusion causes stress, which is acute in societies experiencing rapid economic change and cultural shift. It can be severe among local management in multinational companies. Perhaps most stressed are those senior local managers who have to respond to the different needs and values of expatriate top management above them, and to subordinate local staff below. These managers have the "invisible" role of negotiating and interpreting between different levels of the company.

4.2.5   *The speed of movement in the culture*

Problems of recognizing those culture shifts that promise to have long-term effects on market and workforce values are complicated when the deep values of a culture change slowly.

Why are cultures often slow to shift? First, any change can be painful. People's values are reinforced by habit and a fear of too much novelty. Second, individuals start learning their values in earliest childhood (see 1.3.6). At this age culture is learned without conscious effort and conscious resistance. This learning is extremely deep rooted, and so the individual is slow in modifying his/her unconscious values in later life. This has general implications; not only individuals but the groups to which they belong cannot easily shift their unconscious values.

4.2.6   *Economic change and movement in the culture*

The possession of wealth does not in itself lead to economic development. However, in some circumstances a correlation occurs between wealth and individualism. The wealthier countries tend to be more individualist; for example, the USA and the UK are both wealthier and more individualist than Guatemala and Panama. But this correlation is not exact and an obvious exception is made by the wealthy but relatively collectivist Japan.

A change in economic circumstances can bring about a shift in the culture, and as a country becomes more developed, it also shifts towards greater individualism. Hofstede (1983) found that those countries that had achieved the fastest economic growth were shifting most strongly in that direction. In sum, it seems to be the case that increased affluence is a cause of increasing individualism, rather than individualism causing affluence.

4.3   Economic Change and Cultural Movement in Japan

The relationship between economic change and shift in the culture cannot be precisely mapped, however. Over the past decades, both Indonesia and Nigeria have emerged as major oil exporters; yet slow growth, joblessness, slack investment, institutional disarray and fitful policy change have deepened popular discontent in each country (p. 2).

The organization of the Nigerian state has fostered corruption and rent distribution in ways that are highly detrimental to economic development (Lewis, 2007, p. 285).

Japan since 1945 provides a second illustration. Japan is relatively unblessed with natural resources, yet has developed to a degree unknown in Nigeria and Indonesia. At the end of the Second World War, Japanese infrastructure was devastated, and the country faced massive problems in reconstructing. In order to rebuild and prosper, companies had to depend upon the whole-hearted commitment of their staff, and gave commitment in return. This relationship of mutual dependence and obligation gave contemporary expression to the traditional culture of organizational collectivism, relatively high needs to avoid uncertainty and stress, and relatively high power distances.

The conventional Japanese office worker or "salaryman" built a reputation for loyalty to the company and his boss to the point of giving up evenings, weekends and even vacations in order to serve their interests. This loyalty was expected. In 1967 Hitachi sacked an employee who refused to work overtime. The case went to court and after several years the Supreme Court came to a ruling, in favor of the company; "employees are obliged to work overtime, even against their will, if the request is reasonable".[3] In return, the company did its best to protect the salaryman against redundancy, and in some cases (but perhaps in never more than 40 percent of all companies) awarded guarantees of lifetime employment to management staff. The relationship worked. In the 1980s the Japanese economy had grown to the point at which it seemed likely to dominate the world economy for decades to come.

Nevertheless, values were beginning to shift. Not only were younger managers adopting new attitudes to work. A 1991 survey conducted by an employers' association found that only 3 percent of the 250 managers surveyed still favored such traditional practices as long hours and the arbitrary transference of employees to distant posts where they might be separated from their families.[4] The effects of internal change were magnified by changes in international marketplaces and global competition.

The economy began to slide into recession and by 1998 employees were being laid off and companies were failing. Bankruptcies had never occurred on this scale before. In September 1998, Japan Leasing, a unit of failed Long-Term Credit Bank of Japan, went under with 2.18 trillion yen in debt. In October 2000, Chiyoda Mutual Life Insurance became the nation's biggest corporate bankruptcy to date, with 2.94 trillion yen in debt. These failures meant that the private sector could no longer guarantee its side of the contract, and massive numbers of salarymen were made redundant.

In a culture with high needs to avoid uncertainty, and where growth had been continuous since 1947, the effects were devastating – particularly among middle aged male managers. This is shown by leaps in the suicide rates. In 1990, 5,200 middle-aged men killed themselves; in 1998 around 10,000 committed suicide; and in 2007, the total was 30,093, making Japan the most suicide-prone nation in the developed world. Government figures showed unprecedented levels of suicide among professionals in their thirties and suggested that work-related depression was the prime cause.[5]

4.3.1 *Movement caused by change in employment practices*

The new economic conditions had apparently made the old values untenable. Many insiders and outsiders expected that the traditional structures of life-time employment and promotion by seniority would disappear. It seemed for a few years that the majority of

Japanese firms were indeed attempting to adopt global practice. A Japanese manager reported that whereas top managements were keen to follow American models, middle managers and below were disinclined to give up tradition. The situation was confused. Holzhausen (2000) argued that the long-term development of human capital inside the firm was still the norm; but although seniority was still a considerable influence, wage decisions were increasingly determined by qualification and competence rather than age and tenure. Four years later, Baba (2004) wrote similarly, that the seniority system was breaking down as predicted, but that lifetime employment had remained largely unchanged.

The lack of decisive change in employment practices suggests that the impact on the culture has been correspondingly slight.

4.3.2   Change between the generations?

There have been suggestions that the generations born since the 1960s and without experience of the struggles after 1945 have evolved different cultural patterns. For example, in the 1980s some observers thought they had identified a new generation known as *shinjinrui*, or new human beings. According to a contemporary account, a typical *shinjinrui* was more direct than the traditional Japanese, and acted more like a Westerner. The *shinjinrui* did not live for the company

> and will move on if he gets the offer of a better job. He is not keen on overtime, especially if he has a date with a girl. He has his own plans for his free time, and they may not include drinking or playing golf with the boss.[6]

And by 2001, there seemed to some that a significant break with the past culture of deference to elders had been made. Every year the Japanese have a national holiday celebrating the coming-to-age of their young people who turn 20. Held in every municipality, these ceremonies began after 1945 as a way of inspiring young people with hope for the future and commitment to social structures. They are presided over by civic dignitaries such as governors and mayors, who welcome the young to adult status and celebrate their passage to maturity. But in 2001, not all the ceremonies went according to plan:

> When the mayor of Takamatsu city stood up to address a coming-of-age ceremony...he expected the ritual to be conducted with its usual pomp and solemnity. Instead Shozo Masuda had to deliver his speech while drunken members of the audience approached his podium and fired party crackers at him.[7]

Across Japan other dignitaries suffered similar affronts as young people ignored, heckled and even shouted abuse. But did this really mark a shift in the underlying culture?

4.3.3   Change in the labor market?

In the past, young graduates had aimed at working for one of the giant corporations that dominated the economy. By the end of the century, a rising generation were beginning to challenge this orthodoxy and start their own companies, often in information technology fields. This change seems to have been influenced both by rising affluence and the realization that it was no longer necessary to commit to a lifetime of company drudgery in order to guarantee survival, and also because the large companies were no longer able to guarantee a lifetime job even if one wished it. Among the young it was no longer fashionable to secure a salaryman job, and entrepreneurial successes were widely reported.

In a similar spirit, increasing numbers of young Japanese apparently preferred to work on a part-time basis in preference to a lifetime in the big corporations. Between 1982 and 1997 the numbers of part-timers increased from 500,000 to 1.51 million, 80 percent of whom were in their 20s.[8] However, at the same time the Tokyo Metropolitan Government was holding seminars to persuade middle-aged people to take up full-time jobs, which showed that not everybody was sympathetic. The officials had an economic incentive for resisting the trend to part-time work; tax revenues were falling at a time when the population was graying.[9] It was also perceived that increasing numbers of young Japanese were aiming to start their own businesses. In particular, the young culture of entrepreneurship offered opportunities to women, many of whom had previously been excluded from the managerial workforce (although never from the blue-collar workforce).

All these apparent changes have been widely reported in the Western media. However, they seem to involve relatively few people, and there is very little evidence of major cultural shift. The great majority of young Japanese still show far greater deference to their elders than is fashionable among their American and British counterparts, and most still prefer to look for safe jobs in large companies than to venture out on their own. The problem of finding evidence of significant cultural shift is further illustrated by the questions that arise in trying to chart relations between the sexes.

4.3.4   Change between the genders?

In 1945, women made up about 22 percent of the total labor force. This figure increased rapidly after 1975, and reached 40 percent in 1999.

After 1945, most Japanese females had been expected to marry in their early twenties, then stay at home and rear children, and this usually meant giving up their career. This was typical of a highly masculine culture, in Hofstede's (1997) terms, in which male and female roles were sharply divided. In this situation it was economically realistic of Japanese companies to hesitate in recruiting and training unmarried women to managerial posts when they are likely to quit the job on marrying.

However, the boom years of the 1980s created massive demands for managerial manpower, which the predominantly male labor force was unable to satisfy. New opportunities arose for women. This was particularly the case in subsidiaries of Western firms headed by expatriates who were used to working with female managers. It seemed that the culture was about to shift radically, and that this shift was being propelled by economic factors.

But these expectations were premature. By 1992 the recession and stock market collapse had meant that firms were shedding staff and making fewer appointments. Women suffered disproportionately.

Toyota recruited 1,580 fewer male high school graduates than the year before, a reduction of 7.4%; but the number of women high school graduates fell to 570, a reduction of 25.6%:

> Nomura Securities will halve its annual intake of women from last year's [1991] 800 and the total number of women workers is likely to fall to 3,000 in 1997 from the present 5,000.[10]

Hiring policies were influenced by both internal and external factors. As the boom collapsed, foreign firms often modified their expatriation policies to replace their expensive expatriates with locals. These were usually males, who tended to be more conservative and to revert to traditional priorities in recruitment.

So how far have relations between men and women shifted in response to economic change? The degree of ambiguity is shown by the newspaper story in the Introduction. It further suggests that if Japanese culture is shifting significantly, progress is slow; and more generally, that the influence of economic change is uncertain.

4.4   Other Factors Causing Movement

We have examined the broad effects of economic change, and seen how difficult it is to map their influence on cultural shift with any great reliability. Here are other factors that may be causal in different circumstances:

- the development of education systems;
- development of the media;
- political change;
- technology;
- intervention from outside – see 4.4.1–4.4.9;
- government policy to shift the culture – see 4.4.10.

4.4.1   Drastic intervention

Intervention by an outside power may bring about a major shift in the culture. Occupations by Western colonialists profoundly influenced the cultures of many less developed economies during the nineteenth and early twentieth centuries. In some cases, the effects were entirely negative. Here is an example in which the culture-at-risk and the outsiders comprised subcultures belonging to the same country.

In Brazil, the largest tribe of Amazonian Indians have been pushed close to extinction as the result of contact with outside people (Watson et al., 2000). Time and time again the Guarani have been forced to abandon their settlements in the southwest of Brazil. They have a history of being exploited and murdered by colonists, the Brazilian army and police, traders and ranchers, and even those Brazilian agencies supposed to protect Indian rights. In the past 200 years they have lost about 95 percent of their ancestral territory, and have declined in number from about 1.5 million to 27,000 today.

Indian land ownership rights are not acknowledged by the Brazilian government even though they are established in international law. The sites which they now occupy are too small to support their traditional occupations of hunting and gathering, and too dry to sustain farming. The water is too polluted for fish. Forced to find work to prevent their families starving, many of the men have been recruited by sugar cane factories for as little as £7 a week. Used to a barter economy, they have found it hard to adjust to the rules of the market.[11] Alcoholism is widespread, and many women are forced to prostitute themselves.

The Guarani culture has been devastated. Community and family structures have broken down, and sacred rituals come to a halt. Most serious, the sense of hope-lessness and loss of identity has led to a wave of suicides, particularly among the young. More than 280 Guarani took their own lives in the years between 1990 and 2000, including 26 children under the age of 14, who have poisoned or hanged themselves.

This example indicates the damage that outside intervention can inflict on a once healthy culture. The case of the Guarani is extreme (although not as extreme as that of many other Brazilian tribes, which have been entirely exterminated; see Watson et al., 2000). However, it is not unusual. In Africa, Asia, and elsewhere, many examples can be found of cultures that have been severely damaged by pressures for change.

The concept of the "failed state" is sometimes used to explain those societies that, for different reasons, are unable to manage their own affairs – some because they fail to conform with the orthodoxies imposed by the American-led international order; see 13.2.2.

We now examine two historical examples of intervention in the affairs of an independent power by an outside power. The effects of intervention differed, and the reasons why are explored.

4.4.2 *Intervention in Japan, 1853*

By 1853 Japan had defended itself from Western cultural influences for almost three hundred years; foreign visitors were forbidden, and no Japanese who left the islands could claim readmittance. This isolation only ended when an American sailor, Commander Perry, entered Tokyo Bay, and insisted on rights to trade and representation. Perry's "black ships" refused to leave, and made it clear that they were prepared to use force. This came as a profound shock to the Japanese. By denying its authority, Perry caused the government, the Shogunate, to lose so much face that political change was inescapable. It had been in decline since 1830, and the failure to deal effectively with the threats posed by the barbarian West sounded its death knell (Henshall, 2005). The Shogunate and feudal culture collapsed. A teenage emperor was restored, and after 1868 his Meiji government actively followed a policy of seeking knowledge throughout the world in order to strengthen the country. The Americans were quickly followed by representatives of the different European powers, and the period of modernization and openness to the world began.

4.4.3 Why the intervention in Japan caused movement

Why did this intervention succeed? This analysis gives a lead to understanding the conditions under which intervention by "outsiders" WILL significantly influence the culture:

(a) OBJECTIVE. The outsiders aimed to influence Japanese values, and to secure a long-term involvement in the Japanese economy;
(b) LOCAL LEADERSHIP. The Japanese leadership had been divided for some time before 1853. Powerful groups wanted change, and the Shogun and his supporters had shown themselves incapable of planning and implementing these changes;
(c) OPPORTUNITY. The collapse following the foreign intervention offered the opponents to the Shogunate an opportunity to make the desired change, and modernize;
(d) RESPECT. The outsiders were respected for their efficient government and technological culture;
(e) CONTACTS. The barbarian foreigners were always suspect and often disliked, but they began to have regular contacts with significant groups within the new government;
(f) TENURE. The foreigners stayed.

4.4.4 Intervention in Saudi Arabia, 1990–1991

In 1990, the Iraqi invasion of Kuwait posed a serious threat both to their Middle Eastern neighbors and to Western powers dependent on cheap oil produced in the region. Saudi Arabia was a front-line antagonist, and host to a massive Allied army (led by the USA). As foreign troops flocked in during the run-up to war, many Saudi and non-Saudi citizens were convinced that changes in social values were imminent. Middle class and Western educated Saudis hoped that the confrontation would prompt the Saudi ruling family to side more openly with those who favored the liberalization of religious, social and political institutions. They expected sex roles to be influenced. Traditionally, women had played very little part in the segregated labor market. But now, King Fahd suggested they be allowed to replace expatriate women as nurses, clerks, and medical technicians.

Many observers expected that the mass intervention by Western forces would cause an immediate crisis in the local culture, and that liberal Western values would emerge from the process of adjustment. These observers included both outsiders and some "expert" insiders. But by 1991, after the fighting in which Saudi Arabia had played an important part on the winning side, the country had apparently returned to its pre-war routine. Members of the educated middle class who wanted greater liberalization were relatively powerless and outnumbered. Open access to Western media was allowed for only a short time. The ultra-religious morals police, or *mutawah,* again started harassing those Saudi and foreign women they considered insufficiently covered in public places, and the authorities reneged upon promises to employ women in a wider range of occupations. In the immediate aftermath one Western diplomat[12] estimated that the impact made by Western culture "was just about nil".

4.4.5   Why the intervention in Saudi Arabia did not cause movement

The intervention in Saudi Arabia did not cause a rush to Westernization, for these reasons:

(a)   OBJECTIVE. The outsiders had intervened in order to pursue military objectives, and had no long-term interests in triggering Westernization;

(b)   LOCAL LEADERSHIP. The Saudi leadership was relatively united, and was not interested in change. Traditional structures were capable of integrating tribal and social differences;

(c)   OPPORTUNITY. Given (b) above, the question of opportunity did not arise;

(d)   RESPECT. The outsiders may have been respected for their technological and technical skills. But Saudi Arabia lies at the heart of the Muslim world, and they were not respected for their political and cultural values;

(e)   CONTACTS. The Allied troops were quarantined away from large urban centers. Contacts between Saudis and troops were restricted, and there was no cultural contamination. This quarantining was planned; uncontrolled change was feared by both Saudi AND Western authorities;

(f)   TENURE. The presence of Allied troops in large numbers was short-lived – less than a year.

4.4.6   Some conditions for foreign intervention causing movement

The analyses above suggest some conditions under which foreign intervention can cause cultural shift. These are listed in Table 4.1.

Table 4.1   Some conditions for foreign intervention causing cultural shift

---

- OBJECTIVE. The outsiders aim to cause a shift in values;
- LOCAL LEADERSHIP. The local leadership is sympathetic to the intervention;
- OPPORTUNITY. The local leadership seizes the opportunity posed by the intervention to support or lead the change process;
- RESPECT. The outsiders are respected;
- CONTACTS. The outsiders have regular friendly contacts with influential locals;
- TENURE. The foreigners make a long-term commitment.

4.4.7   Did the intervention in Saudi Arabia meet its objectives?

We saw above that the intervention in Saudi Arabia did not have the objective of causing Westernization, and indeed, this did not occur.

However, it is clear in retrospect that it did have one unwanted effect, and that was to drive some Saudis in the opposite direction. In the wake of the events of September 11, 2001, it became evident that the person responsible, Osama bin Laden, and many of his al-Queda terrorists and financial supporters, were Saudi nationals. Revulsion at the presence of infidel outsiders in the country of the Prophet and the birthplace of Islam has led to a strengthening of traditional fundamentalist values – here and in some other Muslim countries.

This is an example of outside intervention having disastrous effects – and causing unwanted cultural shift – that were not envisaged at the onset.

4.4.8   Globalization as foreign intervention

Globalizing processes represent intervention from abroad. In theory globalization implies the free movement of political, economic and cultural resources between countries, each society influencing and being influenced by every other society. In practice, Western and in particular American values predominate. For example, American values impose on Peru to a far greater extent than Peruvian values impose on the USA. In practice, globalization has effects that have not been predicted, and may be violently opposed by those who feel threatened and perceive that their local economic, political and cultural systems are under assault. The lesson from 4.4.7 is that global interventions may have effects that are unplanned. The effects of globalization are considered more fully in Chapter 13.

4.4.9   Intervention on a company level

This analysis of intervention by one country in the affairs of another country has lessons for the multinational company, in which headquarters intervenes in the organizational culture of the subsidiary, or the foreign parent of an international joint venture company intervenes in that venture. The intervention is most likely to cause a long-term shift in the organizational culture when

- OBJECTIVE. Headquarters aims to cause a shift in values;
- LOCAL LEADERSHIP. Subsidiary management are sympathetic to the intervention;
- OPPORTUNITY. Subsidiary management seizes the opportunity posed by the intervention to support or lead the change process;
- RESPECT. Headquarters representatives are respected;
- CONTACTS. Headquarters representatives have regular friendly contacts with subsidiary managers;
- TENURE. Headquarters makes clear its long-term commitment.

Relations between headquarters and the international joint venture or subsidiary are discussed in Chapters 17–21.

4.4.10   Government policy to shift the culture

Over the years, different national governments have tried to engineer shifts in the values of their national cultures. Attempts have been made in the UK by the government led by Margaret Thatcher, in Australia by Gough Whitlam when an Asian identity was proclaimed, and in Russia after the breakdown of communism.

After the handover of Hong Kong to China in 1997, the government worked to integrate the political and cultural systems of the ex-British colony with the rest of China. But Hong Kong people refused to give up their sense of a separate identity. And when anti-subversion laws were proposed in June 2003, up to 500,000 took to the streets in protest – despite an assurance from the Chinese premier, Wen Jibao, that the legislation "absolutely will not affect the different rights and freedoms that Hong Kong people enjoy under the law". However, two days later the proposed laws were withdrawn.

The leadership of the European Union has a mission to impose homogeneity throughout this new empire. Policies of cultural uniformity have seemed to be the only solution to problems of exerting control. However, the electoral successes of nationalist parties over the last decade and the failure to agree on a constitution show that local national loyalties are still strong.

An explicit attempt to plot a cultural transformation occurred in Japan. On January 18, 2000, a Commission on Japan's Goals for the Twenty First Century reported to the Prime Minister Keizo Obuchi. In order to survive in a globalized world, Japan needed to drastically change its culture. The Commission stressed the need for "individual empowerment". In the past, the emphasis on loyalty, patience and hard work had bred the production line workers needed for Japan's transformation after 1945, but in the new climate qualities of spontaneity, innovation and ambition were needed. The emphasis on homogeneity and uniformity in both the educational system and workplace should be curbed. Reward structures should recognize individual excellence.[13] The Japanese had to accept more foreigners and cultural influences from abroad and not simply stick to "the identity of the past".

This report reflected a growing dissatisfaction with the hierarchies in government and business, the repression of innovation, and complacency in public life. Suddenly it seemed that cultural shift was possible.

The 10-year recession had forced a dissatisfied public to look at their society through critical eyes, and now they expected the authorities to make changes. This was

> simultaneously a national identity crisis and an awakening. The powers-that-be are scrambling to react to pressure.... "We all know that we are facing a crisis and that we have to change," says Kawai Hayao [the chairman of the Commission]. "It is a great opportunity for Japan to take real action."[14]

This illustrates a general point that people are most likely to perceive the need for change – and act on it – in response to crisis, when the cost of continuing without change is prohibitive. However, when the crisis eases, the calls for radical change may become muted. This happened in Japan as the economy began to revive.

In sum, deliberate attempts to plot and engineer cultural shifts seldom achieve their objectives. They may even be counterproductive.

4.5 Implications for the Manager

Under some conditions, changes in the environment may affect behavior and lead to shifts in cultural values.

1 Identify significant economic and other events that have occurred within YOUR OWN culture during the past few years (for instance, intervention by some other country, economic recession or boom, technological innovation, educational innovation).
   - How have these affected people's behavior – if at all?
   - How have these affected your relationships with
     (a) other persons in your organization?
     (b) family, friends and social acquaintances?
2 Do you expect these behavioral changes (if any) to cause a shift in your national culture?
   - If you answer YES, what shift do you expect?
   - Do you expect it to be superficial or long term?
   - Should your organization plan a deliberate response?
   - If you answer YES, what response should be made?

4.6 SUMMARY

This chapter has examined how movement in the culture is caused by changes in the environment. Section 4.2 examined the problems of RECOGNIZING SIGNIFICANT MOVEMENT IN THE CULTURE, and responding appropriately. Section 4.3 examined the conflicting evidence for how ECONOMIC change might cause CULTURAL MOVEMENT, and the problems of identifying significant movement. Japan since 1945 provided a case study. The section examined the very ambiguous evidence that changes had occurred in relations between the generations, in the labor market, and in occupational discrimination between the genders. Section 4.4 examined OTHER FACTORS CAUSING MOVEMENT in the culture. It examined two historical case studies and derived some conditions under which the effects of foreign intervention might cause movement – and applied this to the company. The section also suggested that government policies to cause cultural movement are often unsuccessful if they do not accord with the wishes of the people.

4.7   EXERCISE

Everyone is aware that climate change presents threats (and opportunities) to all parts of the world. This exercise asks you to imagine how climate change might influence culture.

1   Suppose that average temperatures in your country RISE by three degrees over the next 10 years. How might this affect how people live their lives?
2   How might your suggested changes in lifestyle affect cultural values in the long term? Specifically, how might they affect

 • power distances;
 • needs to avoid uncertainty;
 • individualism and collectivism;
 • masculinity and femininity;
 • other values.

3   How might these movements in the national culture influence business conditions? List four possible changes in business conditions.

Notes

1   Reuters, Tokyo. Japan loosens apron strings. *Daily Telegraph*, February 7, 2005.
2   Karin Klenkwe. Keeping control in flat organisations. *Daily Telegraph*, August 21, 2007.
3   Free, young and Japanese. *The Economist*, December 21, 1991.
4   Free, young and Japanese. *The Economist*, December 21, 1991.
5   Suicide rise gives Japan grisly honour. *Daily Telegraph*, June 20, 2008.
6   Ronald E. Yates. Juppies. *Chicago Tribune*, April 24, 1988.
7   Peter Hadfield. Japan dismayed as teenagers insult dignitaries. *Sunday Telegraph*, January 14, 2001.
8   Fumihiro Hayasaka. Tokyo wants part-timers to carry load. *Mainichi Daily News*, November 23, 2000.
9   Fumihiro Hayasaka. Tokyo wants part-timers to carry load. *Mainichi Daily News*, November 23, 2000.
10   Robert Thomson. Future dims for Japanese woman. (*Financial Times–Bangkok Post* Service), *Bangkok Post*, August 31, 1992.
11   Christina Lamb. Rising suicides cut a swathe through Amazon's children. *Sunday Telegraph*, November 19, 2000.
12   Rone Tempest. Change comes, at its own pace, in Saudi Arabia. *International Herald Tribune*, September 4, 1991
13   Jonathan Sprague and Murakami Mutsuko. Japan's new attitude. *AsiaWeek*, October 20, 2000.
14   Jonathan Sprague and Murakami Mutsuko. Japan's new attitude. *AsiaWeek*, October 20, 2000.

CHAPTER FIVE
Organizational Culture

5.1 Introduction

Malee, a Taiwanese, worked as a junior manager in a fabrics manufacturer, based in Taipei. She applied for promotion, but was refused on the basis that her management style was too abrasive, and she alienated junior staff. She decided to study for an MBA in the USA in order to learn how to be a successful leader. Within a few days of entering the class, all students were given a psychometric test to assess their potential. In her feedback, Malee was told that she was not sufficiently aggressive to be an effective manager.

The question is, how far do leadership styles transfer between cultures – and between different industries and organizations? The style used by an effective manager both reflects the organizational culture and influences it, and must be effective within its context.

5.2 Defining and Analyzing Organizational Cultures

The study of "organizational culture" is difficult because the term has no one accepted meaning. Definitions are many and varied; they may include the organizational structure and rules, values, feelings, norms, the organizational "climate". In many cultures outside North America and Europe, the concept is strange to managements which may be primarily concerned with fostering a sense of loyalty among the workforce.

In general, this book uses the term organizational culture in preference to corporate culture; the former term includes the notion of culture in private, state, and not-for-profit sectors, whereas the latter is restricted to the private sector. The book assumes that every organization in whichever sector has its unique culture that can be defined and analyzed.

Three definitions of organizational culture are distinguished here. These are the organizational culture as

- a CONSTRUCTED product (see 5.2.1);
- a set of ORGANIC norms (see 5.2.2);
- a continual process of NEGOTIATION (see 5.2.3).

5.2.1   The organizational culture as a constructed product

This definition treats the culture as the product of structures, systems and regulations, planned and imposed by management. Management tries to manipulate values in the organizational culture so that it supports strategic goals and processes. When the structural changes made are superficial, the assessment of success is also likely to be superficial. But compliance by the workforce cannot be taken at face value; it does not necessarily indicate genuine commitment.

5.2.2   The organizational culture as a set of organic norms

The culture is sometimes defined in terms of the members' sense of "How things are done around here" and the appropriate way to behave. These shared experiences may have been built up and internalized over many years. This implies that the organization does not *have* a culture so much as it *is* a culture, which is embedded. Management may find it very difficult to make any permanent impression on the culture, and any attempts to make radical change may have a negative effect, causing resentment and demoralization.

So although new structures may sometimes influence the culture, management cannot be certain that it is controlling the direction of this change. Hesselbein (2002) comments on his experience:

> Our focus was not on changing the culture – though this was a result. Our focus was on building an organization committed to managing for the mission, managing for innovation, and managing for diversity.   *(p. 2)*

The consultants' work on developing the structures of the company resulted in the members' rethinking their experience of working for it. While such a positive change is never certain, the chances of success are improved when the workforce already trust management. If the workforce do not trust management, then they are likely to respond positively to structural innovation. Hence, if the culture is already positive, management may find it relatively easy to make change; but if the culture is negative, the process will be very difficult.

5.2.3 The organizational culture as a continual process of negotiation

This recognizes that management is seldom able to change the culture unilaterally; in practice only those constructs that take account of accepted norms are likely to be easily accepted. Of course management is sometimes bound to take radical steps to improve productivity and implement new strategy, but unless the members are convinced that the change is beneficial, it is unlikely to be successful. That is, management action can have a positive effect on the culture, but only when conditions are right and members are broadly sympathetic to the proposed changes.

An emphasis on negotiation implies that management may find it easier to modify some aspects of the culture than others, and to influence the effect of the cultural and other environments. This recognizes that management is seldom able to change the culture unilaterally; in practice only those constructs that take account of accepted norms are likely to be easily accepted. Of course management is sometimes bound to take radical steps to improve productivity and implement new strategy, but unless the members are convinced that the change is necessary and in their interests, they may resist.

Which definition is most appropriate? Like so much social science, this may depend on the intended functions of the definition, and the analyst's needs. A top manager, an academic, a consultant, a business journalist, have different interests in the organization and take different viewpoints on its activities.

Top managers are recruited to make changes, and need to feel in control of their organizations. A CEO might take for granted his ability to design and impose the construct that seems most likely to achieve the strategic goal. In recent years, optimism that cultures can be radically changed by management action has been greatly reduced by experience of failure.

At the opposite extremes, strongly organic definitions pay much more attention to factors such as national culture, which lie outside management's control. These may be preferred by sociologists – and perhaps by long-term employees who consider that long-term change is more likely to be forced on the organization by developments in the economic and business environments than from anything that management can devise.

5.2.4 The negotiated process

Management experts increasingly recognize that managers are unlikely to be successful in imposing their vision unless they work with the members to create shared meanings and aspirations. Raelin (2006) refers to this as collaborative leadership, or "leaderful" practice. The interaction is circular rather than from top down. Ravasi and Schultz (2006) have dual responsibilities for making sense of cues supplied by the culture and as a source of sense-giving actions, designed to influence perceptions.

This notion of organizational culture in terms of a negotiated process between the needs and perceptions of top management and workforce reflects a differentiation of roles within the organization. Top management is under the greater obligation than the workforce to plan strategy and make predictions on the basis of changes in the environment, whereas lower levels are immediately concerned with implementing the goals and systems. This distinction is reflected in Trompenaars and Hampden-Turner's (1997) three aspects of organizational culture:

(a)   the general relationship between employees and their organization;
(b)   the vertical or hierarchical system of authority defining superiors and subordinates;
(c)   the general views of employees about the organization's destiny, purpose and goals and their place in it. (pp. 138–139).

Point (a) stresses the importance of the relationship between management and employees. This may fluctuate between cooperation and conflict – when goals and perceptions are far adrift. Top management is able to exert some control on the culture (point (b)), but this is never total (point (c)).

The problems of maintaining cooperation may be particularly severe in a foreign investment when top management belongs to a national culture other than that of the mass of the workforce, or reports to headquarters based in another culture. The multinational organization is always likely to develop different organizational cultures in its different branches, or to interpret headquarters structures and systems differently.

5.2.5   *Distinguishing subcultures*

It has been argued that the definition made of "organizational culture" is always conditioned by the reason for which a definition is needed. The same point applies to the domain of analysis. It is sometimes necessary to distinguish subcultures within the organizational culture. Here are questions that might only be answered by subcultural analysis:

*   why are lower management so ineffective in implementing policies set by middle management?
*   we have two sales departments. Do we need both?
*   how can we merge the accounting and finance departments?

In sum, subcultural analysis helps managers and consultants make comparisons and contrasts in order to assess organizational relationships and differences in efficiency. It shows where improvements can be made, where investment is needed, and which staff can be developed.

Subcultures may be identified in structural units and departments. Different groups have different professional experiences and values, even when they are genuinely cooperating to make the organization successful. For instance, distinctions may be made on

- a HIERARCHICAL basis; top management, as against middle management, as against lower management, as against workforce;
- a FUNCTIONAL basis; the sales department as against the marketing department; engineers as against accountants; line managers as against staff managers;
- a STRUCTURAL basis; one shift against another, one work team against another, headquarters as against subsidiary or joint venture, one subsidiary as against another, one division as against another.

But in cases where the need is to compare different organizations rather than parts of a single organization, analysis of subcultures does not serve a useful purpose.

In practice, some subcultures take more decisions than others, and have more influence on general organizational culture than others. We cannot expect these to have similar weight at all levels, in all organizations, or at all times. Some organizations have reconfigured their general cultures by reengineering relationships between the subcultures, reducing the responsibilities allocated to some groups and increasing others. Top management has always had the job of predicting the business environment, but as the developing pace of globalization gives rise to increasing opportunities and threats, these responsibilities grow in importance.

5.2.6 *Analysis: positive/negative organizational cultures*

Organizational cultures are compared by using a common system of analysis. Two simple models are used here. First, the organizational culture is analyzed in terms of how far it is POSITIVE or NEGATIVE.

The culture is POSITIVE when its members support and trust top management and workforce and top management share a commitment to the organization. Their relationships are good. This occurs when

- official relationships are considered reasonable. Top management communicate effectively and fairly with members. Grievances are listened to, and given a fair response;
- members perceive that they have a stake in company outcomes; when the company benefits, they benefit (and when it fails, they fail). Profits and losses are shared fairly;
- demands for productivity are considered reasonable;
- the reward system is considered fair in terms of internal differentials, and what is being offered by competitors.

When the opposite conditions apply, and relations with management are unproductive, the organizational culture is NEGATIVE.

5.2.7 *Analysis: strong/weak organizational cultures*

The organizational culture is STRONG when

- it is cohesive; group members share the same values, beliefs and attitudes;
- members can easily communicate between themselves;
- members depend on each other in meeting individual needs.

The strength of a culture is shown superficially by uniformity, but more significantly by the tolerance that members show for each others' experiences and ideas. When the opposite conditions apply and relations between members are not cohesive, the organizational culture is WEAK.

5.2.8 *The four alternatives*

The positive/negative, strong/weak models generate four alternatives:

(a) a positive, strong culture;
(b) a negative, strong culture;
(c) a positive, weak culture;
(d) a negative, weak culture.

These alternatives are mapped in Figure 5.1

When the culture is positive and strong, relations between management and workforce are good. Communication is easy, open, and fruitful, morale is high, and productivity climbs. Management focuses on developing and maintaining productive values.

Members need a positive culture and strong culture because they need predictability and certainty. However, in cases, where this is not immediately possible, management may aim for a positive, weak culture – that is, a culture in which relations between management and workforce are good, even if the workforce itself is disunited.

	POSITIVE	NEGATIVE
STRONG	a. positive, strong	b. negative, strong
WEAK	d. positive, weak	c. negative, weak

Figure 5.1 Alternatives for organizational culture

Management most fears a negative and strong culture. Employees are united in their alienation from official structures, their lack of trust in management messages, and their perceptions of management dishonesty. A negative strong culture fosters conflict and strikes.

The implications of Figure 5.1 are that management hopes to modify the organization culture so that it moves from

- a negative strong culture to
- a negative weak culture to
- a positive weak culture to
- a positive strong culture.

But questions must always arise as to how far management is able to make such modifications, and these are considered in the sections below.

5.3   Organizational Culture and National Culture

Management can only exert control over the organizational culture to the extent that they control members' relationships and the factors that influence their attitudes to their work.

However, these attitudes are influenced by a number of factors in the business environment, which largely lie outside management's direct control and which management cannot usually change. Management cannot change the national culture, and only a very powerful organization can effect changes in the legal system. Normally, the most that top management can achieve is to moderate and mitigate these influences.

These environmental factors include

- national economic conditions; macroeconomic factors; government economic policy;
- the legal system;
- industry norms; pay and conditions in similar organizations elsewhere in the industry;
- the NATIONAL CULTURE.

This section focuses on the last factor, national culture, and its influence on the organizational culture.

5.3.1   Comparing organizational culture and national culture

Which has greater influence on members' values and behavior, national culture or organizational culture? The question is important because it leads us to investigate the degree of control that the headquarters of a multinational company can realistically exert on its subsidiary abroad, located in some other culture.

If organizational culture has a stronger influence on members' values than their national culture, then headquarters management can directly determine the behavior of subsidiary staff. If, on the other hand, national culture has the stronger influence, then headquarters has to take local values into account when imposing strategies, systems and structures; and how subsidiary staff interpret and implement these policies is strongly influenced by their culture.

Headquarters might always hope to override local national values but this is not always practical, and the attempt may be time-wasting and damaging to local morale. This does not mean that a headquarters' value system can NEVER be transferred abroad.

Certainly if the cultures are close, or if members already have experience in the values of the national culture of headquarters, the transference may be relatively simple. An example of the second point occurs when, say, an American bank operating in Indonesia recruits Indonesian graduates of American universities. However, in other circumstances (and depending on the values being transferred) staff may need to be trained in the new systems and indirectly in the values they express, perhaps over considerable time.

As a first stage in assessing the relationship, we ask how far Hofstede's definition of national culture (see 1.3.3) can be applied to organizational culture:

> the collective programming of the mind which distinguishes the members of one human group from another. . . .Culture, in this sense, includes systems of values; and values are among the building blocks of culture.

These inferences were drawn for a national culture:

(a) a culture is particular to one group and not others;
(b) it influences the behavior of group members in uniform and predictable ways;
(c) it is learned, and is not innate;
(d) it is passed down from one generation to the next;
(e) it includes systems of values.

These inferences apply to organizational culture in that

• every organization has its own culture, and no two are quite the same;
• management hopes that by building and analyzing the organizational culture it can predict the attitudes and behavior of the workforce in routine situations;
• members of the organization have to learn its culture.

5.3.2 Differences between organizational culture and national culture

But the applications of points (d) and (e) are less straightforward. The values of the national culture are taught by family, friends, school, media, and others. In the organization, perceptions of who is responsible for essential teaching differ according to the definition made of organizational culture. Management hopes to act as the primary "teacher" by building and sustaining a positive culture. However, if one accepts an organic interpretation of the culture, one has to assume that the values of the workforce are largely transmitted informally, for example through gossip, unofficial histories, patronage networks.

So far as point (e) is concerned, values in the national culture are learned from the first weeks of life, and most of this learning is unconscious. It is held at a deep level in the psyche, and provides the individual with values that determine his/her behavior throughout life.

On the other hand, the learning, and impact, of organizational cultures is relatively shallow. This is because

- the individual experiences a succession of organizational cultures throughout life; for example, the cultures of primary school, secondary school, university, first workplace, second workplace and so on, religious associations, social clubs – and many others. These cultures may have common elements, but at some points may be contradictory;
- the individual has instrumental reasons for learning each – to fit in at school, to keep a job, and so on. When the individual moves on to the next stage in his/her life, these reasons may no longer apply. The values of the old organization are largely supplanted by the values of the new;
- the individual usually joins the organization from free will, and usually, is equally free to quit. Members who cannot adjust their perceptions and behavior to the prevailing culture of their organization are likely to quit at an early stage;
- at different times, elements of one organizational culture may be contradictory. For example, a new CEO leads the company towards new strategic goals, and attempts to create new cultural priorities in order to meet these goals.

National cultural values are learned so early in childhood that the individual is largely unaware of his/her cultural conditioning and cannot articulate conscious responses – however it affects his/her unconscious experiences. However, organizational values are learned much later, and are assimilated at a more conscious level. The individual learns many of these organizational cultures in maturity, and adopts an objective and critical attitude towards the learning.

You acquire and shed a series of organizational cultures in the course of your working life. But you cannot shed your national culture.

In sum, at a very superficial level the defining parameters of national culture can be applied to organizational culture. However, the two notions of culture are NOT the same and should not be confused.

5.3.3   *The influence of organizational values*

This leads to the question, are organizational values ever so powerful an influence on behavior as national culture? The point is important because if they ARE, employees can be conditioned to expressing values that contradict national values. For instance, in an individualist national culture employees of Company X can be conditioned to placing a premium on group harmony and avoiding confrontation – connotations of a collectivist culture. But if national values are always likely to overrule contrasting organizational values, there may be little point in investing heavily in systems designed to modify the organizational culture. In this case, headquarters control over the organizational culture of a foreign-based subsidiary is always insecure.

The evidence is ambiguous. There is no doubt that organizational values do influence the employees in the long term, and generate patterns of uniformity among organizational units, regardless of geographic, functional or business boundaries. But this does not mean that they operate as deeply as do the values of national culture, or significantly modify the national culture when the two are in conflict. In practice, the influence on the individual may be determined less by management controls than by the length of time he/she stays in the organization. The "job-hopper", who moves rapidly between companies, is unlikely to be much influenced by their cultures. On the other hand, the person who stays with one organization for all his/her career may be significantly affected. Small family companies can indeed impose this degree of control on members born within the organization.

5.4 Mitigating the Effects of the Environment

Section 5.3 listed environmental factors – including national culture – which influence the values of the members and hence influence the organizational culture. These lie largely outside management's control. But management can take steps to mitigate their effects. For example, management cannot change a collectivist national culture to be individualist, but may hope to influence how the prevailing collectivist values influence behavior in the workplace. This section deals with the mechanisms under management's control, by which it can attempt to modify the effects of the wider environment.

These mechanisms include

- official symbols, projected to members and to the environment. These include official rituals, ceremonies, official history, mission statement;
- formal structures (see Chapter 9);
- strategy (see Chapters 14 and 15);
- leadership and the selection of CEO (see 5.4.1 below);
- HRM factors: the case of recruitment (see 5.4.2);
- mission statement (see 5.4.3);
- technology (see 5.4.4 and Chapter 16).

5.4.1 *Leadership*

At the highest level, the board influence the organizational culture by appointing a CEO who seems likely to provide effective leadership. However, problems arise in defining leadership and in identifying persons who have the necessary qualities until they are tested by practice.

On the one hand, some theories of leadership emphasize the social process and the importance of social context. A manager who is effective in one context may be ineffective in another – the Introduction showed a manager who seemed likely to fail in two different contexts for opposite reasons. In terms of politics, a great peace-time leader may fail to manage a war and a successful war-time leader may be ineffective in peace. In business, the successful CEO of a bank may fail when he/she takes a job running an advertising agency.

Managers also have to meet expectations of the persons being led. In Anglo companies, a new CEO is not normally expected to continue his or her predecessor's strategy other than in the short term during the transition period. The CEO who makes no changes may be criticized for a failure of nerve in responding to shifts in the environment. But the leader who marches too far ahead of unpersuaded followers, and fails to communicate his or her vision, brings confusion.

The emphasis on context indicates that the leader is effective when he/she builds a positive organizational culture; but up to a point this definition is circular, because it can also be argued that for as long as the culture is positive, the leader is likely to be effective.

On the other hand, some theories focus on the skills that the effective leader must have. For example, the CEO provides leadership and influences the culture by

- providing vision. He/she recognizes opportunities and threats before others do, and is already planning how to maximize the first and avoid the second when others have still not seen the need for change;
- articulating goals and communicating;
- building confidence in shared goals;
- finding resources needed to achieve goals;
- motivating members to participate.

A recent study examined five qualities that appeared to be common to all good leaders (Blair, 2008). These are

- the ability to listen to what is being said, and distinguish criticisms of one's policy from personal criticisms – which might be ignored;
- the strength to hold fast to one's overarching ideals;
- taking full responsibility for one's beliefs and actions;
- the skill to communicate effectively. This includes appearing sincere, getting to the point, using pauses, gestures, and eye-contact appropriately;
- the ability to remind followers of one's achievements.

But it is often difficult to find agreement on how concepts associated with personality should be identified and defined in concrete situations.

5.4.2   *HRM factors: the case of recruitment*

Human resource management is discussed more fully in Chapter 19. It is sufficient at this point to note that ALL HR functions can affect the maintenance and development of the organizational culture. The point is illustrated here by paying particular attention to the importance of recruitment.

The HRM managers influence the development of a positive culture by recruiting and selecting persons who show the psychological and professional characteristics needed to

* achieve strategic goals;
* fit in with the existing culture AND/OR;
* contribute to change in the culture.

These last two points are not necessarily contradictory. The HR managers responsible for recruitment may have to decide between needs for continuation and for an influx of new ideas and values, and must hope to find candidates who offer both qualities in the appropriate measure.

Psychometric and other personality tests are widely used in the West to select persons who seem likely to "fit in" and contribute to the culture. In collectivist cultures, informal means of recruitment may still be more important than formal means. In Korea, school culture plays a major part; recruitment by "culture-matching" is a convergence of selection by the employer and self-selection by the applicant in which they match their respective school cultures.

Focused recruitment is not the only weapon in the HRM arsenal. It may be supplemented by more or less formal training, which provides recruits and others with the specialized skills and values they need to work and socialize within the organization. Performance appraisal spells out what behavior is required, and various incentive and reward schemes reinforce the point; see 19.6.

5.4.3   *The mission statement*

Management influence the organizational culture by influencing how it is perceived, both by members and by outsiders. An important tool in modifying these perceptions is the mission statement. The mission statement defines the organization by answering these questions:

* WHO are we?
* WHAT do we do?
* WHERE are we headed?

Mission statements vary greatly in length and content. They might explain the company philosophy, promote ethical policy, celebrate successes, and discuss strategic goals (so long as this does not help competitors). They project the corporate image to a range of persons with interests in the company; these include the media, analysts, customers and suppliers, other persons in the environment, and company members.

When directed at members, mission statements aim to create a positive culture by

- explaining strategic thinking and its implementation;
- providing a sense of common experience;
- defining the scope of operations;
- influencing leadership styles;
- promoting a sense of shared experience and expectations at all levels;
- defining the organization in relation to its environment of customers, suppliers, etc.

The mission statement informs the environment of its goals and its progress towards achieving them. It reflects its members, values, experiences, and future plans. When management wishes to signal a change in the organizational culture, it changes the statement.

The mission statement also contributes to hiring the right workforce. A company that projects a positive culture in the business environment attracts potential applicants looking for an employer with a culture that seems likely to satisfy their professional and psychological needs.

5.4.4   Technology

Influences between technology and organizational culture flow two ways. On the one hand, the organic systems and relationships serve as a framework within which members interpret, adjust to and respond to new technologies; and Kabasakal et al. (2006) argue that the characteristics of the national culture therefore influence how the technology is experienced and applied. On the other hand, management's choice of technology influences interactions between members. An information technology that substitutes for face-to-face interaction may have the effect of weakening social dependencies, and therefore weakening the culture.

5.4.5   Weakening the culture

The culture is weakened when cohesion between members is reduced. Independencies and regular contacts between members are also lessened by introducing

- flexi-time systems;
- work-at-home schemes;

- shared office space. Furniture is no longer dedicated to the particular employee. He is expected to work at any workstation available;
- outsourcing specialist functions to outside consultants, who are contracted to the organization on a short-term basis. Their employees do not belong to the outsourcing organization and have no investment in its organizational culture.

When these mechanisms are reinforced by the introduction of a technology that reduces cohesion between members, the culture may be significantly weakened.

5.5 Implications for the Manager

Answer each of the questions for

- an organization that you know well in YOUR OWN culture; AND
- an organization that you know well in SOME OTHER culture.

1 For each organization, decide whether its culture is
   (a) STRONG or WEAK.
   (b) POSITIVE or NEGATIVE.
      - what factors make it strong/weak?
      - what factors make in positive/negative?
      - how might it be made stronger?
      - how might it be made more positive?
2 In each organization, what subcultures can you find? What values do the following subgroups share?
   (a) top management;
   (b) middle management;
   (c) junior management;
   (d) workforce;
   (e) different functional groups;
   (f) different plants/subsidiaries;
   (g) headquarters staff, expatriate staff, local staff in subsidiaries abroad.
3 In each organization, look for evidence of top management attempting to change the culture.
   - how does top management attempt to change?
   - are these attempts succeeding? If so, why?
   - are these attempts failing? If so, why?

5.6 SUMMARY

This chapter has discussed definitions of organizational culture and has examined the conditions under which top management can control it. Section 5.2 dealt with problems of DEFINING AND ANALYZING ORGANIZATIONAL CULTURES. The problem for the manager is to select a definition of organizational culture that can be usefully applied to the specific situation in question. The extremes are marked by definitions that assume the culture is a product created and controlled by top management, and those that treat it as a set or organic norms arising from the members' experiences and expectations. In practice, most cultures are negotiated between these extremes. Cultures can also be analyzed in terms of their strong/weak and positive/negative characteristics.

Management can only exert control over the organizational culture to the extent that they control members' relationships and the factors that influence their attitudes to their work. However, these attitudes are influenced by factors in the environment outside the organization. Section 5.3 focused on NATIONAL CULTURE. Whether or not values in the organizational culture can supplant the national culture is an important question when a multinational headquarters decide on policies for controlling a subsidiary through its culture. Section 5.4 asked how management can MITIGATE THE EFFECTS OF THE ENVIRONMENT on the organic culture – for example, by the choice of CEO, developing appropriate HRM systems, and issuing a mission statement that motivates members.

5.7 EXERCISE

(a) Examine this list of 12 factors below. How might each factor influence the development of the organizational culture?

   1 the national legal system;
   2 policies and systems designed to implement the strategy;
   3 globalization;
   4 decisions made by competitors;
   5 ethical and religious systems;
   6 decisions made by customers;
   7 the national, regional and world economies;
   8 financial markets;
   9 technology;
  10 the organizational strategy;
  11 factors in the green environment;
  12 industry norms.

(b) How can top management modify the influence of each so that they achieve greater control of the organizational culture?

(c) Can you think of additional factors that influence the development of the organizational culture?

CHAPTER SIX
Culture and Communication

6.1 Introduction

It is sometimes argued that the more communication the better. For example, Franklin (2004) writes

> it is amazing how insatiable employees are for communication. Many organizations fall into the trap of reducing communications, because employees don't seem to be bothered – some stand there looking bored. (*p. 47*)

Certainly, employees react against lack of communication on topics they consider vital, but also dislike being bogged down in communication they consider irrelevant. More communication does not necessarily mean better communication, and quantity alone does not guarantee greater involvement by the receiver. A message that does not hold and persuade the receiver is a failed message, and the cost involved in producing it is wasted.

Here is an example of wasted communication on a massive scale, in the European Union.

Even the general director of the EU's translation service admitted that the situation was getting out of control. Juhani Lönnroth commented that

"If you can't say what you need to say on 15 pages...then it is perhaps better not said at all." His criticism comes as no surprise. There are 23 official languages in the EU now, which makes 506 possible translation combinations, including many absurd ones like from Slovene into Gaelic.[1]

The costs of translating EU papers have risen to hundreds of millions of euros a year. In 2007 they reached 332 million euros.

This chapter deals with the conditions under which the optimal balance is found, and so the point at which the communication may succeed. How far these conditions correspond across cultures must be of concern to the international manager.

This chapter focuses on spoken communication. Electronic communication is discussed in Chapter 16.

6.2   Appropriate Communication Across Cultures

A message is most likely to be efficient and to achieve its purpose when it is appropriate in its context. This means that it should be designed for a particular context, and can be interpreted in that context.

Suppose that a poorly dressed stranger approaches you in the street and says "Have you any spare change?" Superficially this appears to be a request for information to which you might answer "Yes I do" or "No I don't." In practice, most people would guess from the physical situation and his obvious poverty that the stranger is asking for money – although no explicit request has been made.

Suppose that a second stranger approaches you in the street. This man looks prosperous and carries a paper-case, and he says "Have you any spare change?" The contextual clues do not support the earlier interpretation, that he is a beggar asking for a handout. If you are unable to find an alternative explanation and to attach any purpose to the message, you conclude that this behavior is irrational.

We create and interpret messages in terms of their context. When we understand the context, the purpose and meaning of the message becomes clear. If we don't understand the context, the purpose is obscure. Here is another example – a short conversation:

A. Telephone.
B. I'm in the bath.
A. Okay.

These six words tell us very little until we know the situation – which is that A and B were occupying an apartment consisting of a bedroom, living room, bathroom, kitchen. A telephone rang in the living room. A, in the bedroom, heard it ring and shouted at B, whom he assumed to be in the kitchen, asking her to go next door and answer the telephone. B shouted back that she couldn't because she was in the bathroom and therefore could he. He agreed. In full form the conversation might be paraphrased as follows.

A. The telephone in the living room is ringing. I'm in bed and don't want to get up. So if you're in the kitchen please could you answer it?
B. I'm not in the kitchen. I'm having a bath and it's easier for you to answer it than it is for me.
A. All right, I accept your explanation. I'll answer it. [A goes to answer the telephone]

In this example the key factors in interpreting the purpose of the message relate to the physical situation. But in other cases other factors may be as or more important. These are described below.

6.2.1   *The context of communications*

The set of contextual categories in Table 6.1 helps the user decide whether a message is appropriate and likely to be persuasive, and can be used both in creating a new message and interpreting a message already transmitted.

Table 6.1   The context of communications

WHAT is communicated?	What is the appropriate CONTENT of the message?
WHO communicates?	Who is the appropriate ADDRESSOR to send the message?
To WHOM is the message communicated?	Who is the appropriate ADRESSEE? The addressee(s) might consist of a single person or a number of people, inside the organization or in the environment.
WHEN is the appropriate TIME for communicating the message?	For how long should the message be communicated? Does the message need repetition, and if so, for how long?
WHERE is the appropriate location for communicating the message?	LOCATION includes physical and organizational situations.
HOW is the message communicated?	What is the appropriate MEDIUM? For example, print, e-mail, text, face-to-face meeting? What is the appropriate LANGUAGE? What is the appropriate STYLE? Formal or informal? How should content be selected and sequenced? What degree of ambiguity is acceptable? Should the communication be one-way or two-way (6.3)?

6.2.2   *Appropriate and inappropriate selections*

The selection made of any one category influences the appropriate selection of all others.

For instance, when a senior person becomes associated as ADDRESSOR with the CONTENT of a communication, it derives status from his importance. If you need to communicate strategy to the stockholders, this influences your choice of communicator – almost certainly the CEO, supported by senior officers of the company. The choice of a junior secretary would be inappropriate. In that case, the message would lack persuasiveness, and fail.

Similarly, suppose that headquarters has agreed a new strategy for the subsidiary. This is presented to subsidiary managers in a weekend conference held in a luxurious hotel. In this respect, the arrangements are appropriate. Unfortunately, the person selected to make the presentation is a junior headquarters manager. The senior subsidiary managers are insulted. They expect to be addressed on such an important topic by the CEO in person, and interpret this selection of addressor as a signal that headquarters has no confidence in their operations. Morale is damaged.

A message that is communicated inappropriately may be AMBIGUOUS – understood differently by different receivers. Managements sometimes practice deliberate ambiguity, for example, leading the marketing department to believe that "this company is marketing-led and depends centrally on your efforts" and the production department to believe that "this company is production-led...". But this can be a dangerous strategy that undermines trust and morale when representatives of marketing and production meet and compare their impressions. In general, management should aim to communicate as clearly as possible.

6.2.3   *Content*

The content of the communication consists of the information that is communicated. But "information" may mean very little unless it is given for a purpose, and this purpose is clear. The usual purpose of giving information is to persuade. Even a casual, friendly greeting serves the function of trying to persuade the addressee that you are a friendly person who intends goodwill.

The meetings described in 6.2 illustrate the point. The literal meaning of the words used by the second stranger is quite clear, but the PURPOSE which they are intended to serve is obscure, and so the message fails as communication.

A message is persuasive when the addressor selects information that the addressee perceives as relevant – in terms of her experience and needs.

Business deals can go wrong when one person does not understand why certain information is being given or requested – or is not being given, and because her informational priorities do not correspond to those of the other side. In international business, when the two sides express different cultures, the implication is that each must work to present information in terms that the other can recognize. Important points are appropriately highlighted, in terms of the expectations of the other culture.

6.2.4   Addressor

A management message is efficient when the person for whom it is intended (the addressee) believes that it is being communicated by the appropriate addressor, and that this addressor has credibility and can be trusted.

Suppose that you, as CEO of your company, decide to re-engineer operational processes in the production department. Who should give the employees this message? You? Your secretary? The production manager? A supervisor? What factors influence your decision? Who is the appropriate addressor if you decide to change the timing of the lunch break?

Senior managers prefer to communicate positive events that reflect well on their performance. Hence they may prefer to delegate the communication of bad news to subordinates. Giving bad news has negative implications, and no one wants to be associated with an unpopular cause. However, the manager invites criticism when he remains silent for too long in a time of trouble. A CEO who leaves all responsibility for firing redundant staff to a subordinate may appear cowardly. Hence, managers have a delicate task in calculating for how long they can afford to stand aside from bad news and when they have to get involved.

6.2.5   Addressee

You cannot take for granted that the norms governing addressor–addressee relationships in your culture apply elsewhere. Suppose that you have an idea for a new product. In a culture where power distances and needs to avoid uncertainty are slight, you as a junior manager might feel secure approaching the CEO to make your suggestion. In a culture where it is sometimes acceptable to by-pass lines of authority you have no inhibitions about seeking the opinions of colleagues and superiors elsewhere in the organization (assuming that you trust them not to steal your idea). But in contexts where these conditions do not apply, you might have no option but to first discuss your idea with your immediate superior.

6.2.6   Time

Concepts of time affect

- when messages are communicated;
- the length of time devoted to a communication;
- the number of times a message is communicated;
- the time allowed to elapse between a message being received and the response. In Japanese companies, the subordinate is expected to respond immediately to a spoken message from his *sacho* (boss);
- how often one should communicate. Many Anglo companies report their financial status every quarter. Is this frequency always necessary – given that the energy and time spent might be better invested in maximizing the long-term value of the business?

Hall and Whyte (1961) distinguished times:

- SCHEDULE TIME refers to the time by when a job should be completed;
- DISCUSSION time refers to the length of time that should be spent in discussing business;
- ACQUAINTANCE time determines how long you need to know the other person before he/she will do business with you. In a low-context culture acquaintance time might be cut back to a single meeting and the identity of your company may be more significant than your personal identity. In a high-context culture you may need to invest time in building an "insider" relationship;
- APPOINTMENT time deals with the issue of punctuality. How late can you afford to be before you should make an apology? The Japanese should be five or ten minutes early. The Anglo manager may be up to five minutes late for an appointment without feeling it necessary to apologize. Some Scandinavians are more particular; an appointment for 10 o'clock means 10 on the dot.

6.2.7   Location

This parameter determines

- where business is appropriately communicated;
- what sort of communications are appropriate in different locations;
- the symbolic meaning that the choice of location imparts to the communication.

The space where the individual works, the ease with which others can gain access, and how the space is furnished, communicate messages of power and status. In American companies the CEO typically occupies a top-floor office (often on a corner), distancing him/her from the workforce, and aides compete for an office nearby.

6.2.8   Language, medium, style

Language, medium and style determine HOW a message is communicated.

What LANGUAGE is appropriate when dealing with a joint venture partner from another culture when you don't share a first language? What language is appropriate when communicating between headquarters and a foreign subsidiary, within the subsidiary, and at different levels of the hierarchy? The selection is decided by such factors as

- the language of addressor and addressee;
- organizational policy;
- the language associated with the task. English has evolved as the language of computer science, and even non-English speaking computer analysts are bound to use English terms;
- the status of the language in the particular industry and country.

The manager can select from a wide range of MEDIA when choosing the appropriate form for communicating a message. She can use speech (in formal and informal meetings, telephone, video, etc.); text (by reports, memos, fax, e-mail, the net, etc.); pictorial forms; combinations. The selection is decided by situational factors such as

- the number and identities of the addressees;
- the personalities of the addressees;
- the complexity and importance of the message;
- the message function, and whether routine or original;
- distance. Opportunities to ask for and make clarifications;
- the need for accuracy and legal considerations;
- the availability of technology;
- expense.

A Thai financial analyst reported that

> I have to write memos (call reports) to the boss after I meet customers.
>
> Memos are important for investment bankers. [But] talking with colleagues and superiors about what I do is easier. I can express my feeling to them. . . . By talking like this, we can know by his face. From memos, we cannot know his real feeling.

The analyst was adept at switching between media, choosing that which seemed most appropriate to the addressee and the content.

Middle-managers from Indonesia reported that although they might commit plans for a new policy to writing, they always took the opportunity to discuss the content first with their superiors. The low-context American manager might reverse the process, first writing in order to establish legal ownership of the idea, then proceeding to discussion. In general, the international manager needs to consider when speech or text is most appropriate to the needs of an addressor in the other culture.

The notion of STYLE is the third factor associated with how a message is communicated. The notion of style encompasses a range of features, including the structure of the message, and its length. Misunderstandings arise when different cultures associate different meanings to extended or reduced messages. For example, Japanese communication style causes problems for Americans because Americans often assume that the more detailed and lengthy a message is, the more complete and so better it is. In contrast, the Japanese tend to use fewer words to express an idea, and find virtue in brevity:

> A common Japanese expression describing ideal communication is *ichi ieba ju wo shiru* (hear one, understand ten). The idea is that if the speaker and listener are on the same wavelength, then it's not necessary to explicitly state everything in words.   *(Kopp, 2001)*

Formal speech and written styles are appropriate in contexts where authority differences are exaggerated, and less so where they are diminished. In the low-power distance Anglo cultures the manager may try to motivate staff by adopting a less formal style and thus creating a closer relationship with them. This tactic can backfire when applied by

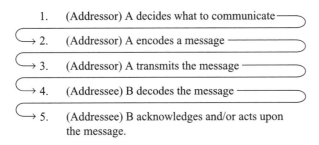

1. (Addressor) A decides what to communicate
2. (Addressor) A encodes a message
3. (Addressor) A transmits the message
4. (Addressee) B decodes the message
5. (Addressee) B acknowledges and/or acts upon the message.

Figure 6.1 One-way communication style

the Anglo manager in high-power distance cultures in circumstances when subordinates expect to occupy a significantly lower place on the hierarchy.

The use of an informal style further risks confusing a non-native speaker of the language who does not have experience of the idioms and slang used by native speakers. Anglo negotiators are happy in searching for a "compromise" - which does not imply a willingness to "compromise" their values; but in Iranian terms, the concepts are less easily separated and the notion of "compromise" implies betraying basic principles.

Such differences occur within one language. The Briton resolves to "table a motion" when he puts a motion before a meeting for discussion; the American interprets this to mean that the motion is delayed. In sum, an inappropriate choice of style leads to misunderstandings and unnecessary ambiguities.

6.3   One- and Two-way Communication Styles

The participants' decision to use a one- or two-way communication style reflects their relationship and their needs to communicate – which may be task based. Figure 6.1 models a ONE-WAY communication between participants A and B, the addressor and addressee.

Participant A plans and makes all significant utterances. B may contribute attention markers and acknowledgments during A's communication ("yes", "I see", "of course", and so on) and otherwise responds only by taking any appropriate action. It is implied that the message given to B is straightforward, and B does not need to ask for clarification.

Figure 6.2 models a TWO-WAY communication between A and B. This time, both A and B contribute significantly to the conversation. Each utterance in the conversation may be expressing one of a range of functions, which include

- requesting and giving information, an opinion, etc.;
- asking for and giving clarification;
- making and responding to a query;
- inviting and suggesting an alternative;
- agreeing and disagreeing;
- requesting and giving support.

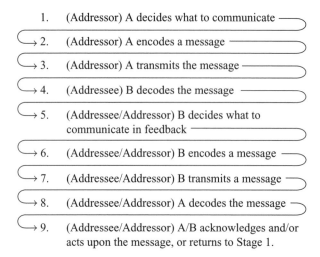

1. (Addressor) A decides what to communicate
2. (Addressor) A encodes a message
3. (Addressor) A transmits the message
4. (Addressee) B decodes the message
5. (Addressee/Addressor) B decides what to communicate in feedback
6. (Addressee/Addressor) B encodes a message
7. (Addressee/Addressor) B transmits a message
8. (Addressee/Addressor) A decodes the message
9. (Addressee/Addressor) A/B acknowledges and/or acts upon the message, or returns to Stage 1.

Figure 6.2   Two-way communication style

In theory, the use of a two-way style suggests that both persons are contributing to the outcome of the communication. In practice, it may be ambiguous. A Chinese manager admitted that his management style was "democratic autocracy. I listen to everyone, then do what I want." But deliberate ambiguity can backfire and cause resentment when the other person stumbles on the truth, that his contributions have not carried any weight.

Figures 6.1 and 6.2 model the extremes, and in practice most communications occur at median points on this continuum. Nevertheless, the question then arises as to what factors influence a move in one direction rather than the other.

6.3.1   How the task influences the choice of a one- or two-way style

Task-based factors influencing the choice of style are listed below:

(one-way style)	(two-way style)
TASK URGENCY	LACK OF TASK URGENCY
SIMPLE TASK	COMPLEX TASK
ROUTINE TASK	NON-ROUTINE TASK
CLOSE-ENDED TASK	OPEN-ENDED TASK

TASK URGENCY can be an occasional factor in all work, and in some tasks – for example, surgery, firefighting, military exercises – is inherent. The key task demands immediate responses to formalized instructions. A one-way style is more efficient so long as all members of the work team share precise understanding of the instructions. Prolonged two-way discussion threatens to impair their efficiency and is avoided so far as possible. But in another situation when no longer engaged in the urgent task – for example, when relaxing off-duty or discussing policy – the medical staff, firefighters and soldiers might prefer a two-way style.

A SIMPLE TASK is defined as a task comprising few stages. An example might be painting a wall, and A, the person requiring the work done, need give only a simple instruction to Painter B. A COMPLEX TASK comprises a range of stages, for some of which there may be acceptable alternatives. Manager A has to meet clients abroad and requests her Assistant B to confirm the meeting venue, check the time of flights, and when a flight is agreed to make flight and hotel reservations.

A ROUTINE TASK is one which B has performed many times before or knows from observation of others; and B needs only a minimal instruction from A. A NON-ROUTINE TASK is new to B and A must be prepared to answer queries, provide clarifications where necessary and to check B's understanding.

The routine/non-routine dimension may override the simple/complex dimension. When the participants are used to performing a complex task, a short one-way communication may be sufficient to trigger its completion. To develop the example above, when Manager A has for many years been visiting her clients on a regular basis (say, every first Monday of the month), always flies at the same time and stays in the same hotel, and Assistant B has been working with her for all this time, perhaps A need give only a brief reminder that the normal procedures apply this month too. On the other hand, if Painter B has never before performed this apparently simple task, A and B may need to participate in a two-way discussion to ensure that the lessons are learned.

A CLOSE-ENDED TASK has one possible satisfactory outcome; for example, I ask you to wash the plates and stack them. AN OPEN-ENDED TASK has a number of possible outcomes, any one of which may satisfy the task goals. For example, a company decides to adapt and manufacture a foreign technology to the local market. A number of departments are invited to send representatives to a meeting to discuss the project, and each contributes knowledge and ideas that the others may not initially share, and the communication has a multi-party two-way style. The contributions include questions, clarifications, opinions, information, arguments and counter-arguments.

In sum; it is sometimes assumed that one-way communications are inherently "bad" and inefficient. This discussion has tried to show that the effectiveness of a communication pattern depends upon how far it is appropriate, given the task being performed and who is communicating with whom.

6.3.2   How culture influences the choice

When patterns of communication in an organization between A and B are normally one way and the superior, A, normally takes the role of addressor, it can be deduced that the organization is hierarchical. When this occurs regularly in a national culture, it can be deduced that power distances are high.

Where power distances are great and where members place a priority on preserving social harmony, the superior's rights to delegate are associated with authority. Subordinates are wary of asking for clarification of ambiguous utterances lest this involve the superior in loss of face – by implying that he/she communicated inadequately the first time. Comments and suggestions might also suggest a challenge.

Here is an illustration. The CEO and his assistant belong to a high-power distance culture, in which the subordinate assistant works hard to identify and serve his/her superior's needs. They are situated in the office:

CEO: "I don't have the figures from sales."
Assistant: "Yes sir." [calls the sales department and requests that figures be submitted].

The assistant interprets the CEO's utterance as a directive; "Get me the figures from sales." Where this meaning is inappropriate to the context, he needs to try again, interpreting it as a question requiring a WH- answer: "Where are the figures from sales?" If this is inappropriate, he might respond as though to a question requiring a YES/NO answer; for example, "Have you seen the figures from sales?" Only if this meaning is clearly not intended dare he interpret it, at face value, as a statement perhaps requiring an acknowledgment such as "Hm", or "Nor me" (see Sinclair, 1980).

When the participants come from a low-context culture the assistant is less inclined to intuit his superior's needs. He is less inhibited in giving feedback responses that make the CEO's meaning explicit. These include

CEO: "I don't have the figures from sales."
Assistant: (a) "Hm." [providing acknowledgment];
            (b) "No, they haven't been issued yet" [answering a YES/NO question];
            (c) "They were e-mailed across this morning" [answering a WH question];
            (d) "I'll call for them now" [calls, obeying the directive].

6.3.3   *Clues that help interpretation*

How does the assistant decide which interpretation to make and which response is most appropriate?

Where power distances are low in a low-context culture, the sensible way to resolve his uncertainty is that the assistant asks for clarification. But in cultural and organizational contexts where a request for clarification is punished, the assistant has to rely on other cues in order to disambiguate the CEO's utterance and identify its purpose. The possible clues include

- clues from the specific task;
- clues from the context of time – see 6.2.6. Is this appropriate?
- clues from the location – see 6.2.7;
- clues from the organizational culture. What is normal practice in this company?
- clues from your experience of this individual; the history of the relationship, his/her psychology, gender;
- clues from non-verbal signaling (see 6.4);
- clues from the national culture.

In a high-context culture, the employee invests effort in observing his/her superior, intuiting needs, and predicting appropriate responses from past experience. In turn, the considerate superior avoids behaving unpredictably. But in a low-power distance and individualist culture, employees need invest less in understanding the boss's psychology. The other side of this coin is that typical relationships with the workforce in his/her own country lead the manager into making assumptions that may not be justified in an expatriate post. For instance, many Japanese working in the United States

> get quietly frustrated with American underlings. Americans, a Japanese boss often feels, need more supervision than their Japanese counterparts, who try to intuit their superior's desire.[2]

The local American employees spend more time in debating instructions and appear less competent than Japanese employees back home.

6.3.4 Unofficial channels for communicating upwards

In all cultures, "unofficial channels" may be used in preference to the formal structures for conveying information around the organization.

The use of these channels is common in high-power distance cultures where it is difficult to communicate unwelcome news and criticisms up the hierarchy. For example, a subordinate wishes to draw the attention of her boss to illegal activity in the workplace. She may choose to send an anonymous note, or to talk to a cousin who passes the information on to a friend of the boss.

In some high-context cultures where the expatriate is not assimilated into social structures, he/she may act as a conduit conveying messages between ranks of locals. His/her equivocal status gives locals the opportunity to pass informal messages around the hierarchy. An American working in a Thai company commented:

> Exchanging gossip with someone's secretary or driver can often be much more informative than going directly to a top executive, as he may feel uncomfortable expressing dissatisfaction directly ... Likewise, most of the Thai executives in my firm use my secretary to convey messages to me or ask my feelings about something rather than communicating with me, even though their English may be better than my secretary's. ... If she gets it wrong, [that is] her mistake, not theirs.

Traditional Japanese achieved the same ends by making rules for after-hours eating and drinking. Japanese culture is relatively tolerant of drunkenness, and once in the bar subordinates could express opinions that would not be tolerated back in the office. Subordinate–superior messages that are inappropriate in the official setting (during working hours, in the office) can be communicated appropriately when different temporal and locational factors apply (after working hours, in the bar).

6.4   Non-verbal Communication

Some scholars estimate that 75 percent of meaning in verbal communications is conveyed by non-verbal signals. They support the verbal message by

- supplementing the meaning of the words;
- modifying and glossing the words;
- mitigating unintended interpretations;
- signaling the significance of features heard or seen in the context. These might include utterances made by other persons present, doors opening and closing, cars, radios and television, overhead aircraft; and visual sights – all of which may either distract or provide stimuli for the communication.

They also facilitate decoding. That is, the addressee uses these signals to show how he interprets the message.

The models of one- and two-way communication (Figures 6.1 and 6.2) imply that verbal communication is a linear process, and that B only contributes when A has ended his turn. However, the non-verbal element is non-linear in this respect, and non-verbal signals pass between the participants in a continual stream. This concept of a transaction recognizes that we often make decisions about sending a message and its content *during* the other person's contribution, and not simply on its completion. And so planning what to encode in your next contribution is influenced by what he is communicating to you and how you decode it.

These signals are usually involuntary. They are transmitted and interpreted uncon-sciously. This means that in any face-to-face interaction, you are sending messages to the other person that are creating impressions of your sincerity, trustworthiness, commitment, etc., and neither of you are fully in control of how the transmission and interpretation processes.

They may have different meanings in different cultures. For example, Anglos greet a new acquaintance by smiling, but the French keep a serious expression. When the French meet a smiling Anglo they may react against his/her apparent insincerity.

6.4.1   Signals

The following are discussed briefly:

- stance;
- gesture;
- eye movement;
- voice quality.

STANCE includes how and where you position yourself in relation to the other person. Stance conveys messages that differ across cultures. In many societies standing with hands on hips might indicate informality and is neutral for mood. In Indonesia it may be interpreted as a sign of bad temper.

GESTURE includes how you use your hands, head, shoulders to reflect and reinforce or substitute for verbal messages.

Many cultures accept physical contact in a business greeting. Anglo males usually resist embracing in public, which is normal in Latin cultures. In Latin America a kiss on both cheeks is accompanied by placing a hand on the other person's shoulder and is known as the "abrazzo". But contact is not universally appreciated. In Muslim cultures, many women refuse to touch the bodies of men to whom they are not related, and so will not shake hands.

EYE MOVEMENT includes length of gaze, maintaining eye contact, dilation, blinking. Eye movement is always significant and some cultures consciously ascribe great importance to feelings communicated by the eyes. These may be avoided, or welcomed.

The traditional Indian woman avoids looking into the eyes of a man to whom she is not related; on the other hand, the Egyptian stands close in order to "read" the other person's eyes. In both Arab and Indian cultures a subordinate averts his/her gaze when communicating with a superior. In Anglo societies eye-contact is crucial to confirm interest and the manager expects it, and is likely to interpret a refusal to make contact as evasiveness. In Japan, and more generally in high-context cultures, face-to-face communication and eye contact is particularly important in initial business contacts.

VOICE QUALITY. Different cultures associate different communicative meanings to such qualities of the human voice as voice quality, tempo, pitch variation, and volume. Cultures respond differently to variations in voice quality. In Latin American cultures, wide pitch variation (ups and downs) indicate emotional commitment to the topic. In West Africa, a wide pitch range is expected among males. Many Oriental cultures prefer a more monotonous style, which indicates respect.

6.5   Implications for the Manager

Compare an organization that you know well IN YOUR OWN CULTURE, and a similar organization in SOME OTHER CULTURE.

1   Assume that you are planning appropriate messages in the two organizations intended to achieve similar purposes (for example, messages used to communicate good news (e.g. a promotion; a reprimand; a query for technical information; a directive; a policy change). What differences occur in your selections of
(a)   appropriate addressor?
(b)   appropriate addressee?
(c)   appropriate content?
(d)   appropriate language, medium, style?
(e)   appropriate time?
(f)   appropriate location?
    •   what cultural and other factors explain these differences?

2 In each of the two organizations, how typical are two-way communication styles between superior and subordinate?
- with what tasks are one-way styles usually used?
- with what tasks are two-way styles usually used?
- how far do these factors explain why two-way styles are/are not selected?
  - (a) task factors;
  - (b) cultural factors;
  - (c) any other factors.

6.6   SUMMARY

This chapter has reviewed aspects of cross-cultural communication. Section 6.2 dealt with the notion of COMMUNICATIVE APPROPRIACY in different CULTURAL contexts. A message is persuasive and effective when it is perceived as appropriate. Appropriacy depends on WHAT content is communicated, by WHOM, to WHOM, WHEN, WHERE, and HOW – that is, in what medium, language, and style. The concept of style was further developed in Section 6.3; ONE- AND TWO-WAY COMMUNICATIVE STYLES. This saw that selection of an appropriate style is influenced by factors associated with the task – whether it is urgent or non-urgent; simple or complex; routine or non-routine; close-ended or open-ended. The influence of national culture was also examined. Section 6.4 dealt with NON-VERBAL COMMUNICATION, and emphasized that non-verbal signals may have different meanings in different cultures, and are often made and interpreted unconsciously.

6.7   EXERCISE

This exercise examines the notion of appropriacy. Work with another person, then discuss your answers with the group. Assume that the company employs 300 persons. You have two subsidiaries, in a country that does not share your national language. You are CEO, and take responsibility for communications.

In each case, decide

- whether the situational factors are appropriate in order to communicate the specified content efficiently;
- what might be the penalties for mis-communication;
- which of these factors you might change so that the communication is more persuasive – and you avoid being penalized.

1 You aim to introduce the annual strategy to the board.

a. ADDRESSOR(s)	Your personal assistant
b. ADDRESSEE(s)	The board
c. LANGUAGE	Language of headquarters
d. MEDIUM	Question and answer session
e. STYLE	Informal
f. TIME	Lunchtime
g. LOCATION	The works canteen

2 You have to inform the workforce that one of your subsidiaries will be closed, followed by mass redundancies.

a. ADDRESSOR(s)	You, as CEO
b. ADDRESSEE(s)	Your board, and all staff in the subsidiary
c. LANGUAGE	Language of the subsidiary
d. MEDIUM	Text message
e. STYLE	Formal; legalistic
f. TIME	The day before the redundancies are made
g. LOCATION	(does not apply)

3 You aim to inform all employees in your foreign subsidiary of changes in working practices and new staffing policies consequential on new strategic planning.

a. ADDRESSOR(s)	Senior manager of the subsidiary
b. ADDRESSEE(s)	Subsidiary managers
c. LANGUAGE	Language of the subsidiary
d. MEDIUM	Speech
e. STYLE	Formal
f. TIME	All day – for as long as is needed
g. LOCATION	Subsidiary board room

4 You aim to announce changes in parking regulations at the headquarters.

a. ADDRESSOR(s)	You, as CEO
b. ADDRESSEE(s)	The workforce in headquarters and subsidiaries
c. LANGUAGE	Language of headquarters
d. MEDIUM	Printed notices
e. STYLE	Informal
f. TIME	Six months before the regulations come into force
g. LOCATION	Canteen

5 You aim to develop new training programs that can help achieve the new strategic goals.

a. ADDRESSOR(s)	Chairperson of the board.
b. ADDRESSEE(s)	All trainers in headquarters and subsidiaries
c. LANGUAGE	Language of headquarters
d. MEDIUM	Meeting
e. STYLE	Informal
f. TIME	A week before the date of the meeting

Notes

1 Europe continues to generate mountains of paper. *European Foundation Intelligence Digest*, April 2008.

2 John Schwarz, Jeanne Gordon and Mark Veverka. The "Salaryman" blues. *Newsweek*, May 9, 1988.

Motivation

7.1 Introduction

In China, international subsidiaries compete actively in recruiting and retaining the Chinese executives. The country president (China) of Carrefour was interviewed about his success in finding and holding the loyalties of the best. He had devised an incentive system that was unlike anything applied in Europe or the United States.

The company fully trained their managers at considerable expense and guaranteed their immediate future, but in return asked them to sign a three–five year contract. If they chose to leave Carrefour and to work for a competitor they would be expected to repay the cost of training. But managers are given another good reason for *not* leaving:

> If people stay for five years, I give them a super bonus – two, three, or five months' salary. In the end, we have a very low turnover of executive staff. Today 50 of the 73 hypermarkets are managed by Chinese managers, who are very good.[1]

Motivators must operate to the advantage of both the employees and the company in order to be effective in the long term. In this company bonuses are linked to training, and so the motivational appeal of both is reinforced.

This chapter deals with a range of factors that motivate employees' performance. It first examines needs, and then shows why a careful analysis of the employees' needs is essential when building an incentive system. The analysis and the system must be closely related An incentive system directed towards meeting needs that employees do not experience is bound to fail.

7.2   Needs

The individual's needs are influenced by factors associated with his/her personal situation (age, experience, and so on) and with factors in the environment, including moral values and culture. People living in different economic and cultural systems have different needs, and an incentive system that motivates performance in one situation may be useless in some other. This has international implications; an analysis of the needs felt by headquarters staff may be inaccurate as a reflection of the needs felt by staff in a foreign subsidiary.

When the individual thinks that his/her needs are likely to be satisfied by a particular activity, he/she may commit to this activity, at least until the need is satisfied or the activity seems unlikely to achieve satisfaction.

However, not all the individual's needs will correspond to company needs. Some needs may be neutral to company goals and relate entirely to the individual's private life over which the company has less control than in the workplace. For example, my strongest need is to play football. So long as I do not pursue this interest in office time, I am not stealing time from my employer, but unless the company decides to organize a company team, it may be unable to harness this drive.

Some individual needs may appear to correspond to company goals but in practice are not productive. For example, the company expects high quality, and this is an aim that I share. I work so carefully at reducing my margin of error to 1 percent of my output that I produce only 100 items a day. However, the company tolerates a 5 percent margin so long as I can produce a 1,000 items.

In extreme cases, the contradiction may be negative; I am motivated by a need to destroy company plant and products, and management may have no alternative but to dismiss me.

It follows that the company has the staged tasks of

1   specifying company goals;
2   identifying the employee's needs;
3   motivating the employee to achieve his/her needs in ways that also achieve company goals.

7.2.1   Identifying the needs of the employee

This section deals with two points:

- the employee's identification of his/her needs;
- the company's identification of the employee's needs.

Table 7.1 Kovach (1987): employees' needs from their work

1986		(1946)
1.	Interesting work.	(6)
2.	Full appreciation of work done.	(1)
3.	Feeling of being in on things.	(2)
4.	Job security.	(4)
5.	Good wages.	(5)
6.	Promotion and growth in organization.	(7)
7.	Good working conditions.	(9)
8.	Personal loyalty to employees.	(8)
9.	Tactful discipline	(10)
10.	Sympathetic help with personal problems.	(3)

Over the years there have been many studies made of employees' perceived needs. These include an American study first made by Kovach in 1946. The informant pool consisted of industrial employees, including unskilled blue-collar and skilled white-collar workers, in American manufacturing companies. Kovach repeated the survey in 1986. The results show some changing priorities over the years but also surprising consistency. Table 7.1 gives Kovach's list of what employees claimed to need from their work, ranked first for 1986, then in parentheses for 1946. Despite the age of these studies, they point to general questions about how needs change over time and why.

Two points to note are that "interesting work" becomes much more important, and that "good wages" was not the most important on either occasion.

This second point may contradict conventional thinking about the importance of the wage, and certainly contradicts what the informants' direct supervisors thought about their subordinates' needs. Kovach also reported on rankings made by these direct supervisors. They were asked to order job rewards as they believed that their subordinates would rank them. Their ranking remained almost the same for 1946 and 1986, and are given in Table 7.2.

These findings have an important implication for the international manager. Kovach's informants were all American; and if managers fail to perceive, or to act upon, the needs

Table 7.2 Kovach (1987): supervisors' perceptions of employees' needs

1	Good wages.
2	Job security.
3	Promotion and growth in organization.
4	Good working conditions.
5	Interesting work.
6	Personal loyalty to employees.
7	Tactful discipline
8	Full appreciation of work done.
9	Sympathetic help with personal problems.
10	Feeling of being in on things.

of subordinates with whom they share the same cultural profile, they are even more likely to mistake the needs of members of another culture. That is, the manager posted from headquarters to a foreign subsidiary may have even greater difficulties in understanding the needs of the local workforce, and thus difficulty in designing an incentive system that is motivating.

7.2.2   *Factors determining the employee's needs*

Of course, not all employees shared the same priorities, and this study revealed the following factors as likely to cause differences:

- age;
- wage levels;
- gender.

Age groups   Kovach (1987) found that informants aged under 30 listed good wages, job security, and promotion and growth as their first three choices. The older workers still gave high ranking to job security, although this declined in importance over time – perhaps because they no longer had to support young children, and had built up investments to carry them through retirement.

Different wage levels   Kovach's figures show that among the lowest paid employees (under $12,000 in 1986) good wages were ranked as most important. But they are ranked as increasingly less important among the better paid, and among the best paid (earning over $25,000 in 1986) they had slipped to tenth place; and interesting work was ranked top.

Genders   Kovach's work found few differences were found between the preferences of men and women. Women ranked "full appreciation of work done" in first place, while men placed it second. However, this does not mean that gender differences are never significant. In other cultures and other industries, the work needs of men and women may be far apart

Other factors influence individual differences. These include education; professional identity (see 7.3); and factors in the organizational and cultural contexts (see 7.4).

7.3   Intrinsic and Extrinsic Needs

Evidence has been produced to show that in developed countries, technical and professional employees are more likely to be motivated by intrinsic (that is, internal or mental) factors rather than by extrinsic factors (from outside ourselves). Intrinsic factors include the need for achievement and the opportunity to do interesting work. Extrinsic factors include needs for food, shelter and money Chen et al. (1999) argue that R&D professionals are more likely to be motivated by intrinsic factors, and in a parallel study using Greek data, Manolopoulos (2006) argues the greater importance of extrinsic factors.

Needs are frequently described in terms of a hierarchy. The most influential hierarchy produced is still that designed by Maslow in 1954. This continues to influence theories of motivation and the design of incentive systems. It shows how behavior is motivated at certain points by opportunities to satisfy intrinsic needs and at other points by opportunities to satisfy extrinsic needs. Maslow describes needs on five levels:

Level 5 and highest: Self-actualization and achievement needs.
Level 4: Esteem needs – both self-esteem and the esteem of others.
Level 3: Belonging and social needs.
Level 2: Safety and security needs.
Level 1: Physiological (existence) needs.

Cartwright (2000) proposes a new highest and sixth level – the "unattainable" – what the individual strives for and can never entirely reach. Because this is unreachable, it suggests that however many other goals the individual achieves, eventually he/she cannot be entirely satisfied.

Needs at Levels 1–3 are basic needs which are satisfied by extrinsic outcomes external to person, such as food, money, praise from others. The ego and self-actualization needs at Levels 4–5 (or 4–6, if Cartwright's suggestion is accepted) are satisfied by intrinsic and internal outcomes, such as a sense of achievement and competence. These spring from personal feelings of worth and cannot be given by someone else.

A satisfied need is no longer motivating, and you satisfy needs progressively. This means that when you have satisfied needs at one level you try to meet those at the next level up, and a higher level need is usually only experienced when those below have been met. Assume that a man needs to buy a car. He knows that if he completes his job he will be rewarded with the money with which to buy the car, and so he works. When the effects of behavior are valued, the individual continues to repeat that behavior; and so he continues to work until his monetary needs are satisfied. When he has enough money he stops working – unless, of course, he finds a new need. This implies that the model is not only hierarchical but also sequential.

7.3.1 *Maslow and money*

Assuming that the company does not have the capacity to accurately identify the needs of each individual and then to satisfy these on an individual basis, it has to make a generalization. This means that an incentive system based on the generalized is bound to offer some individuals more of what they want, and to disappoint others. One solution is to offer money. Everyone can use money, even if the uses they put it to are very different.

Maslow's 1954 model does not include "money", which might suggest that he does not think that needs for money are important. In practice though, money plays a part at every level of the model, which helps us recognize how monetary reward functions as a means to an end, rather than an end in itself.

Money enables me to purchase the necessities of life, thus satisfying needs at Level 1. And when I have consumed sufficient food and drink, any extra money is invested in accommodation to meet safety and security needs at Level 2. The purchase of an expensive car, a house in a good locality, restaurant reservations, new clothes, serves to impress others and build relationships. Thus money helps satisfy social needs at Level 3. Opportunities to satisfy intrinsic needs are expressed by Levels 4 and 5.

But in practice it may be very difficult to entirely separate extrinsic and intrinsic needs. For example, your expectation that you will be paid more reflects extrinsic needs but the size of your pay packet also has symbolic values. It justifies your sense of self-esteem, and reflects your achievement. It serves as a measure of keeping score against other people (are you more or less successful?) and with yourself (have you achieved more this year than last?)

People buy cars, houses, restaurant reservations, clothes for more than their utilitarian worth. They also serve as symbols of success. In modern China many employees seemed to have the same ambitions as do many Anglo workers – the ambition to drive a good car. Your ownership of an expensive car tells the world "I have achieved, I am a success". And a British newspaper reporting on a businessman jailed for plundering his company's accounts noted that

> The defendant and his wife Clare dressed in the latest designer fashions and he rubbed shoulders with the rich and famous at Royal Ascot. . . . He lived in a £750,000 house in Reading, which he extended using stolen money.
> He threw lavish parties to impress his rich friends. . . .[2]

In a developed economy top executives can earn salaries of many million dollars a year. These sums project powerful messages to the media, their colleagues, employees, customers, and competitors. No one needs so many millions in order to meet existence needs; yet these executives might feel humiliated if it were suggested that next year their compensation should be reduced by, say, a million dollars. The deprivation would not be physical but psychological. That is, the hope of a larger pay packet can drive both extrinsic and intrinsic needs.

Research by Vohs et al. (2006) indicates that enhanced possibilities to earn monetary rewards increase motivation to work but have negative influences on relationships with other persons. Individuals become more self-sufficient, and less dependent on those with whom they work and less willing to interact with others. The implication is that the organization may benefit from a more motivated workforce, but suffer from a weakening of the organizational culture. This points to a need to restructure working relationships.

7.4   How Context Influences Needs

Maslow's model was based on data collected in the United States. How far does it apply to other cultures, and in different economic and political contexts?

Members of a society suffering economic hardship or political disturbance typically place greater priority on their security needs than do members of a society that is economically and politically secure. Onedo (1991) found that samples of both Australian and Papua New Guinean managers regarded a sense of achievement as their most important needs but the Papua New Guineans were more dissatisfied with their levels of security and placed security needs higher than autonomy needs.

7.4.1   Industry norms

Long-term employees in stable and conservative industries are more likely to be motivated by the security which attracted them to the industry in the first place. Employees in new and relatively insecure industries – such as in some areas of finance and communications – may be prepared to trade career security in return for immediate financial rewards. To a degree, workers select the occupation that seems most likely to supply the incentives that appeal to their personalities. Chow (1988) found that public sector managers in Hong Kong most valued job security, and private sector managers most valued opportunities for high earnings. Both sectors valued opportunities for promotion. The national culture might be irrelevant; that is, these findings might be duplicated among public and in private sector workers elsewhere.

In Greece, Bourantas and Papalexandris (1999) studied employees in public and private organizations, and found no differences in needs for pay and security. This might seem to contradict Chow's findings. But, the authors suggest, public sector employees compensate for their lower pay by the greater opportunities for tenure, while private sector employees accept their lower security by the greater range of opportunities on the job market. Perhaps all employees are attracted to the ideals of generous pay AND full security, but in practice few jobs offer both and most employees have to choose one or the other.

7.4.2   The influence of organizational culture

Section 5.2.3 defined a positive organizational culture as one in which workforce and management share a commitment to the organization. They are motivated by opportunities to achieve strategic goals. In a negative organizational culture, the values of management and workforce do not correspond, and in an extreme case the workforce may be negatively motivated, to frustrate management and to sabotage company interests. Similarly, employees are motivated by a cohesive and strong culture in which they communicate successfully with colleagues.

7.4.3   The influence of national culture

The employees' national culture influences their needs, and Hofstede's model can be read as a ranking of motivational factors in different cultures. This model is not only explanatory; it enables the manager to predict what incentives are likely to attract in different contexts. Here are some examples.

More INDIVIDUALIST cultures value opportunities for individual promotion and growth, and autonomy. Hence employees are more likely to be attracted by an incentive system that provides these opportunities. Traditionally, highly COLLECTIVIST cultures value opportunities to belong to an influential group, and members may not be given individual recognition if this means shining above other members of the group. Bozionelos and Wang (2007) found that as economic growth in China increases, Chinese workers grow more positive to individually based performance-related reward systems; but traditional needs to avoid losing face (*mianzi*) and interpersonal relationships (*guanxi*) still have to be taken into account when designing an incentive system.

In Malaysia, a project was established between a British educational charity and a Malaysian training school. Those Malaysian teachers who were most productive would be awarded support to study further in the UK, and to return to immediate promotion. However, this did not succeed in motivating performance, and even had the opposite effect; promising teachers declined in productivity. It was discovered that they feared being estranged from their friends both by being so long abroad and by promotion to a level in which they would be expected to manage them. The problem was resolved by reducing the time abroad to three months and not making promotions on return.

Cultures with HIGHER needs to AVOID UNCERTAINTY value job security, and may value a guarantee of long-term employment over the offer of a pay rise. Females may not wish for promotion when this seems likely to bring them into conflict with male colleagues, and so are demotivated from making the effort to win promotion. Cultures with LOWER needs to AVOID UNCERTAINTY value job variety.

Cultures with WIDER POWER DISTANCES value opportunities to work for a manager who shows loyalty to subordinates and gives clear instructions. A Japanese manager with long experience of working in China noted that "Chinese workers care about the reputation of their boss more than the result of the business." Cultures with NARROWER POWER DISTANCES value opportunities to work for a manager who maintains a consultative relationship with subordinates.

More FEMININE cultures strive for tender, welfare societies and focus on domestic values. They tend to value shorter and convenient working hours. More MASCULINE cultures value opportunities to compete for promotion – but males may not be motivated by competition with females.

In sum, needs felt by one group in one context may be considered insignificant in some other. And this means that incentives designed successfully to stimulate performance in one context may be meaningless and unsuccessful in some other context. This has implications for the management of performance across multinational organizations.

7.5   Designing Incentives

Management applies its analysis of needs in an incentive system. This aims to stimulate desired productivity by offering employees the opportunities to satisfy their needs in ways that help to achieve company goals.

We have seen that individual needs differ. Employee A is motivated by opportunities to earn more, B by increased responsibility, C by a title, D by a good relationship with management, E by the use of a company car, and so on. In practice, a company employing a large workforce cannot design a different incentive system for each individual, tailored to his or her particular needs profile. And so it is unlikely that the company can ever provide optimal motivation to every individual.

7.5.1   *Cost as a selection criterion*

All systems designed to motivate performance have to be assessed in terms of their economic value. How much will a system cost to design and implement? And by how much can the organization expect to benefit from its success? An incentive system that costs more than the income it yields (and has no other compensating benefits) does not make economic sense and should be scrapped.

The size of the investment in designing and implementing motivators is determined by labor market factors; the value added by scarce labor and the cost of hiring on the labor market. When many companies are competing for a small supply of labor and the company depends on holding the loyalty of its key employees, it invests more in identifying their needs and providing opportunities by which these can be satisfied. When supplies of the labor required are plentiful, the company invests less.

7.5.2   *Applying needs analyses*

Management is under pressure to generalize needs, and to assume that members of a group share common needs. This approach makes savings, but is bound to provide inaccurate reflections of some individuals' needs, and perhaps is fully accurate for no one person. On the other hand, a company competing for labor in an expanding economy may decide that it has to invest in greater attention to individual needs in order to retain those skills that are in great demand

Analyses of needs suggest that in some circumstances, some groups of employees may give priority to non-financial needs. It seems clear that in such cases, opportunities to satisfy these needs might be highly motivating. These include opportunities to do interesting work, win appreciation of work done, feel that they are in on things, and so on. The company applies these alternatives when

- they are as effective as the wage rise;
- the costs they incur are less (including the costs of implementation);
- they are implemented consistently over time, and when applied to different individuals and groups.
- they are credible.

Here are some of the incentives that management might offer. The following sections examine why each might or might not be selected:

- the pay rise – see 7.5.3;
- the bonus – 7.5.4;
- interesting work – 7.5.5;
- opportunities to learn new skills - 7.5.6;
- recognition – 7.5.7;
- factors associated with the organizational culture – 7.5.8.

How management exploits the motivating qualities of work are discussed in 7.6.

7.5.3   *The pay rise*

In practice though, these conditions are often difficult to meet. Companies find it easier to motivate and reward using salaries, bonuses, stock options. They apply a system of monetary rewards both as a recognition of past performance and as an incentive to future performance for three reasons. One example is a pay rise:

- First, it is relatively simple to administer. Pay packets can be easily calculated and paid to a large number of employees.
- Second, the individual employee is easily able to convert financial rewards into the goods and services that satisfy his/her particular needs.
- Third, a salary rise sends out signals about the status of the company and the individual rewarded.

7.5.4   *The bonus*

The worth of a bonus as an incentive depends on industry and company factors. Smith (2002) argues that efficiency wage benefits are effective if there is fear of dismissal. When the same bonus is paid every year it becomes taken for granted as though an element of the basic reward structure. This has two effects. First, the bonus no longer motivates greater effort in the future; and second, any decrease in the level paid – perhaps caused by adverse trading conditions which the workforce are unable to control – causes disappointment and may be demodulating. When Sanyo (Thailand) was forced by an economic downturn to cut its end-of-year bonus from 5.75 months in 1995 to 3 months in 1996, workers burned down a warehouse containing 500 new refrigerators and started fires in the production facility and company headquarters.[3]

Section 6.3.1 distinguished between an OPEN-ENDED task, which has many possible outcomes, and a CLOSE-ENDED task, which has one correct outcome, and the objective can be precisely stated. For example, you have to sell 100 units of a particular product. Either you succeed or fail. When the task is close-ended, performance-based incentives can be clearly formulated, and incentives influence performance, and are effective. The incentive system can be closely linked to strategic goals, and it gives management close control on performance and output. But where the employee must use complex skills to perform an open-ended task for which the best possible outcome cannot be defined in advance, performance is less easy to measure. Hence, performance-related incentives are less effective. Incentive systems cannot be effectively applied and so are less useful as a means of controlling performance and output.

In some relatively stable industries, bonuses may be taken for granted as part of the reward package. A failure by the company to pay a bonus – or even a lower bonus than in the previous year – may be resented as a major disappointment, and lead to a fall in morale. The financial services industry, on the other hand, is very sensitive to market swings; profits vary enormously from year to year. Experienced employees soon learn why their bonus payments fluctuate. Hence when the company in this industry pays a low bonus that fairly reflects the state of the market and their lack of success, these employees accept the fact and are not necessarily demotivated.

7.5.5   *Interesting work*

Kovach's (1987) early research shows that employees value the opportunity to work on tasks that interest them – see 7.2.1 above. Further, employees challenged by interesting work are more likely to stay in their jobs. Bored workers show frustration, aggression, ill health, and may withdraw from the labor force. Thus there are several respects in which the company benefits from making tasks more interesting.

However, defining interesting work and then structuring is not easy. Individuals have very different ideas about what makes work interesting, and these are influenced by personal taste, experience, and culture. Even if there is agreement, the ideal may not be possible to achieve. One person's improved work may cause difficulties for those working alongside him. Some tasks are very difficult to make interesting to all but a few. How many people derive a sense of achievement from washing dishes in a restaurant? And how can this task be redesigned? In practice, task restructuring may involve giving the employee more responsibility for deciding his/her own priorities.

7.5.6   *Opportunities to learn new skills*

Anglo cultures place great importance on personal change and achievement. An opportunity to learn new skills may be valued.

GE is a company that focuses on encouraging learning rather than formal teaching. The chief learning officer explained the company's continuing success by its focus on a culture based on achievement and self-critical reflection on how to improve. Training systems empathized employees' needs to learn rather than the company's capacity to teach:

> "No one is satisfied with just doing good enough," he said . . . . (He) admitted that another critical element of GE's learning culture and continued success had been the type of people it had recruited, from factory workers to highly trained professionals. "We always look for people who are very bright over-achievers."[4]

The company searched for recruits who asked questions about their world.

But there are disadvantages. Learning divorced from formal teaching systems is difficult to measure. Learning that contradicts present practice and policy may not be rewarded – and may even be punished, which does not encourage further experimentation. The danger is that learning is rewarded only when it conforms to what has already been learned and applied.

An accent on training is not always welcome. In the UK, an employee working for a global telecommunications company complained that she was being constantly taken off her desk to go on training courses. Often these taught skills that she had already acquired through experience, or new skills that she did not expect to need in the immediate future. Training does not always guarantee increased financial rewards. In a Taiwanese textile factory, the production staff were paid on a piecework basis. They much resented being asked to work on new products when these necessitated training. Their new skills were not recognized and inevitably they lost time in practicing them, which lowered their productivity and hence lowered their earning potential.

The Introduction shows a case where executive training is apparently effective in motivating productivity and loyalty to the company.

7.5.7   *Recognition*

Recognition can be motivating, and may be costless, but it is difficult to use effectively, and if misused can cause demoralization that costs much more.

For example, suppose I congratulate a new employee on his productivity; "Thank you. You're doing a really great job." This costs the company and may be motivating the first time. But if I make the same comment every day thereafter, the employee is likely to become disenchanted. This means that appreciation for work done must celebrate real achievement. Appreciation of trivial success rings false, and is unconvincing. Second, the appreciation must be sincere, which may mean that it has to be demonstrated selectively (Pettinger, 2001, p. 76). Similarly, a title only motivates when it carries real status. Titles do not motivate if they do not give genuine authority. In Kroll Associates, in 1996,

> status titles were dispensed as an inexpensive way of retaining top staff but, ultimately they failed to prevent dissatisfaction. At one stage the company had seven managing directors in its London office.[5]

This is not credible. Staff resent being fobbed off with empty status.

7.5.8   *Factors associated with the organizational culture*

Companies hope to build a positive culture that give employees the sense that their and management interests are aligned. Day et al. (2002) argue that employees are less motivated by excessive financial incentives than by a culture that promotes the individual's sense of commitment to the company, and to thinking not only about present circumstances but also about innovatory systems to develop in the future. The disadvantage lies in the difficulty in creating a motivating culture.

Some of the factors associated with a positive culture are discussed in Chapter 5. These include

- a LEADERSHIP STYLE that is appropriate to the national culture and the organization, and the needs of its members. The attributes of good leadership are not constant. The roles adopted by the successful leader vary in different contexts – see 5.4.1;
- RECRUITMENT of motivated individuals who contribute to building the culture – see 5.4.2;
- a MISSION STATEMENT that expresses the aspirations of members – see 5.4.3.

7.6   Work as a Motivator

The findings made by Kovach (1987) and Maslow (1954), discussed in 7.2 and 7.3 above, make clear that factors associated with the work in which people are engaged can motivate them. People need to win esteem and recognition, and they value work that promises these rewards – under certain conditions. This section examines research that suggests how these conditions may be put in place. Two classic theories are discussed here:

- Herzberg's two-factor theory – see 7.6.1–7.6.2;
- McClelland's achievement motivation – see 7.6.3.

7.6.1   Herzberg

Herzberg et al. (1959) and Herzberg (1968) distinguished two types of motivational factors, "hygiene" factors and motivators.

The hygiene factors include wages, good working conditions, good company policy and administration, good relationships with supervisors and peers, and job security. The presence of these factors does not guarantee satisfaction and productivity. But if they are absent, the employee will be dissatisfied and demoralized.

Satisfaction and productivity are only possible when the employee is positively motivated. Possible motivators include feelings of achievement, responsibility, and recognition.

Herzberg applied his theory in the following techniques:

- JOB ROTATION. This involves planning the employee's time so that he performs a variety of tasks. For instance, he spends a period of time working in Process A, then moves to Process B, then moves to Process C. Job rotation introduces variety to the employee's routine, and helps develop a multi-skilled workforce. Employees may also be rotated to perform the same task in different settings. Japanese primary school teachers can expect to be rotated between schools every three years until, in their fifties, they are sent to the district office.
- JOB ENLARGEMENT involves reorganizing the job specification so that the employee now performs all the tasks required to complete the process. Rather than have Tasks C, D, E performed by employees P, Q, R, respectively, all three tasks are allotted to each of P, Q, R. In theory, the individual derives greater satisfaction from completing all tasks contributing to production and seeing the completed unit than from specializing in a single task.
- JOB ENRICHMENT means making a job more interesting and more challenging, which in practice usually means more complex. First, responsibilities are pulled down from above, and the employee is trained to take new responsibilities for aspects of the task that previously were performed by a supervisor. Second, earlier work stages are pushed forward into the job. Third, later work stages are pulled back so that the

employee is made responsible for up-stream and down-stream activities that were previously handled by other persons. Fourth, parts of the task are pushed down to a lower job level and are performed by lower grades (whose jobs are thus enriched by these responsibilities being pulled down). Fifth, parts of the job are rearranged and reordered.

7.6.2   Making Herzberg work

There can be no doubt that these proposals suggest useful opportunities to motivate employees. However, they do not guarantee success. First, they assume that jobs can be structured to be enriched. It was noted in 7.5.5 that not all work can be made more interesting, and the same point applies. Second, in cultures where status differentials between roles are significant, problems arise in identifying jobs of equivalent status when enlarging and enriching them. Third, job rotation is less likely to be effective in a collectivist context where a sense of belonging to a group is essential. Opportunities for individual achievement and responsibility may not be attractive in contexts where their achievement isolates the individual from his group. Job rotation is also unlikely to succeed where employees prefer specialist to general careers. Fourth, these models have cost implications. Employees are more likely to make mistakes and work at a lower level of productivity when learning new skills. Fifth, employees may not want their jobs to be enriched. The models were developed from data gathered where needs to avoid uncertainty are low – in the United States. Elsewhere, employees may not welcome so much change and novelty.

In other words, the attempt to enrich jobs in inappropriate contexts may not only fail to increase motivation, it may actually have adverse effects on creative achievement, and demotivate performance. Then, if enrichment has the effect of giving workers "a property right to their jobs they will substantially lose their incentive to work" (Smith, 2002, p. 182). This opens up questions about how long enrichment problems can succeed and if they have to be continually enlarged in order to retain a motivational pull.

7.6.3   McClelland's theory of achievement motivation

McClelland's (1976) theory of achievement motivation argued that the greater the need to achieve in a society, the greater that society's economic growth and tendency to innovate. The need for achievement is defined as a desire to meet and exceed performance standards, and to succeed in the face of competition.

High achievers seem to have in common

*   a preference for taking moderate risks;
*   a need for immediate and frequent feedback on performance;
*   a preference for specific performance criteria;
*   a dislike for leaving tasks incomplete;
*   a sense of urgency.

McClelland argued that motivation to achieve could be taught by focusing on goal setting. Trainees should be taught to think in terms that relate to achievement and to consciously dismantle those assumptions in the culture that inhibit achievement; they should develop communication norms that focus positively on achievement, and group systems that give emotional support in achieving their goals.

McClelland's theory has had a great influence, particularly in the Anglo world. But it may have to be modified to other cultures. It associates achievement with the satisfaction of individual needs and responsibilities, and relatively low needs to avoid uncertainty in taking initiatives. Hence it cannot explain achievement in cultures where achievement is associated with group effort and where individual effort is associated with avoiding punishment for mistakes.

7.7 Implications for the Manager

Compare an organization that you know well in YOUR OWN CULTURE with a similar organization in SOME OTHER CULTURE.

1 How do members of the two organizations (at the same level of seniority) rank these rewards for working?
   (a) good wages;
   (b) interesting work;
   (c) good job security;
   (d) feeling of being in on things;
   (e) opportunity to learn;
   (f) appreciation for work done;
   (g) promotion and growth in organization;
   (h) good working conditions;
   (i) personal loyalty to employees;
   (j) sympathetic help with personal problems.
      • Explain any differences.
2 Rank the rewards listed in (1) in terms of how effectively they motivate performance within the two organizations. Take into account such factors as
   (a) the target behavior required;
   (b) cost;
   (c) ease of implementation;
   (d) (any other significant factors).
      • Explain any differences in the rankings.
3 How can jobs be enriched within the two organizations? For each organization, take into account
   (a) the nature of the jobs to be enriched;
   (b) what factors in the organizational and national cultures favor enrichment programs;
   (c) the expense of planning, communicating and implementing the program.

7.8 SUMMARY

A need felt in one context may not be significant in another and a successful motivator in one context – say, headquarters – may be less motivating elsewhere.

Section 7.2 examined the problem of identifying NEEDS. People have different needs, and managers are often inefficient in recognizing needs. An incentive system based on an inaccurate analysis of needs is unlikely to be effective in motivating performance. Section 7.3 discussed INTRINSIC AND EXTRINSIC NEEDS and focused on needs for money – which are not explicitly accounted for in Maslow's model. Section 7.4 saw HOW CONTEXT INFLUENCES NEEDS and dealt with the importance of industry norms, organizational culture, and national culture. Section 7.5 discussed the DESIGN of INCENTIVES, and first examined the economic context. Most systems to motivate employees have a financial cost, and the company cannot invest more in motivating its employees than it expects to benefit. Hence the selected system must generate a profit. The alternatives to the obvious solution of a wage rise carry both advantages and disadvantages. Section 7.6 asked about the circumstances under which WORK acts as a MOTIVATOR, and discussed the applications and limitations of theories produced by Herzberg and McClelland.

7.9 EXERCISE

This exercise gives practice in analyzing and developing an incentive scheme.

1 Investigate the incentive schemes used to motivate employees in an organization that you know well – for example, your business school.
2 Distinguish different segments; for example, different age groups, genders, professional groups.
3 What incentives are currently used to motivate each of the segments you choose? List them.
4 Are the following incentives used? If not, add them to the list you made in (3):

(a) opportunities to develop new skills;
(b) improved facilities;
(c) greater responsibility;
(d) study and other visits abroad.

5 From the total list, select three that you think are NOW most effective in motivating each segment?
6 How might these schemes be improved in order to motivate employees more effectively? Design an improved incentive scheme for each segment you have chosen, using the list of incentives prepared in (3) and (4).

Notes

1 McKinsey. Lessons from a global retailer: an interview with the president of Carrefour China. *McKinsey Quarterly: 2006 Special Edition*, p. 73.
2 Court seizes assets from executive who robbed firm. *Western Morning News*, August 20, 2008.
3 Anucha Charoenpo and Wuth Nontarit. Workers put Sanyo HQ to the torch. *Bangkok Post*, December 18, 1996.
4 GE takes training into the 21st century. *The Nation*, November 19, 2002.
5 Stewart Dalby and Richard Donkin. The gumshow and the City. *Financial Times*, April 1, 1996.

CHAPTER EIGHT
Dispute Resolution

8.1 Introduction

In 2006 Nicholas Sarkozy won the French Presidential election with a promise to modern-ize the economy, which in part meant reforming the system of pension rights for public sector employees. Until then the rights had allowed some employees, including rail and energy workers, to retire on pensions at 50.

Earlier attempts at reform had ended in humiliating defeats for the Presidency. But Mr Sarkozy seemed to be adopting a more subtle approach than those taken by his predecessors.[1] *The Economist* identified three points of novelty; first, he had hidden nothing from the French and had always made his intentions clear. Second, there had been a marked change in the public mood, and now a majority were in favor of reform. Third, in his talks with union bosses he had made clear that he would not budge on the basic principles, but was happy to negotiate details.

In November 2007, the rail workers went on strike in protest, but this caused deep divisions between the militants prepared to fight to the end and the moderates who were more in tune with the public mood. By the second week the number of strikers had fallen to 26.2% of union memberships. The government had chosen the tactic of fixing the deadline for negotiations, and indicated that it was only prepared to negotiate with the six striking rail unions when rail traffic was renewed.[2] By the ninth day, a poll showed that 68 percent of the public thought that the strike was "not justified". By the end of the second week, it had collapsed.

Mr Sarkozy chose a time to fight that best suited him. He prepared his electoral constituency for the conflict, and showed himself willing to negotiate – but at the time of his deciding. He had attempted to manage every stage of an unavoidable conflict.

This chapter deals with factors that influence how disputes emerge and how they are resolved. One way of resolving dispute is by negotiation.

8.2   Reasons for Dispute

Disputes arise within organizations when members COMPETE or ARGUE. They compete for resources, responsibilities, promotions, the use of facilities, and so on. They argue about how to exploit strengths and opportunities, answer threats and compensate for weaknesses, how strategies should be designed and implemented, how tasks should be performed, and so on.

These competitions and arguments arise for a range of reasons. Members may have genuine differences of interest and viewpoints. Or they may have clashing personalities. They try to meet their own agendas that they hide from others. They communicate inappropriately. They fail to agree on procedures for how disputes should be conducted and ended. A dispute might arise from misunderstandings; for example, information used is inaccurate or incomplete. In multinational organizations, cultural differences mean that the danger of misunderstanding is particularly acute.

8.2.1   *Interest in the dispute*

People's attitudes towards a dispute depend upon their proximity to it and how closely it affects their interests. When they feel distant from it, they may be indifferent. If I see two people fighting in the street, maybe I watch for a few minutes and walk on when my interest peaks. If they suddenly involve me in the fight, I experience a wider range of emotions; anger, fear, anxiety, the need to win or perhaps escape. Similarly, if my neighbor is made redundant, I feel mild sympathy. But if my employer goes bankrupt, I become worried.

The persons immediately involved in a dispute may feel pain, anger, embarrassment, a sense of being damaged. Their colleagues are perhaps confused and distressed that the harmony of the workplace has been upset. For their senior manager, the dispute represents another problem that must be resolved appropriately. An outside consultant may find in it the symptoms of a general malfunctioning in the organization. The disputants are perhaps most at risk – they may lose their jobs.

8.2.2   Factors influencing interest

Factors that influence your interests in a dispute include

- RELATIONSHIP FACTORS. These include the personalities of the disputants, any knowledge they have of each other and previous history, involvement of third parties;
- STAKE. How badly do you want to win, and how serious would be the cost of losing? In the Introductory case, Mr Sarkozy needed to win a satisfactory result in order to keep his promise to the French electorate.
- EMOTIONAL INVOLVEMENT. The more involved I am in defending my interests or achieving my goals, the more I commit myself to the dispute.
- URGENCY. If I want a problem resolved quickly, I may force a solution, or at the opposite extreme, withdraw quickly.
- PRECEDENT How does the individual or organization usually behave in these circumstances? If there is a precedent, then this may give an example of how the dispute can be resolved. In the Introductory case, Mr Sarkozy had learned important negative lessons from previous unsuccessful attempts to reform the welfare system – how NOT to fight the French rail unions.
- CULTURE – see 8.3.

8.3   Culture and Dispute

Western cultures have always been interested by the paradox of dispute, and how it can have both positive and negative outcomes. The Greek historian Plutarch, who lived between about AD 46 and 129, wrote that

> the natural philosophers believe that if the forces of conflict and discord were eliminated from the universe, the heavenly bodies would stand still, and in the resulting harmony the processes of motion and generation would be brought to a dead stop.   *(1973, p. 29)*

8.3.1   Dispute in the Anglo cultures

This attitude still holds among cultures most influenced by ancient Greek philosophy. Anglo cultures, in particular, perceive some degree of dispute as a necessary condition for creativity and initiative. This reflects the Anglo value of individual growth through creative "doing". But other cultures are much less accepting of disagreements.

This does not mean that *any* level of dispute is accepted in Anglo companies. Every organization must impose some limits to aggression, and the person who passes beyond them, for example by bringing a gun to work and shooting up the opposition, may be referred to legal or medical officers. But so long as negative effects can be limited and dispute seems to aid productivity, tolerances are wide.

The tolerance given to dispute in Anglo cultures means that it can arise in any relationship, and therefore persons skilled in their culture have to become adept at compartmentalizing aspects of their relationship. Persons may disagree in some areas while maintaining their friendship in others. In her biography of the British art critic and spy Anthony Blunt, Carter (2001) explains how in the late 1930s Blunt disagreed with the critic Herbert Read and artist Roland Penrose over the work of Pablo Picasso. This war was fought publicly in journal articles. But Read and Blunt belonged to the same club. Blunt later explained:

> We used frequently to meet there by chance, and one would say to the other "I hope that you did not take my saying you were stupid and wrong etc. in my last letter in any personal matter", and we would go and have lunch together.   *(Carter, 2001, p. 208)*

8.3.2   *Dispute in collectivist cultures*

But in collectivist cultures, aspects of a relationship are less easily compartmentalized and disputes in one area have repercussions in others. Dispute is feared as likely to destabilize the harmony between individuals, within a group, and between groups. Rather than welcomed as a positive stimulus, it may be regarded as inherently dangerous. For example, hostile takeovers which are accepted in American business as necessary and normal are disliked in Japan. During the boom years, they almost never occurred. Ishimuzi (1990) reported that when an American finance company attempted to take over a Japanese high-tech company, it was unable to find a local securities firm prepared to act as tender offer agents. The recession is now forcing the Japanese to conform with globalized Anglo standards, but sometimes unwillingly.

In Thailand, a Buddhist critic of Western economics commented:

> Modern economics is based on the assumption that it is human nature to compete. Buddhism, on the other hand, recognizes that human beings are capable of both competition and co-operation.
>
>   Competition is natural: when they are striving to satisfy the desire for pleasure – when they are motivated by *tanha* – people will compete fiercely. At such times they want to get as much as possible for themselves and feel no sense of sufficiency or satisfaction. . . . This competitive instinct can be redirected to induce co-operation of a particular group by inciting them to compete with another group. For example, corporate managers sometimes rally their employees to work together to beat their competitors. But this competition is based entirely on competition. Buddhism would call this "artificial cooperation". True co-operation arises from a desire for well-being – with *chanda*.   *(Payutto, 1994, pp. 53–54)*

An aversion to overt dispute in Buddhist and other Asian cultures does not mean that disputes do not arise there. (A quick review of Asian history over the past hundred years makes this clear.) Rather, cultures deal with possible or actual disputes differently. That is, cultures make different recognitions of dispute and may adopt different approaches to resolving disputes.

Each develops approaches to prevent or minimize those aspects of dispute that members find most threatening. For example, collectivist cultures are more likely to discourage OPEN dispute by tolerating LATENT dispute, which is ignored or overlooked. Implicit challenges are smoothed over so that perhaps all involved can deny that any challenge was intended. Communicative style maintains an appearance of harmony.

8.3.3   *Explaining tolerance of dispute by cultural analysis*

Laurent (1983) asked managers from a range of countries to respond to the statement "most organizations would be better off if conflict could be eliminated forever" (p. 86). He elicited agreement from 4 percent of his Swedish respondents, from 6 percent of the Americans, 24 percent of the French, 27 percent of the Germans, and 41 percent of the Italians. These findings indicate that tolerances of conflict vary across cultures.

Similarly, Hofstede's (2001) model can be interpreted as a study of different attitudes towards dispute. At the extremes:

- In COLLECTIVIST cultures, harmony should always be maintained, and direct confrontations avoided. In INDIVIDUALIST cultures speaking one's mind is a characteristic of an honest person.
- In wide-POWER DISTANCE cultures, latent conflict between ranks is considered normal – and always feared. Peers are reluctant to trust each other. In narrow-power distance cultures, harmony between the powerful and powerless is valued; peers are relatively willing to cooperate.
- In high UNCERTAINTY AVOIDANCE cultures, disputes within the organization are considered undesirable; conflict is disapproved of, perhaps because it is felt that disputants are unlikely to accept compromise readily. In low uncertainty-avoidance cultures, conflict in organizations is considered natural. Competition may be fierce, but afterwards the opponents find it relatively easy to reconcile.

In strongly MASCULINE cultures, disputes are resolved by fighting them out. In strongly FEMININE cultures, conflicts are resolved by compromise and negotiation.

Because attitudes towards dispute vary across cultures, it follows that tolerances vary and that a disagreement that causes little reaction in Culture A (or may even be considered positive) gives rise to serious conflict in Culture B. Here is an example. An American manufacturing company operating in Thailand was structured so that five teams reported to their supervisors, who reported to a manager. Then the manager resigned and the company decided to hold a competition between the supervisors to decide which deserved promotion to the vacant post. After two months, Supervisor A was promoted. Supervisors B and C perceived that they had lost face before their work teams, who had all been committed to their respective leaders, and immediately resigned. Supervisor D left a few weeks later. Only Supervisor E was prepared to continue. The company had used a competitive system that worked well in the individualist United States. However, by spreading the competition over two months in this relatively more collectivist culture where face mattered, it had created a condition of conflict which cost it three skilled supervisors.

8.3.4 Distinguishing levels of dispute

Handy (1985) distinguished types of dispute:

- COMPETITION for resources serves a useful purpose WHEN it
  - sets standards;
  - sorts out the best from the field;
  - motivates and channels energy.
- An ARGUMENT is constructive and helps people learn WHEN
  - the sides are arguing about the same thing. Issues are properly framed;
  - information to resolve the issue is available;
  - personal attacks are avoided;
  - the rules for conducting and resolving the dispute are clear and are accepted by the two sides;
  - communication is full and accurate;
  - differences are resolved, and the resolution is accepted.

However, CONFLICT occurs when competition or argument fails to reach a successful outcome and spirals out of control. Neither participant is prepared to accept a closure, and no superior or third party is capable of enforcing closure. The conditions occur when

- there is no perception of common interest;
- one or both of the two sides refuse to accept arbitration;
- the responsible superior refuses to arbitrate, or botches arbitration;
- the procedures for deciding a "winner" are obscure and unacceptable;
- the cost of losing is greater than the cost of continuing the conflict;
- personality clashes cannot be overcome;
- information is inadequate; communication breaks down; the sides are unable to communicate essential information, or disagree on how it should be interpreted.

The cross-cultural implication is that levels of argument or competition accepted in Culture X may be unacceptable in Culture Y, where tolerances of dispute are lower. The case in 8.3.3 gives an example of a competition quickly deteriorating into conflict in a context where tolerances of this type of competition are low.

How do members deal with conflicts? Some may be resolved by goodwill, ignored, and finally forgotten. Some may be unresolved, and not forgotten and lead to greater problems in the future. Others are decided by management, or resolved by negotiation.

8.3.5 Disputes within the group

When dispute occurs within the more individualist group, the disputants may be un-inhibited in trying to secure support from outside the group. In collectivist cultures, dispute in a group may be resolved by its non-disputing members either trying to ignore it or, at the other extreme, enforcing a resolution. When a peace formula is agreed the disputants downplay their disagreements. If one party continues trying to force its own solution after the group has intervened, he risks being expelled from the group.

Because a group is weakened by dispute, in a collectivist culture members try to maintain the appearance of a united front before outsiders. The Chinese cultures focus on protecting and building consensus. Compromise may be preferred to competition, at least as an initial move. But an apparent withdrawal cannot always be taken at face value. It may imply that the "loser" is making a tactical retreat in order to retaliate at a future time when conditions have changed in his favor.

8.4 The Manager Resolves a Dispute

The manager hopes to control disputes by

- clarifying strategic priorities;
- applying strong but flexible structures;
- setting resource priorities and task descriptions;
- communicating clearly and accurately and encouraging clear and accurate communication from subordinates;
- discouraging personal attacks;
- ensuring that information is freely available to conduct the argument or competition fairly. Restricting the use of privileged information;
- enforcing procedures for controlling arguments and competition that are clear and appropriate to the cultural and organizational context.

These conditions occur in a strong, positive culture where persons and groups communicate well and are happy to accept their mutual dependencies. They are far less likely in a weak, negative culture, where members feel less responsibility or capacity to halt the deterioration of competition or argument.

8.4.1 Intervention by a superior

When a dispute reaches the point at which relations between the disputants seem about to break down and the dispute may deteriorate to open conflict, the manager has to decide whether to avoid the issue or intervene.

The manager declines to intervene, and AVOIDS the issue when it seems likely that

- the two sides can reach a satisfactory solution on their own; OR
- involvement will make the dispute worse; OR
- involvement will cause her loss of face. Values in the culture may be significant. Where power distances are wide, she risks loss of authority if an intervention is unsuccessful. In that case she may either decline to become involved in a problem at a subordinate level, or delegate the responsibility to find a solution.

But avoidance, or withdrawal, is more or less acceptable in different contexts. It is more acceptable where harmony is valued highly, but less so in where it may be interpreted as a fear of asserting oneself. In Anglo contexts, the manager who regularly ignores subordinates' disputes is in danger of losing their respect.

If the manager decides to INTERVENE and confront the dispute between her subordinates, she can choose from a range of options, all of which carry risks:

- IMPOSE a solution. This is a highly risky strategy; if one or both disputants refuse to accept the imposed solution, the manager suffers a major loss of authority;
- SEPARATE the disputants; for instance, by moving one to another office or work unit. But in many situations, this may not be practical – and even if it is, does not remove the cause of dispute and signals a failure to control;
- COUNSEL between the two sides, providing advice and support, in the hope that they can then resolve their difference on their own. But if the disputants refuse to accept the counseling, the manager loses authority;
- MEDIATION takes a stronger position than counseling in that the manager becomes involved as a participant, even though not taking one side or the other. Both counseling and mediation become more forceful when the disputants are given a deadline by which they must find a solution, or risk punishment.

Mediation does not depend on the participation of a superior. In some circumstances, a peer or an outsider will be asked to mediate. An outsider knows least about the situation, and has to start by asking each side (together, or separately) to explain their understanding of the situation and point of view, and of the other side's point of view. This discussion of the facts of the case is useful when it reveals misunderstandings and ambiguities.

What is important is that both sides accept the mediator as an honest broker, who has no personal interest in one or the other side winning. The mediator acts as a disinterested third party, who tries to persuade the disputants to climb down from forcing positions and encourages a bargained or negotiated solution:

- NEGOTIATION – see 8.5.

8.4.2   Timing the intervention

In ALL cultures and organizations, the manager has to decide WHEN to intervene. Timing is crucial, and bad timing may make the conflict worse. The superior who waits too long before involving him/herself may cause as much damage as he/she who jumps in too quickly to impose a solution. A lack of action may be interpreted as a signal that an increase in conflict will go unpunished. The manager may sometimes so fear losing face that he/she hesitates unduly. On the other hand, in Anglo cultures, the manager who wants the reputation of an effective "troubleshooter" may intervene too early. Premature intervention is fruitless when one or both sides still think that more can be gained by forcing their solution than by negotiating and accepting a compromise.

8.5   Negotiation

The Introductory case shows negotiation used to resolve a dispute. Of course, many negotiations have a positive aspect. For example, two companies have identified the chance to develop a new product by working together, and they negotiate the terms of their alliance. Each side stands to gain, but each must be prepared to cover their share of the costs. Whether negotiation is pursued to overcome a problem or to take advantage of an opportunity, many of the same points apply.

Every negotiation expresses a paradox. It involves the participants in both actual or possible confrontation and in cooperation. If there were no confrontation, they would have no need to resolve differences; if they were unwilling to cooperate, they would not try to resolve these differences through talk.

8.5.1   Preparing to negotiate

PREPARATION is the essential first stage. The negotiator prepares by

- identifying his own priorities and position;
- trying to predict the priorities and position adopted by the other side.

In a commercial negotiation, priorities are bound to be influenced by factors in the competitive, economic, and political contexts. What contextual factors constrain each side's needs to counter perceived threats, and take advantage of significant opportunities?

Relevant factors in the other COMPANY include:

- its ownership and legal status. History;
- equity structure; current financial circumstances;
- size;
- strategic interests and scope; labor relations; technology;

- suppliers; customers; partners; competitors;
- organizational structure, systems, and culture;
- commitments abroad.

Preparation also involves being certain about your answers to these questions:

- WHY negotiate? – 8.5.2;
- WHERE to negotiate? – 8.5.3;
- WHEN to negotiate? – 8.5.4;
- HOW to negotiate? – 8.5.5;
- WHO negotiates? – 8.5.6;
- WHO has authority to decide? – 8.5.7.

8.5.2 *Why negotiate?*

The disputants choose to negotiate as the preferred alternative to either avoidance or any of the other forms of intervention discussed in 8.4.1.

The question "why negotiate?" is also answered by listing desired outcomes. Fisher et al. (2003) show how goals can be prioritized – first your goals (Y), then their goals (T). Your goals in negotiating can be ranked:

Y1. What you MUST achieve.
Y2. What you HOPE to achieve.
Y3. What you WOULD LIKE to achieve.

Obviously you would like to achieve all Y1s, all Y2s, and all Y3s, but in the real world this is very unlikely. A negotiation from which you achieve all your Y1s, some Y2s, and no Y3s must be counted as a success. A negotiation that wins you Y3s, a few Y2s and no Y1s has failed – however many Y3s.

The next stage is predicting THEIR goals – so far as you are able:

T1. What they MUST achieve.
T2. What they HOPE to achieve.
T3. What you WOULD LIKE to achieve.

Your analysis of goals tells you where to focus your resources of time and energy, and also helps you decide on concessions that you are able to make in order to secure your goals:

Ya. What you are MOST WILLING to concede in order to achieve your essential objectives.
Yb. What you are MODERATELY WILLING to concede.
Yc. What you are LEAST WILLING to concede.

And, for their side, what you predict:

Ta. What they are MOST WILLING to concede.
Tb. What they are MODERATELY WILLING to concede.
TC. What they are LEAST WILLING to concede.

You hope for a match between Y1 and Ta; what you value most, they are most willing to concede. For instance, your priority is that neither of the disputants should quit the firm. To obtain that, you are prepared to revise their job descriptions.

In a commercial negotiation, financial goals may not necessarily be the most important. When negotiating an international joint venture, a foreign partner may be most interested in gaining experience in the new environment and the local partner in securing the transfer of technology. Or one side or both might prioritize developing a long-term relationship that guarantees a source of supplies on generous terms. Trust reduces expense in drafting detailed contracts, and in making economic transactions. However, the negotiator may need to be cautious in accepting at face value the other side's expressed desire for trust, which should rather be earned by demonstrations of good faith.

A company that overvalues promises of long-term relationships may have itself to blame, particularly when product or service quality is an issue. The mistakes can be avoided. It should be common sense to prepare for a negotiation by developing a realistic picture of what the other side can deliver, and how far you have the resources to make a long-term commitment. But this is not easy when understanding is obscured by differences in language and culture.

8.5.3   *Where to negotiate?*

Negotiating at your place may give you the territorial advantage. However, meeting at their place gives you insights into how they manage their operations and their capacities, and enables you to hide from your constituents should you prefer the negotiation to be secret. Meeting in a neutral territory (a hotel, a chamber of commerce) offers a compromise when both sides are reluctant to give the other a territorial advantage. It also removes negotiators from pressures from their own constituents. Or, you may decide to alternate between your territories; or, both sides negotiate from their own premises linked by information technologies.

8.5.4   *When to negotiate?*

The nature of the problem or opportunity over which you are negotiating and the persons involved decide when the time is ripe. Negotiating prematurely, or too late, may be fatal. Here is an example. In the United Kingdom, in 1984, the powerful National Union of Miners went on strike in opposition to pit closures. The Prime Minister, Mrs Thatcher, had predicted the strike, and perhaps even provoked it. Certainly it occurred at a time that suited the government best, in March when winter was over and demands for coal were relatively low. The government had stockpiled massive supplies at power stations and so the effects on the economy were minimized. Support for the union dwindled and the strike collapsed. The NUM never recovered and the entire British trades union movement was weakened.

The timetable is affected by practical issues such as company routines, when budgets are normally set and labor contracts signed. Timing also involves planning how often you should meet, and at what intervals. How much time do you need between meetings to discuss progress with your persons in your organization? How much time should you give the other side to bring their constituents on side – or can you benefit from their disagreements? How much time do they need to consult with their superiors? What is the likelihood of hold-ups and delays and how much time can you allow for them?

If you are traveling to negotiate abroad, are there climatic features that influence your schedule? Are there any religious or national holidays set for that period? Is this a culture in which members expect to negotiate outside regular working hours and over weekends? How much time should you allow to recover from jet lag before going into a meeting?

8.5.5   How to negotiate?

Like all other communication structures, a negotiation must be appropriate to be effective. It is likely to express a number of communication functions, including

- developing the relationship between the two sides (particularly if they have not worked together before). A Chinese businessman said "I join a negotiation in order to negotiate a relationship. When we feel that we can trust each other, agreeing on the business takes no time."
- exchanging information, attitudes and interests – so far as is necessary to give the communication direction and without giving away confidential information;
- exploring divergent needs, expectations and assumptions;
- persuading;
- making and accepting concessions;
- reaching agreement;
- implementation.

It is tempting to map these functions into a sequence of stages, and this may be appropriate in some formal negotiations. But often it oversimplifies. In practice, these functions may be expressed at various points throughout the process. For example, persuasion occurs throughout; even when first introducing yourself, you hope to persuade the other party that you are a trustworthy person.

Information may have to be exchanged in requests for, or offers of, a concession. Any offer to concede must be supported by either a demand for a reciprocal concession or some reason for making the concession. If the offer is not supported, it appears weak. As 8.5.2 showed, you hope to concede only what costs you least, but this does not mean that you announce them as such; on the contrary, they must appear to cost you dearly, particularly if you are using them to demand significant concessions in return. Needs to reach an outcome by a tight deadline increase the pressure to make concessions.

In Anglo negotiations the activity of creating a relationship may be passed over relatively rapidly but elsewhere, in high-context cultures and when the negotiators hope to build a long-term relationship, it may always be of prime importance. And when the two sides have developed a sense of the each other's interests and their shared experiences, they are quick to resolve issues such as (in a commercial negotiation) terms of payment, delivery, and quality – details which the Anglo business person tends to prioritize. To the Anglo it would seem obvious that implementing the contract must always be final – but the circumstances under which implementation may be lead to new negotiation are noted in 8.5.8.

Where needs to avoid uncertainty are high, negotiators have a greater need for signals distinguishing stages in the structure, particularly where the relationship is new and therefore stressful. Where these needs are less important, participants are comfortable with an emergent structure.

In Anglo cultures a concern about the time spent – for example, by looking at your watch – almost always gets things moving along. Elsewhere this behavior may be interpreted as impatience which causes apprehension, and this may cause the other side to spend even more time sounding out your interests and commitment.

8.5.6   Who negotiates?

In any negotiation, the identity of the persons representing you and the other side may be crucial. What specific interests do they represent?

First, HOW many people should represent you? One person or more? A negotiator from the individualist Anglo cultures typically wants to project him/herself as the person with authority who does not need to check with headquarters. An organization in the People's Republic of China may be represented by a large team. This may include not only functional experts and administrators, but also representatives of local, provincial and national authorities. Similarly, a Japanese team represents a wide range of units and functions, whose interests must be taken into account.

What AGE is most effective? Anglo companies often select their brighter more energetic member, but this may be a mistake when negotiating with a Chinese or Japanese team, which may be led by a senior and older person, who has high status and loses face by dealing as an equal with a younger person. He may play little part in the detailed discussions, but plays an important "figurehead" role.

What company RANK should the negotiator have? The ranks of team leaders, like their ages, should be equivalent. But matching leaders is complicated by the different meanings of ranks in different countries.

In trade negotiations, an alternative to using a member of the organization is to use an AGENT. An agent may perform a number of functions beyond negotiating on your behalf. These include

- identifying organizations with which you might wish to do business;
- making introductions to possible partner organizations;

- arranging negotiations;
- preparing background information and advising on strategy;
- arranging documentation in preparation for a negotiation and for conducting business (e.g. arranging visas, work permits, customs clearance, etc.);
- resolving disputes.

In an international negotiation, an agent who understands the cultures of both sides is particularly useful when neither side has as much experience.

8.5.7 *Who has authority to decide?*

In many cultures the person who takes the final decision on whether or not to accept the other side's offer is typically the leader of the negotiating team. For instance, company owners in the high-power-distance cultures of Greece and Latin America wish to keep personal control and not to delegate. Individualist Anglo negotiators similarly insist that headquarters give them the power to accept or reject. But this is not the case everywhere. The real decision-maker may be absent. An American team negotiating with a family company in Brunei discovered that permission for the deal was given by elderly family members who never appeared at the meetings. In the People's Republic of China the technical representatives often contribute most to the discussions, but distant bureaucrats make the decision.

8.5.8 *Implementing the negotiated contract*

In some cultures, the negotiation process effectively ends when the contract is signed; elsewhere, it may not. In Anglo cultures the action of signing a contract symbolizes an intention to fulfill the stated terms. In the United States, it is expected that the contract should be implemented as signed regardless of changes in the environment. A legal advisor may be included in order to reduce the level of misunderstanding and conflict after signing. The business person with a reputation for attempting to renegotiate contracts is not trusted.

Elsewhere, the contract may not represent finality in the discussions so much as an honest intention to do business along the lines agreed, all other things being equal and in the light of foreseeable events. In Thailand, implementation, rather than signing the contract, is the final stage of negotiation. It involves a continuing process of discussion and adjustment in response to environmental changes which could not have been foreseen at an earlier stage.

Similarly, the Japanese try to resolve disagreements by compromise and consensus. Trade contracts avoid stressing rigid performance criteria and typically include a clause such as "All items not found in this contract will be deliberated and decided upon in a spirit of honesty and trust." Third parties may be brought in to mediate agreement and avoid conflict. In a business negotiation where both sides are Japanese, the winner incurs future obligations towards the loser, and unless these are paid off the disharmony affects not only their future relationship but also the attitudes of observers. The knowledge that the loser may be capable of retaliation at some future date acts as a constraint on winning too clearly.

8.5.9 Renegotiation

An American businessman with extensive experience of negotiating with family companies in Southeast Asia reported:

> When the Chinese negotiate a contract, they never argue at the beginning, they argue when they implement it. In an American negotiation, you argue at the beginning and keep quiet when the contract is signed.

Thus the American negotiator cannot assume that once a contract has been signed, his/her responsibilities are at an end. Rather, he/she needs to keep aware of what is happening in all stages of implementation and always be prepared to return to the table.

In many cultures, the implementation process is the point at which the practical bargaining starts. Unfortunately, it is then that many Anglo headquarters assume that all the serious problems have been resolved and that they can safely turn over responsibilities for the international joint venture (IJV) to a new hire or junior staff member who lacks commitment, knowledge or competence. Perhaps the problems that arise can be avoided if a senior manager involved in the original negotiation continues to keep a watch on developments.

8.6 Implications for the Manager

1 Disputes (arguments, competition) occur in all organizations:
   • Disputes can be positive, and of value to the organization.
   • But when disputes are not resolved (or cannot be resolved) they deteriorate into conflicts which can be damaging in the long term.
2 Tolerances of dispute vary. What might be considered trivial and even creative in one context is perceived as highly threatening in some other. National culture is one of the factors that influences tolerance levels. It also influences the use of tactics to manage disputes and to prevent or resolve conflicts. These include negotiation.
3 Every negotiation involves the participants in both confrontation and cooperation. The negotiator prepares carefully in order to identify where cooperation is possible, and where confrontation is necessary.
4 The negotiator makes decisions for his own side, and predicts for the other side,
   • the best location to negotiate;
   • the best time;
   • the best members of the team;
   • the persons with authority to decide on a settlement;
   • the priorities in negotiation;
   • the best styles and tactics.

8.7 SUMMARY

This chapter has examined how disputes arise and how they are resolved. Negotiation is one way of resolving a conflict, and also of exploiting an opportunity.

Section 8.2 discussed REASONS FOR DISPUTE. It distinguished competition and argument, and examined the factors that influence one's interest in a dispute. Section 8.3 dealt with the importance of CULTURE in influencing tolerances of different forms of dispute, and applied Handy's model in distinguishing levels of dispute. When argument and competition get out of control, they spiral into conflict. Section 8.4 discussed what the manager can do to RESOLVE disputes, and noticed the importance of timing when making an intervention. Section 8.6 dealt with NEGOTIATION.

8.8 EXERCISE

This exercise gives practice in preparing for a negotiation, then negotiating.

All students: Read the case below, then form small groups in order to solve the PROBLEMS that follow.

NOTE: keep any material that you produce in this exercise. You will need it again when you do the exercise in 18.8, on international joint ventures.

THE ACME HOTELS NEGOTIATION

You have been appointed to the post of international officer in your business college. You have just received a message from a hotel chain in Country X – a tropical country that has a large tourist industry.

Acme Hotels are the leading hotel chain headquartered in Country X. They propose that your college join them in a joint venture to establish a school there for hotel and tourist managers. This will produce staff to work for Acme Hotels and for other hotels in Country X and neighboring countries. (For a definition of an international joint venture or IJV, see 17.2.2).

Here are more details of the proposal:

1 Acme Hotels propose establishing a two-year MBA (hotel management) program, which your college would validate.
2 Your college would also be responsible for staffing the project with one full-time manager, one full-time assistant manager, and 10 visiting faculty.
3 The visiting faculty will be responsible for teaching 10 core courses in the first year of the program. These first-year courses are: introduction to management, organizational analysis, accounting, finance, human resource management, statistics, marketing, sales and advertising, international management, production management. Each course consists of 40 hours' instruction. A further 10 second year courses will be taught by locally recruited faculty.

4 Acme Hotels expect to recruit 80 students a year from Country X and neighboring countries.

5 Acme Hotels and your college will share equity on a 50/50 basis, and will be jointly responsible for all financing.

6 The school will be situated in a building leased from Acme Hotels.

This proposal has immediate attractions. It enables you to develop international interests in a country where you do not have experience. If satisfactory financial terms can be agreed, it might be very rewarding. And you are sure that your faculty will enjoy the opportunity to work in Country X.

But there are a number of issues that need to be resolved:

• Formulating a satisfactory financial structure.
• Guaranteeing the standards of student recruitment and of second year teaching. You have to protect your local market and cannot afford to associate your college's name with a substandard operation.
• Meeting your teaching needs in the college. You are planning a new program on your own campus. If this goes ahead, your staff will be teaching to capacity.
• Timetabling. Your staff must be present in the college during the examination months of May and June. They are normally on vacation between July and September, and your new teaching term begins in October. Acme Hotels propose teaching between August and the following June every year.
• Administrative and secretarial staffing.
• Facilities, including technology, teaching material, etc.

ACTIVITIES

Acme Hotels have invited you to their headquarters to negotiate a deal. What more information do you need? Prepare a draft e-mail to be sent to them, outlining your information needs:

(a) Give your draft e-mail to some other group, and ask them to invent appropriate answers that help solve your information needs. Some other group will give you THEIR draft e-mail.

(b) Invent and supply the information that they need – but be realistic. Put yourself in the position of Acme Hotels, and decide what information you should NOT give the college because it is confidential.

(c) Prepare your college's position for the negotiation.

(d) What position might Acme Hotels prepare? Try to predict their position.

(e) Meet with some other group and negotiate. One group negotiates on behalf of the college, the other on behalf of Acme Hotels.

(f) Switch roles.

(g) The instructor will ask you to explain your results to the full class. If your groups cannot reach a conclusion, say why.

Notes

1 Let battle commence. *The Economist*, November 17, 2007.

2 For the General Secretary of the CFDT, M. Chérèque. We could not hasten the pace. *Le Monde*, November 19, 2007.

CHAPTER NINE
Formal Structures

9.1 Introduction

An Iranian consultant was interviewed on how efficiently formal structures operate in the organizations of his country:

> When you talk to a secretary and ask to speak to the top manager the first thing he asks is "What do you want to know? What do you want that for?" Once I was representing a client who was proposing changes to the company. As soon as the secretary realized that this might affect his own position he said "he's not here, he's very busy" – and blocked entry to the manager while talking for an hour on why the proposed changes were not needed.
>
> In Iran, secretaries derive power both from position and by use of informal power derived from their status in the mosque.
>
> Top managers may want to make changes but the workforce are far more conservative.
> (INTERVIEWER) "What factors influence the attitudes of middle managers?"

(CONSULTANT) "If they got their jobs through family connections and power in the mosque, and they don't know their jobs well, they side with the workforce. But if they are qualified and efficient they side with top management."

How formal structures work is influenced by factors associated with the organization and with the persons concerned. This chapter deals with these structures, and examines how they are modified in practice.

9.2   Defining Structure

FORMAL STRUCTURES are governed by impersonal rules that apply to all members of the organization, regardless of the members' personal identities. INFORMAL SYSTEMS – discussed in the following chapter – express felt obligations operating between more and less powerful persons and express "rule by personality". In practice, the distinction is not as clear as it might seem; the Introductory case shows that the individual's personal interests can influence how the formal structure is implemented, and informal systems sometimes correspond with formal structures. However, this broad distinction is sufficient for our purposes here.

9.2.1   *The functions of structure*

Every organization is a distinct unit of economic action, in which a range of related activities or tasks have to be performed in order to achieve its strategic goals. The tasks are structured so that they can be integrated with each other, and this means that the use of human, financial, technological and other resources has to be coordinated systematically. Thus the company can derive maximum value from the use of these resources.

A formal structure regulates

- the TASKS or duties for which each member is made responsible. Responsibilities are more or less specialized. An employee appointed as a marketing assistant can normally expect to perform marketing tasks and not to act as accountant transport manager.
- the RELATIONSHIP that each member has with other members; for example, who manages who, who reports to who, and who works alongside who. Normally, the assistant marketing manager reports to the marketing manager, not to the production manager, an accounts clerk or the office cleaner.

This definition in terms of tasks and relationships has four important implications.

First, formal structures channel communication processes; how members communicate, with whom they communicate and what they communicate about. By implication, they also reduce less desirable communication options; who does not communicate with whom and what topics are not normally introduced in particular situations. Second, clear structures that are understood and accepted by all have the effect of reducing the possibilities for conflict and of establishing the norms by which conflicts are resolved. Third, they influence the opportunities for the growth of the organizational culture, considered in terms both of relationships between members and of management and staff. An effective structure meets members' needs for coordination and motivates them so that they are optimally productive. Each individual knows how he contributes to the well-being of all. Fourth, appropriate structure provides control, a framework within which performance is generated and assessed. This point is developed below.

9.2.2   *Appropriate structure*

Structure is appropriate when it responds to the needs of the organization in that particular time and context. Overstructuring stifles creativity, and understructuring causes confusion and uncertainty. Here are two examples, one of a company which suffered from too much, and one of a company which fell apart because controls were insufficient.

A Chicago-based manufacturing company had branches around the world. The branches were organized on a regional and national basis. The Asian region had regional headquarters in Hong Kong, to which branches in China, Thailand, Singapore and Malaysia reported; and a regional headquarters in Sydney, to which branches in Australia, New Zealand and Indonesia reported. Manufacturing staff were encouraged to work overtime. However, claims for overtime payments were only authorized by Chicago when they had been checked first by the office of origin, then by the national branch headquarters, then by the regional headquarters. Because no overtime payments were authorized until all national and regional offices had signed them off, there might be a delay of several months between an employee working overtime and receiving payment. This excessive red tape had the effect of reducing employees' interest in working overtime.

An example of a company that was understructured is given by a Thai firm that imported and manufactured office furniture. Demand boomed, and the company grew from two to 300 employees in three years. The entrepreneurial founders devoted far more energy to seeking new business opportunities than to developing structures by which operational problems could be resolved. As the company mushroomed, different units increasingly disputed their areas of responsibility. The market began to change and the company decided to start new product lines, but first the sales force had to be retrained. Both the human resources department and the sales department claimed this as their responsibility. But the company lacked any procedures for deciding the issue, and for resolving the ensuing conflict, which badly damaged morale. The company was unable to take advantage of the new opportunities.

As the context changes, needs for structure changes, which means that a structure that worked well at one point may no longer be appropriate. When people complain about an organization being "too disorganized", or "too bureaucratic" and having "too much red tape", they are often expressing a sense that the formal structures are no longer appropriate. Effective structuring has to be flexible; and the strong manager does not hesitate to modify it when necessary.

9.2.3 Examples of structures

Here are some common types of structure:

- In a FUNCTIONAL STRUCTURE, the organization is based on the performance of essential tasks. For example, there are departments of marketing, finance, production, and so on. This structure is appropriate when the firm produces a narrow range of products or services, and needs to link functional experts together within units.
- In a PRODUCT STRUCTURE, different departments are responsible for a wide range of different goods or services. In a food company, there may be different departmental responsibilities for bakery products, breakfast cereals, preserves, and so on. Each of these product departments includes managers for marketing, finance, production, etc.
- A CLIENT STRUCTURE. Departments are organized in terms of the clients they serve; e.g. wholesale, retail.
- A DIVISIONAL STRUCTURE is adopted by a large company with interests widely separated in terms of geography or product (or both) – Asian division, European division, etc.; toiletries division, food division, publishing division. The division has an internal structure; e.g. functional, product, etc.
- A HEADQUARTERS – SUBSIDIARY STRUCTURE. Relationships between headquarters and subsidiaries are discussed in Chapter 18 and subsequently. In a highly centralized organization, headquarters retains greater control of how the strategy is implemented. In a more decentralized organization, the subsidiary is allowed greater freedom to interpret the strategy in terms of its own needs.

9.2.4 The cost of structure

Because the structure constrains both the tasks in which members should be involved, and how the members communicate in performing these tasks, it functions as a system for exercising control.

Tight control is not necessarily the ideal. All control costs money, and a large investment in tight control does not guarantee greater productivity. One way of controlling the workforce is to implement a structure that uses more managers in proportion to the workforce; but managerial time is expensive, and may constrain rather than encourage creativity. By analogy; it costs a government more to control a lawbreaker by locking him in prison than by giving him a conditional discharge.

In sum, a company calculates the value of investing in control mechanisms. If tight control is likely to increase profitability and to give protection against internal and external threats, the investment is justified. If the expected rewards do not balance the costs, the company might look for an alternative route to increasing profitability. In sum, control should be aimed at regulating task performance, and not in developing rules that are perceived as oppressive and demotivate the workforce. Here we deal with control in terms of centralized and decentralized structures; this discussion is developed in Chapter 18, where we examine structures by which headquarters controls its subsidiaries abroad.

9.2.5   *Centralized and decentralized control*

Control is more or less centralized and decentralized. In a highly CENTRALIZED company, units and individuals depend on decisions taken by the CEO (or a small group). Communication tends to be on a vertical axis between superiors and subordinates.

The advantages are that decision-making is more likely to be coherent and to provide a single interpretation of strategy. Coordination between units can be highly regulated – if this is needed. Centralization may be essential in a company that produces a global product for a global market, and where headquarters needs to retain a high degree over subsidiaries abroad. The disadvantage is that top management has greater difficulty in responding rapidly to messages from below and to local events outside the immediate environment of headquarters. In a large and complex company, centralization places excessive responsibility on one person, who cannot be expert in all aspects of the company's activities.

Control is DECENTRALIZED when the opposite conditions apply. For instance, a multinational company might diversify in order to produce for different markets. It decentralizes its country-based subsidiaries, giving each the authority to make marketing and policy decisions previously made by headquarters, and building structures for greater communication between them. Decentralization may be achieved by widening spans of control, giving managers greater control over budgets, and in a foreign subsidiary, appointing from local as opposed to headquarters staff.

The advantages of decentralization are that units have greater capacity to make their own decisions and respond immediately to events in their environments. This can have the effects of giving lower levels greater responsibilities, motivating them, and stimulating their capacities to manage. It has the disadvantages that activities are less easily coordinated, and may be replicated by different units.

9.3   Bureaucracy

The structure is expressed in BUREAUCRATIC rules. Although the terms "bureaucracy" and "bureaucratization" have taken on negative connotations, Weber and other sociologists used them in a neutral sense to describe how modern organizations should work. Bureaucratic rules are designed to make members' behavior predictable and to reduce uncertainties and inefficiencies; and this need for order applies also in the private sector. All organizations, whether in the state, voluntary or private sectors, have some needs for bureaucratic rules.

9.3.1   *Weber's model of bureaucracy*

The earliest and greatest of the writers on bureaucracy was the nineteenth century German scholar, Max Weber. Rules determine

- **WHO joins: ENTRY to the organization.** Entry qualifications typically include age, educational achievements, and professional expertise. Different qualifications are required for different jobs and ranks.
- **WHAT the member does: JOB DESCRIPTION.** The member is expected to perform specified tasks and not to meddle in the duties allocated to others. The accountant cannot choose to spend one day marketing, the next in sales and the third on the production line. If he/she wishes to change jobs, the bureaucratic procedures must be followed.
- **WHO works with WHOM: RELATIONSHIPS.** Formal relationships with superiors, subordinates, and peers are regulated. The member cannot choose to spend one day as a secretary, the next as CEO, the third as canteen manager. Relationships influence his/her options for communication. If he/she wishes to change position in the hierarchy, the bureaucratic procedures must be followed; e.g. when applying for promotion.
- **HOW the member works: PERFORMANCE SPECIFICATIONS.** There are rules and procedures for doing the job.
- **HOW work is regulated positively: REMUNERATION and INCENTIVES.** Pay and allowances (including sick pay and pensions) are paid for satisfactory service, depending on the member's job description, rank, length of service. Performance is motivated by incentive systems – e.g. bonus payments, company car (see Chapter 7).
- **HOW work is regulated negatively: PUNISHMENT.** Rules make clear what behavior can be punished and what punishments can be imposed. Punishment is rule governed and should not be arbitrary – as when people are punished differently for the same offence.
- **HOW members move up to higher ranks: PROMOTION.** Criteria for promotion include length of service, good performance, and qualifications.
- **WHEN the individual works: TIMETABLE.** Rules set the length of the working day and week, opportunities for breaks, flexi-time, vacations, etc.
- **WHEN the member leaves: EXIT FROM THE ORGANIZATION.** Many organizations have rules regulating when staff must retire – usually 60 or 65. In public sector organizations, rules determine how staff are made redundant and how they are compensated.

9.3.2   How far do bureaucratic rules apply in practice?

Weber's model of bureaucracy expresses his notion of an "ideal" organization. It is RATIONAL in the sense that it is based on rational, sensible rules, and IMPERSONAL in the sense that relationships are decided by individual's formal rank and responsibilities. Relationships are rule governed and apply to all members, whatever their identity (social status, family membership, etc.) outside the company. The individual is employed to serve the company's interests and not to serve any other member.

How far does this ideal apply in practice? Perhaps no organization can ever match it entirely. Organizations working in different industrial, economic and cultural contexts are bound to have different priorities. Practice is swayed by different opportunities and risks, and so organizations have different needs for structure and emphasize different rules. And the individual's implementation of the rules is also modified by personal factors, likes and dislikes which may be rooted in factors outside the organization but within the context; the Introduction gives an example.

What factors determine what aspects of bureaucracy an organization needs, and how it implements them? Culture is one factor – discussed in the next section. But it is not the only factor, and may not even be the most important – others are discussed below.

9.3.3   The characteristics of the industry

A structure that meets the needs of any one of these organizations may not suit the others:

- a traditional government ministry;
- a private law firm;
- a hospital;
- a bank;
- a single-product manufacturer;
- a multi-divisional firm.

These have different needs for structure. The ministry and law firm lie at opposite extremes. The ministry operates through a mechanistic and centralized structure. Responsibilities and relationships must be precisely formulated, and a hierarchical structure is appropriate. An early study of US government public personnel agencies and finance departments found that when administrative authority was invested in expert personnel, there was a tendency to generate tall hierarchies with narrow spans of control (Blau, 1968).

The law firm may consist of partners who work relatively independently of each other, with a minimum of administration. Goals are formulated loosely, to provide legal services, perhaps in a specific area of law. Knowledge based organizations such as hospitals depend on the inputs of independent specialists who route their communications directly, rather than through superiors. This has the effect of flattening the organization. But banks – which are also knowledge based – need centralization in order to standardize rules and so give legal protection, and to reassure clients. Joint venture partners control the joint venture through agreed specifications and deadlines, and depend upon trust relations. Licensing and franchising firms control their franchisees through formal financial agreements and monitoring of service standards.

9.3.4   The strategic response to the environment

Top management is responsible for assessing opportunities and threats in the business environment and for deciding how the organization should respond to them. This means taking account of factors that include

- customer demands;
- the pressure of competition, market share and strategies followed by competitors, new entrants;
- possibilities for strategic alliances with other organizations;
- new technologies;
- availability of resources, finance, staff.

Management develops the bureaucratic systems that enable the members to achieve the strategic goals as efficiently as possible, making optimal use of the resources available

9.3.5 *Personality of the top manager*

In any organization the top manager has considerable power to interpret the rules. A strong single owner may be at liberty to decide on strategic goals and how these should be achieved, and hence to set structural priorities. In the entrepreneurial organization, influence spreads from the central figure along functional and specialist lines. In all cultures, the founder of a family business may give preferential treatment to his/her children when making appointments.

9.3.6 *Labor force*

A small three-person company and a multi-divisional multinational company have different needs for rules. A new company may have very few members, and responsibilities and relationships are flexible. As numbers grow, the structure becomes more formalized. If structural adjustments are NOT made, chaos follows. Section 9.2.2 above gives an example of a Thai company that outgrew its original structure.

9.3.7 *Technology*

Whether or not this is intended, the introduction of technology affects relationships between members, and in time this leads to a modification of the existing formal structures and possibly the design of new structures. For example, when a computer rather than a supervisor is used to communicate standardized data, operating procedures and quality controls, supervisors become redundant. This has the effects of reducing human interaction and of removing a managerial layer. The use of information technology (IT) leads to standardizing processes. Supervisory rules are replaced by covert control administered through the organization culture. When expert information is located within the technology, human specialists are replaced by generalists. And this "de-specialization" of functional departments means that formal boundaries between them can be dismantled. Those experts remaining find that their status is enhanced, and expertise and accomplishments (rather than span of control and seniority) decide how they are rewarded.

9.3.8   *Labor-force factors*

Needs for structure are also influenced by factors associated with the labor force. Experienced and educated workers may be better able to plan and manage their own tasks – and may strongly resent too-much supervision. Inexperienced employees need more supervision. In some developing countries, workers have migrated to find factory work in cities. Migration causes family units to break down, and family strife may be reflected in uneasy work relationships.

The implication is that there is no simple answer to the old question of the ideal span of control. An "ideal" span is one that achieves optimal results in practice, and this depends on a range of cultural and non-cultural factors.

9.3.9   *Complexity of the task*

The complexity of tasks allocated to members of the organization influences their needs for supervisory control and how they communicate. Figures 9.1 and 9.2 show that the same FORMAL relationship between A, B and C can be implemented differently in different contexts, and have different outcomes. Different implementations are influenced by factors associated with task and culture. The complexity of tasks allocated to members influences their needs for relationships on both horizontal and vertical axes.

For Figure 9.1 assume that

- the task is close ended. There is only one way of correctly performing it, and one correct outcome;
- A has expert knowledge of how the task should be performed;
- B and C do not have this expert knowledge;
- in this cultural context, close supervision is welcomed. Chapter 3 showed that where power distances are large, supervision is positively evaluated, and the superior is expected to be directive.

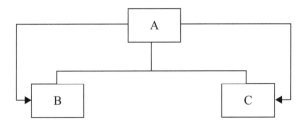

Figure 9.1   Communicative focus (1)

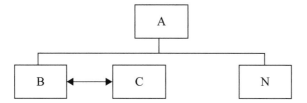

Figure 9.2 Communicative focus (2)

A invests time and energy in giving instructions, advice, and checking B and C's understanding. B and C may take little or no part in planning the task, deciding on operating procedures and performance criteria. A controls the information flow. The dotted lines indicate the communicative focus, on a vertical axis.

In narrow power-distance cultures which do NOT welcome close control, close supervision is NOT positively evaluated and a participative superior is preferred. For Figure 9.2 assume that

- the task is open-ended and there are many possible outcomes;
- B and C know more about how to accomplish the task than does A;
- B and C must collaborate in order to accomplish the task.

In this context, efficient communication between B and C is of prime importance and either's relationship with A is of less importance. Hence in this context, a broader span of control is possible. A gives less supervision to each subordinate, and so can supervise more of them (N).

Figures 9.1 and 9.2 show the same formal structure can be implemented in different ways, and that one additional factor influencing implementation is national culture – see below.

9.4   Culture and Bureaucracy

Culture also influences needs for structure, its design and how it is implemented.

Hofstede's model (2001) provides a guide to the work relationships valued and disvalued by members of the culture group, and to different types of tasks valued and disvalued. In an Anglo culture (lower power distances, individualist, lower needs to avoid uncertainty) and in a typical organization, structures are relatively flat, facilitate communication between all levels and units, reward members for taking initiatives and promote on the basis of achievement. In this context, these are likely to be more effective than structures that are deeply hierarchical, discourage communication outside the vertical axis, reward members on the basis of group achievement and promote on the basis of years' seniority – all other factors being equal.

Top management in Japanese companies still focuses on providing "top-down" strategic guidance, which gave a framework within which policy details were formulated. Levels below contribute "bottom-up" interpretations of policy; for instance, by suggesting process modifications, which were reviewed at higher levels. These can eventually lead to the development of and perhaps stimulate strategic development – although this decision is taken by top management. Thus influence moves in both directions. But this does not mean that formal authority is delegated downward. Strategic decision-making processes tend to be centralized, regardless of organizational size and technology.

The employee is motivated by a structure that reflects his values within the work relationship, and is applied appropriately in the cultural context. Culture influences how Weber's bureaucratic "ideal" is implemented in practice, which means that the same elements of structure may be implemented differently in different cultural contexts. Hofstede (2001, pp. 376–378) argues that the dimensions of power distance and uncertainty avoidance are the most crucial in determining organizational structures and systems. His model (see 2.5) indicates four quadrants, where needs to avoid uncertainty are high and low, and where power distances are wide and narrow:

- THE MARKETPLACE BUREAUCRACY. This typifies organizations in national cultures where needs to avoid uncertainty and power distances are narrow – for example, in the Scandinavian countries, the United Kingdom, Australia, New Zealand, the United States. Members depend more upon personal than bureaucratic relationships to achieve results – and may feel free to by-pass the hierarchy and cross departmental boundaries. Formal structures and functions may be ambiguous, and members are not sure of the precise limits to others' authority. They negotiate for influence on the basis of individual expertise and need, creating alliances by trading support. The underlying assumption is that "if you scratch my back, I'll scratch yours". Support staff play a key role in helping the different parts of the organization adjust to change. Job rotation and matrix structures are commonly implemented.

- THE FULL BUREAUCRACY typifies organizations in national cultures at the opposite extreme, where needs to avoid uncertainty are high and power distances are wide – for example, in Italy, Taiwan, France, and Guyana at the extreme. It comes closest to Weber's model of making members' behavior predictable and reducing uncertainties. Responsibilities and relationships are standardized and impersonal, and emphasis is given to staff roles (technocrats who supply ideas). Members understand the limits to their own and other people's authority and responsibilities. They respect the unequal distribution of power and have a strong need to avoid ambiguous procedures. Centralized structures and routine tasks are more readily accepted – Hofstede (2001) likens these organizations to pyramids. Vertical communication is the norm, and departments perhaps communicate with each other only at the highest levels.

- THE WORKFLOW BUREAUCRACY typifies organizations in the relatively few national cultures where needs to avoid uncertainty are high and power distances are narrow – for example, in Germany, Austria and Israel. Structures depend heavily upon professional bureaucrats occupying senior posts in the operating core where the productive work is centered. Operating procedures are standardized. Hofstede uses the metaphor of the well-oiled machine. Needs to avoid task uncertainty are high and so specifications for job performance are tightly controlled. On the other hand, power distances are relatively low. In Germany, large companies, executives and workforce may share common canteen facilities. German unions, management and government find it relatively easy to cooperate and avoid conflict – for instance, in organizing training programs and implementing new technologies.

- **THE PERSONNEL BUREAUCRACY** flourishes in national cultures where needs to avoid uncertainty are low and power distances are wide – for example, in the Confucian cultures, India, Indonesia, the Philippines, and Malaysia at the extreme. Hofstede (2001) likens organizations in this quadrant to the family. They often have a simple structure built around a strong leader who controls by direct and close supervision, and authority is associated with this person. The leader may be perceived in terms of his social position and personal qualities rather than of the responsibilities associated with his/her bureaucratic rank – the opposite to the full bureaucracy. Ranks are tightly differentiated and in a family company, non-family members have few opportunities for promotion. The manager must demonstrate expectation in order to hold the loyalty of subordinates, and must behave according to their expectations of his/her rank and role.

Any "stepping out of place" may be disruptive. The manager thought to be acting outside the limits of his authority becomes the object of suspicion. Writing in an Indian newspaper, an Indian manager made the point:

> Relationships often fail due to misunderstandings and lack of role clarity, as can be seen in the example of the old employee trying to play the role of adviser to a new employee who misinterprets this as being "bossed" by one who has no business to do so![1]

Managers who do not understand or misinterpret their role boundaries soon find it difficult to persuade others, and become ineffective.

9.4.1 The matrix structure

The matrix structure gives a vivid example of how culture affects the design and implementation of a structure. In essence, the individual (A, below) reports to two superiors (B and C); see Figure 9.3.

The matrix is the chosen structure of many project-focused companies (such as NASA, and many engineering and construction companies), where

- tasks are non-routine;
- relationships and responsibilities have to be continually changed in order to meet the needs of new project.

In Figure 9.4, A is a project engineer and reports to both the project manager (B) and the engineering manager (C). The other members of the project team (D, E) also have dual reporting relationships – to B, and to their own functional managers.

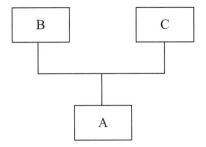

Figure 9.3 The matrix

However, cultural factors may prove a major disincentive to applying a matrix structure. The tables above imply that the multiple superiors collaborate on planning A's budgets, and on how his time should be spent. And so must balance their decision-making powers in relation to A. All participants have to cooperate and share information and other resources in a relationship of trust. The implication is that they work best in cultures where colleagues trust each other more – in cultures with low-power distances and low needs to avoid uncertainty.

In all cultures they are always very difficult to operate smoothly; they are most likely to work in the marketplace bureaucracies, for example Sweden and the United Kingdom, where there was most agreement with Laurent's (1983) proposition that bypassing the hierarchical line is often necessary – see 3.3.1. They are least likely to work in the antithetical cultures, the full bureaucracies, where needs to avoid uncertainty are high and power distances are wide. Laurent's (1981) data indicate that "rejection of the dual-boss principle appears much stronger in the Latin cultures [France and Italy] than in others [Northern Europe and the USA]" (p. 108). But even in the United States, success is not guaranteed. A study of American hospitals that had abandoned matrix structures showed that the most common reasons were financing, turnover and staffing problems, and conflicts between physicians and nurses.

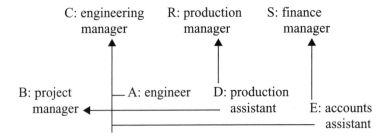

Figure 9.4 A project matrix

9.4.2   *Applying the four-quadrant model*

The model, derived by Hofstede from his dimensions of uncertainty and power distance, is not making rigid predictions. It is not saying that all organizations in the same quadrant are of the same type. Not all organizations in, say, Ireland follow the market bureaucracy model or that all in, say, Belgium follow the full bureaucracy model. In both of these countries you could expect to find examples of all four models. Small family companies can be found across the world; and a multinational might try to replicate significant features of its structure wherever it establishes subsidiaries. Rather, it indicates tendencies.

It is most useful when like is compared with like, for example when an advertising agency in Denmark (marketplace bureaucracy) is compared to an advertising agency in Portugal (full bureaucracy) of approximately the same size. It may not be accurate if used to compare a small Portuguese advertising agency with, say, a large Danish bank.

9.4.3   *Different needs for structure*

Different cultures have different needs for structure in order to function efficiently. This means, first, the same structure may be implemented differently in different cultures, and a multinational company cannot expect that even a simple structural arrangement will yield the same results in different national subsidiaries. Perhaps the members of Culture A are highly collectivist, and they will give more emphasis to those aspects of the structure which foster the development of group loyalties. Members of Culture B give greater respect to high power distances than do members in Culture C, and supervisors in the two subsidiaries have different relationships with their juniors.

Second, this suggests that an MNC needs to consider the implications of imposing the same structure on different investments in different cultures. What different interpretations of the structure can it expect to develop?

Third, when members experience the formal structure as failing to serve their needs, they make increased use of informal structures, including patronage arrangements – discussed in the next chapter.

9.5   Implications for the Manager

Compare an organization that you know well in YOUR OWN CULTURE with a similar organization in SOME OTHER CULTURE.

1   In each of the two organizations, which of these are rewarded? Which are not?
   (a)   the employee follows his job specifications to the letter;
   (b)   the employee departs from his job specification when this seems likely to accomplish the task;

    (c)   the employee always follows official reporting procedures;

    (d)   the employee bypasses the hierarchy when this seems likely to accomplish the task.

2 Which organization is more active in each of the following?

    (a)   differentiating the functions performed by employees;

    (b)   imposing formal systems for controlling performance;

    (c)   imposing formal communication systems.

3 For similar departments in the two organizations, compare and contrast the following: RELATIONS BETWEEN PEERS. In which organization are they more likely to

- cooperate?
- come into conflict? Over what issues?
- socialize outside the workplace?
- What factors OTHER than culture influence their relationships?

RELATIONS BETWEEN SUPERIOR AND SUBORDINATES. In which organization

- do subordinates expect more supervision? Why?
- do subordinates have more freedom to plan, implement and evaluate their own work?
- are subordinates more likely to bypass the hierarchy when they need to communicate?
- What factors OTHER than culture influence their relationships?

4 How far can differences between the organizations be explained by differences in their national cultures?

- What other factors explain these differences?

9.6 SUMMARY

This chapter has examined those factors that influence the design of formal structures and how they are implemented. Most emphasis has been given to cultural factors, which may radically influence the implementation of the same structure in different contexts.

Section 9.1 dealt with the needs for and FUNCTIONS OF STRUCTURE and focused on how tasks and communication responsibilities are structured in order to achieve the organizational goals as efficiently as possible. The structure gives members information about what communications are necessary or preferred, and what communications are discouraged or even prohibited in routine circumstances. Section 9.2 discussed needs for BUREAU-CRATIC STRUCTURE and argued that a wide range of factors influence how structures are implemented in different contexts. Section 9.4 focused on how factors in the national CULTURE influence needs for different types and degrees of structuring, and on how structures are implemented in practice. Hofstede's model shows that a country's culture influences implementation.

9.7 EXERCISE

This exercise role-plays a resolution to a conflict, and then the design of structures aimed at preventing such a conflict recurring in the future. This is a pair and class activity.

1 The class divides into pairs. Each pair consists of
   - the sales manager;
   - the production manager.
   You work for a small engineering company.

   SALES MANAGER. The production manager never cooperates with you when you have a rush order. You have to fight with him/her every time you want to make a change in the production schedule. You can't understand why he/she won't be more cooperative. After all, if you can't cooperate to keep the customers happy, you could both lose your jobs! You have requested a meeting with the production manager in order to resolve this problem.

   PRODUCTION MANAGER. The sales manager never cooperates with you when there's a rush order. Every time he/she expects you to change the production schedule, and entirely overlooks the problems you face in procuring materials, tooling up, organizing work details, etc. If you have to rush an order ahead of schedule to get it finished, you cannot guarantee quality, and other scheduled jobs are delayed, which affects other customers. After all, if you can't cooperate to keep your customers happy, you could both lose your jobs! The sales manager has requested a meeting with you today in order to resolve this problem.

2 EACH PAIR: develop any further data you need about a recent incident in order to give your role-play greater realism.

3 (a) ALL sales managers meet together to discuss your problems and strategy.
   (b) ALL production managers meet together to discuss your problems and strategy.

4 EACH PAIR: ROLE-PLAY and negotiate a solution to the immediate problem.

5 (a) ALL sales managers meet together to discuss the solutions you have just negotiated. How can such problems be prevented in future, assuming that the company is operating within
      - a market bureaucracy?
      - a full bureaucracy?
      - a personnel bureaucracy?
      - a workflow bureaucracy?
   (b) ALL production managers meet together to discuss the solutions you have just negotiated. How can such problems be prevented in future, assuming that the company is operating within
   - a market bureaucracy?
   - a full bureaucracy?
   - a personnel bureaucracy?
   - a workflow bureaucracy?

6 ALL PAIRS: ROLE-PLAY AS FOLLOWS. Design a structure/formal rules/informal rules which will

prevent such problems recurring in the future, given a specific cultural context or contexts. (Choose one or more of the four bureaucratic contexts listed in 5.) Your recommendations will be passed on to top management for their decision.

7 FULL CLASS DISCUSSION. Compare and contrast your recommendations.

Note

1 Dr V. V. R. Sastry. Know thy role. *Times of India*, May 29, 1991.

CHAPTER TEN
Informal Systems

10.1 Introduction

Yasser Arafat, Chairman of the Palestine Liberation Organization, died in 2004 at the age of 75. He had been a controversial figure. Newspaper obituaries had different opinions on the ups and downs of his career during the half century in which he had embodied Palestinian demands for a state. However, they broadly agreed on his skills in developing a wide patronage network.

Some critics argued that he prized personal loyalty of his officials over their managerial and administrative competence. He used posts in institutions as his own property, with which to reward his followers. Despite his radical reputation, he had the effect of retarding the growth of Palestinian society. Aid organizations, the Americans and the Israelis regarded him as untrustworthy. But none of this affected his relationship with the Palestinian masses. For them, the idea of life without him was dreaded:

> even when opinion polls showed little support for his policies. His position as Palestinian leader included the traditional role of arbitrating among local families in disputes over land, marriages and property, and his shrewd ability to hold together a wide consensus in Palestinian society never faltered ...[1]

An American paper argued that Arafat was accessible and beloved by many for restoring to Palestinians a nearly lost sense of nationhood after the disaster of 1948; like a father his mistakes were usually forgiven. He behaved like a tribal chieftain, handing out money and favors. He earned loyalty but he also bought it.[2]

These stories indicate how patronage – or *wasta* in Arab cultures – may have both positive and negative affects. On the one hand, Arafat provided cohesion and coherence within his fractured community, and his use of power corrupted bureaucratic structures – at least in the eyes of these (Western) commentators.

This chapter deals with the mechanics of informal power, and on the cultural and economic conditions which lead the individual to invest in these relationships. It focuses on developing and applying a model of patronage. Sections also compare two variants – *guanxi*, practiced in Chinese societies, and *wasta*, practiced in Arab societies.

10.2 Informal Relationships

Chapter 9 showed that organizations establish formal bureaucratic structures in order to provide bureaucratic discipline to control tasks and communication.

These structures are designed to be rational and rule governed. They are adopted in order to help the organization reach its strategic goals, and to motivate members so that they contribute efficiently. Both these aims are achieved in a positive organizational culture.

Formal structures and informal systems have limited correspondence. Informal systems set priorities for certain personal relationships. These relationships determine what tasks the participants perform in order to meet each other's needs, and what communication is appropriate. Informal systems also serve the function of meeting individual needs, but these may only coincidentally correspond with the needs of a formal organization in cases where the participants both belong to one.

In some cultural and ethical contexts, informal relationships may benefit the firm. They create the conditions under which strategic goals can be achieved and plans implemented – or, if necessary, modified. They oil the wheels of business.

Lall and Ghosh (2002) studied a hundred and eight Mexican firms in three cities: Guadalajara, Hermisillo and Tijuana. The purpose of the study was to see which external factors affect the firm's productivity. These factors were trade, availability and quality of infrastructure, informal networks and exchange of knowledge, competitors of the firms and regulation climate surrounding the firms. The study concluded that the most important factor was the formation of informal networks. Companies benefited from investing time in having business lunches with local buyers and suppliers, competitors, government officials; see Lall and Ghosh (2002). But elsewhere – particularly in the Anglo cultures – there may be a cultural bias against the use of informal and personalized relationships.

Three types are discussed here. They have in common a number of characteristics, chief among which is that they are not fully legal or contractual – which distinguishes them from formal relationships. They are

- FRIENDSHIP RELATIONSHIPS (10.2.1).
- PATRONAGE (10.3).
- VARIANTS on patronage – *GUANXI* AND *WASTA* (10.5).

10.2.1   Friendship relationships

Friendship relationships include:

(a) Horizontal relationships between peers based on affection rather than on service and mutual obligation.
(b) Vertical relationships between superior and subordinate. Resources – such as birthday presents – may occasionally be exchanged, but do not commit the parties to further obligations. Such relationships may be of only short duration.
(c) A friendship clique – for example, persons who were in the same class at school. After graduation, members typically help each other by arranging reunions, parties, and helping find work. For instance, an employee informs her friends when her company is recruiting. Perhaps she asks the recruitment manager to give their applications special attention.

It becomes clear below that the line between friendship and patronage is imprecise, particularly in (b) vertical relationships between superior and subordinate and (c) friendship cliques; and the line between friendship and *guanxi* in respect of (a) horizontal relationships.

10.3   Modeling Patronage

We have seen that members of a strictly formal structure are recruited on an impersonal basis, and are selected on the bases of their experience and paper-based qualifications. But participants in patronage relationships are selected on the basis of personal qualifications, and for their readiness to accept and reciprocate personal obligations. The participant meets these obligations by utilizing his economic and other resources, social contacts and power in the other's service.

The most important similarity in formal structures and informal systems is that both provide means by which individuals can satisfy their needs. When informal systems prove to be more rewarding than formal structures in meeting needs, the individual may prefer these. When formal structures operate efficiently, these are preferred, the importance of patronage declines.

This section contributes a general model of patronage, and Sections 10.3.1–10.3.6 describe categories that explain how patronage operates. Where a relationship does not express these categories, there must be some doubt as to whether it is best described as one of patronage, and further examination is needed. Variants are common; in China, *guanxi*

(10.6) provides an example of a system that fits the model in most but not all respects. Should it be treated as a patronage system or as a related but different phenomenon?

10.3.1   Vertical relationship

Patronage relationships include a patron and at least one client. The patron plays a relatively senior role — both within the relationship and in other interactions. That is, they are unequal in rank.

10.3.2   Exchange of resources

Patronage provides a means by which patron and client acquire the resources that they need. Each side expects to obtain what is not otherwise available and contributes something valued by the other.

The patron needs the client's loyalty and service, and the client needs justice, protection, opportunities to work, and so on. Thus patron and client are mutually dependent. For example, when patron and client work in the same company, the patron might arrange that his client manager is given interesting and rewarding assignments; the client reciprocates by taking on additional work in the weekends and evenings; the patron arranges the client's promotion; the client acts as informal personal assistant to his patron; the patron attends the client's wedding; the client pays respects to his patron on his birthday; and so on. Each side advances the interests of the other and comes to his assistance when help is needed.

10.3.3   Dissimilar resources

The resources exchanged include

- ECONOMIC resources, such as money, employment, choice of work detail, a contract.
- SOCIAL and POLITICAL resources, such as loyalty, support and protection. The patron mediates in disputes – as in the case or Arafat (10.1) – and protects the client against outsiders, including the bureaucracy. Clients reciprocate by participating loyally in the patron's family ceremonies – for example, a birthday, wedding, or funeral.
- SEXUAL favors. For instance, a politician rewards his client mistress with political and business influence – with which she can reward her family and own clients.

Usually, each party reciprocates the other's contribution with a DISSIMILAR resource. That is, a vote is not usually exchanged for a vote. Because they play different social roles the patron and client have access to different resources.

Reciprocity does not mean that the items exchanged have equivalent cash value. When the patron is rich and powerful and the client poor, material balance is impossible. But the client is able to reciprocate by demonstrating loyalty and giving service. What is important is that there should be a symbolic balance.

10.3.4   *Duration*

A patronage relationship takes time to develop. Because it is not governed by impersonal rules that can be enforced by law, each side makes sure of the other's trustworthiness before making a commitment. The stream of exchanges creates new obligations, and the relationship may continue for the lifetimes of the participants – and even in some cases over their succeeding generations.

10.3.5   *Obligation*

Each side is obliged to respond to favors given by the other. Failure to meet this obligation brings shame to the persons concerned, and is punished. For example, the client who denies a justifiable request for service, or who fails to reciprocate a favor, or who seeks a new patron, may be labeled a traitor. The client who betrays his or her patron acquires a reputation for unreliability and risks social estrangement. This makes it very difficult to find a new patron. Similarly the patron who fails the clients may lose them and hence lose his or her power base.

The relationship should not be perceived as a simple commercial transaction. Conditions such as "if you find my son a job I'll vote for you in the next election" are unstated; patron and client are NOT bound as seller and buyer. That is, the individual cannot buy in and out of patronage relationships as easily as you change your orthodontist or management consultant.

10.3.6   *Insiders and outsiders*

When a patron has a number of clients, and a client also functions as patron to her own clients, patronage relationships involve a wide range of people tapping into different sources of power and influence. These linkages build into a NETWORK of influence based on the patron. The net protects members against non-members or outsiders.

Patronage is both an INCLUSION and an EXCLUSION mechanism; economic and social resources are channeled to the favored few and kept out of the grasp of outsiders, however well deserving. Insiders and outsiders are distinguished on the basis of their relationship with the patron, not on the basis of formal qualifications. For example, the patron–manager accelerates the promotion procedures of members of his/her "supporters club" while non-members find that their own promotion prospects are delayed.

Members of a university-based friendship clique (10.2.1) behave like a patronage network when they control access to jobs within an organization which they channel to junior classes, and so deny employment opportunities to persons with other backgrounds. The organization may benefit in that it secures a homogeneous workforce with similar qualifications and is knit by bonds of friendship and shared experiences; it may lose in that alternative perceptions and unorthodox viewpoints are excluded and not heard.

Table 10.1 Formal structures and patronage networks

	Formal structures	*Patronage networks*
Qualifications to join:	Bureaucratic criteria	Social relationships
Scope of influence:	Restricted by task/role specifications	Unrestricted
Source of influence:	Bureaucratic rules	Control of resources
Senior/junior status decided by:	Bureaucratic criteria	Perceptions of social status and control of resources
Purpose:	To serve the needs of the organization and its customers	To serve the needs of members of the patronage network
Relations to other members of the organization determined by:	Organizational structure	Membership or not of the patronage network; in- and out-groups
Decision to reward/sanction determined by:	Performance of formal tasks; position in the structure	Needs to reciprocate favors, and to make future exchanges

Whether such control is inherently unethical is an open question; but, like all patronage, it creates the conditions for corruption.

10.3.7 *Relationships in formal structures and patronage networks*

Table 10.1 summarizes the differences between how formal and informal systems operate within an organization.

10.4   Patronage, Culture and Society

In ALL societies there are SOME conditions under which patronage networks thrive – for example when they supply persons' needs more effectively than would the formal alternatives. Most people in the world depend on patronage at some points in their careers and lives.

Anglo cultures adopt strong attitudes towards patronage, and treat it as at best undesirable, and at worst evil. However, many people in the world today depend on patronage in order to secure a living. In some situations it may represent the most practical alternative to anarchy. An article dealing with the 1994 genocide in Rwanda argued that in many African countries the individual could only hope to become rich and exercise control of his life by participating in government and benefiting from the rewards, which are then distributed to dependents. And so he, rather than the abstraction of state, becomes the object of primary loyalty within his society:

And a man who, being in a position of power and influence, fails to help his relatives, villagers and tribesmen, is regarded not as incorruptible, but as cold-hearted and unfeeling – a wicked man, in fact.[3]

The opportunity to belong to a powerful patronage network is always attractive in a culture where stable group membership is most valued and group exclusion most feared. But patronage offers more than this. It provides the individual with a precise place in the social jigsaw, and reinforces identity and function. Hence, examples of patronage can be found very widely, particularly in societies that lack cultural coherence.

10.4.1   The cultural context

Patronage is founded on a personal relationship, which places a premium on face-to-face contact. In contexts where social mobility is low, patron and client meet on a relatively regular basis, and feelings of trust and loyalty are developed and maintained through face-to-face interactions. This is not an absolute condition and there are cases of patronage relationships where the participants meet only occasionally. But in general such dependency relationships develop where there is only limited geographic and occupational mobility, and where competing relationships are few.

Patronage links may be exploited in order to restrict mobility. In an unstable labor market, the owner of a small business may fear losing skilled workers who might gravitate to work for a competitor, or start their own businesses in competition. In such contexts the employer is naturally inclined to take a personal interest in their employees' behavior, even when this is not directly related to work, and to develop personal links of obligation with them. A Hong Kong student told one of the authors that for several years she had worked for a family to whom she was not related. Her bosses valued her contribution, and suggested that she might be interested in marrying their young son. If she had accepted, she would have been bound to the company – perhaps, to their mutual advantage.

The other side of the coin is that informal patronage ties become less important under conditions where labor markets are stable and there exist opportunities for employees to move to better paid jobs and for employees to recruit the staff they need.

10.4.2   The social context

Patronage is more likely to be accepted in social contexts where

- public officials do not protect individual rights and liberties;
- officials are corrupt;
- welfare services have few resources;
- individuals do not have easy access to welfare services;
- available services are delivered too inefficiently to be effective;

- individuals do not have opportunities for social and occupational mobility. They cannot escape from traditional relationships;
- concepts of collective responsibility by state officials are weak;
- systems for disciplining state officials are weak;
- codes governing the conduct of state officials and their relationships with business people are inadequate or not enforced.

It may also be common in societies to experience extraordinary growth, where development programs offer unusual opportunities for personal enrichment.

Several of these conditions explain the rise of one of the best known instances of organized patronage, the Mafia in the United States. The Mafia originated in Sicily among small landowners anxious to protect their estates against royal (and alien) authority. When large numbers of Sicilians migrated to New York and the United States in the nineteenth century, the *padrone* or sponsor advanced money for the immigrant's passage and found him work – in return for a fee. Most of these immigrants knew no English and did not understand the new society. They were defenseless and alienated. They could communicate with neither welfare agencies nor potential employers. They had very few opportunities for mobility outside their own community, and hence were forced to depend on the *padrone*. The Mafia emerged from the *padroni* system as a set of linked criminal gangs. The early scenes in the film *The Godfather* brilliantly demonstrate the patronage relationship between a Mafia chief and his dependent clients.

10.4.3   *The industry context*

The industrial context influences how far patronage is tolerated and even welcomed. In some industries patronage is unlikely to be significant in making appointments and promotions. For example, an engineering company is unlikely to reward the individual who lacks technical engineering skills, which can be precisely specified and evaluated by bureaucratic procedures. But other industries place a far higher premium on personal attributes and connections. In politics, the necessary skills cannot be precisely specified and certified, and we expect successful politicians to control informal networks. In the United States, all recent presidents have been highly skilled in granting favors and calling in debts.

Patronage may link the professions of politics, the army and police. In Thailand for many years, all governments have relied on either the army or the police and sometimes both to hold power. This culture of close dependencies between civil, military and police authorities is well established, and the same families enjoy dominant positions in these institutions.

"You find the same few surnames wherever you look," writes Michael Nelson, a political scientist in Bangkok.... Thai public servants are less loyal to the institutions that employ them than to their loose network of connections – relatives, ex-classmates from military training or old university chums.[4]

10.4.4   Government–business patronage

In essence, a patronage relationship occurs between individuals rather than between institutions. Nevertheless it links them when the individuals belong to different institutions and use it in order to advance their institutional interests. Government and business are linked by patronage when the business person plays the role of client to a powerful patron in politics or the government bureaucracy.

The political/bureaucratic patron

- steers government contracts towards his client business person; secures government funding;
- provides inside information about government policy;
- supports legislation favorable to the business person, and opposes unfavorable legislation;
- gives protection against other arms of the bureaucracy attempting to implement legislation which threatens the business person's interests;
- gives protection against business competitors, and helps the business person secure a monopoly position;
- acts as a consultant and middleman.

The client business person reciprocates by

- making straightforward payments – perhaps disguised as "consultancy fees";
- giving favorable stock options;
- paying election expenses (in cases when the patron is an elected politician);
- demonstrating loyalty and respect. For instance, the patron is invited as guest of honor to family celebrations;
- providing leisure opportunities such as holidays and golf weekends.

These relationships have been labeled differently; for example, "cronyism" in the Philippines, "sweetheart deals" in the United States. They have in common that they discriminate against those who do not belong to the circle of influence. In the eyes of the outsider, these relationships are unfair. After the 1997 financial crisis, they were judged to fail the new criterion of "transparency". They are particularly non-transparent to foreign companies which are trying to break into a close-knit local market, and which are incapable of developing the long-term personal links essential in developing a patronage relationship.

10.4.5   The costs of government–business patronage

These relationships convey obvious benefits to both parties when both parties are able to satisfy the other's needs. However, they carry risks:

- the bureaucratic patron loses legitimacy when the relationship is condemned as unfair or corrupt by outsiders;
- either party may find him/herself locked into a unprofitable arrangement when the other's influence wanes.

And broader society may suffer when:

- the official steers contracts towards a business client, and free trade is stifled;
- the benefits of competition are restricted;
- consumers may be forced to pay monopoly prices.

10.5   Some Variants: *Guanxi* and *Wasta*

The notion of patronage has been explored above in general terms. Many variants can be found, each conditioned by the particular cultural and economic conditions of its society. Two examples are dealt with here; *guanxi*, found in Chinese cultures, and *wasta*, found in Arabic societies. In what situations should these be sharply differentiated from the patronage model and treated as distinct systems?

10.5.1   Guanxi

Informal *guanxi* relationships constitute a major social dynamic in the People's Republic of China, Taiwan, Singapore, and in Chinese societies elsewhere.

Guanxi has been defined as

> the set of personal connections which an individual can draw upon to secure resources or advantages when doing business or in the course of social life.   *(Davies, 1995)*

This definition is broad, and in practice the term is used with many different meanings. At one extreme it may indicate no more than that the individuals concerned are favorably inclined to each other, and that a basis exists for a relationship. At the other extreme it might refer to the relationship and even that the individuals share membership of an informal association.

Guanxi relationships are used in order to secure personal, business, and political advantages, and are important in all aspects of business life in the Chinese world. The business person approaching local government with an application to establish a new company hopes that a *guanxi* relationship with someone in authority will make the procedure much shorter and smoother. When he decides to build a new office, good *guanxi* helps secure a good location and a lower price than otherwise. *Guanxi* with a client speeds up the deal at the best possible price. In business, *guanxi* is a form of social capital owned by the business person and associated with his/her organization (Chen 2001).

10.5.2   *How can* guanxi *and patronage be differentiated?*

There are grounds for arguing that *guanxi* and patronage are essentially the same, and grounds for arguing that they are distinct. *Guanxi* and patronage relationships are similar in that, first, both are based on interpersonal trust. Second, they join individuals in informal relationships that have no contractual basis. Third, they set a pattern of mutual obligation and provide a channel for the exchange of different resources. Fourth, they have no fixed duration. Fifth, they distinguish insiders from outsiders. Sixth, both patronage and *guanxi* may reflect a high cultural context – although, as we have seen, patronage arises in all national contexts.

However, in other respects patronage and *guanxi* have to be distinguished. Whereas patronage is based on a vertical axis, *guanxi* can function on either a vertical or horizontal basis. For example, classmates of equal status may be joined by *guanxi* obligations, without any one of them having superiority or dominance. Second, the economic motive may sometimes be far less important than the basis on loyalty and affection. Thus *guanxi* may be less coercive than patronage.

The problem that arises in using *guanxi* as an analytical tool is that the concept is often used very generally, both by Chinese and non-Chinese. Sometimes the term is employed so loosely that it lacks any descriptive worth, and sometimes with so narrow a reference that the meaning is distorted. Some *guanxi* relationships are said to exist between family members, between personal friends, and between business associates who might not normally be counted as personal friends. But in all cultures, positive personal ties are based on affection and a sense of personal obligation – for instance, between family members, friends, and classmates. How can the relationship between father and child in Iraq, Guatemala, and China be significantly distinguished in practice, other than by the fact that the latter finds its justification in Confucian ethics? Iraq and Guatemala are not Confucian societies but they also have ethical systems that stress the importance of healthy parent–child relationships

The outsider faces an additional difficulty in that when the Western media show interest in *guanxi*, they tend to use the term too narrowly, implying only corrupt practice. This tendency has grown stronger since the 1997 recession in Asian economies, and Western observers have developed a taste for lecturing Asians on how they might correct their business practices. For example, in 2001 a magazine article cited a Chinese–American academic who was hopeful that China's entry to the World Trade Organization would foster the growth of a system in which bureaucratic systems and structures would grow in importance as the legitimate way of getting things done, and in which *guanxi* connections would count for less:

> The Chinese government has already made progress in diminishing the role of *guanxi*, Li says, explaining it this way: "Banking reform is getting rid of relationship banking, the smuggling crackdown is getting rid of relationship trading, the separation of the army from business is ending relationship business."[5]

Of course it is to be hoped that business criminality is punished by the Chinese courts – just as it is in the United States, the United Kingdom and elsewhere. However, there is little point in calling for a ban on a total cultural system that is also expressed in innocent relationships between family members and friends.

In sum, the international manager needs to discriminate between malignant forms of *guanxi* (and patronage) that harm the organization and benign forms that help foster strong, positive relationships and organizational cultures.

10.5.3 Wasta

Patronage in Arab cultures is generally described as *wasta*, but the practice varies in different societies. *Wasta* is often rooted within the family and then involves using third person parties; if I want to find a job I speak to a relative and ask him to recommend me to his *wasta* contact who has influence in the organization in which I am interested.

In Jordan, the public sector has become bloated by the number of people hired through using *wasta*. This has the effects that the public sector is burdened with salary bills that inhibit development, and that the labor pool available to the private sector is reduced. When a person hired through *wasta* has powerful contacts in the public sector and elsewhere, his company may benefit greatly. But persons hired at the lower levels, without useful contacts, drain resources, particularly if they are not productive. Attempts are being made to rectify this situation, and to enforce bureaucratic standards.

10.6   Managing Informal Systems

This section deals with the management of informal systems, whether characterized as patronage, or some variant – including *guanxi* and *wasta*.

10.6.1   *Informal systems in the public sector*

In many developing societies, dependence on a central bureaucracy as a vehicle of development has sometimes meant that the very societies that lack good administration are the ones most likely to try to establish a comprehensive array of administrative controls over every aspect of investment, production and trade. That is, the bureaucracy creates more and more structures in order to safeguard itself. But the more complex these grow and the greater the demand for staff to run them, the greater the opportunities for development of informal patronage systems, by which individuals are able to maneuver themselves around the formal structures.

Efforts to build a modern bureaucracy are undermined when the loyalty of members is divided between the formal system and the patronage networks by which they secured the appointment.

Often, of course, the organizational superior and subordinate are linked in both systems. And when formal and patronage roles do correspond, the reporting and controlling functions of the formal structure are reinforced. But when the formal superior and the patron of a network of clients are different persons, and when these two persons are in conflict, the loyalties of subordinates are divided. The greater the disparity in patronage network and formal structure, the greater the danger to the organization.

The contradictions between patronage and impersonal criteria for recruitment and promotion are most acute in countries that have not yet fully developed a modern bureaucracy. In Pakistan, efforts to combat terrorist groups are compromised to the extent that patronage (or *sifarish*) is still important in social and political life. As a rule, political leaders are tribal or clan leaders and when they achieve power are expected to find employment for their clansmen – who helped them win their positions.

When unqualified clients are appointed, the bureaucracy suffers in three ways. First, the client placeholders are not competent to perform their jobs, and this reflects on their bureaucratic superiors rather than on their patrons. Second, the professional reputations of all other members are devalued. Third, tensions arise when those bureaucrats who have secured their posts through years of hard work and bureaucratic excellence find themselves subordinated to less competent newcomers who have gained their posts through patronage.

Of course, patronage occurs in all bureaucracies. In the United States and the United Kingdom, long-time supporters of the ruling elite may expect to be rewarded with posts in the administration. But the greater the numbers and influence of these patronage appointees, the greater are the risks.

10.6.2 *Informal systems in the private sector*

It might appear that business patronage is in decline. The growing dependence on information technology seems to be leading to a greater standardization of work structures. Anglo companies with multinational commitments have become less tolerant of local anomalies, and Anglo notions of "transparency" in business behavior are increasingly treated as an ideal.

But these informal systems are unlikely to be easily banned – except perhaps in instances of outright criminality. They are not limited to serving narrow economic ends; they express broad social functions within their cultural environments. And because they reflect deeper values associated with communication within high-power contexts, and power distances and collectivism, legislation is unlikely to achieve much.

The conditions for patronage to flourish were set out in 10.4.2. It is logical to argue that when these conditions are reversed, individuals will be more attracted to the option of formal structures as a way of satisfying their needs, and less attracted to informal systems. That is, patronage will diminish in importance and formal structures will gain when

- they are perceived top be effective and impartial;
- bureaucrats observe the bureaucratic rules. Corrupt officials are punished;
- officials are freely accessible;

- welfare services are effective;
- opportunities for social and physical mobility are present;
- public resources are channeled equitably.

This means that in the private sector the bureaucratic rules described in 9.3 apply. In particular, all recruitments and promotions are determined by impersonal criteria. The individual's responsibilities reflect his/her qualifications and are formalized in his/her job description, which can be formally compared to the responsibilities of other individuals.

10.6.3   The "outsider" manager and informal systems

The cross-cultural manager trained in a culture relatively free of patronage may find it difficult to adjust to a culture and organization where informal power arrangements are normal.

By their nature, patronage, *guanxi,* and *wasta* systems are not transparent, and outsiders face a particular problem in understanding if they do not have a working knowledge of the language used by the participants. But insiders are well aware how the system operates, who is involved and what resources are exchanged.

The Anglo manager has been conditioned to think of informal systems as necessarily unethical. The immediate Anglo response is that any form of patronage is inherently corrupt and should be banned.

However, this may be jumping the gun. The outsider first needs to understand how the system works within the organization and effects task and communication relationships among members. Second, she needs to understand why the informal system might be preferred – that is, why it seems to promise greater rewards than does the formal structure. An ethical response might then be appropriate, but only when the dynamics of the system have been examined.

An outsider manager may hope to outlaw the use of patronage relationships. But the members' overt compliance with a ban does not necessarily signify that they accept the change, or that the organizational culture has been reformed. Attempts to directly eliminate patronage have to be weighed against possible short-term loss of morale and weakened vertical linkages.

The outsider manager might be more successful in modifying the conditions that make the informal system a preferred alternative to formal structures. This means improving formal structures, and making them more rewarding and more accessible. Formal structures attract members when

- the bureaucratic rules are accepted;
- implementation of the rules is accepted as fair. For example, rewards and punishments are fair;
- rules governing relationships between peers, superiors and subordinates are accepted;
- task specifications are accepted;
- the organizational culture is positive and strong.

10.7   Implications for the Manager

How important are informal relationships within your own culture and in some other culture? Compare between

- a typical organization that you know in YOUR OWN CULTURE.
- a typical organization that you know in SOME OTHER CULTURE.

1 What cultural features explain the significance and functions of patronage relationships within each organization?
   - Take into account such cultural features as power distances, individualism/collectivism, needs to avoid uncertainty and fears of outsiders, high-/low-context features.
2 What organizational features explain the significance and functions of patronage relationships within each organization?
   - the quality of management;
   - the existence of welfare services and staff support;
   - the organizational culture;
   - pay and other rewards;
   - opportunities for training;
   - opportunities for promotion.
3 Within each organization, identify a patronage network:
   - who are involved, as patron? As client(s)?
   - what resources are exchanged between patron and clients?
   - in what respects does the organization as a whole benefit from the activities of this network? (Consider factors including motivation, loyalty, speed of communication.)
   - in what respects does the organization suffer?
4 Compare your answers for the two organizations. How do you explain differences?

10.8   SUMMARY

This chapter has examined informal systems. The emphasis has been laid on understanding patronage and variants as systems that meet participants' needs and respond to factors in their cultural, social and economic contexts.

Sections 10.2 and 10.3 discussed various INFORMAL RELATIONSHIPS and distinguished formal bureaucratic structures from PATRONAGE NETWORKS. Patronage relationships express mutual obligation between patron and client(s) and may distribute a stream of resources on a reciprocal basis over a lengthy period of time. Outsiders to the network are excluded. Section 10.4 examined how CULTURAL and SOCIAL conditions influence the growth and decline of patronage. Section 10.5 dealt with *GUANXI* and *WASTA* and asked how far they should be regarded as local variants and how far as distinct phenomena. Section 10.6 dealt with the problems of MANAGING members of a formal structure when they are also participating in INFORMAL SYSTEMS.

10.9 EXERCISE

1 What relationships are exemplified between the participants in each of the following? Decide between
- friendship
- formal
- family
- patronage
- *quanxi*
- *wasta*
- (any other).

For each, give your reasons.

2 Which of these relationships do you think are unethical? Why?

(a) In Asian Country B, Charnvit has worked in his company for seven years. All this time Sanet has been his boss. Sanet is a good-hearted man, who regularly asks Charnvit for news of his family. He passes on his best wishes to Charnvit's wife and children, whom he once met at a company New Year party.

(b) In Latin American Country Y, Paulo is illiterate, but nevertheless was appointed to his present position of clerk in the provincial government. He reports directly to the governor, who is his wife's cousin and hired him. He is responsible for turning out the vote in his village. He is always proud to attend family celebrations hosted by the governor.

(c) In African Country K, Tamba and Musa are distant cousins, and were in the same class at school together. Since then Tamba has secured a safe job in a local government department. Musa has a small company producing low-cost stationery products. He has a history of illness and the business has not been a success. Tamba tries to help by recommending his low-cost products to the purchasing manager of his department. He sometimes has to lie in order to give his friend an attractive reference. The purchasing manager has to choose between competing stationery companies, but in order to oblige his friend and colleague Tamba, sometimes buys from Musa.

(d) In Central European country H, Sandor and his girl-friend Rosa have been close for many years. Rosa has a good job in the buildings department of their local district government office. Sandor has a business importing and selling low-cost building materials. He has a history of fighting with his ex-wife, who still owns a share of the company, and this has distracted him from giving the company his full attention. Recently the company has been operating with low profit margins. Rosa is trying to help by recommending Sandor's products to her boss, the buildings manager. She never lies about the quality of the products. The building manager is new to this job and this town. His chief responsibility is providing cheap but adequate housing for the many refugees in the district. He does not yet know Rosa well, but has been told by others that she is trustworthy, and so he is increasingly happy to act on her recommendations. This simplifies his time-consuming chore of selecting between the many competing suppliers and means that he can devote a greater share of his energies to rehousing the refugees.

(e) In Taiwan, Mr Leung and Mr Wang were students in the same class and have been business associates for many years. They do each other favors when the opportunity arises. Last week Mr Leung asked Mr Wang to help him find a job for his son, Leung Qi. By chance, Mr Wang is looking for someone with Qi's qualifications to work in his company, and he was able to oblige.

(f) In New York, Mr Smith and Mr Brown were students in the same class and have been business associates for many years. They do each other favors when the opportunity arises. Last week Mr Smith asked Mr Brown to help him find a job for his son, Peter Smith. By chance, Mr Brown is looking for someone with Peter's qualifications to work in his company, and he was happy to oblige.

(g) In European Country X, traffic policemen tend to demand bribes from motorists stopping at lights. Every demand is justified by claims that the motorist has been seen driving dangerously, or that the vehicle is not road worthy. Motorists who refuse are taken to the police court where they waste considerable time waiting for their cases to be heard, at the end of which they are usually found guilty and fined.

Notes

1 Obituary: Yasser Arafat. *Daily Telegraph*, November 12, 2004.

2 James Bennet and Steven Erlanger. Palestinians mourn a loss of icon. *Interational Herald Tribune*, November 12, 2004.

3 Anthony Daniels. A continent doomed to anarchy. *Sunday Telegraph*, July 24, 1994.

4 The Thai police: a law unto themselves. *The Economist*, April 19, 2008.

5 Bruce Einhorn. Trading despotism for democracy. *Business Week Online*, October 16, 2001.

CHAPTER ELEVEN
The Culture and Politics of Planning Change

CHAPTER OUTLINE

Introduction

The Meaning of Planning

The Classic Planning Model

How National Culture Influences
  Planning

How Organizational Culture
  Influences Planning

The Politics of Planning

Implications for the Manager

Summary

Exercise

Note

11.1   Introduction

Chapter 9 saw how the organization uses structures to control how members perform tasks and communicate. This chapter deals with organizational planning as an attempt to control activities in the future. In general, organizations don't invest much in planning when the conditions are good and there seems no need to break with routine. But when serious threats or extraordinary opportunities appear, radical planning may be needed.

A consultant commented:

> I do most of my work for [a London-based engineering company]. Top management can see how the industry is developing and has been trying for years to change practices in its [Gulf state] subsidiary. Consultants are hired to make plans and then go out to implement them. But local management and workers don't see how they can benefit from the changes that are proposed, and they don't want them. They never say no, but they use a range of delaying tactics. They know that eventually the consultants will give up, or be recalled, and nothing

will happen. Then, a new team of consultants are sent out – and we go through the same process all over again.

Planning alone is not enough. Plans have to be implemented, and achieving this is a political process – in the sense that it involves different people with different interests. These interests may sometimes conflict, as the example above shows.

This chapter focuses on planning as a reflection to environmental disturbance, and as a political event within the organization. An effective plan takes account of changes in the environment and tries to predict how these will effect implementation. This topic is developed in Chapter 13, which focuses on the environment of increasing globalization, and Chapters 14–15 on the design and implementation of strategic plans.

11.2   The Meaning of Planning

We can't plan the past. I can't plan what to eat for breakfast yesterday. All planning deals with events in the FUTURE. In this sense, planning is a symbolic activity. In present time, events in the future are not known, cannot be predicted with absolute accuracy, and cannot be entirely controlled. This means that planning is also an OPTIMISTIC activity but it implies that planning can influence the future.

But this does not mean that planning is entirely utopian. There must be REASONABLE grounds for supposing that the planned goal can be realized. Business planning therefore makes more sense in conditions of MODERATE predictability, for instance where markets and institutions are stable.

Note that planning is a less valued activity in conditions of absolute predictability, and, at the opposite extreme, absolute lack of predictability. The factors that might persuade the businessman that planning for a particular event might be a wise investment include the nature of the business, markets, the behavior of competitors, available technologies, and factors concerned with the organizational culture and the national culture.

The investment made in planning is influenced not only by the likelihood of success but also by the importance attached to the outcome. When it is very important that the outcome is achieved, the investment is greater. When the outcome is not important, the outcome is less. When there is a 1 percent chance that the company will fail, resources may be used in different activities than in planning against failure. When there is a 50 percent chance, this becomes a much more important item.

The term "planning" is used with different meanings which reflect different assumptions about the relationship between the planner and possible future events. The purpose of this chapter is to examine these assumptions and to distinguish different types of planning. This chapter is primarily concerned with planning for radical change. But before we move into that main topic, other types of planning are briefly discussed.

This section deals with

- planning as forecasting
- routine planning.

11.2.1   Planning as forecasting

At one extreme planning makes predictions about the future; weather forecasting is one example. This describes possible future events and leaves individuals free as to how they might respond. Whether or not they wish to change their behavior in response to the prediction is up to them to choose.

Planning-as-forecasting includes

- CONTINGENCY PLANNING. This explores the impact of a single hypothetical event on a given situation.
- SENSITIVITY ANALYSIS. This examines the impact of a change in one variable when all other variables do not change. The planner tests for a series of variables in succession.
- COMPUTER SIMULATIONS. These make objective simulations when a range of variables are manipulated.

11.2.2   Routine planning

Routine planning occurs when an operation is performed regularly, but needs to be slightly reorganized each time in order to take account of slight changes in the context and the participants. For instance, the human resources department organizes the annual training program for new sales staff. Although the basic model is unaltered, no one year's program is entirely like that of the previous year. The number of trainees and the syllabus varies; new trainers are hired; new topics may be introduced; facilities may need to be changed (a new hotel, more teaching rooms) and budgets adjusted.

This planning is routine and does not enjoy high priority. It is conducted by relatively junior managers and experienced senior management may be involved only in overseeing and monitoring roles.

11.2.3   Planning for change

This chapter is less concerned with routine planning than with planning to make significant change. It focuses on the cultural influences on planning priorities, and the political considerations that have to be taken into account in order to get a plan accepted and implemented. Planning for change is often termed "strategic", and the formulation and implementation of strategic plans is dealt with in Chapters 14 and 15.

11.3   The Classic Planning Model

When routine planning is unable to respond to internal changes or to changes in the environment, the company may resort to traditional routines. These are modeled in

Table 11.1 The classic planning model

1. proposing an objective for change; the goals to be achieved;
2. collecting relevant data;
3. analyzing the data and projecting past and present conditions into the future;
4. designing a set of alternative plans by which the objective can be achieved;
5. selecting the best alternative;
6. implementing the selected alternative;
7. monitoring and evaluating the implementation stage;
8. making necessary modifications, based on stage 7 output.

Table 11.1. The model has eight stages, 1–5 concerned with formulating the plan and 6–8 with implementing it.

This model depends heavily on the collection and analysis of accurate data. Increased access to the web has reduced some barriers to sharing information. This gives companies in the developed, information-rich economies a planning advantage over companies in less developed economies. The use of research facilities, consultants and specialists is expensive and these facilities also tend to be located in the developed economies.

When this model is implemented in consecutive stages and in full, it allows the user to continually check previous decisions. For example, assume that you have reached stage 8, and you recognize that problems have arisen, and so modifications must be made. Your next step is to make a check at stage 7; have you properly monitored and evaluated the implementation? If not, then make the correction. But if you find no problem at this stage, go back to 6. Did you fully implement the selected alternative? If you did, then look for the problem in stage 5. Are you sure that the selected alternative was, in fact, the best? If you are, then reconsider stage 3. And so on. When the problem has been located and resolved, revert to the original sequence.

This model is "ideal" in the sense that it provides a rational system which is often modified in practice. A number of factors intervene, and these include

- ENVIRONMENTAL FACTORS. In a competitive and rapidly shifting business environment, there may not be sufficient time to check and recheck every stage in order to locate a fault. There may not be time to fully analyze the data and design a number of alternatives. There may not even be time to collect reliable data. In such a situation, the user is forced to plan on the bases of intuitions and hunches, and treat any experience gathered from conducting early experiments as the only guide to future activities. The problems of making strategic plans in a discontinuous and post-modern environment are discussed in Chapter 15.
- INDUSTRY and products/services. For example, the advertising and petroleum industries adopt very different planning horizons. In advertising, much planning is very short term, perhaps for no more than one or two years. In the petroleum industry supply contracts can run from 15 to 50 years, with 20–25 year terms being the most common in the case of a major gas export scheme. This time is needed in order to put

the project together and to cover the duration of the sales contract (see Wybrew-Bond and Stern, 2002, p. 280).

- SIZE. Small companies that lack resources lead a hand-to-mouth existence. They are far more vulnerable than are their large competitors to external and internal changes. A large company may lose one customer and one member of staff and be little effected; a small company suffering the same difficulties could be wiped out. The owner of a small company may be willing to make short-term plans only, and lack the skills and resources to invest in the long term.
- LEVEL OF EXPERIENCE. A young company may lack understanding of what information it needs in order to plan, and have little experience of available data sources. Although planning aims to establish areas of certainty in the unknown future, it can be based only on what IS known — past and present conditions – and succeeds only to the extent that future events conform to projections made from past events. The inexperienced planner with no precedents from which to project may be at a disadvantage. On the other hand, the experienced planner may be hamstrung by historical precedent and be less equipped to respond to new opportunities and threats. He/she stumbles when the unexpected occurs. Planning based on projections of existing conditions did not help governments and companies foresee the collapse of communism in the Soviet Union and Eastern Europe after 1989, and when this collapse occurred existing business and political planning had to be scrapped.
- The planner's PERSONALITY; optimists and pessimists plan towards different goals.
- RELIGION and philosophy; a dislike for long-term planning may be influenced by a fundamentalist religious belief that only God can see the future, and that any attempt to do so challenges God. In Morocco, a Muslim society, futurity for many Moroccans was not something that could or should be rigorously planned for in advance. To attempt to secure the future, the day after next, was close to being sacrilegious (Finlayson, 1993, p. 224).

  In many Muslim societies, hopes and plans for the future are qualified by "Insh' Allah" – as God wills.
- NATIONAL CULTURE – discussed in 11.4 below.
- ORGANIZATIONAL CULTURE – discussed in 11.5 below.

11.4 How National Culture Influences Planning

Values in the national culture influence decisions about

- WHAT is planned;
- WHO plans;
- HOW planning is done;
- WHEN: timetables;
- WHEN: planning horizons.

11.4.1   What is planned

In cultures where needs to avoid uncertainty are high, members may invest in planning to protect themselves against the possibilities of, say, unemployment and sickness, and give less emphasis to planning how to optimize their salaries.

Where needs to avoid uncertainty are lower, members may stress planning to optimize their salaries and pay less attention to planning long-term employment. Planning may be less detailed and more long term. There is less emotional resistance to change. However, it does not follow that all proposed changes are equally welcomed any more than, at the opposite extreme, all changes are equally feared.

11.4.2   Who plans

Culture influences perceptions of who has rights to plan. Where power distances are relatively wide, subordinates are not trusted to make effective plans and planning is left to the superior – which, in a family company in Latin America or Southeast Asia, means the owner and perhaps his/her close family members. A subordinate who pushes too strenuously to implement his/her personal agenda may be seen as challenging their rights to control.

Where power distances are narrower, lower levels might expect to have opportunities to provide the vision. In practice, this may not often happen. Only exceptional companies encourage "intrapreneurial" initiatives below the level of departmental heads.

Where tolerance of uncertainty is low, planning is more detailed, and may be made the responsibility of specialist planners. Because uncertainties need to be resolved as quickly as possible, short-term feedback systems are emphasized.

In Japan, planning at the top level may be intuitive, incremental and empirical. At lower levels it is treated as a formal process, and comparisons between Japanese and Hong Kong planning show that the former demanded more detailed information.

11.4.3   How planning is done

Traditionally, Anglo cultures have interpreted the classic planning model by emphasizing the importance of objectivity. This has meant depending on hard data and computer models in collecting and interpreting them

In many cultures, as much emphasis may be placed on shared understanding of the environment, historical precedent, and "best guesses". In highly collectivist cultures, it may be difficult to formulate a plan without taking into account the interests of powerful members of the group.

Superstition can play a part. In Hong Kong when starting a venture, business people may gamble heavily on the lucky number eight which in Cantonese translation sounds like *faat*, or "prosperity".

11.4.4   Timetables

Trompenaars (1993) distinguished between sequential and synchronic cultures. In SE-QUENTIAL cultures, time is perceived as measurable and planning is treated as an important activity. Trompenaars gave examples from the United Kingdom and the Netherlands, and discussed the influence on the conduct of business in north-western Europe and North America. The implications for planning are that

- an initial plan is preferred, and straight paths are made to achieve it;
- management by objectives (MBO) is popular;
- employees are motivated by schedules for achieving their plans, and by career planning.

But in SYNCHRONIC or polychronic cultures, members prefer to juggle various activities in parallel and straight-line planning has less importance. Examples include cultures across the Middle East, Latin Europe, Africa and much of Asia. Plans are changed according to circumstances. Past experience, present circumstances, opportunities and possibilities cross-fertilize to decide the best course of action.

This distinction is too broad to differentiate specific cultures – for example, how planning routines vary across South East Asia, in Thailand, Malaysia and Indonesia. But it is useful, first, if it alerts the international manager to the possible problems of trying to impose headquarters planning models on a subsidiary where the culture has other temporal priorities. Second, it has implications for organizational structures. Sequential planning models reflect notions that the flow of information to the planners is likewise sequential.

But increasingly in today's business world, this is not the case. The flow is continual and of varying (and uncertain) reliability. Bush and Frohman (1991) argued that American companies had depended for too long upon a conceptual model of the innovation process that emphasizes the sequential involvement of groups of specialists. They propose as an alternative a CONCURRENT MODEL in which communication between different specialists is both simultaneous and spontaneous:

> The result is interactive learning that covers technology, customer needs, distribution, financial strategy – in short, all the elements needed to complete innovation.   *(p. 26)*

11.4.5   Planning horizons

Short-term planning tends to be less comprehensive and detailed. Monitoring procedures are taken less seriously than where planning is long term, and planning is restricted to narrower groups of managers. Long-term planning is more strategic, and makes greater use of strategic information sources, such as data banks, trade journals, reports, conferences. Almost by definition, planning schedules adopted by top management, with strategic responsibilities, tend to be longer term than those of middle and junior levels who have different responsibilities.

Cultures vary in the emphasis they give to short term and long term planning. However, there is some uncertainty over which cultures can be categorized as short term and long term. Early research (Neghandi 1979) suggested that time horizons were longer in the United States than in three Asian countries (India, the Philippines, and Taiwan), and that these were longer than in three Latin American countries (Argentina, Brazil, and Uruguay). On the other hand, the Hofstede (2001) concept of the "Confucian Dimension" classified the Asian cultures of China (ranked first), Hong Kong, Taiwan, and Japan as having the longer-term orientations of the 23 classified, and Pakistan (ranked 23rd, Nigeria and the Philippines) as having the shorter-term orientations, with the USA and UK at 17th and 18th places.

It may be the case that just ALL cultures tend towards longer-term planning for some activities and shorter-term planning for others, but that cultures do not correspond in what activities they consider worth longer-term planning. That is, the question arises, what activities merit strategic planning? For example, Thai family businesses respond rapidly to changing market conditions and in this respect planning is short term. But Thai managers often show long-term priorities in planning their careers (Mead et al., 1997). Hampden-Turner and Trompenaars (1997b) found that the then "Asian tiger" economies (including Singapore, Malaysia, Taiwan, Thailand) were very long term in developing knowledge and elaborating core competencies.

In circumstances where culture has an important influence on planning priorities, the implication is that systems proven in one country may be counterproductive in some other. This means that systems that work well in headquarters may be counterproductive in a subsidiary.

However, in industries that are most susceptible to the speed of change in global markets, planning horizons are likely to be shortened, regardless of cultural factors. Industry and market factors become increasingly important, and planning may be based on trial and error as much as on data that is quickly outdated.

11.5 How Organizational Culture Influences Planning

Organizational culture influences attitudes towards planning styles and responsibilities. Each organization has its own culture, and hence its own attitudes towards planning, but Table 11.2 gives four broad types, and suggests attitudes to planning in each:

- the entrepreneurial company;
- the family-owned company;
- the full bureaucracy;
- the old-established company.

Table 11.2 Organizational culture and planning

CULTURE	Entrepreneurial	Family owned	Full bureaucratic	Established
PLANNING INTERESTS	Innovation	Owner's needs	Rule-bound; safety first	Experience
PLANNER	Innovative planning group	The owner	"Expert" planning group	Established seniors
ATTITUDE TO RISK	High tolerance	Fear of losing face	Low tolerance	Low tolerance
STATUS OF THE PLAN	Flexible	Determined by the owner	"Legal"	Justified by precedent
COMMUNICATION	Ideas and counter-ideas debated throughout	Only as directed by the owner; no counter-ideas	Formalized and rule governed	Determined by precedent

In practice, these four types are not discrete. That is to say, the culture and planning systems in any one company may be influenced by more than one type. A family company may also be entrepreneurial and risk taking, or old-established and influenced by its history.

In the ENTREPRENEURIAL type, structures are relatively fluid and employees feel more confident in communicating across structural boundaries than they do in, say, in the bureaucratic type. Particularly if the company is new, there may be no culture of long-term thinking, and planning is made in response to immediate circumstances.

In a FAMILY-owned company, the owner may do all planning. If planning decisions do not have to be justified to other members, he may find it convenient to overlook or run together the formal stages in the Classic Planning Model (Table 11.1). Rigorous monitoring of the implementation process is unlikely if this threatens the owner's face. Some family companies do no coherent plan at all, and decisions are made in accordance with the owner's whim.

In the FULL BUREAUCRACY, planning procedures are determined by established formal procedures at each stage of the planning process. Planning is made the responsibility of a nominated group of expert planners, and other members are not normally expected to contribute. Monitoring and feedback processes may be restricted to checking that these procedures have been correctly followed. Failure is routinely blamed on circumstances outside the planners' control – for example, the actions of competitors or government. The danger lies in the culture of formal planning becoming so powerful that too many resources are invested in it and other systems are hobbled. For example, committees are formed and no decision can be taken until they report.

In the OLD-ESTABLISHED company, innovation may be disliked if this contradicts the accumulated wisdom of experience. Structures become fossilized and are unable to respond to changes in the environment. Planning becomes a matter of routine.

11.6   The Politics of Planning

Except when the planner is the sole owner of a one-person company and planning only for him/herself, all planning involves other people. In order for the plan to be accepted and implemented successfully, these others have to agree that it is of value, is achievable, and serves their interests. Persuading them calls for powers of persuasion, and in this respect all planning is political.

In theory of course, the owner of a large company may force through his/her ideas regardless of opposition, but an unpopular plan does not usually inspire the support needed.

Planning becomes necessary when there is a clear perception that change is needed, EITHER

- to overcome present WEAKNESS. Levels of dissatisfaction are intolerably high; OR
- to exploit a significant OPPORTUNITY; OR
- to meet a significant THREAT.

These three categories are derived from the framework for doing SWOT analysis; the analysis of weaknesses, opportunities, and threats (see 14.5.2). The first of the SWOT categories, STRENGTH, has been omitted. Planning for radical change is usually not necessary when the organization is in a position of strength. Calls for change are not persuasive when everybody is comfortable with the current situation. However, in such cases the planner may have the problem of convincing other members of the organization that the apparent success is illusory, and actually masks serious difficulty.

Commonplace examples occur when a company depends too heavily on a highly skilled staff member who is likely to leave. A few years ago, an insurance company in Thailand enjoyed the services of a well-known reinsurance expert, who enjoyed a pre-eminent position in the industry. However, he was by then an old man and obstinate, and refused to pass on his skills and contacts to other members. It was clear that in these circumstances, the company could expect to lose much of its highly successful business when he eventually left. Hence the owner was forced to treat this present strength as a future threat.

It is a characteristic of a good leader that he looks ahead to possible changes in the business environment, and plans against threats and for opportunities that others might not recognize. By 2001, assets of the global bank HSBC had been growing by 20 to 25 percent over the past 30 years, and the return on equity was exceptional. Making change is always painful and understandably, few within the bank saw any reason for taking radical steps when the existing model seemed to be so successful. The then new CEO, John Bond, realized that he needed

> a convincing rationale to shake things up. . . . He explained "I keep telling my colleagues that there is no such thing as static success. To be successful, you have to be dynamic and you have to keep changing."[1]

Table 11.3   Conditions for winning acceptance of the change plan

1. There is a clear perception that change is needed, EITHER
    to overcome present WEAKNESS. Levels of dissatisfaction are intolerably high; OR
    to exploit a significant OPPORTUNITY; OR
    to meet a significant THREAT.
2. Senior (and other influential) members of the organization believe that change is possible.
3. A specific change can be formulated.
4. The proposed change is welcomed.
5. Initial implementation procedures can be identified.
6. Resources for implementing the change are available – including change agents, training
    facilities and capital.
7. Persons taking part in and affected by implementation processes can be motivated to take part.
8. Environmental forces are supportive of change, or at worst neutral.
9. The likely cost of change appears less than the cost of EITHER
    (a) continuing under present conditions of weakness; OR
    (b) failing to overcome the threat; OR
    (c) failing to exploit the opportunity.

In general, top managers often have problems "selling" radical plans to managers at middle and lower levels, who are not mainly responsible for analyzing the environment and predicting long-term business cycles.

11.6.1   Political conditions for planning change

Table 11.3 shows the conditions under which resistance to making change can be overcome, so that members will agree to implementation of the proposed change. Unless all these conditions can be met, the likelihood of success is doubtful. The first condition – a clear perception of the need for change – has been discussed above.

When any one of these nine conditions is NOT present, the odds are stacked against your implementing a plan. Put another way, this means that change plans are unacceptable when the perceived cost of making the change is greater than the expected benefit.

11.6.2   Participants

Persons in the organization involved in this political process of planning include

*   The PLANNER.
*   A CHAMPION is a person with authority and influence. The champion secures support at senior levels and commits the organization's resources to achieving the plan.

- SUPPORTERS among superiors, peers and subordinates. Their support must be reinforced. NEUTRALS must be won over to support. If OPPONENTS cannot be persuaded to support you, you hope to move them to a position of neutrality.
- CHANGE AGENTS are responsible for implementing the plan and leading the change in each unit. They will also be responsible for communicating the plan.
- MANAGERS who are responsible for running the organization during implementation and after the changes have been made.
- AFFECTED PERSONS who will live with the consequences of the plan. They may feel anxiety when the change is proposed and they see their interests threatened. How can they be involved in the process?
- PERSONS IN THE ENVIRONMENT. Customers, suppliers, financial analysts, journalists, officials and politicians may all be affected by the plan.
- OTHER STAKEHOLDERS. Other persons or organizations with an interest in the outcome.

11.6.3   Barriers to change

Possibilities of making decisive change are reduced when the conditions listed in Table 11.3 do not apply, or are negated by opponents of change; see Table 11.4.

11.6.4   How opponents kill the plan

Opposition to the plan develops when

- members perceive that it threatens their existing or future interests. Some may lose their jobs;
- it threatens members' status and self-esteem;
- it creates unacceptable degrees of uncertainty;
- it promises unequal benefits; some units will benefit less than others;

Table 11.4   Barriers to change

(a) there is NO perception that change is needed;
(b) senior (and other influential) members of the organization do NOT believe that change is possible;
(c) NO specific changes can be formulated;
(d) proposed changes are NOT welcomed;
(e) initial implementation procedures CANNOT be identified;
(f) resources for implementing the changes are NOT available;
(g) persons taking part CANNOT be motivated;
(h) environmental forces are NOT supportive of change;
(i) the likely cost of change appears GREATER than the cost of continuing under present conditions.

- it involves unwanted retraining;
- it seems not to recognize the legitimate worries, ideas and opinions of members;
- the needs for planning and implementation procedures are badly communicated and are misunderstood.

Opposition may come from various quarters. Here we consider opposition shown by subsidiary staff to a plan developed in headquarters. Because they belong to the same organization, they appear to have interests in common. But headquarters managers make a mistake if they overestimate the degree of this common interest, and underestimate disparities in how they and subsidiary staff perceive the business environment. Particularly if they have been empowered in other respects, subsidiary staff wish to protect their independence. They may feel that they are doing their best in their particular circumstances, and do not see any need to change their agenda.

Here are tactics by which subsidiary management may prevent implementation of a plan introduced by headquarters managers or outside consultants acting on behalf of headquarters.

- They DENY factors in the model (Table 11.3). For example, they deny dissatisfaction with present circumstances, that change is possible, that specific changes can be formulated.
- Acquire a right to decide on change in certain key areas – for example, human resources.
- When any plan seems likely to involve changes in the human resource function, local management have the right to VETO it. In practice, they sometimes apply this veto only late in the implementation process – which creates extreme frustration for headquarters change agents
- DELAY. Suppose that change agents are expatriated by headquarters on short-term contracts. Local managers know that if they continue to delay in implementing the plans, these change agents will give up trying, or return to headquarters.
- Insist that every detail be discussed in committee, and TALK endlessly. They may arrange the composition of the committee so that opponents outnumber the supporters and neutrals.
- CONFUSE the issue by circulating misinformation and conflicting information.
- WRECK the communication structures so that the plan is not effectively communicated.
- Insist on PREREQUISITES for change – such as training – and then make sure they don't happen. Potential trainees are discouraged or prevented from attending training.

11.7 Implications for the Manager

1 Review Table 11.1 (the classic planning model). Use this to evaluate a change plan developed in an organization that you know well. How far does your plan match the model? What factors restrict its application? Consider these factors:
- national culture;
- organizational culture;

- identity of the planners; champion; change agents;
- size of the organization;
- industry factors;
- other factors in the environment.

2 Review Table 11.3 (conditions for winning acceptance for the change plan). Use this to evaluate a change plan developed in an organization that you know well. How far do these conditions explain the planners' success (or lack of success) in implementing the plan?

3 Review planning priorities, procedures and implementation in an organization that you have known over the past few years.

What factors have caused changes in these priorities, procedures and implementation? Consider the following:

- technological change;
- competitors and competition;
- human resources and staff;
- customers and change in the market.

11.8 SUMMARY

This chapter has examined the theory and practice of planning. All planning represents an attempt to control future events, and therefore has symbolic and optimistic dimensions. Section 11.2 examined the MEANING OF PLANNING, and focused on planning as forecasting, scenario planning, and routine planning. The "ideal" classic planning model was introduced in 11.3. In practice, this may be seldom applied in full – in part because attitudes towards planning are influenced by factors associated with the NATIONAL CULTURE, discussed in 11.4. Culture effects expectations of what it can achieve in a given situation. Different ORGANIZATIONAL CULTURES (11.5) typically apply different priorities and systems in planning. The effectiveness of planning may be decided by POLITICAL processes, in which different participants have interests which may conflict.

11.9 EXERCISE

This exercise asks what value planning has in different contexts and what factors need to be considered.

What plans would you typically make NOW for each of these events? What other plans might you make at later times? What factors explain the different levels of planning?

(a) Next week you have to meet an important business client at the airport. You have never met him before, and have not seen his picture. He is arriving on an international flight. The precise date and time of arrival is still unspecified.

(b) Tomorrow (or the next working day), you hope to go to work/study as usual, at your normal time. You expect to eat your normal food, and dress as usual.

(c) In two weeks the government publishes its budget. You own a company employing 500. If business taxes rise by more than 2 percent you will be forced into bankruptcy. If the taxes are unchanged you expect a small expansion of business over the next year – provided that you do not make unnecessary financial commitments now. If taxes drop by 2 percent or more you can earn large profits provided that you rapidly increase your product range.

(d) You are planning to make two presentations to major clients. These presentations are designed to elicit investments in the same research and development project. The first client comes from Culture X, whose members typically have high needs to avoid uncertainty and tolerate high power distances. The second client comes from Culture Y, whose members have low needs to avoid uncertainty and tolerate low power distances.

(e) Every year, your country is afflicted by very heavy monsoon rains, which regularly wash away large quantities of farming land. You are a poor farmer like your ancestors before you. The monsoon season starts next week.

(f) A consultant's report predicts that your company can only survive if your ten sales people acquire advanced new IT skills. You know that the team will resent losing time in training and would rather be out selling. They are a tightly knit group and loyal to each other – and to you. Three of them may be too old to acquire the skills, and in this case the CEO will expect you to replace them.

Note

1   Assif Shameen. Hold on tight. *AsiaWeek*, January 26, 2001.

CHAPTER TWELVE

When Does Culture Matter? The Case of Small/Medium Sized Enterprises

12.1   Introduction

Wang (2004) compared the problems faced by start-up entrepreneurs in the UK and Taiwan. She based her UK analysis on a survey of the literature, and the Taiwanese analysis on government reports and a small-scale interview survey, conducted in Chinese.[1]

Like the Anglo entrepreneurs discussed in 12.1, some Taiwanese entrepreneurs will fail in the immediate future. In 2002, the Taiwanese Ministry of Economic Affairs calculated that 8.3 percent of start-ups survived less than a year (Ministry of Economic Affairs, 2003).

But also like the Anglo entrepreneurs, they are driven on by psychological needs for independence and control over their own destinies. One of Wang's 12 informants said that he could never be happy with any job for more than a few weeks, and that his decision to start up stemmed from this dislike of working for others. Of course he hoped to make a profit from running his own business, but other than that his main reason was to satisfy my need for achievement. . . . I think my parents would always prefer me to stay in their plastics business and work together with them. But my wife and I think we can do something new, as we have the ability to do so.   *(p. 51).*

Wang's (2004) study is discussed further in 12.3, which examines how far cultural factors influence this stage of small business development.

This book warns against the dangers of overgeneralizing the importance of national culture. Section 1.1 raised the question WHEN IS NATIONAL CULTURE IMPORTANT, AND WHEN NOT? This question has been revisited a number of times since, and here we ask it again, in reference to start-ups and one family companies; when does national culture have a significant influence on the development of a small company, and when not?

12.2   The Start-up in the United Kingdom and United States

The START-UP is defined as a business in its first year of operations. Unless it has been hived off from a large, ongoing concern, it usually counts as a small business.

12.2.1   The small business

The SMALL business is defined differently in different countries. In the United Kingdom, the Companies Act of 1985 defined it as one with a maximum turnover of £2.8 million and a workforce of no more than 50 persons. In Taiwan it has fewer than 200 employees, but industry differences occur; in some industries (including agriculture, forestry, fisheries, water) a small business is classified as one with 50 or fewer employees (Ministry of Economic Affairs, Taiwan, 2003). The European Union defines a company with a workforce of less than 50 as small and less than 10 as micro (Johnson, 2007). In China, the small company employs no more than 100 persons. (Harvie and Lee, 2002) The Singaporean government defines the manufacturing small business in terms of investment (enterprises with at least 30% local equity, and fixed assets valued up to Singaporean $15) and the service small business in terms of staff numbers – no more than 50.

Both start-ups and small businesses tend to be family owned and managed. The FAMILY COMPANY is defined as a company started by an individual, and ownership and financial control is held by members of the family. Because they own all or a substantial share of the equity, they are able to control the financial and operating decisions. When the owner leaves the company, ownership is passed on to other members of the family. Family members may also work for the company.

Most companies everywhere count as small (or micro). In the European Union in 2003, 98.8 percent fitted into these two categories, and accounted for 56.8 percent of total employment (Johnson, 2007, p. 47). In the United Kingdom in 2000, almost two-thirds of all businesses provided work for only one or two people (Burns, 2001).

Leaving aside those spun off from large companies, the great majority of new start-ups count as micro (perhaps operated by the owner alone) or small.

12.2.2   The challenge in the United States and United Kingdom

In all cultures, entrepreneurial individuals prefer to go into business on their own, working for themselves and taking orders from no one. An American survey by Padgett Business Services USA, Inc. found that small business people valued independence (72 percent) most, control (10 percent), and satisfaction (10 percent).[2] A study conducted by the National Bureau of Economic Research in the United Kingdom found similarly that 46 percent of the self-employed were "very satisfied" as against 29 percent of those working for others (Megginson et al., 2003, pp. 24–25). Start-up owners tend to have a strong desire for independence. They expect concrete results.

Whether or not these concrete results are achieved depends in part on how the new company positions itself in the market. The start-up depends heavily on a small number of customers, which means it is far more vulnerable to the loss of a single customer than would be a large competitor and cannot influence price. Typically it operates in a single market and offers a very limited range of products. This means that the scope of operations is relatively very limited, and that it has greater problems than would a large competitor in diversifying business risk. The fight for day-to-day survival restricts opportunities for long-term planning. Taking on a single additional employee means that fixed costs are massively increased, and this may make the difference between making profits and very quickly going out of business.

In both the United States and the United Kingdom, manufacturing labor costs have risen to the point where start-ups with limited resources cannot compete in manufacturing sectors – and cannot compete with East Asian firms. In 2004, the CBI predicted that by 2014 there would be no jobs for unskilled workers in the United Kingdom:

> The prediction is based on the growth in "outsourcing" manufacturing and sales jobs abroad to economies where staff are hired at a fraction of the cost.[3]

In the service sectors, the Anglo start-up can flourish by delivering personalized service in tightly limited niche markets, and by innovating. If costs prohibit product innovation, opportunities may arise to introduce a new process, open up a new market, identify a new source of supplies, create a new type of industrial organization. However, the struggle for survival is bound to be difficult.

Any start-up is most at risk in its early life. In the United Kingdom almost 50 percent cease trading during the first three years (Small Firms Statistics Unit, 2000). In the United States, only four out of 10 small businesses survive more than six years (Megginson et al., 2003).

12.2.3   Explaining the problems

What problems can occur? An old survey conducted by Minota Corporation of 703 American businesses with fewer than 500 employees explained start-up failure by

1 Lack of capital
2 No business knowledge
3 Inadequate planning
4 Inexperience
5 Inadequate planning.[4]

And reasons for failure have not changed significantly over the years. In 1995, Birley and Niktari (1995) gave 24 reasons for start-ups failing in the UK, the first eight being

1 Capital structure
2 Management team
3 The economy
4 Customer diversity
5 Financial management
6 Owner attitudes
7 Rising costs
8 Lack of planning.

This list shows some correspondence with the Minolta survey – inadequate capitalization, poor management and lack of planning being common.

Megginson et al. (2003) argued that success factors in developing and managing a small business depended on a range of factors, which include the following (in summary):

- defining a market for the product;
- securing adequate capital;
- recruiting and using human resources effectively;
- obtaining and using timely information;
- coping effectively with government regulations;
- having expertise in the field;
- being flexible. (p. 31)

It may be inferred from this that problems are likely when the start-up owner

- fails to define a market for the product;
- fails to secure adequate capital;
- fails to recruit and use human resources effectively;
- fails to obtain and use timely information;
- fails to cope effectively with government regulations;
- lacks expertise in the field;
- fails to be flexible

But how far do these reflect the cultures of their Anglo environments? How far do the same challenges arise elsewhere? And in these other environments, what is the significance of culture?

12.3 The Start-up in Taiwan

The Introductory section quoted Wang's (2004) study of start-ups in Taiwan. This opens up the question of how far cultural factors influence the process of starting a new company.

In the past, start-up entrepreneurs in Taiwan depended on their own or family savings, and avoided government institutions that might render them liable to interference and taxation. These attitudes are changing, e.g. the erosion of family structures and the new importance of competing in international markets (most particularly with China – Taiwan's great economic and political rival). Some government funding was available, but was spread among all "small" companies – which in 2004 constituted 97.72 percent of all Taiwanese companies.

Wang's (2004) informants had little to say about government policy, and instead focused on the practical problems of operating with insufficient resources:

> You must keep a tight control of cash flows. Payment terms determine whether your cash flow should be tight or loose. ... Interest rates also affect cash flows. The flexibility of the cash flow also depends on the industry category. *(p. 56)*

> So far, the company hasn't reached its break-even point. We still have a lot of debt even though the company is earning. ... It will take us three years to balance the books. *(p. 56)*

> Small and medium sized companies don't earn enough profits to support their survival. They have to keep reinvesting. *(p. 56)*

The entrepreneurs may have been given moral support by their families, but little specific advice:

> None of my family members has start-up experience. ... I don't think I gained much business experience from my family because electronics are very different from plastics. But I definitely get full support from them. *(p. 57)*

> Many of my family members have managed their own companies in different industries. ... They offer me some tips. ... But for most of the knowledge on how to start-up I relied on myself. *(p. 57)*

They faced the common difficulty of finding a market niche that was wide enough to attract an adequate number of customers, yet not so wide as to involve direct competition with a larger company that is better resourced. They faced a further problem of maintaining their positions against very rapidly developing competitors in China:

> We may lose our strength in a few years as China can catch up very quickly. ... We are always on notice to change our lines very soon. So we have to strengthen our R&D capacity. ... If

the government can pay attention to this and give us some advice to help us keep one step ahead of China, we may be able to keep our strength for a little longer.   *(p. 62)*

Many responded to the problem of competing with low-cost producers in China by basing their own production there. But dealing with the Chinese bureaucracy was sometimes a problem. According to one:

> The three main [problem] areas are finance, law and government regulations, and managerial systems. We have to cooperate with a local agent because under this arrangement we can set up a company with RMB 100,000. Otherwise, setting up a foreign sole ownership needs US$200,000 capital. This is a typical law constraining ... a small start-up.   *(p. 55)*

They also complained about their own government regulations:

> The reason that the company chose not to stay in Taiwan was not because of costs but because labor law and social welfare is not fair to employers. ... This is why many companies now hire contract workers instead of offering permanent jobs. But this reduces staff loyalty to the company. So the real managerial problems don't come from the company itself but from government legislation.   *(p. 62)*

Staffing problems arose from the entrepreneur's lack of managerial experience, and from the difficulty of competing for trained staff with larger and wealthier competitors, and providing training to those who needed it:

> We don't have proper staff to develop new customers abroad. We have no budget to hire good staff.   *(p. 64)*

> Now we divide the whole process into many parts, one person just needing to know how to do his or her part of the job and this requires fewer skills and knowledge. Just like an assembly line, everyone needs to do a single part, so we don't need to train everyone to do everything. Thus we reduce training costs and keep staff loyalty as they feel less frustrated.   *(p. 66)*

12.3.1 *The relative unimportance of culture when starting up*

In sum, Wang (2004) found that most problems stemmed from the need for start-up capital, a lack of experience, identifying a secure market niche, government regulations, and finding adequate human resources.

Start-ups in different countries are influenced by local economic, legal and administrative factors. In many other respects, though, the problems are common. They often have difficulty in securing adequate capitalization. They can offer little security, and banks may prefer to lend to large, established businesses. In any situation, the start-up entrepreneur must

- define the industry in which the company will operate;
- define the market segment;

- decide how to serve the market segment;
- secure a position that can be defended against competitors;
- sustain this position.

Cultural factors may not influence this basic strategy, but may affect how the strategy is implicated.

The next sections discuss family companies in the Anglo, Chinese and Middle Eastern regions. It examines how far internal and external constraints are influenced by national culture and how far by business priorities.

12.4   The Anglo Family Company

Family companies can be found wherever they are permitted by law. Klingel (2002) cites figures showing that they comprise 67.2 percent of all in Malaysia, 66 percent in Hong Kong and 66.9 percent in Germany. In the United Kingdom, about 66 percent describe themselves as family owned.

Nevertheless, our understanding of them is constrained. Bjerke (2000) argues that the available theory is largely based on western scholarship, and in particular on US thinking. Similarly, Al-Rasheed (2001) argues that

> empirical research on Arab management has mostly applied standardized Western instruments of measurement in its investigation.   *(p. 30)*

This literature may not be sufficiently flexible. First, it tends to be prescriptive, showing how family companies might be established and managed with optimal efficiency according to Western criteria. Second, it pays little attention to factors in the local environment that might derail attempts to transplant Western models.

In all cultures, family entrepreneurs need to protect the company from conflicts arising between relatives when they work together in management. In 2003 a London business school report warned that in the United Kingdom

> family tensions will remain the key threat to these enterprises and anyone ignoring the issue could end up out of business.[5]

The typical Anglo response to this threat is to impose bureaucratic systems that have the effect of separating family and management roles by bureaucratizing the latter. But in cultures this overlap may be precisely the reason for preferring family members, who can be expected to show greater loyalty to the shared enterprise.

The standard advice made by Anglo consultants to family companies is that you avoid this threat by NOT employing family members if possible, and if you have to, employ ONLY when this person has appropriate work experience and qualifications needed for the position. If hired, the family member should

- be paid a fair market salary;
- be promoted, rewarded and if necessary terminated on the basis of job performance;
- NOT participate in the hiring of other family members;
- NOT directly supervise other family members.

In sum, impersonal job-related factors determine employment policies. The fact that Joe is your son-in-law or even your son is no reason to hire him unless he is qualified. Rather, your relationship is a reason for NOT hiring him. The alternative to employing family members is employing outsiders on the basis of their professional qualifications and experience.

Anglo management scholars recommend that the board of directors include professionals recruited from outside the family. Outside directors are defined as directors who are NOT

- members or close associates of the controlling family;
- present or retired employees of the company.

Their particular values lies in their ability to

- introduce new expertise and skills;
- give impartial advice which is not influenced by personal relationships;
- move the business to a more accountable system of corporate governance and greater transparency;
- advise on succession issues.

Succession issues are sensitive because familial and business relationships intersect. Decisions need to be made about

- who succeeds as controlling owner;
- the status of minority family owners;
- the obligations that the new controlling owner has in respect to his predecessor's policies;
- the rights held by the previous controlling owner, for as long as they live, to interfere in day-to-day operations.

This final point is contentious. The owner may delay retirement for as long as possible, and even then insist on retaining some authority. An American study comparing family company CEOs to senior managers in non-family companies found that

> even after retirement they hung around; 57% of them retained an office at the firm for at least two years (compared with 23% of senior managers).[6]

Leach (2007) proposes that there should be at least three outsider directors. But he recognizes that to many small family businesses, this is unpalatable. Practice does not correspond with expert advice, and research conducted in 2003 found that 61 percent of family companies in the UK had no outsider involvement at board level.[7]

12.4.1   How culture influences the Anglo family company

In individualist and low-power contexts, the entrepreneur derives much authority from his function or expertise rather than from family status. Here, "laws and rights are supposed to be the same for all" (Hofstede, 1997, p. 73). This means, first, that group interests, including family interests, are unlikely to be given automatic priority; and, second, that family connections may be less efficient than institutions in securing economic resources. Individuals are assessed on the basis of their skills and experience. Family membership does not automatically qualify the individual for employment, and competent outsiders are readily recruited.

Where collectivism is relatively low, notions of family loyalty are weak. Compared to members of a Chinese family company, family members may not feel driven to hang together in response to outside threats. Because family membership does not guarantee a shared body of experience and opinion, communications may be no faster or more reliable than in a public company managed by unrelated outsiders. Communications are bureaucratized and perhaps expressed by text and e-mails that have legal status, rather than by word of mouth.

Relations with the environment tend to be calculating and unemotional, being determined by impersonal and economic criteria rather than by family and clan emotions. The family company joins trade associations with similar firms, attends conferences, and shares information on market opportunities and threats.

In cultures where needs to avoid uncertainty are low, conflicts and competition – for example, between board members and different levels of the hierarchy – are expected, and are tolerated for so long as they are productive. Also, "citizens are positive towards institutions" (Hofstede, 1997, p. 134) – which include government and bureaucracies such as banks.

This has implications for financial policy. The entrepreneur does not make himself entirely dependent on personal savings and loans from friends and family, and is relatively willing to seek loans and investments from outsiders who require financial information relating to the firm's core interests.

12.5   The Chinese Family Company

The traditional Chinese company has a simple structure; either as management "spokes" around a powerful founder, or as a management structure on two levels. Table 12.1 shows a hypothetical company in which the entrepreneur has staffed all management posts with close relatives.

Table 12.1   A traditional Chinese family company

President: Tan Soo Sin (father)

Production manager L K Tan (son)	Marketing manager John Tan (son)	Finance manager Amy Tan (daughter)	Administrative manager Henry Siew (son-in-law)	Purchasing manager Lee Tan (son)
:	:	:	:	:
:	:	:	:	:

N O N - F A M I L Y W O R K F O R C E

Section leader Wong	Section leader Chung	Section leader Oi	:	:

The company is organized on a strongly vertical basis below top management levels, and very little information is communicated between functions; perhaps Wong, Chung and Oi scarcely know each other.

At the level of functional management – and assuming that family relationships are good – information is communicated relatively quickly. John Tan and Lee Tan are un-married and live in their father's house; L K Tan and his wife, and Amy and her husband Henry Siew, occupy houses nearby. They eat together several times a week. Hence Mr Tan is able to collect information and to relay his decisions quickly, and any decisions for which he invites participation are efficiently made.

We have seen that the Anglo company responds to the dangers of conflict between family members by limiting their participation. Professional and bureaucratic relation-ships and standards are emphasized in the hope that these restrict the play of familial emotions. The traditional Chinese response is the reverse. Family participation is valued because family members seem more likely to be trustworthy and show loyalty than do outsiders, and communication with them is easier and faster.

The bureaucratic controls exerted in an Anglo company may be absent – so that, in extreme cases, no regular salary is paid. A young Hong Kong Chinese commented:

> I used to work in the family business. But my brother didn't pay me. I complained to my Mum and she said you should be doing it as a favor.

The family assumed that its junior members should be willing to work from a sense of loyalty and be contented with room and food. In their terms, they were properly respecting her family membership, and so her complaints were inappropriate. But – like many of her generation – this particular individual had studied in the West and had been exposed to Anglo work values. She preferred to be paid a market rate for the job, whatever the identity of her employer.

12.5.1   Employing outsiders in the Chinese model

The Confucian Chinese company aims to maintain its family harmony and needs managers who offer both loyalty and expertise. A close family member who satisfies both criteria is preferred to an outsider. Difficult decisions have to be made when the family member lacks skills, or the preferred expert does not belong to the family.

The traditional company fears that a non-family member might

- leave to set up business on his/her own, and compete;
- be poached by a competitor;
- supply confidential data (e.g. accounting and financial data, customer and supplier lists, process secrets) to a competitor;
- supply confidential information to the authorities.

These fears are acute if the outside employee uses his experience in the company to develop skills that are valued in the labor market. The company may be unwilling to train a non-family member – and so the repertoire of skills available is restricted to those held by family members. This constrains the development of strategic goals and planning.

However, generalizations about traditional recruitment practices cannot always be taken for granted in the fast-changing economies of modern Asia. Employment decisions are increasingly complex and may involve permutations of family relationship, emotional ties, education, skills, market competition, the stage of company development. A student research project conducted in Taiwan by Wang (1998) suggested that the desirability of professional skills varies across functions, being very high in finance and relatively lower in human resource management. A non-family member might be more trusted in production and sales, then in finance, then in personnel management, and least in general management. This raises the question of who belongs to the family.

Liang (2007) found that Cantonese businesses interpreted the notion of "family" relatively strictly, often limiting it to parents and their children, whereas the Shanghainese include other family members.

12.5.2   Succession in the Chinese family company

In a traditional company, the controlling owner derives authority from his (or her) position rather than from function or expert power. He can take decisions quickly and without fear of a challenge. His authority is usually decisive, whether or not he has greater knowledge of the problem or not, and whether some other family member is better qualified. In his absence, the spouse or senior child temporarily assumes authority. The senior child can normally expect to succeed, perhaps under the tutelage of a surviving spouse. This pattern is complicated in cases where, for example, a junior child is more competent, or the controlling owner has two or more families and the children of the second – or subsequent – family demonstrate greater aptitude for business than do those of the first.

The children of Chinese family companies may start working in the business from an early age, regardless of regulations restricting child labor. Where this practice applies, the child may succeed to controlling ownership of a company in which he or she has already gained considerable practical experience.

12.5.3   Building an international identity

The successful Chinese family company or group of companies may be spread over a range of countries and continents. Wherever there are family members to participate in managing subsidiaries and related companies, the company looks for opportunities to establish itself.

A Chinese family company builds an international identity by developing its cross-border family and clan connections. First, this offers financial advantages. The wider the network, the easier it is to move capital to the points of greatest safety and of highest profit. Second, this arrangement offers production and marketing advantages. Suppose that an entrepreneur employs his eldest son in the family shop in Hong Kong. He trades gems with his uncle and cousins in Los Angeles and Singapore and buys property from a clan member in Thailand. He sends his younger sons to study in the United Kingdom, Canada and Australia, where they seek residence. A daughter works for a cousin in Amsterdam. Eventually, these children return to work for the flagship company or to establish their own companies.

Guanxi links are formed beyond the family with government and business leaders who can offer business deals, protection and privileged information. Suppliers, subcontractors and customers are courted. However, these skills in developing business links may not guarantee success in other cultural settings. Anglo business people do not recognize the meaning of *guanxi*, and the Chinese company cannot depend on its traditional tactics of relying on networks to arrange financing and reduce transaction costs. Fewer market niches can be accessed through connections in Anglo countries because information is distributed more evenly than in Asia.

Those Chinese companies that DO succeed abroad develop business skills and relationships appropriate to the non-Chinese environments in which they hope to operate. Pananond (2001) sees how four multinational Thai companies have used selective networking to offset their lack of financial and technological assets. Yeung (2000) shows that Chinese companies headquartered in Hong Kong often give their foreign affiliates considerable autonomy in running their own affairs, and exercise control and coordination through informal networks. That is, control is less centralized than in non-international Hong Kong companies.

Finally, despite the efforts made to protect their interests over time, Chinese family companies may be no more successful than family companies elsewhere. A Chinese proverb says that "Wealth doesn't last more than three generations." A similar Italian saying is "*il primo fa, il secondo porta avanti e il terzo mangia*" ("the first creates, the second carries forward and the third eats").[8]

12.6   The Middle Eastern Family Company

The Middle Eastern company employs family members and close friends in part because they owe loyalty to the family, and are likely to work more productively than would an outsider. One of Al-Tamini's (2004) informants reported

> We have a general rule, if there are two people who meet the qualifications, and one of them is a relative or a close friend, then we give the priority to that person.   *(p. 8)*

The need for trust often proved more important than the need for top qualifications when deciding on an appointment. This means that employing from your family and social circle offers an advantage – that they are less likely to betray you. They are more likely to be trustworthy than outsiders because they are themselves at risk if they prove unreliable. The second of Al-Tamini's informants gave the example of one employer who hired persons only from his own town because he knew them and their families

> so they weren't going to run away. He knew where they lived and where there their Moms lived, they grow up together.   *(p. 8)*

The entrepreneur feels most confident when able to keep close supervision on his managers, even though these may be family members.

In Middle Eastern and in Chinese companies the problems of maintaining loyalty are complicated in cases of

- MULTIPLE FAMILIES. When the owner takes a number of wives, either in sequence or at the same time, and each produces children, conflicts arise over succession rights.
- GENERATIONAL CONFLICTS. At one time father and children shared experience and expectations. Of late the younger generation is better educated – often abroad – and those with management qualifications are less willing to accept policies based on experience. Generational conflict is particularly dangerous in a time of rapid economic change.

The strategy adopted by many Middle Eastern owners is to protect one's power by limiting what information is made available to others. Another of Al-Tamini's informants suggested that

> Delegation ... does not come easily to most controlling owners. Typically they retain control of critical decisions regardless of the size of the company.   *(p. 7)*.

They may only delegate authority when the company reaches a size and complexity at which centralization is no longer productive.

12.6.1   Succession in the Middle Eastern family company

Typically, the controlling owner is followed by his oldest son. This has implications for the organizational culture. The son does not have the same degree of status – particularly if his father was the founder. He is obliged to negotiate with his brothers, and management style shifts from the autocratic to a coalition. The company structure shifts from a pronounced hierarchy to a triangle, with the successor at the apex. In societies where experienced middle managers are in short supply, the triangle may be relatively flat.

The company is most profitable when outsiders assume that the controlling owner has exceptional qualities. When he grows old and these qualities desert him, the company loses prestige. These problems of confidence become acute at the point when control passes to the heir-apparent. Some companies try to overcome these by following a long-term policy of training and monitoring the heir apparent – although this may mean sharing confidential information.

In Middle Eastern cultures, where age is more respected than in the Anglo cultures, the new generation have even greater problems in resisting the continuing influence of an experienced but no longer competent father.

12.6.2   The family company in Saudi Arabia

In some countries the structures of family companies not only typify the business world; they reflect and underpin the social structures. The Kingdom of Saudi Arabia, remains an absolute monarchy; the King is the dominant political figure, and the main arms of government are controlled by a tight network of royal princes and their dependants. Society is bound together by

> bonds of family and ties of honor that often go back several generations to their roots in Bedouin culture. Many of the prominent corporations are still in the hands of their original founding families such as the Olayans, Juffalis, Kanoos, Bin Ladens, Ali Rizas and Algosaibis   *(Al-Tamini, 2004, p. 2).*

These factors influence conservative attitudes towards developing new ideas and practices. New management systems are suspect; companies tend to recruit senior managers from family members:

> Saudi companies are slow to change. They have no proper recruitment systems, and management has not matured.   *(Malik, 2004, p. 130)*

On the other hand, the Kingdom is being forced to deal with the changes in the labor markets. Younger Saudis returning from training abroad increasingly expect to replace the expatriates and their seniors, who may have been in post for many years. A state of tension exists, as older managers have problems breaking with the old local ways, and younger managers are frustrated by failures to implement change in the face of resistance. The process of adjustment between traditional and global practices is painful and uneven.

12.7   Assessing the Influence of National Culture

This chapter has examined the management of small companies. Factors in the national culture seem to have little impact on some decisions, and much more influence over others. It has been argued that the problems facing start-up entrepreneurs are essentially the same across cultures. The responses chosen are also very similar, and differences may be explained by market factors and legal requirements rather than by culture. In any society, a successful company responds to a range of events in the business environment, and the influence of culture may be far from obvious.

On the one hand, it is a mistake to overestimate the impact of culture. This leads to mystification, and suggests major differences where they do not exist. For example, Huang (1999), finds these differences (among others) between how succession issues are handled in Chinese and Anglo companies:

- In Chinese companies, the process of succession is governed by top-down decision-making.
- Mutual trust is built around *guanxi*. The importance of personal relationships means that close relatives are usually chosen to succeed to general management positions.

But, to take the first point, succession issues are also decided by top management in Anglo companies. Although the opinions of lower levels may be taken into account, juniors do not make the final decision. And the second point; family business people in Anglo cultures may not articulate the principles of *guanxi*, but they are also far more likely to choose the new CEO from the controlling family.

On the other hand, it is hard to overlook the differences that occur between Anglo, Chinese, and Middle Eastern attitudes towards employing family members and outsiders, and these can be explained by reference to models of culture.

The point is that the influence of culture is seen to be variable. Whether or not it matters in any one instance depends both on the company interests involved and on the needs of the person making the analysis. As an example of the latter, Rutten (2000) examines the strategies employed by small entrepreneurs in India, Malaysia and Indonesia, and finds striking similarities. He argues that there are no significant differences between these and Western strategies. He focuses on the flexibility of these firms' strategies in adjusting to both commercialism and productive investments, and finds no evidence of cultural differences. This is not surprising, given the self-imposed limitations of his enquiry.

12.8   Implications for the Managers

1   Research recent start-ups in your culture and another culture. For each, rank these problems in order of difficulty.
- getting adequate financing;

- identifying a market niche;
- dealing with government regulations;
- finding good staff;
- owner's lack of experience.

How do you explain differences in your rankings for the different companies?

2 Research family companies in your culture and another culture. How does national culture influence start-up strategy within these different companies?

3 In each of the two family companies,
- Are family members employed?
- If you answer YES, in what positions are they employed?
- What criteria are used in appointing them?
- In what positions are non-family employed?
- How quickly and efficiently do members communicate?
- What disputes arise between family and non-family members?
- Compare your analyses of the two companies.
- What significant differences do you observe?
- How far can these differences be explained by
  - (a) the national cultures?
  - (b) the business environments?
  - (c) (other factors)?

4 Which of (a)–(c) do you think is most important in explaining the differences?

12.9 SUMMARY

This chapter takes up the point made in Chapter 1; that national culture is often but not necessarily an influence on decision-making, and that the problem for the manager is to identify WHEN culture matters and to respond appropriately. The chapter focuses on factors influencing small companies.

Section 12.2 examined THE START-UP IN THE UNITED KINGDOM AND UNITED STATES and saw that a range of non-cultural factors may be very important. These include access to finance, finding a market niche, dealing with regulations, acquiring staff, and the owner's experience and skill. Section 12.3 reviewed small-scale research into the START-UP IN TAIWAN and noted the importance of factors that might be found anywhere, regardless of culture.

On the other hand, cultural influences are clear when employment and succession issues in the small family company are considered. Comparisons were made between companies in the ANGLO region (12.4), the CHINESE region (12.5) and MIDDLE EASTERN region (12.6). Section 12.7 warned against overestimating the importance of NATIONAL CULTURE when explaining events in a company.

12.10 EXERCISE

This exercise asks you to suggest hypotheses that might explain differences in employment in SMEs.

Judt (2008) wrote that

> 65 percent of European jobs in 2002 were in small and medium-sized firms, compared with just 46 percent in the US.   *(p. 397)*

1 On the basis of what you know about the different cultures of Europe, and of the US, and about their business practices, develop hypotheses that might explain the difference.

2 What information might you need in order to test your hypotheses?

Notes

1 We are grateful to Wang Yen Chuan for permission to quote extensively from her study.

2 www.Dbtech.net/Padgett

3 Malcolm Moore. Unskilled jobs to go in 10 years. *Daily Telegraph*, November 8, 2004.

4 *USA Today*, March 13, 1987, p. 13.

5 A report by London Business School, cited by Richard Tyler. Family firms run risk of tensions. *Daily Telegraph*, September 22, 2003.

6 Passing on the crown. *The Economist*, November 6–12, 2004, pp. 83–85.

7 Family firms run risk of tensions. *Daily Telegraph*, September 22, 2003.

8 We are grateful to Kim Anne Barchi for this example.

Cross-cultural Management

CHAPTER TWO **Analysing Cultures: Making Comparisons**

CASE   RELATIONS BETWEEN MANAGER AND EMPLOYEES

An Indonesian manager was discussing labor relations with a manager from their British joint venture partner. The visitor said that he had recently officiated at a football match as a linesman. The senior official, the referee, happened to be his subordinate at work.

The Indonesian said that in his country this was not possible. In Indonesia, the boss and a low-level employee were always more distant outside the workplace than are their British equivalents: when the visitor asked why, he explained.

"In your country, the boss and the worker can still respect each other, because they separate the relationship at work from the personal relationship. But in Indonesia, that isn't possible. The person's status at work is carried out into the other things he does. In the culture he is the boss, wherever he is, and the staff will think that he is the boss, even outside office hours. This means that if his workers see him outside the office, they don't have to behave any differently than they usually do at work. So the boss must also be the boss at the football match, he would be the referee."

QUESTIONS

1 In your culture, does the manager carry his or her authority into other activities unrelated to the place of work?
2 What advantages do you see in the manager carrying his authority into other activities?
3 What disadvantages can you see?
4 Which aspect of which model discussed in Chapter 2 does this case illustrate?

DECISIONS

5 *Assume that you are a British manager working in your project based in Indonesia. How would this insight influence your behavior?*
6 *Assume that you are an Indonesian manager working in your project based in the United Kingdom. How would this insight influence your behavior?*

CHAPTER THREE   **Analysing Cultures: After Hofstede**

CASE   THE VENEZUELAN MANAGER

An Australian engineering company appointed a local manager to run its subsidiary in Venezuela. A few months later your consultant visited the branch and reported back to you.

"Sanchez knows everything about the business, and knows the customers well. The problem is, he's a micro-manager. He is always telling his subordinates how to perform the details of their jobs, and whether they're right or wrong. He expects to be consulted about every decision."

"And so?"

"In this day and age, that doesn't work. Employees expect to be given the power to decide for themselves how to do their jobs. You don't give that close supervision here, and there's no reason why your manager should in Venezuela. You should replace him."

"Did you see any signs of our local employees resenting his management style?"

"No. But how could I? I don't speak Spanish."

QUESTION

1   Does Sanchez's management style surprise you? Why? Why not?

DECISIONS

2   *What do you decide to do? You may choose more than one, but justify your choice.*
    (a)   Replace Sanchez immediately.
    (b)   E-mail him, saying he has three months in which to improve his management style (and how he should improve) or he will be replaced.
    (c)   Do nothing for three months, then make a check in person.
    (d)   Send Sanchez a message congratulating him on progress, and otherwise do nothing.
    (e)   Replace your consultant.
    (f)   (Any other. . ....)

CHAPTER FOUR **Movement in the Culture**

CASE   YOUTH OR AGE, OR YOUTH AND AGE?

Research shows that the proportion of over-50s in the European workforce will rise sharply after 2010, and after 2010, for the first time there will be more 50-year-olds than 30-year-olds working. Birth rates are declining and life expectancies increasing. The implications for European companies are reviewed in Garz and Gerdes (2007).

QUESTIONS

1 How do you think the ageing of the European workforce will influence the cultures of these countries?

2 How do you think it will influence the economic competitiveness of companies within these countries?

Now read the case.

Bente Johansen is human resources director for an engineering company based in Norway. The company was born in 1920, and manufactures lathes. There is a continuing market for traditional models, but plans are put forward to apply advances in laser optics into a range of new models. Sales to long-standing customers in Europe are still strong. But increasing efforts are being made to develop new markets in East Asia.

Bente has to develop a long-term human resources plan for presentation to the board, In the past, most new recruits to the marketing and engineering departments were fresh graduates in their 20s. Typically these persons worked with the company until reaching the obligatory retirement age of 65.

But recently, there have been increasing applications from older employees to continue working after 65. And there have also been applications made by over-60-year-olds made redundant or about to be made redundant by competing companies. Many have valuable expertise.

These two extreme age groups offer advantages and disadvantages. The YOUNG group have up-to-date technical know-how. They are more flexible, mobile and career-oriented. On the other hand, they need career planning, and lack practical and commercial experience. The OLD group offer experience, expert knowledge, business contacts, and proven commitment and loyalty. On the other hand they lack up-to-date technical know-how, flexibility and mobility, and have to be shown how to transfer their knowledge within the organization.

DECISIONS

3 *What should Bente advise the board? Taking into account your answers to (1) and (2) above, choose one or more of the following. Be prepared to justify your suggestions.*

(a) *continue the traditional policy of only hiring fresh graduates, and enforcing retirement at 65;*

(b) *hire at all ages but still enforce retirement at 65;*

(c) *drop the requirement that retirement is obligatory at 65;*

(d) *hire outsiders at 65;*

(e) *establish different policies for marketing and engineering (specify what. . .);*

(f) *(Any other. . .).*

CHAPTER FIVE **Organizational Culture**

CASE THE VIETNAMESE BANK

A bank in Vietnam employs young MBA graduates, and allocates them to two departments, domestic business, dealing with Vietnamese customers, and foreign business, for the most part dealing with foreign customers wishing to invest in the developing economy.

In the domestic business department, the organizational culture is group oriented and hierarchical. Members tend to stay in that side of the bank for many years – sometimes for all their careers.

The foreign business department has a different culture. Members expect greater individual autonomy, and operate relatively flat structures – at least in terms of standard banking practice in Vietnam. The attrition rate is greater than in the domestic business department, but top management accept that this is the price of attracting the ambitious, upwardly mobile graduates.

Graduates from Vietnamese business schools have relatively limited experience in foreign business practice and in using foreign languages. They are happier dealing with local customers, who appreciate their understanding of local business and society. On the other hand, graduates from foreign business schools are comfortable using foreign languages, and in some cases have extensive experience of foreign business practices. In general, they work effectively with their foreign customers.

The graduates of Vietnamese MBA schools are employed in the domestic business department, and the graduates of foreign schools in the foreign business department.

QUESTION

1 What does this arrangement tell you about the corporate organizational culture?

DECISIONS

The bank has hired you as a consultant to advise on whether or not it should restructure. The bank aims to compete more actively in global markets.

2 *What is your tentative response, and what new information do you need in order to make a considered proposal?*

3 *What advice do you give your client in respect of the organizational culture?*

CHAPTER SIX   **Culture and Communication**

CASE   BAD COMMUNICATION

In the United States, Connie Maxton was widowed four years ago and inherited her husband Jack's small furniture factory. She had never made any secret of her ambition to pass the business on to her son, Gary, as soon as he completed his education and had some experience. While waiting for Gary to graduate, she employed general managers, one of whom was Spike.

Sales grew at first. But after a year, Spike resigned and left for Florida. Connie tried to run the business by herself but she lacked the skills and decay set in.

Then she was introduced to Julia, who has a good record as a competent general manager, and hired her. Julia applied herself to learn as much of the business as she could. At first, her relations with Connie were good, and she received all the assistance she needed. The two women became friends, and began to socialize. The business was rejuvenated and the sales graph looked up again.

But then communication between them began to break down. Connie did not pass on vital documents. She refused to take Julia's advice about reinvesting profits. Julia decided not to give further credit to a long-time customer who had failed to pay his recent bills. She was horrified to discover that Connie had countermanded her decision.

"Why did you do this? Harvey is a crook and will never pay what he owes."

"Harvey was an old friend of Jack's, and he's a friend of mine. Family matters don't concern you. If you want to continue here, you must recognize the limits to your authority."

QUESTIONS

1   On the basis of the information given you, suggest what factors might have caused this breakdown in communication.

2   How far might the values of their shared American culture been a factor?

DECISIONS

3   *What advice would you give Julia?*
4   *What advice would you give Connie?*

AFTERWORD

Julia decided that the relationship could not be salvaged, and she resigned. She left for a vacation in Florida, and by coincidence, met Spike. They began to talk about their common experiences of working for Connie.

"The same things happened to me", Spike said. "There's a pattern. Communication was good. Then without warning, not. Sales dived, and I was put in a position where I had no choice. I quit."

QUESTION

5   *Do you want to revise your answers to (1)–(4) above?*

CHAPTER SEVEN **Motivation**

CASE   MOTIVATING WHO?

In the UK, a telecommunications company employed teams of engineers to make installations around the country. In the first years of the company's life, productivity had rocketed, but now was leveling out and in some regions, declining. Quality measures indicated a growing level of dissatisfaction among the teams. Absenteeism was a problem. Increasing numbers of these highly skilled experts were leaving, often to work for competitors.

It seemed possible that these morale problems had arisen from faulty service by the sales department, who were responsible for making and confirming orders, and scheduling the engineers' visits. However, an investigation showed this was not the case. On the contrary, the sales department had been winning industry commendations. The problem was restricted to the engineering department, and the company embarked on a crash program of generous incentives designed to keep these staff and attract new recruits.

Salary levels were raised, and bonuses paid for increased productivity. Easier working conditions were introduced and new cars provided. The most successful teams were awarded vacations abroad. The program succeeded, and productivity once again hit record levels.

But morale fell correspondingly among the sales force. A sales manager commented:

We work closely with those engineers so we know what's happening. They're being rewarded for doing their jobs and no more. But what about us? We were the best in the country, but the company never recognized us. Now they've sent out this message that only the engineers are valued and we're not. My best staff are leaving and I don't blame them. The moment the right job comes up, I'm off too.

QUESTIONS

1   What mistake has the company made?
2   How could this mistake have been avoided?

DECISION

3   *You are a consultant hired by the company to find a solution. What do you propose?*

CHAPTER EIGHT **Dispute Resolution and Negotiation**

CASE   THE NIGERIAN FAMILY FIRM

In Lagos, Umaru Engineering was started in 1947 to serve the auto industry. The founder passed away 10 years ago, and since then the firm has been run by his widow, Madame Umaru, Her three sons and a daughter-in-law shared the different management tasks between them, depending on where work was needed. This overlapping led to some confusion, but in general the firm succeeded in a competitive environment.

For instance, the eldest son was usually found in the showrooms, but also shared importing responsibilities with the third son, who had trained as an engineer. The daughter-in-law was book-keeper and accountant and reported directly to Mother Umaru, but sometimes helped her husband in dispatching

The second son Sanni was ambitious to develop his skills and enrolled on a weekend MBA program. He kept the family informed on the courses he was following, and before long argued that they needed more structure. "We must have a formal structure, which details each person's specific responsibilities. If everyone knows who is responsible for what, we won't have so many misunderstandings. Also our customers will be happier."

The family agreed to his plan. The eldest son should restrict himself to the sales and dispatch; the second son became import manager; the third son engineering manager, the daughter-in-law accounts. Mother Umaru took on the title of managing director.

Difficulties arose when the eldest son became bored with dispatching consignments to their customers. The third son was not prepared to take this responsibility, although was clearly underemployed in managing his team of skilled engineers, and moved out of the family compound. The second son demanded that his imports office be expanded, but this would have meant reducing the space allowed for accounts – which his sister-in-law resisted. She instructed her staff to collaborate only minimally with the imports department.

Soon, the family was wracked by conflict. A family friend attempted to mediate, but his offer was rejected by all. The final straw came when the daughter-in-law left her husband in order to live with an old boyfriend. Without an efficient accounts manager, the firm could no longer function effectively, and eventually collapsed.

QUESTIONS

1   What evidence is there for the cause of this conflict? Consider each of the following:

    (a)   inappropriate use of structure;

    (b)   personality problems;

    (c)   lack of negotiation;

    (d)   communication problems;

    (e)   lack of technical competence;

    (f)   the history of the firm before structures were introduced;

    (g)   (Any other...).

DECISION

2   *A similar family business asks for your advice in introducing formal structures. What advice do you give?*

CHAPTER NINE **Formal Structure**

CASE NO JOB DESCRIPTION

May Chung was from Hong Kong. She was being interviewed for a place in a graduate management program in a business school. She is about to graduate from her first degree program, and her teachers expect her to gain a top degree. But the second requirement for entry is that the student should have worked for at least two years. The interview went as follows.

"Have you any work experience?"

"None," admitted May.

"What do your parents do?

"They have a business. They import home furnishings. "

"Do you ever help them?"

"All the time. When I was 10 my parents started the business and they asked me to sweep and keep things tidy. Then I went on to stocking the shelves, and when I was a bit older I served customers. Now I help my father with the accounts and when he deals with suppliers."

"How do you find time for all this?"

"When I was at school I worked in the evenings and weekends when I'd finished my assignments, and also in the holidays. I still work there in university holidays."

"So you've been working in the business for about 12 years. You must know a lot about running a family business in Hong Kong."

"I do, yes. My parents told me everything. But they never gave me a rank or a precise job description. So I can't say that I have work experience."

QUESTIONS

1 Do you consider that the parents' treatment of May was unethical in this cultural setting? Explain your answer.

2 How is May interpreting the notion of work experience?

3 By what criterion should May be denied a place in the management program?

4 What problems might arise if she is admitted?

DECISIONS

5 *Suppose that you are dean of the business school. You wish to recommend to your colleagues that special consideration be given to applicants who do not meet all your formal requirements but have practical experience. What conditions will you set?*

6 *How will you justify your recommendation to your colleagues?*

CHAPTER TEN **Informal Systems**

CASE   PATRONAGE IN EUROPE

Based on your reading of Chapter 10, decide whether you AGREE or DISAGREE with each of these statements.

1 Patronage occurs only in societies that are economically underdeveloped.
2 Patronage occurs only in societies that have strongly collectivist cultures.
3 Patronage can occur in any society that lacks a strong sense of national identity.

Now consider the case of Belgium. This wealthy country lies at the heart of the European Union. Yet since its birth in 1831 the country has been divided and federalized between its two cultural groups, the Dutch-speaking Flemings and the French-speaking Walloons. Very little is shared by members of these two communities or "pillars", and there is very little shared feeling of Belgianness. The communities provide parallel administrations, and Judt (2008) describes the effects.

All political, military, civil service and even police appointments are made on a basis of "proportionality", which means that they are assigned to the pillars on a proportional basis. And the gift of these appointments lies in the hands of the leaders of these pillars, who distribute these through their personal networks. Political parties are thus reduced to acting as

> vehicles for the distribution of political favors. In a small country, where everyone knows someone in a position to do something for them, the notion of an autonomous, dispassionate, neutral state barely exists.
> *(p. 236)*

4 How far does Judt's example justify your answers to (1), (2), and (3)?

DECISION

5 *Your headquarters in New York is sending you to manage an international joint venture in Belgium. No one can tell you whether the project will be located in a Flemish or Walloon region. How do you prepare?*

CHAPTER ELEVEN **The Culture and Politics of Planning Change**

CASE   IMPROVING QUALITY CONTROL

Pierre is an organizational planner working for a French food production company. He has been given a two-year posting to a subsidiary on the Gulf. Headquarters in Paris is concerned about the quality controls currently been operated, and the legal risks involved. Pierre's task is to restructure the manufacturing teams so that standards of quality control are raised, the range of operations liable to inspection is increased, and externally based quality control officers can be introduced at critical points.

The problems are not new. Neither of the previous planners succeeded in getting their plans accepted within the time of their assignments, and both have since left the company – but unlike Pierre, neither spoke Arabic fluently.

The staff of the subsidiary are all Arab.

Pierre's proposals were accepted enthusiastically by headquarters, and by the subsidiary managing director, Mr Faisal. Pierre was initially optimistic that he would succeed where your predecessors failed. But unhappily, a few days after accepting the proposals this Mr Faisal was hurt in a traffic accident and has been hospitalized since. He is visited every day by his young son Hamad, who is working in your office and with whom you are on good terms. Hamad supports your ideas, but he is still young and not yet in top management. He tells you that his father is unlikely to return to work for another six months.

Mr Faisal has been replaced by a cousin, but he is a weak man heavily influenced by senior managers, none of whom has committed himself to or against – Pierre's proposals. But at supervisory levels and below opposition is beginning to grow, and senior management is bound to be influenced.

The opposition is centered on a quality officer and production manager. Neither has the technical qualifications for their jobs, and they can ex-

pect demotion if the proposals are implemented. When questioned directly, both claim to support the proposals – subject to certain conditions. The conditions they propose would have the effect of delaying any implementation by at least eighteen months, by which time Pierre would have exhausted his contract. These two persons have persuaded the workforce that if the proposals are implemented,

- they will be required to undertake more training;
- the training will be conducted in French – which few of the workforce understand;
- those who fail to pass the training will be sacked without compensation.

Only the first of these statements is true.

Headquarters are as frustrated as Pierre, but until now have been unwilling to become directly involved. He thinks that his customers would approve of the changes if they knew more, but he has no clear evidence.

At present Pierre's campaign to get the proposals accepted and implemented has stalled. There is no movement.

QUESTIONS

Pierre is an old business friend of yours, and at one time you worked with him in Paris headquarters, so you know some of the people involved. He has asked you to propose a plan by which he can revive the decision-making process, and get his proposals accepted.

1 Review the political factors involved. Which factors are positive? Which are negative?

DECISION

2 *Suggest a plan of action.*

CHAPTER TWELVE **When Does Culture Matter? The Case of SMEs**

CASE EXPLAINING DECISIONS MADE BY SMALL BUSINESS OWNERS

Decide how far each of these factors explains the decisions made in the cases below.

- social norms influenced by national culture;
- business practice;
- factors associated with personality;
- (any other factors).

(a) Forty years ago, Mr and Mrs Choo emigrated to the UK from Hong Kong. Now they own a small and very successful Chinese restaurant in Camden Town, London. They love cooking but both are in their sixties, and have grown tired of the business responsibilities. They decide to gift the restaurant to their eldest son, on condition that he employs them as his cooks.

(b) Mr Ahmed owns a small family engineering business in Cairo. For reasons of ill health, he has decided to retire. He wishes to hand on the business, which involves entertaining visitors, to one of his children. Fatima, the eldest, is very bright. She has a good understanding of business. Mahmoud, his son, graduated from school two years ago and is dull. Mr Ahmed chooses Mahmoud.

(c) In Taiwan, Annie Wong wants to start a small business manufacturing costume jewelry. She has 12 years' work experience in different industries, but has decided to branch out on her own, doing something that interests her. She succeeds in her application for a small government grant, but most of her financing comes from family members. Three of her uncles have agreed to act as directors on the board. All family members give her moral support, but none of them have any experience in this industry and they do not work for her. She staffs all levels of the business from non-family members.

On the advice of her father, she has selected Marvin to act as her (part-time) finance director. Marvin is an American, who also works for an international bank. He has no family or other business links in the country.

PART THREE

International Management

CHAPTER SIXTEEN   **E-Communication**

In comparison to face-to-face (FtF) communication, electronic communication offers the organization economies of time and economies of cost. However, it can also bring problems. The importance of cultural influences cannot be overlooked, and the organization may need to invest in training its members in cross-cultural use of e-mail. In practice, e-communication and FtF may complement each other.

CHAPTER SEVENTEEN   **Forming an International Joint Venture**

Participating in an international joint venture (IJV) is one means by which the company aims to achieve its strategic goals by investing abroad. It offers a range of benefits other than the possibility of making large profits. The IJV is always bound to be risky, in part because the partners operate in different national environments, both of which may be undergoing rapid change. Success and failure factors are discussed.

CHAPTER EIGHTEEN   **Opportuinity and Risk: Headquarters and Subsidiary**

Establishing a subsidiary is another means by which the company aims to achieve its strategic goals. By investing abroad, it incurs certain risks, and to protect itself implements control systems that protect and take optimal advantage of the opportunities. This chapter focuses on some of the systems by which a headquarters controls its subsidiary. Control exercised through staffing is discussed in the next two chapters.

CHAPTER NINETEEN   **Managing Human Resources**

Control exercised by staffing involves appropriate use of human resource management (HRM). This chapter focuses on local staffing. It asks how far HRM techniques developed in Anglo contexts are appropriate in contexts constrained by other historical, political, cultural and economic factors. A number of standard Anglo HRM practices are examined.

CHAPTER TWENTY   **Controlling by Staff**

This chapter deals with how the company uses staffing policies when exercising appropriate control in its investment abroad – whether a subsidiary or an international joint venture. Bureaucratic and cultural control techniques are discussed. A range of factors determine the choice of a local and or an expatriate as top manager.

CHAPTER TWENTY ONE   **Managing Expatriate Assignments**

The concepts of expatriate success and failure are flexible, and are understood differently by different people in different circumstances. But one point on which the experts agree is that the commitment of the expatriate's dependants is vital for success. This chapter emphasizes the importance of selection, training and support.

CHAPTER TWENTY TWO   **The Expatriate Brand Manager**

This chapter deals with the importance of brands to the multinational company, and shows the importance of brand management to the headquarters–subsidiary relationship. It shows the importance of ethical cause-related marketing, and examines the role of the expatriate brand manager in controlling brand communication.

CHAPTER THIRTEEN
Globalization and Localization

13.1 Introduction

In the sixteenth century, the Portuguese established a coastal trading empire between India and Japan. Their monopoly was then challenged by the increasingly efficient Dutch and East India companies. Between 1500 and 1800, Asian commodities such as tea, textiles, porcelain and luxury goods flooded into Western markets. The European traders found it difficult to export European products in bulk, and paid for Asian products with silver. This also led to the export of European scientific and artistic technologies to Asia. The East occupied an important place in the Western imagination. The reverse was also true. European objects and artifacts, sometimes reworked to suit Asian lifestyles, created a corresponding vision of a mysterious and exotic West.[1]

Large-scale trade across national borders is not a new phenomenon. A definition of globalization made simply in terms of a quantitative increase of trade does not explain why it is so important an issue today. The question is whether the trend that we are living through is simply a stage in this same pattern, or a new phenomenon. And if a new phenomenon, what factors distinguish it from traditional patterns, and how can it be explained?

13.2   Defining Globalization

Why does the concept of GLOBALIZATION excite so much interest? We are beginning to think about the world in new ways. The importance of borders between different countries is reduced, and cross-border structures are strengthened. The power of organizations operating only within the nation state is weakened. Individuals who possess the necessary skills find it easier and faster than before to implement complex interactions. By pushing computer keys a banker can almost instantaneously transfer sums of money between London and New York, between New York and Bangkok, between Bangkok and Paris, and so on. The political and legal institutions of these different countries no longer present insurmountable obstacles to doing business between them.

Despite offering these commercial advantages, the set of financial and technological factors that power globalization also have negative aspects. They radically influence how we lead our lives, and it seems that the changes can be neither fully controlled nor reversed. Individuals find it impossible to plan their futures more than a few years or months ahead.

The problems of predicting the effects of globalization in part stem from uncertainties about how the notion should be defined. These uncertainties arise because the terms are used in many different ways. Gowan (1999) reflects on this ambiguity in the introduction to his text:

> The 1990s have been the decade of globalization. We see its effects everywhere: in economic, social and political life, around the world. Yet the more all-pervasive are these effects, the more elusive is the animal itself. An enormous outpouring of academic literature has failed to provide an agreed view of its physiognomy or its location and some reputable academics of Right and Left even question its very existence.   *(p. 3)*

However, the term "globalization" is ambiguous, and this gives rise to confusion. In reference to Held et al. (2000), one reviewer argued the term has fallen into misuse, and social scientists of all disciplines needed to define precisely what they meant by it.

As the authors acknowledge, the term is "in danger of becoming the cliché of our times, the big idea which encompasses everything from global financial markets to the internet but which delivers little substantive insight into the contemporary condition.[2]

This chapter examines some of the different uses of the term. It is not necessary to agree on a single definition. What is more important is that the manager recognizes that different definitions are in currency, and identifies that which serves his/her purposes.

13.2.1   Uses of the term

The most general sense of the term is "applying to the whole earth". For example, in March 2003 the senior London representative of the Taiwanese government complained in a newspaper letter about reporting of the SARS pneumonia, then spreading across the globe has prompted the World Health Organisation to issue a "worldwide health alert". It has sent experts to the East Asia region to investigate and yet has still to respond to three similar cases Taiwan reported this month.

The writer complained that this was obvious discrimination against Taiwan, which the WHO did not recognize. The Taiwanese had as much right as anybody else to research findings into the disease, and to resources for prevention and cure. Furthermore, at a time when the world is growing smaller and killer bugs develop more virulent strains,

Taiwan's exclusion poses a serious danger to global health.[3]

Mr Yang's complaint about the WHO's political agenda (not recognizing the existence of an independent Taiwan) used the terms "globe" and "global" with an everyday sense equivalent to "worldwide". However, different specialists use the term with other meanings focused on their particular interests.

The specialist meanings examined below are as follows:

- globalization for politicians and political scientists (see 13.2.2);
- globalization for economists (13.2.3);
- globalization for industrialists (13.2.4);
- globalization for marketing managers (13.2.5);
- globalization for sociologists (13.3).

13.2.2 Globalization for politicians and political scientists

In politics and international relations the term "globalization" refers generally to increasing dependencies between national and international bodies. Barriers between nation states are reduced in importance and hence the autonomy of nation states is undermined. National governments and their agencies lose responsibility for and control over local decision-making, and individuals are even further removed from the locus of power.

This decline in local autonomy encourages the emergence of anti-state groups, including terrorist groups. For example, al-Qaida (the network) has operated over a range of countries throughout the world, and has itself taken on a global identity. In response to the new sources of conflict, nation states collaborate in building new forms of security by which they can be contained.

The political meaning of globalization has taken on the specific connotation of development of a New World Order which is dominated by the United States. The United States justifies its control of the global political and economic processes by claiming a need to protect its own interests and prevent instabilities in the wake of the collapse of the Soviet system. It employs its financial and military power to build its unchallenged position as a superpower, able to exert unequalled influence on other countries. In some eyes, this gives the right to determine events across the globe.

A journalist interviewed the former head of the CIA in the Carter administration, Admiral Stansfield Turner, and asked him if America was fit to be an imperial power. The Admiral was obviously irriated by the question, but put forward three reasons for a positive answer. First, the United States had won the Cold War decisively. Second, the United States was the most democratic country in the world and the best example of free trade, all other countries were following in the same direction and those that attempted to stand out against the trend would be trampled under foot. Third,

> the world needed a leader, and no one else can do it. The EU didn't stand up on Bosnia. We did. The EU couldn't stand up on Kosovo. We did. So it doesn't make much difference whether we're fit or not. We're there, and no one else is.[4]

Anyone who disputed this should be prepared to show why.

Governments that accept American political priorities are rewarded with trade agreements and development aid. Governments that do not are denied these opportunities and in extreme cases may be actively destabilized. States such as Cuba, North Korea and Myanmar (Burma) have refused to subscribe to American authority, and have paid an enormous cost. In 2007, the United States waged a financial war on Iran designed to isolate its economy and to compel it to abandon its dangerous nuclear programme. American, European and Japanese banks agreed not to conduct business with Iranian clients. It was reported that as a result,

> Iranian companies had seen their import costs rise by 20 or 30 percent because they had to employ middlemen to evade financial restrictions.[5]

13.2.3   Globalization for economists

Managers sometimes limit their definitions of globalization to perceptions of a quantitative increase in international trade – whether measured by value or volume.

But this phenomenon is not new. The Introductory section describes international trade between Europe and Asia since 1500, but in fact the history is far longer. The Silk Roads between China and the West were garrisoned during the Han Dynasty, over a hundred years before the birth of Christ. At one time or another, Phoenicia, Carthage, the Hellenic world, and Rome all stood at the center of trading networks that steadily grew to dominate their regions.

One effect of competition has always been to punish a loser and to drive it out of the market. In general, the firm able to produce at the same standard but at lower cost is likely to prevail. The novel factor is that when firms compete on a global basis as opposed to a local or national basis, the loser is as likely to be driven out by a competitor based in some other country as by a neighbor.

Globalization theory commonly refers to the ever-increasing mobility of capital across the globe, and the impact that this has on national economies. However, it involves more than simply a quantitative increase in capital enterprise. "Capitalism" is defined as the investment of finance in creating new productive capacity, and hence international or global capitalism means the investment of funds earned from one country in a project based elsewhere. This is not the same as global trade; the profits derived from trade only constitute capital when they are reinvested or are available for investment.

Capitalism was internationalized centuries ago. For example, the Rothschild banking family was founded in Frankfurt by Mayer Anselm (1744–1812). His five sons established branches in Vienna, London, Paris and Naples. The company continues to be based in Frankfurt but funds move easily between the original branches and many new branches. Also the many complexities have historical roots:

> The whole canopy of forms of capitalism – commercial, industrial, banking – was already deployed in thirteenth century Florence, in seventeenth century Amsterdam, in London before the eighteenth century. *(Braudel 1984, p. 621)*

Gowan (1999) points to a recent shift in modern capitalism that can be associated with globalization. He notes the difference between money-dealing capitalism and the employment of capital in the productive sector. In the first case, the capitalist aims to make profits from trading funds regardless of the sector from which these profits arise, and in the second case, the capitalist invests money in the production of goods and services which are sold at a profit and possibly contribute to social life. These two functions also have long histories. But Gowan argues that the phenomenon of globalization is characterized by a massive increase in money-dealing capitalism and a relative decline in productive capitalism.

We need a definition that captures the unprecedented changes that are occurring in our political and economic lives. Notions of globalization which fail to explore the political and cultural dimensions of international monetary regime that has existed since the mid 1970s will miss central features of the dynamics of globalization.

13.2.4 *Globalization for industrialists*

A GLOBAL INDUSTRY is commonly taken to mean an industry which is able to operate across national boundaries with a minimum of disruption. This is made possible both by a lack of government regulation and by common operating procedures and structures. That is, firms in the industry have the same or very similar priorities and do not distinguish between competitors in their own country and competitors elsewhere.

The need for dependability and trust has led the banking industry to adopt procedures that can be recognized and applied everywhere. For many years the Japanese industry stood out against accepting the global structures; however, the increasing fragility of the industry after 1970 forced it to conform with American and European norms. Developments in information technology now mean that capital transactions can be made almost instantaneously to anywhere in the world. An electronic capability also reduces needs for large investments in premises and staff.

A global identity may simplify procedures and reduce misunderstandings, but cannot eliminate all weakness. A report by the Electronic Banking Group of the Basel Committee for Banking Supervision (2001) noted that in addition to those traditionally associated with strategic and business uncertainty, credit, liquidity, markets and foreign exchanges, some risks were increased. These included

- operational risks – including risks associated with the technological;
- infrastructure, security, the integrity of the data, system availability, internal controls and auditing, and outsourcing;
- reputational risk;
- legal risk.

International transportation industries, such as air transport, also have to develop systems that have global applications in the sense that they can be used in different countries, and the language used with certain procedures may also be in common usage. Air pilots are required to use English when communicating take-off and landing priorities with air traffic control staff everywhere. Other industries have far less need to apply the same systems; there may be no need for department stores serving local markets in Tokyo, New York and Sao Paulo to follow common operating procedures.

In general this book refers to "multinational" companies rather than to GLOBAL companies. This is to avoid confusion; companies with multinational interests relate to their investments and customers in a range of ways, and in Section 18.3 the term "global company" is used with a specific meaning to refer to one type of multinational relationship. In general, multinational companies are defined as those that own and manage investments located in countries other than that of headquarters. The factors that influence the ownership structure of any one company include

- the legal requirements of the country of headquarters;
- the legal requirements of the country of investment;
- the industry norms;
- the organizational culture;
- the organizational strategy.

Management structures may vary widely. Different companies have different needs to control relations between headquarters and foreign investments, and these needs are reflected in how control is centralized and decentralized. The factors influencing these relationships are discussed in Chapters 17 and 18.

13.2.5 *Globalization for marketing managers*

A GLOBAL PRODUCT is developed and sold in response to common demands in different nations. When the marketing manager identifies shared customer aspirations and similar marketing infrastructure (in terms of distribution system, logistics, media and regulations) the company can develop a standardized good or service that appeals to the shared needs. A global product creates a sense of shared interest and identity among its producers and purchasers, whatever their country, and differences between national and foreign markets disappear. For example,

> Coke has successfully purchased the once civic-minded song "We are the World" on the way to "eliminating the very concept of a 'domestic' and 'international' Coca-Cola beverage business". *(Barber, 2001, p. 294)*

In practice, the list of truly global products is short. It includes certain makes of automobile, electronics, cigarettes, some leisure products including drinks sold on the basis of the lifestyle they project. And of even the most widely used products, few are global in all respects. In different countries, a product claimed to be the same everywhere may be produced from different materials; in Muslim countries, burgers might be made from lamb or chicken and never from pork which is forbidden. The same electronic device may be produced from slightly different components, perhaps less in response to local taste as to local licensing regulations.

Marketing managers might wish otherwise, but in practice even a global product may be purchased by different market segments, or valued for different reasons. In Chicago, fast food may be consumed by office workers as a rapid lunch at midday, perhaps in the street. In Bangkok, students may sit for hours in the fast food outlet. They value the restaurant as a symbol of youthful modernism, and they meet there in order to participate in it.

> The marketing strategy may reflect local demographic and socio-cultural features. Although McDonald's has used drive-through outlets in the US since 1975, these have only recently been introduced to China, where changing lifestyles and a growing acceptance of more diverse foods are creating a fertile environment for the drive-through business. . . . Among customers visiting our drive-throughs, 30 percent choose to use the drive-through facilities instead of going inside the stores, compared to 65 percent in the United States.[6]

13.2.6 *Globalization for sociologists*

Sociological interest focuses on the how far there can be said to be a global culture. It is sometimes argued that all national cultures are converging – and this is sometimes advanced as an argument for not wasting time in cross-cultural analysis and training. Not all scholars agree. Gray (2000) has argued that

> The belief that modern societies will everywhere converge on the same values does not result from historical inquiry. It is a confession of faith. In fact late modern societies show little evidence of any such consensus. They differ from each other too much.
>
>   There are many ways of being modern. Different societies absorb science and engender new technologies without accepting the same values. The idea that modern societies are much the same everywhere which is still defended by Enlightenment fundamentalists, has scant support in history. *(p. 24)*

In respect to management studies, many years ago, Child (1981) reviewed the arguments advanced by both sides. One group of scholars were arguing that convergence focused on increasingly common use of the same structures and technologies, while those claiming a lack of convergence or even increased divergence dealt with the behavior of people in organizations. Different cultures apply technologies and structures in different ways, even in cases that they appear to converge.

13.2.7   Is there a global culture?

Globalization reflects an ideology of modernity and the assumption that a single, universal community can be established, founded on principles of reason that are accepted by everyone. The assault on traditional value systems is spear-pointed by global organizations and, on a human level, by those who decide strategy in these organizations.

The persons responsible for taking these global decisions include

- the owners of prominent global companies in the private sector; the large capitalists and shareholders;
- senior managers of these global companies;
- senior managers of international not-for-profit organizations. These include organizations with an extra-national identity such as European Union, the United Nations and the World Bank, national organizations such as embassies, and international non-governmental organizations such as OXFAM and Care.

How far do these elites constitute an international "class"? This depends on your concept of the notion "class", but they certainly have powerful common interests. They spring from their own national bourgeoisies, but are increasingly alienated from them, and appear to have more in common with each other than with members of their national groups. They share broad economic and political interests and have interlocking directorships. They communicate by using a shared global language (English). They have shared global tastes in food, clothing, cultural pursuits, and sports. (Golf appears to be most general.) Many have studied at the same elite universities and business schools.

How far do they constitute a culture group? This can be argued either way. Applying Hofstede's definition of a national culture (1.3.3) it can be claimed that the global culture

- is common to those categories listed above and not to others – but that these categories do not share a common geographical area, as do members of French culture, Japanese culture, and so on;
- is learned, and is not innate. But this learning may be heavily institutionalized, from school age. The European Union budgets over £160 million a year to provide free education for the children of EU officials and accredited diplomats. In 2005, 20,000 children were enrolled in the 13 schools, in which £8,000 a head is spent on pupils annually:

> The European schools teach a special curriculum with a strong emphasis on foreign languages, as well as the culture and values of the EU. . . . The schools' mission statement says

"pupils shall become European in spirit, while preserving their love and pride for their own countries, and shall be well prepared to complete and consolidate the work undertaken by their fathers, towards the creation of a united and prosperous Europe."[7]

- is passed down from one generation to the next. The story above supports this;
- includes systems of values. But how far are do these correspond to Hofstede's notion of values in the national culture, and how far to the more superficial values consciously espoused by an organizational culture?

13.3   The Social Effects of Globalization

The globalizers (whether or not considered a "class" or a "culture group") do not exercise direct rule on national governments, but through exercising influence on national governments. They use their organizations to persuade national governments to conform with the dictates of globalization. They exert influence through control of their companies and other organizations, by formulating and implementing strategies for globalization. These strategies are always likely to be antagonistic to local and particular interests, at least in the long term. In this respect members of the globalizing class are opposed to the democratic theory that major decisions are made by politicians responding to the will of the national majority, and expressed through democratic processes.

Key decision-makers have increasingly less need to reflect and respond to national interests. Their local commitments are increasingly driven by marketing considerations. The overall effect of this drive towards a globalized rationalism, outside the control of local politicians, is to devalue local political action. Local politicians who fail to support local interests lose local trust. Those who fail to meet the needs of the globalized class risk attack from that quarter and may be unable to hold onto power. In either case, the capacity of the politician to adequately represent his or her constituency is endangered, and so democratic institutions in general are endangered.

13.3.1   *Local responses*

Responses to globalization can take benign forms in the rediscovery and development of local arts and culture. The past few years have seen the massive growth in regionalized "world music", although the technologies used to record and transmit it are common everywhere.

But reactions may be more sinister. Over the past few years there has been a sense of frustration among those who are losing control over their power to make decisions, and processes that were once welcomed may be increasingly resented. This has been the fate of the EU project, for which support across Europe is in decline. This fear of losing local identity is even more evident elsewhere, and may be resisted with violence – for example, in Arab countries concerned with American influence in Palestine and the region.

The activities of extremist groups such as al-Qaida do not simply express fundamentalist Islam. They can be read as a measure of the powerlessness felt by those unable to compete with the cultural stereotypes projected from outside, and this powerlessness is expressed through that aspect of the local culture that stands apart from the all-encompassing values of globalization – in this case, militant Islam. Stern (2003) discusses a number of Islamic, neo-Nazi and White supremacist groups and argues that they

> view the September 11 attacks as the first shot in a war against globalization, a phenomenon that they fear will exterminate national cultures.   *(p. 38)*

This argument suggests that terrorist and revolutionary ideologies will become increasingly attractive wherever people feel that they have been displaced from their accustomed economic, political and cultural systems. Extremism provides meaning to the disoriented and culturally deprived.

Rather than leading to an equal sharing of prosperity, globalization seems likely to cement differences between rich and poor countries rather than dissolve them.

Globalization has contributed to growth in many countries, but not in all, and has the effect of creating a new division of labor. African countries are economically furthest removed from the main globalizing powers and have benefited least. The continent's share of world trade continues to decline, and this has had the effect of isolating these countries from

> the global economy and its detachment from growing world prosperity. Over the past decade, sub-Saharan Africa's trade has grown 39 percent, while world trade has increased 85 percent. In the same period, African GDP grew less than 8.5 percent, against a global figure of over than 44 percent.[8]

In terms of orthodox theories of globalization, this shouldn't be happening. Grey (1990) described the underlying belief thus:

> Western capitalism will soon be accepted throughout the world. A global free market will become a reality. The manifold economic cultures and systems that the world has always contained will be redundant. They will be merged into a single free market.   *(p. 1)*

Grey argues that this enterprise is impractical. Similarly, Elsom (2007) points out that cultural engineering attempted on a global scale is most unlikely to meet its supposed objectives. Rather than leading to a fairer world order, it increases ever greater disparities between those countries that can contribute and those that cannot. Those outside the loop cannot grow enough food for their populations nor afford to import it. What has made matters worse is that their traditional social structures, such as tribal and family loyalties, have been undermined by the poor imitations of Western management models imported with the investment and development aid.

13.3.2 *The movement of labor*

Large-scale migration causes problems in both the country from which the migrants come and the countries to which they move. In their original home countries, the traditional social structures are undermined by the mass emigration of the working population when only the very old, very young, and those unable to emigrate are left to depend on earnings remitted by their relatives working abroad. The loss of working people in their prime endangers social and cultural structures. In the target countries, mass immigration inflames resentments and insecurities among those locals who feel their economic and cultural identities at risk.

Most people prefer to emigrate to where the standard of living is highest, and the economic opportunities greatest. This means that they would prefer to move to, say, the wealthier nations of North America and Africa than poor African nations. When the better qualified people of working age emigrate from the poor nations, their productivity results in the rich growing ever more prosperous and developed. Their intellectual and artistic cultures are enriched by the influx of new ideas and values. Hence they attract yet more skilled migrants. And so the gap between more and less developed countries widens rather than narrows. The less developed countries lose twice – once because their competitors have gained additional talent, and secondly because they have lost whatever skills they had.

13.3.3 *Labor markets*

This pattern of migration from the poor to the rich nations is partly counterbalanced when jobs are moved from regions where the cost of labor is high, to where it is lower. When the same skills are available at lower prices (and all other factors being equal), the company may be able to relocate at least part of its operations.

Jobs are transferable under conditions that

- production processes can be fragmented without loss – say process A performed in a Country X location, process B in a Country Y location, and so on;
- the production output can be transferred between locations without incurring significant losses;
- the same skills are available in different locations.

And the jobs are transferred to the lowest-cost location when all other factors are equal – skills levels, other resources, and so on.

The call-center industry provides examples. In 2002–3 the Bank of America slashed 4,700 of its 25,000 tech and back office jobs. These jobs had not been eliminated because business was failing. Rather, many were outsourced to companies in India where work was then costing only $20 an hour, as compared to $100 in the United States. Indian labor might be relatively cheap, but it was expert. Indian suppliers recruit staff from the massive numbers of knowledge graduates trained by local technology universities.

Similarly, in 2003 HSBC – the world's second largest bank – moved 4,000 British jobs to India, China and Malaysia in the biggest single export of finance positions to Asia. The jobs involved mainly processing work and telephone enquiries. At this time the bank employed 55,000 people in the United Kingdom. Some experts predicted then that in the financial industries overall up to 3.3 million jobs in the US and 2 million in other Western countries would be lost to lower costs countries such as India.[9]

The dependence on non-local staff who may have no experience of the conditions in the country of the customer has led to a reaction in some sectors, and in the UK some banks now advertise that all enquiries are answered in local call centers. This may give opportunities for further business.

13.4   The Roots of High Globalization

We have seen that notions of "internationalism" are too weak to define the recent rapid development. But how do we explain the trend towards HIGH GLOBALIZATION over the past 30 years?

High globalization has specific historic and cultural roots that can be located precisely in time. This aspect of globalization arose from the

- internationalization of finance;
- internationalization of production;
- development of information technologies.

13.4.1   The internationalization of finance

In the early decades of the twentieth century, capitalist production tended to be restricted to the nation in which the headquarters was located. A capitalist might have far more in common with capitalists from his own country – whether or not they belonged to the same industry – than with capitalists from elsewhere. This affinity extended beyond culture; they depended upon and contributed to the same financial system, which were in many ways still local.

The disasters of the First World War, the slump of the 1930s and the Second World War eroded the autonomy of national financial systems. After 1945 the least damaged of the major belligerents, the United States, led the development of security and economic systems which would safeguard the world from further destruction. Also, Washington needed trade partners, and the economic recovery of Japan and the major European powers seemed the best way to block the progress of communism. In Europe, the United States invested in the highly successful Marshall Plan. The Bretton Woods system was designed to create financial stability. Exchange rates were fixed within 10 percent. The dollar acted as an international currency, and its value was fixed in gold. Each country's government exercised its own exchange controls. The World Bank and IMF were established under American controls to police and stabilize this system.

It seemed that in 1972 the American guarantee of world peace, Pax Americana, was beginning to break down. The United States had overspent in financing the wars in South East Asia, and in response to the emergent Eurodollar. Washington stopped honoring its promise to transfer every dollar into gold and the Bretton Woods agreement collapsed. The financial game changed radically. Freed from centralized controls, foreign currencies could be traded for each other across borders like any other commodities. Speculators made the best of their opportunities and wealth was increasingly created from paper money rather than from production.

Financial markets grew at rapid rates. The total value of financial assets traded in global markets in 1992 was $35 trillion, twice the GDP of the 23 richest industrial countries. Estimates put their value at $83 trillion by the year 2000. In the past, a far greater proportion of wealth was derived through the creation of goods and services that served social needs. But in the era of financial globalization, wealth is increasingly derived from trading financial assets, so that this activity now offers the greater return on capital. Increasingly, the commercial value of information about money outstripped the value of productive investment.

In the 1990s, the growing strengths of some European and Asian economies forced the United States into a greater awareness of its needs to protect its own economic superiority. The Washington Consensus developed cooperation between the Treasury and those international organizations that the United States dominated, such as the World Trade Organization and the International Monetary Fund (IMF). The IMF ideology of free-market economics and foreign direct investment was increasingly used to give American companies access to foreign markets without necessarily facilitating foreign investments in the United States. That is, the IMF was most active in pushing for those structural adjustments that best suited American interests.

The internationalization of finance means, first, that business people everywhere should be able to move capital around the world almost instantaneously and without hindrance from national governments. In practice American influence over the international regulatory authorities gives American companies a leading edge. Second, the drive towards globalization has been led by the financial industries and other service companies; with the exception of the oil producers, most businesses that sell a manufactured product have been outstripped.

13.4.2   The internationalization of production

In the first half of the twentieth century, economic leadership passed from Europe to the United States. After 1945, the American economy emerged as the major international creditor, owed vast war debts by the previous leaders, the United Kingdom and France and far more productive. American production systems became increasingly global, designing goods for a world market, producing in several countries at once and targeting their financial and marketing strategies to the world economy, not only to the American economy. But it was still the case that in any one production center, all aspects of the production process were centralized under one roof; raw materials were fed into one end of the factory and the completed automobile emerged from the other.

This philosophy dominated manufacturing systems until the 1970s when Toyota and other Japanese manufacturers began to experiment with the internationalization of production. The principle of this new post-Fordian system was that the manufacture of a complex good could be diversified to different locations. Each manufacturing center depends upon good relationships with local suppliers and good communication with up- and down-stream centers. The different parts of the good are then assembled at a location conveniently close to the sales outlet. This means that different aspects of manufacture and assembly can be located outside the home country – just as Toyota cars targeted at South East Asian markets were assembled from engines, gearboxes, chassis, and so on, produced in different countries across the region.

The Japanese automobile and electronics industries were the first to develop this international division of labor. Manufacturing plant in each country specialized in producing those parts for which the local resources of talent, materials and capital investment best suited it. This globalization of production meant that Japanese companies could produce and sell almost anything anywhere. Their success in pioneering the techniques meant that by the 1980s Japan seemed to be the only economic giant set on a course of continuous expansion. The United States was facing a crisis of archaic manufacturing plant. Having rebuilt its industrial base since the Second World War, European countries apparently enjoyed an advantage, but were hobbled by continuing fuel shortages.

The globalization of production was facilitated by the globalization of finance. The breakdown of localized exchange controls meant that capital could be moved across national borders to purchase new plant and materials, hire a new workforce, or acquire a competitor. Both aspects of globalization did more than make adjustments to the prevailing economic system; they introduced major structural changes. They were made possible by a third factor, the development of information technologies.

13.4.3   The development of information technologies

In the 1970s, readjustments in the US manufacturing sector caused a shift in economic power from the traditional heavy industries to the development of new industries associated with information technologies. In geographical terms, this meant a shift from towns like Detroit and Chicago to Silicon Valley. America's competitive edge in the development of the micro chip technology helped rebuild the US economy. Developments in IT enabled the United States to restructure industry and organizations and to take advantage of its leading role in the financial sector. Capital is easily transferred around the world by pressing a few computer keys. The United States was quickly followed in exploiting the technology by its principal competitors, and increasingly, by middle-ranking economies that had previously played little part in international business other than by hosting multinational subsidiaries.

At a time when developed national markets were saturated and the structural limits on real wage increases reached, this technological revolution has allowed capitalists to escape national restrictions. Mittelman (2000) comments that

> with new technologies, especially space-shrinking systems of transport and communications, the sites of manufacturing are increasingly independent of geographical distance. Capital now

not only searches for fresh markets, but also seeks to incorporate new groups into the labor force. *(p. 38)*

IT not only frees production from geographical dependence on headquarters, but also gives the company greater facility in transferring production from one location to another.

13.5   Implications for the Manager

How does globalization effect your organization?

Decide which of these statements APPLY to your organization (company, business school, or other). If necessary, check your answers with people who have worked there for longer.

(a)   Ten years ago it was possible to predict major changes in markets a year ahead. This is no longer the case.
APPLIES / DOES NOT APPLY.
(b)   Ten years ago it was possible to identify our main competitors in the year ahead. This is no longer the case.
APPLIES / DOES NOT APPLY.
(c)   Ten years ago, it was possible to keep our understanding of new technology up to date. This is no longer the case.
APPLIES / DOES NOT APPLY.
(d)   TEN years ago, how long did you expect the majority of newly appointed staff to stay with your organization?
NOW, how long do you expect the majority of newly appointed staff to stay with your organization?

How do you explain changes to your organization over the past 10 years?

13.6   SUMMARY

This chapter has examined the phenomenon of globalization. This influences how far companies can plan their futures in rapidly changing business environments, and is fundamental to the remaining chapters.

Section 13.2 argued that different DEFINITIONS OF GLOBALIZATION are used in different contexts. This need not be a problem for the manager so long as he/she is certain of the definition being employed in any case. Precision is important. Section 13.3 developed the final section of 13.2 and focused on the SOCIAL and human resource EFFECTS OF GLOBALIZATION. Section 13.3 dealt with the ROOT factors that have been responsible for the development of HIGH GLOBALIZATION over the past 30 years.

13.7 EXERCISE

How global is your organization?

1 How global is
   (a) your product range?
   (b) the market segments that it serves?
   (c) the resources used in producing the product range?
   (d) the workforce?

2 Supposing that your organization decided to
   • serve only local market segments;
   • depend on only local resources;
   • employ only a local workforce;

   what would be the effects of this new policy?

Notes

1 Flier for a 2004 exhibition at the VAA, London, "Encounters: The Meeting of Asia and Europe, 1500–1800".

2 Nigel Gromwade, Time you globalised? *The Times Higher*, May 26, 2000; review of Held, D., McGrew, A., Goldblatt, D., Perraton, J. 2000. *Global Transformations: Politics, Economics and Culture*. Polity.

3 Waili Yang. Taiwan's warning. In Letters to the Editor, *Daily Telegraph*, March 20, 2003.

4 Graham Turner. An American odyssey (part one). *Daily Telegraph*, June 16, 2003.

5 David Blair. Banks recruited to wage financial war on Teheran. *Daily Telegraph*, September 18, 2007.

6 Will drive-throughs drive McDonald's growth in China? *People's Daily Online*: http://english.peopledaily.com.cn/200610/11/eng20061011_310618.html

7 David Rennie. UK challenges subsidy for elite Euro-schools. *Daily Telegraph*, April 1, 2005.

8 Tom Nevin. 2003 gains offset 2002 pains. *African Business*, July 2003, pp. 37–38.

9 Jane Croft. HSBC to cut 4,000 jobs in switch to Asia. *Financial Times*, October 17, 2003.

CHAPTER FOURTEEN
Planning Strategy

14.1 Introduction

One of the authors was teaching in Hong Kong. He gave his class of executive MBA students a practical research exercise; investigate small family companies and find out how far they apply Anglo notions of strategic planning. The students conducted the survey and reported back. The professor asked one of the students to describe his experiences.

"Every company that I approached said that they were very happy to use Anglo planning routines," he said. "They see these as modern and scientific. However, a few problems arise. One owner told me 'I follow all stages of the planning model up until the implementation stage. The reason is that these Anglo models tell us that we must be prepared to dismiss staff who are redundant to our new strategic goals.'"

"But how can I dismiss old Wong there? He has served our company for 40 years. It's true that he's no longer very productive and he doesn't understand our new goals. But if I did send him away, what would my customers say? That I am a cold and heartless employer. And how would my other employers feel? They'd be frightened that the same thing might happen to them – and this anxiety would affect their productivity. So I have to keep him on."

This case shows an Asian company needing to compromise between the formal management model borrowed from the West and the expectations of the local environment. This and the next chapter examine this ambiguity.

14.2   The Formal Strategic Plan

Chapter 11 discussed the cultural and political implications embedded in planning. This chapter focuses on the factors that influence how the plan is formulated. The next chapter deals with implementation.

In Anglo cultures, the model has been that only top management took responsibilities for strategic planning. Conventionally, lower levels might be consulted and asked for suggestions, but the final responsibility for making decisions on design stayed at the top.

Although the notion of strategy has been applied to business only in the past 60 years, a complex system of models and practices has developed. The organization adopts that model which seems most likely to achieve its long-term goals. These might be to safeguard and develop its financial basis, identify and meet customer demand, compete with rivals, attract and develop a skilled workforce, and so on; but in the private sector, a company is most concerned with building a reliable financial strategy. This becomes increasingly difficult in a time when the internal world of the company and its environment are changing at an unprecedented rate.

This chapter distinguishes emergent and formal strategic planning. EMERGENT or incremental strategic planning is made in response to small shifts in the environment, and the manager may not be aware of how far his stream of small adjustments is committing the organization to a future position. Emergent strategy is discussed further in 14.8; the preceding sections focus on formal strategy.

14.2.1   Formal planning

The company formulates a strategic plan in order to

- resolve observed correct weaknesses; AND/OR
- exploit opportunities; AND/OR
- counter apparent threats.

This may involve formulating new goals, or aiming at existing goals by a new route. In either event, the strategic plan involves making a radical change from the past.

The formal strategic plan may be formulated as

- a response to particular events;
- a matter of routine (see 14.2.2);

- a response to a decisive event in the company – say, the arrival of a new CEO (14.2.3);
- a record of incremental changes and emergent strategy (14.8).

This planning is a deliberate activity, which may emphasize

- applying existing or targeted resources (see 14.5);
- positioning the company in relation to the environment of markets and competition (see 14.6).

The company is unlikely to focus entirely on one or the other. The balance that it makes depends on such factors as its perception of the market, competition, its future potential, its history.

14.2.2   Routine strategic planning

Formal strategic planning is sometimes made a matter of bureaucratic routine. For example, the organization assumes that at regular intervals corrections to the existing strategy will be needed in order to respond to the expected stream of change in the environment.

During the growth years of the 1950s and 1960s, many organizations produced five-year plans, and some governments still do. Making strategic planning a routine process may be efficient, but carries the risk of restricting the scope of possible goals and of underestimating the importance of novel factors that do not fit the planning model. It presupposes that conditions within the organization can be tightly controlled and that the environment remains stable. These conditions are difficult to obtain in a rapidly changing world. In practice, much routine planning needs to be continually reviewed and modified in order to keep up to date.

14.2.3   Strategy exploiting internal change

In any culture, the appointment of a new CEO constitutes a major internal change in the organization. In Anglo cultures where higher levels of individualism are tolerated the CEO is often expected to signal his/her arrival by embarking on strategic planning. In these contexts a new CEO might be very uncomfortable if asked to continue his/her predecessor's policies in the long term. The new strategy sends messages to both insiders and outsiders that one chapter in the life of the organization has closed and another opened, and as such has symbolic value. The appointment of the new CEO may have been made BECAUSE the board sees the need for a new strategy – although this is not the only reason for CEO change.

14.3   Stages of Planning

In Anglo companies, formal strategy at the corporate level aims to achieve a single goal or a cluster of closely related goals. It is cross-functional in that it is made for the entire organization and commits all functional units. It depends on all making inputs of relevant data in the analysis and design stages, and on participating appropriately in the implementation stage. This means that there have to be effective cross-organizational links by which the departments can communicate.

This corporate strategy is then recycled at the departmental level, and all departments develop planning for their own specialist interests; the marketing department develops a marketing plan, the production department a production plan, and so on.

These departmental plans are coherent in that they all reflect the interests and analysis expressed in the corporate strategy and contribute to the same strategic goal. They deepen and develop aspects of the corporate strategy but do not posit alternatives to it. They must be integrated. An organization that has different units pursuing different goals is doomed to strategic failure – for example, if the finance department aims at budgetary restraint in the next year, and the marketing department aims to make massive investments over the same period. Departmental plans are then be recycled at lower levels – down to the level of the individual.

14.3.1   Stages in formal planning

Conventionally, formal planning is developed and implemented in stages, given in Table 14.1 These reflect the priorities of the Classic Planning Model, Table 11.1.

14.3.2   The scope of operations

The notion of SCOPE helps the organization identify those industries in which it already participates and those industries in which it should aim to participate. If the scope is not clearly defined, the selected strategy is in danger of focusing on the wrong product, misusing internal resources, and misreading the market and competitive factors. Faults in defining the scope occur when it is delineated either too broadly or too narrowly. In the former case, the company is likely to scatter its resources too finely across a range of products and markets. In the latter case, it is blinded to alternative uses that its products can serve and hence to new markets.

Table 14.1   Stages in formal planning

(a) identifying the existing SCOPE of operations (see 14.3.2);
(b) defining GOALS (14.3.3);
(c) collecting relevant DATA and projecting future conditions. Where adequate data cannot be found, possible futures might be projected from devised scenarios (14.9);
(d) analyzing DATA on internal resources (14.4);
(e) analyzing DATA on the environment (14.5);
(f) designing the STRATEGY (14.6–7);
(g) IMPLEMENTATION – including evaluating implementation to data and making modifications (Chapter 15).

This shows the importance of keeping an open mind on scope. If you define the question "What business are we in?" too rigidly, you are in danger of overlooking changes in markets and the environment. A wider question is "What business could we be in?" This means asking what new capabilities does the company have to take advantage of changing conditions. This has implications for examining the firm's resources in relation to its environment.

Here is an example of an industry that rethought the scope of its products. By the end of the twentieth century the Japanese fertility rate was among the lowest in the world, and so the demand for baby food was plummeting. At the other end of the age range, Japanese adults were living longer. One in five Japanese was aged 65 or older, and it was estimated that by 2014 one in four would be.

Japanese baby-food executives needed to reconsider their strategies in order to save their companies from a difficult future. Then someone in the industry realized that they weren't simply in the business of selling food to babies. The soft, small morsels with low salt that could be easily prepared were also attractive to the elderly.[1] They were in the business of selling to people who could not digest rich food and didn't have teeth.

The decline in the baby-food market constituted a threat; the growth in the elderly food market presented opportunities. The companies were able to maintain their core product lines while readjusting their perceptions of their industry and their marketing strategies.

This example suggests that a correct appraisal of scope can sometimes only be made when the relevant data have been analyzed – indicating that the model should not always be applied sequentially.

14.3.3 *Goals*

Goals are the objectives or outcomes that an organization seeks to achieve, and the formal strategic plan has the functions of identifying them, then mapping the most efficient route to achieving them. Strategic goals are simple and long term.

Every organization has the minimal goal of survival. Usually this can be taken for granted and is not articulated, although here is an example when the urge to survive was made clear. A director of one of China's largest private steelmakers claimed that

> the company's aim is not to make money yet – it is simply to survive. But given Fosun's rapid growth, from a standing start with its first steel investment in the late 1990s . . . it may be the survival of the group's rivals that is more on line.[2]

Different types of goals may be specified. These include

- FINANCIAL GOALS. The main financial goal is always the maximization of value to the owners and shareholders. Other financial goals contribute to this;
- MARKET GOALS: e.g. to win or maintain a position as market leader;
- POLITICAL GOALS: e.g. to win cooperation from other bodies within the environment;

- ETHICAL GOALS: e.g. to contribute to society, to achieve social and humanitarian goals;
- CULTURAL GOALS: e.g. to build a positive organizational culture;
- HUMAN RESOURCING GOALS;
- TECHNOLOGICAL GOALS;
- and others.

In any company, the FINANCIAL GOALS are most important. However successful it is in achieving the subordinate goals, the company goes out of business if it fails to make sufficient profit. Subordinate goals are designed to help achieve the financial goals, at least in the long term. For example, only those marketing goals are selected that promise to make more money. The company aims to build a culture that improves productivity so that it can make more money. And a keen sense of ethical purpose improves morale and gives the company a strong image in society, even if in the short term this involves investment.

The need to make money may not be an explicit priority for non-profit-making organizations; these include charities such as Amnesty International and Medicins sans Frontieres, international organizations such as the United Nations, and government organizations including ministries and embassies. Nevertheless they also need to pay for rent, utilities, staff salaries, expenses, and so on; and are in danger of closure if expenditure regularly exceeds income.

The goals directly influence the strategies selected; financial strategies are directed to meeting financial goals, marketing strategies to marketing goals, and so on.

14.4   Strategic Planning Based on Resources

The strategic process always involves analysis of two sets of factors:

(a) those internal to the organization; AND
(b) those in the business environment.

Any strategic decision-making process must pay some attention to these two areas of analysis. In some companies, greater attention is paid to (a), in others to (b). The precise balance in any one case depends on how far the company is looking for a strategy by which to apply its internal capabilities more effectively within its industry, or is reconsidering its position within the industry, or move to a new industry in which it can earn a higher rate of return than do its competitors.

14.4.1   Core competencies

The organization's core competencies consist of a combination of technologies, skills, experience and knowledge that the organization has applied to reach its present position in the market. It reviews these competencies in order to identify the roots of its competitive position, and understand how these may be exploited strategically in the future. The review also tells the company how these competencies should be developed and augmented by new competencies. In the event that an existing competence is redundant to the strategic plan, it may need to be reduced or terminated.

Any changes in the configuration of competencies cause change in the investments of staff, technology, and capital, and so the review has direct implications for the strategic budget.

14.4.2 *Analyzing and auditing resources*

A resource-based approach indicates that the organization sees itself primarily as a bundle of resources and capabilities, and that these will determine how it can manage a long-term strategy most effectively.

ANALYSIS of resources needed in order to achieve its strategic goals takes account of existing resources and those that should be acquired. For example, the decision to widen its product range may mean acquiring new materials, new technologies, and new skills.

An AUDIT of the resources already under its control helps the company to decide whether it is using its resources efficiently and whether they might not be better applied in developing new products or even in a new industry.

Different types of resources may be audited. These may be codified in different ways, but a simple system is to distinguish

- the FINANCIAL status of the company. This means
  (a) appraising all financial data relating to current performance;
  (b) on the basis of this appraisal, predicting the financial potential of continuing the present strategy into the future, AND predicting the financial potentials of new strategic alternatives;
  (c) then selecting the optimal financial strategy;
  (d) finally, setting financial targets for those whose task it is to implement the strategy.
- other TANGIBLE resources; materials, location, plant, technology-as-artifact, etc.
- INTANGIBLE resources. These include:
  (a) capacity; patents, research capacity;
  (b) reputation; brand image, reputation of senior officers; ethical image;
  (c) skills; intangible technology, human resource skills, commitment of employees;
  (d) employees' KNOWLEDGE (see 15.2).
- SYSTEMS. This component includes the internal arrangements discussed in earlier chapters; the organizational culture, management, structures and systems of communication, systems to motivate and resolve dispute, informal relationships, planning systems.

Grant (2002) argues that for most companies:

> Intangible resources contribute much more than do tangible resources to total asset value. Yet, in relation to company financial statements, intangible resources remain largely invisible...   *(p. 141)*

The reason is that intangible resources cannot be reliably costed.

14.4.3   Intangible resources of knowledge

Intangible resources include KNOWLEDGE, which is applied both in planning a strategy and implementing it. Knowledge is dealt with at greater length in the context of strategic implementation, see 15.2.

14.5   Balancing Resources and Position

A position-based approach focuses on the importance of positioning the company in relation to its existing or probable competitors. The company seeks to become a market leader within an industry which offers the best opportunities for profitability. This means analyzing the factors that influence the development of those industries in which it aims to participate. The strategist uses current and projected figures to assess their present and future profitability, market growth rate, and the opportunities for product differentiation.

The business environment includes a range of factors associated with

- competitors; the threat of new entrants to the market; the threat of substitute products and services;
- customers and their bargaining power relative to that of producers; the different market segments that they represent;
- suppliers;
- the degree of government interference;
- corruption;
- official grants;
- preferences given to local competitors;
- political personalities.

14.5.1   Resources and environment

In practice, a resource-based approach and a competitive approach are not strict alternatives. They give different emphases to the same strategic question; how can the company match its capabilities to the changing business environment? In practice, analysis of resources and analyses of the environment must proceed together.

We now deal with two analytical systems which take into account both approaches.

14.5.2   *Strengths, weaknesses, opportunities and threats*

A correct analysis of its present strengths and weaknesses tells the company what it COULD do in the future; and of opportunities and threats, what it MIGHT do.

Problems arise in using SWOT analysis. First, planners increasingly recognize that within an unstable environment a single factor might quickly change from being, say, a strength to a weakness, or an opportunity to a threat. Second, individuals might classify factors differently, an optimistic personality finding a strength where a pessimist sees a threat. Third, these subjective impressions are influenced by national culture; for example, headquarters managers with relatively low needs to avoid uncertainty perceive opportunity whereas subsidiary managers where even low levels of uncertainty are poorly tolerated sense a threat.

This system has value, however, so long as an analysis is constantly reviewed. The analyst needs to keep asking how far the situation has changed, and the attributed values need to be revised – for example, whether factors that once indicated a strength now suggest weakness, or an apparent opportunity has disappeared.

14.6   The Influence of Enviromental Factors

This section examines how factors in the environment influence attitudes towards how strategy is planned and implemented.

Industry factors may be decisive. In reference to the oil industry, Stern and Wybrew (2002) write:

> The relevance of the western model of a fully liberalized market open to competition remains to be demonstrated in Asia. This is not simply because of cultural differences but because the creation of new markets requiring new pipeline infrastructure, both on a national and regional basis, will be such a large factor in the region's development over the next two decades.   *(p. 4)*

The writers imply that cultural factors may work in conjunction with others. The point is developed below.

14.6.1   *Cultural differences influence strategic planning*

Anglo writers dominate current thinking on strategy. Mintzberg (1994) cited evidence of planning being most common

> and most formalized in the United States, followed closely by England, Canada, and Australia, with Japan and Italy at the other end of the scale. . . . Thus the propensity seems to be not just American but Anglo-Saxon, although the Americans have certainly been in the lead. *(p. 415)*

This might be interpreted to mean any of the following:

- companies in other cultures do not perform strategic planning;
- companies in other cultures do perform strategic planning but do not write about it;

- companies in other strategies perform other, non-Anglo, forms of strategic planning.

The third interpretation is adopted here.

   Aspects of formal strategic planning in Anglo companies reflect the culture in a number of other ways. Formal strategy is

- directed to achieving a SINGLE GOAL or a cluster of related GOALS.

   BUT OTHER CULTURES may accept greater ambiguity. Japanese companies tend to distrust the notion of a single strategy, and different sections of the company may have different priorities (Saxton, 2004).
- a DELIBERATE process, derived from conscious analysis of specified data and rational processes of discussion by planners.

   BUT OTHER CULTURES place greater reliance on knowledge of the situation derived from personal relationships and intuitions. These are informal sources that often cannot be justified as rational.
- a high tolerance of explicit COMPETITION and CONFLICT. The typical Anglo company uses strategy as a means of differentiating itself from its competitors, by performing or similar activities in different ways.

   BUT OTHER CULTURES are less tolerant of OPEN EXPRESSIONS of conflict – for instance, where needs to avoid uncertainty are higher. This does not mean that their strategies are not competitive, but rather that this aspect is covert. A Japanese company might communicate its goals in terms of releasing the creative energies of its members, and fulfilling a universal mission.
- a relatively BUREAUCRATIC company structure – although in any culture, strategic planning in a small company is likely to be less bureaucratic than in a large company.

   BUT OTHER CULTURES may give less importance to bureaucratic priorities. Chapter 13 shows that Chinese family businesses tend to center strategic planning in the hands of the owner, who may make decisions without consulting other family members. And Japanese companies may have no corporate strategy teams and strategic planning processes. Strategy is viewed in terms of whatever capabilities help the company adapt successfully to its environment, and this means assimilating inputs to the final plan from a range of sources. Rather than depending on specified strategy teams and planning processes, they depend on a range of different sources from different levels in the company. Senior levels may focus on guiding and orchestrating inputs from other members (including production and sales staff) and from outsiders (such as dealers) rather than steering the organization along a predetermined strategic course (Saxton, 2004).
- a tolerance of RADICAL CHANGE, and a belief that this can achieve dramatic improvements in performance. Hammer and Champy (1993) title their most famous book *REENGINEERING THE CORPORATION: A MANIFESTO FOR BUSINESS REVOLUTION*

   BUT in OTHER CULTURES, where tolerances of uncertainty are lower, radical change is not welcomed. Members prefer to make small, incremental changes that respond to immediate conditions rather than to analytical models.

In sum, it is argued here that the assumptions underlying formal planning in Anglo companies are not universal. The implication is that a strategy planned in an Anglo headquarters may not be automatically understood in a subsidiary set in some other cultural setting. Where the values are significantly different, strategic thinking has to be mediated before it can be effectively transplanted.

The Introductory example suggests that even when an Anglo model is applied elsewhere, implementation priorities may differ.

14.7 Growth Strategies

Coulter (2008) describes four basic alternatives for the firm when trying to grow the market for its products:

- Product market exploitation, by increasing the same current production in the current market – for example, by offering three for the price of two;
- Product development, by creating new products to sell to the current market – for example, by first developing modifications to the current product;
- Market development, by selling current products in new markets;
- Product – market diversification, by creating new products to sell in new markets.

Questions then arise about how long a product can be sold on the market. the length of The lifecycle of a product can be envisaged as a number of stages, as in Figure 14.1

technological development $\longrightarrow$ introduction to the market $\longrightarrow$ growth $\longrightarrow$ maturity $\longrightarrow$ decline

Figure 14.1 Product life cycle

In the technological development phase, resources are invested when no sales are made; the company only earns a cash return when the product is introduced to the market. Sales and cash flows reach their peak in the growth phase, level out in maturity, and then decline until the company withdraws the product.

If the company were offering only a single product, then that product's lifecycle would coincide with the company lifecycle, and when the product reached maturity and declined, so would the company. The company might accept that situation, keep reinvestment to a minimum and extract as much cash as possible before decline leads to expiration. Coulter's four strategies, above, provide alternatives.

The Boston Consulting Group has distinguished four product types:

- A STAR product has high growth and a high market share relative to competing products in the industry;
- A CASH COW has low growth but high market share, and so generates significant cash – which may not be reinvested in the same product;
- A DOG has low growth and low market share. These products are often found in mature markets, and are likely to be discontinued;
- A QUESTION MARK – also termed a "problem child" – has a small share of growing market but perhaps can develop into a cash cow at one extreme or a dog at the other. Question marks make enormous demands for cash, and are growing rapidly, but have relatively poor profit margins.

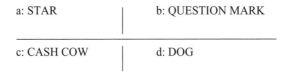

a: STAR	b: QUESTION MARK
c: CASH COW	d: DOG

Figure 14.2   Growth-share matrix

Figure 14.2 shows the matrix (derived from The Boston Consulting group 1970). In many cases, the STAR might be earning well but in actual fact contribute little to profits, since earnings have to be continually reinvested in development. Growth and profits are not necessarily compatible; Chakravarthy and Lorange (2007) cite research showing that even in the boom years of the 1990s, nine out of 10 companies failed to sustain growth and only 13 percent were able to grow as fast as GDP growth and inflation combined (p. 1).

This model helps guide strategic planning in different ways. It provides a snapshot of the present situation, particularly in terms of relative market share and market growth. It guides thinking about the strength and resources associated with a product, and what resources must be invested in order to justify further development. It helps predict the lifecycle of a product over time.

14.8   Emergent Strategy

Non-Anglo cultures may prefer to make strategy on an incremental basis, by responding to opportunities in the environment – or in order to protect themselves from apparent threats. This opportunistic mode of operation may drive them towards greater diversification than would be expected in an equivalent Anglo company.

For example, the son of a business family in the Philippines reported to one of the authors "We never write a strategy. We make decisions every evening at the family dinner." When this was reported to a group of businessmen from Saudi Arabia, they commented "Here it is entirely different. We make our business decisions over breakfast and review them when we eat in the evening." In practice, of course, the differences were slight. In both cultures the business people were managing their future directions on a strictly incremental basis. Data were collected from observations of the markets, meetings with customers and suppliers, reactions to the media. The sum of recognizing and understanding the opportunities and threats was continually being modified. Action was taken on a day-by-day basis, in response to principles and this learned knowledge.

In some cases this approach can be explained by cultural factors, such as low tolerance of uncertainty. But increasingly Anglo companies are being forced by circumstances to adopt a similar attitude to making change.

Everywhere, the new global environment is increasingly unpredictable. Change has become discontinuous in the sense that the unexpected is now ordinary, and our reservoir of experience is no longer adequate to deal with it. For example, we have recently been faced with the unexpected failure to resolve conflict in Iraq, the upsurge of terror, and the imminence of collapse in the green environment. Michaud and Thoenig (2003) describe the implications of turbulence for the business world:

> Protection against competition has been reduced. Time horizons have shortened. The economic battlefield has changed radically. Financial death is now more sudden and more certain for anyone who does not know how to state and restate strategies and actions, a daily position and a future. *(p. 14)*

The increased rapidity of globalization means that getting goods to market as fast as possible becomes increasingly the one priority. In order to satisfy local markets as quickly as possible, decision-making has to be localized and the functions of centralized control are eroded (Allee, 2003, pp. 29–30). The planning function is among those weakened.

For example, traditionally the data collection stage has preceded planning, which has preceded implementation. This linear process has presumed a stable business environment, and for many industries this condition applies less and less. In these cases, changes are made in advance of long-term planning. The company adopts a provisional plan and acts on that basis – or responds to the action of a competitor. The process of monitoring and checking provides the basis for further activity.

In sum, fluid, emergent strategy may always have been preferred in some cultures. Increasingly it is being forced on companies operating in those cultures which at one time naturally chose a long-term model. The changes brought about by globalization force the company to continually reappraise the scope of its activities and its place in the market, and hence to rethink goals.

14.8.1 Recording the emergent strategy

Emergent strategy is recorded when the manager needs *post hoc* justification for the steps taken. The strategic direction is made clear for the benefit of stakeholders, including investors who need to be assured that they will benefit, and managers who need a clear picture of the point from which they have traveled and the possible destinations ahead. An accurate record raises morale.

On the other hand, if the management and investment team are small, possibly comprising family members, only a modest record may be considered necessary. The strategic direction of the company is manifested in its activities, the financial records, lists of customers and suppliers.

14.9 Scenario Planning

The company develops scenarios of possible futures when the available data are inadequate, and it cannot project from these with any reliability.

SCENARIO PLANNING explores the impacts of a range of uncertainties, possibly changing at the same time. Scenarios are built on a basis of historical data and project significant trends into the future. They can include the planner's subjective interpretations, and factors such as a shift in cultural values, which cannot be formally modeled.

Scenario planning tries to compensate for two common errors in planning: overpredicting, which leads to overconfidence; and underpredicting, which leads to restricting the possibilities for action too narrowly. Given a question, the planners develop a number of plausible scenarios – sometimes three, one predicting a positive outcome, one a negative outcome, and one a middle-of-the-road outcome.

An example of a scenario question might be "How will the growth of the Chinese economy effect our Southeast Asian subsidiaries in the next 10 years?" The positive scenario might find evidence for expecting growth, possibly in cooperation with Chinese producers or developing niches that they overlook. The negative scenario might develop the notion that Chinese dominance will drive the company out of the market. The third scenario finds both positive and negative expectations.

The scenario planner is a facilitator and educator who produces material that can be applied by top managers when designing strategies. Scenarios do not themselves constitute strategies, but they push managers into considering alternative futures, and how they would behave under these conditions. They express a "What if...?" condition; for example, what might happen to the industry if the Chinese economy collapses? What might happen if the company is unable to hire sufficient numbers of local specialists? They aim to stretch managers' imaginations outside what is the conventionally accepted as probable.

Lindgren and Bandhold (2003) describe scenario planning as a form of responsiveness:

> A powerful tool for anticipating and managing change on an industry level or environmental level, and scenario thinking is the strategic perspective necessary in today's turbulent business environment.   *(p. xi)*

This responsiveness reflects, and fosters, a "thinking and playing culture" (p. 2) within the organization.

Robson (2002) focuses on scenario planning as a communication activity. This implies that the precise forms and functions are bound to differ, each more or less appropriate to the needs of the participants. He found differences in scenario plans made by Shell in Kenya and China. In Kenya

> native Kenyans produced the scenarios because the issues raised were close to their hearts and affected both themselves and their families at a very personal level. . . . The method of creating the scenarios leant heavily on group work and storytelling which has a strong tradition in African cultures.   *(pp. 31–32)*

But his China data showed that severe problems could arise in the notion of scenario planning into the language and culture. In the Shell subsidiary, outside consultants were almost always responsible for the scenario planning, and they developed scenarios that placed and emphasis on readability.

Scenario planning helps the company develop its capacities to learn about the contexts within which it operates; learning organizations are discussed further in 15.2.2. However, it cannot help the company prepare for the highly improbable, the "unknown unknowns".

Taleb (2007) refers to these as "black swan" events. Two examples are the September 11, 2001 terrorist attacks in the United States and the rise of Google. Both these events can be explained logically in retrospect but at the time they were largely unpredicted, and changed the landscape.

14.10   Implications for the Manager

Show how this model can be applied in an multinational corporation that you know. Use it to propose how a strategic system might be transplanted from headquarters to a target subsidiary.

MODEL FOR TRANSPLANTING A STRATEGIC SYSTEM

1 (a) DEFINE your strategic goals.
  (b) DEFINE your aim in transplanting the system. How might the system help you achieve your goals?
2 COLLECT INFORMATION about the system.
3 ANALYZE THE SYSTEM. How does it reflect the cultural and non-cultural characteristics of its home context? (Take into account factors associated with the economy, industry, market, national culture, and organizational culture.) What is the system expected to achieve within its home context?
4 ANALYZE THE TARGET CONTEXT. How closely does the system reflect the target context? What are the relevant cultural and non-cultural characteristics of the target context that will affect implementation?

14.11 SUMMARY

This chapter has discussed a range of approaches in planning strategy. At one extreme, a strategic plan is designed in a formal process; at the other, strategy emerges from an incremental process of small changes. The factors which influence the approach taken include the emphasis given to resources held within the company as a means of securing advantage, its need to position itself within the competitive environment of its industry, cultural factors and the perception of how far ahead the company can plan in response to change.

Section 14.2 dealt with THE FORMAL STRATEGIC PLAN. This developed the arguments for formal planning given in Chapter 12, and focused on the different situations in which formal planning might be needed. Section 14.3 examined STAGES IN STRATEGIC PLANNING and presented a simple model showing how the stages of goal setting, analysis, planning, and implementation follow sequentially in a conventional plan. The financial goals always have prime importance, and determine which subordinate goals are feasible. . Emphasis was given to examining the scope of the company's activities and the goals of planning. Sections 14.4 and 14.5 examined RESOURCE priorities and the need to BALANCE PRIORITIES AND POSITION within the business environment. A SWOT analysis can be useful so long as it is continually revisited and revised in the light of change. Section 14.6 discussed the INFLUENCE OF ENVIRONMENTAL FACTORS on strategic planning, and focused on cultural factors. Section 14.7 briefly examined HIGH GROWTH STRATEGIES. Section 14.8 dealt with one alternative to formal strategic planning, EMERGENT STRATEGY. Section 14.9 saw how planners apply SCENARIOS of possible futures when reliable projections cannot be made from the available data.

14.12 EXERCISE

Research how organizations plan strategy in your home culture, or some other culture that you know well.

1 Research planning in a range of organizations – for example
   - a small family company;
   - a large company;
   - an organization in the state sector;
   - a non-governmental organization.
2 In each of these organizations, how far does strategic planning follow the stages in formal planning modeled in Table 14.1?
   (a) identifying the existing SCOPE of operations;
   (b) defining GOALS;
   (c) collecting relevant DATA and projecting future conditions;
   (d) analyzing DATA on internal resources;
   (e) analyzing DATA on the environment;
   (f) designing the STRATEGY;
   (g) IMPLEMENTATION.

What differences can you find between strategic planning in these organizations and as modeled?

What factors explain the differences that you find? In particular consider
   - national culture;
   - industry;
   - competition.

Notes

1 Chester Dawson. No kidding – a new market for baby food. *Business Week*, January 27, 2003.

2 Richard McGregor. Surviving drives the strategy at Fosun. *Financial Times*, September 22, 2003.

CHAPTER FIFTEEN
Implementing Strategy and Applying Knowledge

CHAPTER OUTLINE

15.1 Introduction

Implementing a strategy gives rise to difficulties when it is not clear what ideas express the strategic plan and what express the system for implementing the plan.

The problems of confusing plan and implementation system are made clear in the movie *DIE HARD: 4* (2007). Detective John McLane, played by Bruce Willis, and his friend are outside the perimeter of a government building where a terrorist gang are holding McLane's daughter Lucy:

> FARRELL: When we get inside, do we have a plan?
> McLANE: Find Lucy, kill everybody else.
> FARRELL: I mean a plan of how to do that?

McLane understands the "plan" to be the goal. But Farrell intends the term to mean the route to this goal.

A plan that does not take into account the means by which it can be achieved may not have much value other than as a desirable dream; "I'm going to make my first 10 million before I'm 30." On the other hand, too much attention paid to implementation can lead to the overriding goal being obscured. This is a weakness when the environment changes and the plan is no longer relevant, yet the organization continues to pour resources into resolving problems that arise in achieving it.

Deciding how a strategic plan can best be achieved and designing appropriate systems depends first on being able to utilize knowledge. This chapter therefore deals first with the problems associated with defining and managing knowledge, and then examines implementation issues more generally.

15.2   Identifying and Applying Knowledge

Section 14.4.2 noted that KNOWLEDGE constitutes an intangible resource, invaluable both in planning and implementing strategy.

Knowledge is defined here as the capacity to select relevant items of information and to understand how these can be applied in order to formulate and implement strategy. It includes knowledge of the INTERNAL arrangements of the company. This includes knowledge of the structures and organizational culture and how these function in practice. Knowledge of the EXTERNAL environment.

Knowledge should not be mistaken for information. Information is readily available on the net, and the manager can very easily trawl the internet to access the information required as the basis for decision making. The problem is the reverse; often, too much information is available, and the manager needs the skills to decide what information is significant and how it can be used. A letter to a UK newspaper makes this point. The writer stated that he did not know of any businesses that had too little information, but

> I know plenty that are drowning in it, staffed by people who simply don't have the skills to process it. Too often, we ask interviewses, "So what do you actually think?" and they're like rabbits caught in the headlights. It should be the most exciting question you can ask.[1]

The French philosopher Jean Baudrillard argues that "We live in a world where there is more and more information and less and less meaning" (Baudrillard, 2006, p. 79). By this he means that information circulates to such excess and so freely, that it no longer signifies but has the reverse effect. When people are not able to fit the swill of information into mental structures that they understand, they may try to justify it in ways that are illogical and irrational.

15.2.1   Developing knowledge resources

The strategist develops mental patterns and priorities for processing and applying information. These processing skills themselves constitute a body of knowledge, and create further knowledge. Processing skills include the abilities to

- distinguish relevant and irrelevant information;
- analyze, evaluate and prioritize the relevant information;
- predict changes in the business environment;
- visualize how information can be applied to the benefit of the company.

These skills demand personal attributes of judgment, maturity, and creativity.
Relevant information is garnered from

- employees' experiences and skills; these may not be skills for which the employee was hired, and may not be revealed on the CV or job description.
- websites, electronic media, other data sources;
- employees' understanding of the organizational culture and of the company's history;
- employees' ideas and suggestions;
- debriefing expatriates returning from assignments abroad; see 21.6.9.

Here is an example of knowledge derived from information provided by an employee. An oil company heard that the United States was about to auction more oil leases in the Gulf of Mexico, and immediately began planning an expensive seismic survey.[2] At the last moment, an executive recalled that the company had previously surveyed the area and had even drilled some inconclusive wells before giving it back to the government. Thus his memory saved the company from repeating the exercise and making an expensive mistake in implementing its strategy.

The company needs to develop systems for recognizing what special knowledge its members have (which may never appear on their CVs or job descriptions), and then finding ways of applying it to meet company goals. That is, knowledge must be developed and managed.

15.2.2   The learning organization

The learning company is defined as one which has the capacity to change itself and deliberately establishes dynamic systems which adapt to the environment and develop knowledge that can assist its operations.

Members' knowledge is applied in formulating and implementing strategy. A learning culture is reflective in the sense that members learn from their experiences, both successes and failures. They become adept at identifying new goals, creating new solutions and at sharing knowledge (Sugarman, 2001). Planning and implementation layer over each other, and the planner learns from attempts to implement early stages of the plan as much as from data. Goals and plans are determined by the organization's capacity to learn from its environment and its own culture, and so are continually modified. The resources of data and their analysis available to the organization determine the formulation of goals, rather than goals determine data analysis. This process of adapting to the environment may result in the organization adopting new structures and systems (Forte et al., 2000).

The company is more likely to need a learning culture when it operates in an environment in which

- change is increasingly rapid;
- competition is fierce;
- essential skills are scarce (and so expensive).

15.2.3   *Learning from members' knowledge*

The knowledge held by expert members is a valuable resource which the company is under growing pressure to exploit. Investments are made in retaining and motivating these people, and to develop and apply their knowledge throughout the company.

A learning company needs to develop a positive and strong culture in which members are aware of their mutual dependencies and able to communicate freely. Where these conditions do not apply, members are likely to be inhibited in developing and communicating their knowledge with each other or with management.

The structural implications are, first, control can no longer be strictly maintained within departmental boundaries, and tight departmental structures may need to be reengineered away. Second, the company may decide to appoint a dedicated "knowledge officer" to develop and organize its knowledge bank.

However, it is not easy to identify knowledge which might be useful now or at some indefinite time in the future. The process might sound simple, but in practice, organizations usually only recognize and absorb new' experiences when these relate to what they already know. This means that a company is most likely to reject precisely those experiences and ideas that might offer the best opportunities for developing in radical new directions. Only a senior manager who is confident of holding onto his/her position might be prepared to take a risk and back a radical proposal based on knowledge that is unorthodox.

Applying lessons from experience implies a capacity to see parallels between the present problem – for example, how to achieve a particular goal – and a similar case in the past. But the analogies may not be exact; Gavetti and Rivkin (2005) discuss the problems of committing too deeply to superficial similarities when other factors make the cases fundamentally different. The use of knowledge is never risk free and analogies need to be assessed and tested at every stage of application.

15.3   Organizational Capabilities and Competitive Advantage

Success in implementing a strategy depends largely on the company developing the ORGANIZATIONAL CAPABILITIES needed to exploit its resources – including resources of knowledge.

Capabilities consist of capacities to produce, and the concept is relative; the company is more or less capable of producing X in comparison to competitors who also produce X.

That is, the company focuses on developing and exploiting those internal resources that will give its products competitive advantage in the marketplace.

Capabilities must be used effectively within their limited life span. The value of any resource is determined in part by how easily it can be imitated by a competitor; the easier this is, the less contribution it makes to developing competitive advantage.

15.3.1 *Competitive advantage*

A company gains COMPETITIVE ADVANTAGE when the customer favorably distinguishes the company and its product from competitor and its competing product. That is, the company's strengths and weaknesses are defined either relative to the competition or relative to the alternative investments that the company might make.

Three points arise. First, competitive advantage is always relative and never absolute. It does not mean that the product meets any absolute criteria of quality, only that it is best in the eyes of the customer, who prefers it to competing products.

Second, the factors giving this advantage must be apparent to the customer so that they influence his/her purchasing decision. A competitive advantage is based on such values as quality, price, breadth of product line, reliability, performance, after-sales service, styling and image, regular deliveries. Relatively higher quality at a relatively lower price gives competitive advantage.

Third, different products project different advantages. A sandwich is sold on the basis of its freshness and taste, and a book for its quality and appearance. On the other hand, if the customer wants to purchase a dishwasher, the after-sales service offered by the manufacturer may be an important factor in swaying the purchasing decision. Different brands of the same product may offer different advantages. Automobile X is valued for its low cost; automobile Y for its sophisticated engineering, regardless of cost; automobile Z for its safety record.

Competitive advantages are developed through application of organizational capabilities, but these capabilities do not of themselves give the product any advantage. Supposing that Company A's competitive advantage is through delivering a low-cost product to the market with minimum delay. Company A's human resources policy supports this advantage if it produces staff who are sufficiently skilled and motivated to achieve this objective. But it does not normally constitute competitive advantage in itself because

- the consumer does not base his/her decision to purchase on it; AND
- does not choose the product offered by Company A in preference to that offered by Company B because it prefers A's human resources policy.

That is, these capabilities are complementary assets that do not directly sway the consumer's purchasing decision. But exceptions occur in cases where a company is able to project an ethical policy in terms that give the product exceptional value in the eyes of the consumer.

15.4   Implementation and Communication

In the past, management theorists placed greater emphasis on strategic design and less on implementation. Many textbooks on strategy still treat implementation as less important than formulating the strategy.

Modern theorists have moved towards redressing the balance. Increasingly, implementation is seen as a vital stage, and the formulation of a plan cannot be sensibly discussed without taking into account how it will be put into practice. For example, Grant (2002) discusses examples of successful strategies, and derives four common elements; the fourth makes the point (our emphasis);

1   Goals that are simple, consistent, and long term;
2   Profound understanding of the competitive environment;
3   Objective appraisal of resources;
4   *Effective implementation. (pp. 11–12).*

Several factors explain this change of emphasis. First, in increasingly heterogeneous organizations, shared understanding cannot be taken for granted and more attention has to be paid to the political aspects of persuading members to accept the practical implications of a plan. This means that developing a constituency favoring change and communicating with the various interested groups becomes a priority.

Second, there is a growing awareness that in an increasingly globalized world, the long-term impact of strategic planning cannot be predicted with any accuracy. Increasingly an initial stage in strategic development consists of experimenting with alternative solutions to problems that may still be only vaguely articulated. That is, early implementation contributes towards planning. All the different stages of the strategic process tend to be run together and overlapped.

Third, when the process of globalization leads the company to change its organizational structure, middle managers responsible for implementing the changes come under increasing pressure.

Both Percy Barnevik (once voted top executive in Europe) and Jack Welch (described in *Business Week* as the top US executive) agree that success depends on the company not only designing appropriate strategies by implementing them appropriately. They agreed that the implementation phase should take at least 90 percent of the total effort necessary to carry out a change program adequately. Barnevik says that the challenge to get people to support and then to accomplish the strategy is 95 percent execution and that the differences in execution are what differentiate the successful companies from the less successful. (See Flood et al., 2000, p. 31)

15.4.1   *Implementation systems*

IMPLEMENTATION SYSTEMS are established with the purpose of turning the strategic plan into practice. They offer a means to an end, but THEY ARE NOT STRATEGIES IN THEMSELVES. For example, management forms a joint venture in order to improve its financial position, to increase market share, to develop useful knowledge and skills, but NOT simply for the excitement of participating in a joint venture. Management does not re-engineer for its own sake unless there is a clear perception of what that mechanism can achieve.

Implementation systems detail

- the routes to achieve the strategic goals;
- the implications for structural development;
- needs for HR planning. What new training is needed? What categories of new staff should be recruited? What categories of existing staff have to be made redundant? These topics are discussed in Chapter 19;
- other changes in resourcing, including the financial, technological and other resources needed;
- the costs of implementation;
- rewards and sanctions offered;
- the management systems required including the communication systems – 15.4.3-15.4.9.

In addition, they provide measures by which progress is monitored, and indicate routes to take if changes to the strategy are required.

15.4.2   The problems of implementation

Implementation may always be traumatic. For example, the new strategy calls for the termination of outdated brands and the development of new ones. This means that some staff are dismissed and new staff hired, new skills learned and old skills forgotten. The design of new tasks and relationships has structural implications. In order to coordinate and monitor developments, new committees, task forces, liaison and integrating roles are established.

The problems of implementation are multiplied when a strategy is designed in one branch of the company to be implemented elsewhere. For example, a headquarters strategy is exported for implementation in a subsidiary located in a different culture. A model for transplanting implementation systems between cultures is discussed in 15.6.

15.4.3   Communicating the strategy

The benefits offered by the strategic plan appear obvious to the planner, but perhaps less so to the other persons affected. They may be entirely invisible to employers in a distant subsidiary, whose interests are influenced by other economic and cultural factors. This wider constituency has to be persuaded. This means that the planner, or the delegated agents of change, must efficiently communicate the plan. This process aims to prepare members of the organization so that they can efficiently contribute to the implementation phase. Those who can contribute derive a sense of control over the process, and are more disposed to accept the strategy as a contract.

The communication process is ineffective when

- its importance is not recognized;
- systems for communicating and implementing the strategy are not in place;
- resources for communication are not available and the planning budget does not allow for the expense;
- the communication is mistimed;
- communication is not followed up with action. Repetitions do not substitute, and the more often the plan to change is repeated and no attempt is made to implement it, the less believing grow the audience.

15.4.4   The notion of stakeholder

Strategy is communicated to those persons who are directly affected by the change. These persons are sometimes referred to as "stakeholders" of the plan. However, the concept of a stakeholder, much beloved by politicians, is very imprecise and is falling out of favor. In 1993, David (1993) defined stakeholders as

> the individuals and groups of persons who have a special stake or claim on the company. Stakeholders include employees, managers, stockholders, boards of directors, customers, suppliers, distributors, creditors, governments (local, state, federal, and foreign), unions, competitors, environmental groups, and the general public.   *(p. 98)*

But these categories cover almost everyone; if everyone is to be treated as equally "special", no one is special. And, as David does go on to recognize, not all stakeholders' claims can be pursued with equal vigor. That is, stakeholders are bound to be ranked in order of importance.

Perhaps the point is what different categories are likely to be most favored in a particular organization. A marketing-oriented company is likely to treat its director of marketing and his senior staff as leading stakeholder. A production-oriented company has other priorities. There may be industry differences, and cultural differences. An Anglo company is likely to prioritize persons of power and influence, including owners and board members. When it seems that employees and customers can easily be replaced their stakeholder rights are treated as of lesser significance. But other cultures may be more likely to balance the interests of stockholders. Yoshimori (1995) notes that Germany and to some extent France hold a "dualistic" outlook; a premium is placed on shareholder interests, but the interests of employees are also taken into account. At the time Japan took a "pluralistic" approach. This assumed that

> the firm belongs to all the stakeholders, with the employees' interests taking precedence. This . . . manifests itself in the form of long-term employment for employees and long-term trading relations among various other stakeholders (the main bank, major suppliers, subcontractors, distributors), loosely called *keiretsu*.   *(p. 33)*

However, since the crisis of 1997 Japanese business has been forced to conform with global norms, and the power of employees has declined.

The notion of "stakeholder", then, is general. It is more useful to identify as precisely as possible those categories of persons within the particular organization who need to be informed of the strategy. These include

- stockholders;
- the board and senior management;
- those who manage the implementation process;
- those managed, who are involved in the process;
- those whose job procedures are changed;
- those who need to learn new skills or retrain;
- those whose career prospects are changed;
- those in the external environment who need to know; financial markets, customers, suppliers, analysts, etc.

Some of these categories can exert great power, at different points. Birkinshaw et al. (2006) argue that the demands of global financial markets and shareholders may lead to the multinational company shifting its corporate headquarters to another country. A major strike by the workforce may also have extreme consequences – perhaps leading to closure. Several of these categories may coincide. Those involved in the implementation process may also need to learn new skills, and may find that their career prospects are changed.

15.4.5 *Who communicates the strategy?*

Top management are usually responsible for deciding on strategy at the corporate level and for communicating it to the board and to the external environment. Mid- and lower-level managers have responsibilities for communicating to those in the organization who will be directly involved in putting the strategy into practice. They direct the new operations, instruct those who need training or liaise with specialist trainers, reassure those worried about having to take on new skills, deal with the implications for human resource processes, and so on.

These communications are vital. Unless they are efficient, implementation will fail and the organization will not develop new learning.

However, research based on the views of 1,003 managers in organizations with 60 or more employees showed that their work was often complicated by poor communication (CHA, 2007). Problems arose in working with levels above them and in communicating with their teams. They supported a number of suggestions for removing communications blockages, including the following:

- "Tell me clearly what the organization's plan is so I understand it and feel able to pass on the message" (supported by 51 percent of the respondents);

- "Give me time to do it" (50.5 percent);
- "Give me the mechanism with which I can feed back employees' comments" (41 percent).

Only 40 percent of middle managers in the private sector felt involved in developing business plans, as against 27 percent in the public sector.

15.4.6   Communicating to those who need to know

Efficient communication of the strategic plan does NOT mean that the same message is sent to all those in the categories listed in 15.4.4. To take extreme examples, the board need detailed projections of the effects on the proposed change on their subsidiaries and the likely responses of competitors, but these issues may be of little or no interest to workers on the factory floor. Those on the factory floor need to know what new skills they will have to master and how their pay packets will be affected, while this may be incidental to the board's considerations. Production and marketing have different priorities, but probably need some information about the new route that will be taken by the other department. Each category is chiefly interested in those aspects of the strategic plan that influence their work and their interests.

Although different aspects of the message are communicated to different audiences and in different ways, this does not mean that their contents are unrelated. It should always be clear how the different emphases relate. If different audiences sense contradictions between different messages sent to different categories, they become confused and demoralized. Managers need to avoid ambiguity as far as possible.

In sum, at an early stage in the implementation process top management decides

- what different stakeholder categories need to know;
- what each category need to know;
- how this information should be communicated to each;
- when this information should be communicated.

15.4.7   Appropriate timing

Appropriate timing in communicating the strategic plan is essential to successful implementation. When it is communicated too slowly it is in danger of being bogged down in bureaucratic inertia, and pockets of resistance have a chance to grow and to undermine the radical change process. By implementing the plan quickly and "routinizing" it, you may outflank your opponents before they mobilize their forces. But if you act too quickly, employees may not be committed. Rather, they feel insecure and resist both your sleight of hand and the policing necessary to safeguard an unwanted change. It is important to allow time in situations where resistance will fade as more people become used to the notion of change and more understanding of how they can benefit.

Values in the national and organizational cultures may influence the speed with which change can be made. In a context where experimentation is welcomed, your audience is more receptive, and time spent in teaching new routines is reduced. Industry values may also be significant. For example, high-tech industries are often tolerant of change made with little lead-in time, whereas heavy industry is less so.

A further problem may arise in giving members time to forget the old priorities and routines which are being replaced. If the old has become second-nature and automatic, a longer time is spent in their forgetting it and learning the new.

15.4.8   *National culture and the communication of planning*

Cultural factors influence norms for communicating planning. In low-context cultures where written text is treated as more reliable than speech, greater reliance may be made on written documentation which provides input to meetings where the plan is then discussed. In high-context cultures the order might be reversed and documentation prepared only after a spoken agreement has been reached by the interested persons.

Culture also influences what STYLE is most appropriate. Where power distances are narrow and the organizational structure is relatively flat, plans are communicated so that they build a broad consensus. This means inviting suggestions and comments, even from categories whose interests are only marginally affected. Informal channels may be as least as important as formal ones. But where power distances are wide, only senior members are consulted, and subordinates are informed of change plans.

Where power distances are great, subordinates may not expect to be informed in any great detail. Decisions are then cascaded down, perhaps using both formal and informal channels.

In Anglo management theory, a participative style may secure employee commitment to the plan and so foster a common sense of ownership of the change process. This raises the odds on making the change successfully. But in some cultural contexts, where power distances are wide, the notion of employee participation may attract little interest – at least until the workforce have been trained to participate.

15.4.9   *A model for communicating the strategic plan*

In sum, the model given in Table 15.1 for communicating the strategic plan adapts the model of the Context of Communications, Table 6.1. These questions have to be answered.

15.5   International Mergers and Acquisitions

The company may decide to implement a strategy of growth by merging with or acquiring another company from another country. MERGERS combine two companies so that they

Table 15.1 Communicating the strategic plan

- TO WHOM should (different aspects of) the plan be communicated? These persons include the categories listed in 15.4.4.
- WHO should communicate with each of these persons?
- WHAT aspects of the plan should be communicated to each?

These include

- the REASONS for making the change;
- the LIKELIHOOD of success;
- DETAILS of the change process; procedures; responsibilities; resources available;
- implications for TRAINING;
- how forces in the ENVIRONMENT can be expected to respond;
- the COSTS of change as opposed to the greater costs of not changing.

- WHEN should the plan be communicated?
- WHERE should the plan be communicated?
- HOW should the plan be communicated? What medium and style are appropriate?

---

form a new, single legal entity. In an ACQUISITION, a company takes over the assets of a foreign firm without expunging its separate legal identity. An acquisition is attractive when the costs of purchasing a going concern and making any necessary changes to its operations are still less than the projected costs of buying a greenfield site, building, installing equipment, hiring and training a workforce, and so on.

MERGERS and ACQUISITIONS (M&As) are attractive when they offer opportunities to

- increase stock value;
- enter a new market;
- diversify;
- fill gaps in a product line;
- create synergies;
- acquire a needed resource – for example, a technology;
- acquire a company that is perceived to be undervalued;
- make economies of scale. By combining, firms eliminate costs by eliminating redundant resources and make efficiencies – which might mean reducing the workforce.

Here is an example of the advantages that firms might hope to reap from an international merger. In 2008, GfK of Nuremberg, Germany, and Taylor Nelson Sofres of the United Kingdom planned a merger that would create the world's second-biggest market information company.[3] One analyst commented that the merger would give both entities greater power in the market. They would find it easier to operate on a global basis, which was what their customers want. A second noted:

We believe and deal would bring both revenue and cost synergies.

And Credit Suisse analysts said:

> After 20 years of consolidation, the still relatively fragmented market research industry still appears to have further to go. ... Benefits such as shared technologies, consolidation of accounts and brand globalization all lend themselves to extend this trend further.

Nevertheless it was reported later that in Nuremberg, there were fears that the union would damage the local economy. The deal was expected to lead to the loss of 500 jobs globally, as duplication would be eliminated and the headquarters moved to London.

Mellahi et al. (2005) distinguish three directions in M&A:

- horizontal, involving two competing firms from the same industry;
- vertical, involving two firms in the supply chain. For example, a distributor merges with a manufacturer;
- conglomerates. Two firms from unrelated industries combine. The writers note that

> Conglomerate M&As were very popular in the late 1980s, but have been declining ever since as firms retreated to their core businesses during the 1990s and early 2000s. As a result, the share of conglomerate M&As fell from 42 percent in 1971 to around 27 percent in 1999 [reference given]. *(p. 197)*

But not all M&As succeed, and they can fail for a range of reasons. The target is wrongly selected, or the price is miscalculated. Relationships between the two managements deteriorate, or the organizational cultures of the two firms prove incompatible.

15.6 Transferring the Implementation System

It is often expected that implementation systems effective in headquarters can be easily transferred to subsidiaries abroad. But these subsidiaries operate in different cultural and economic systems, and assumptions of compatibility may be unrealistic. In practice, the problems may be severe.

Two examples are given by attempts to transfer systems:

- re-engineering;
- quality circles.

15.6.1 Transferring re-engineering

Hammer and Champy's (1993) system for RE-ENGINEERING organizational processes aimed to achieve dramatic improvements in performance by discarding existing structures and systems, and replacing them with new ones. Born in the United States, it reflected values of American culture:

- low needs to avoid uncertainty. It called for ambiguity in job responsibilities, tolerance of change and restructuring processes, conflict and dismissals. It was highly stressful;
- high individualism and low collectivism. It called for the erosion of departmental boundaries and demanded individual initiative and decision-making;
- low power distances. It called for reductions in middle management and management authority, and a flattening of the hierarchy.

Attempts to transfer this to Thai companies have been described by Colin Jones and one of the authors (Mead and Jones (2000)). They caused considerable unease among employees who perceived their jobs were on the line. Cultural differences may in part explain the failures. Relative to American culture, Thai culture has

- high needs to avoid uncertainty;
- low individualism and high collectivism;
- high power distances.

That is, the cultural conditions necessary for assuming the radical changes envisaged by Hammer and Champy were not present. And McKenna (1995) concluded that

> the message of business re-engineering is inappropriate in certain environments and cultures at present, although it may indeed be the message necessary in the future.   *(p. 16)*

15.6.2   *Transferring quality circles*

Whereas re-engineering aimed to overhaul management systems, the concept of the QUALITY CIRCLE had more modest aims, to make existing systems more efficient. The quality circle contributes to achieving strategic goals of producing more efficiently and maximizing profit margins. It was invented by an American, W Edwards Deming, and in the 1950s was adopted by firms in Japan, where it made a major contribution to production between the 1950s and the early 1990s. A small group of employees, usually in a manufacturing unit, took responsibility for analyzing and recommending improvements to their technologies and processes. They typically met after regular working hours and did not expect overtime payment.

When Japanese companies first began to transfer the quality circle from the United States, they prepared at length. They analyzed the cultural implications of the technique and the conditions under which it could be grafted on to their existing structures and within the cultural context. In transplanting, they adapted.

But during the 1970s, American companies were slipping back in the race against Japanese competition. In an attempt to emulate their rivals they began "re-importing" the Quality Circle, but usually without attempting to re-adapt it. Most failed. This was in spite of warnings. Schein (1981) argued against solutions that did not sufficiently recognize the differences in the environments in which Japanese and American companies operated. Japanese cultural practices could not be transplanted to an American setting as though they were rice seedlings.

When an implementation system is borrowed inappropriately and no attempt is made to adapt it to the new context, one of three things happens:

- the system is rejected;
- the system functions as planned, but its operation transfers the problem elsewhere in the total system – as when a new road designed to alleviate traffic pressure creates new pressure points elsewhere;
- the process functions as planned, but its operation causes new problems.

Japanese success in adopting the American concept of Quality Circle demonstrates that strategic implementation systems CAN be successfully transplanted. But every system reflects the cultural priorities of its original context, and adaptation may be necessary before it can be transplanted. The next section gives a model for transferring a system.

15.7 Implications for the Manager

This model covers the steps needed to transfer a strategic implementation system from headquarters to a subsidiary in some other culture. Apply this model to an MNC that you know.

MODEL FOR TRANSFERRING AN IMPLEMENTATION SYSTEM

1 (a) REVIEW your strategic goals.
   (b) DEFINE your aim in transferring the system. How might the system help you achieve your goals?
2 COLLECT INFORMATION about the system.
3 ANALYZE THE SYSTEM. How does it reflect the cultural and non-cultural characteristics of its home context? (Take into account factors associated with the economy, industry, market, national culture, and organizational culture.) What is the system expected to achieve within its home context?
4 ANALYZE THE TARGET CONTEXT. How closely does the system reflect the target context? What are the relevant cultural and non-cultural characteristics of the target context that will affect implementation?
5 (a) DESIGN PLANS for ADAPTING the system so that it can achieve your goals (stage 1) and be appropriate to the target context (stage 4).

   (b)   DESIGN PLANS for communicating the adapted system within the organization in the target context and to appropriate parties in its environment.
   (c)   DESIGN PLANS for any necessary training.
6 IMPLEMENT the adapted system; implement stage 5.
7 MONITOR the implementation – stage 6.
8 MODIFY as necessary, depending on the stage 7 output.

15.8 SUMMARY

This chapter has discussed problems that arise in implementing strategy. Section 15.2 argued that successful implementation depends upon the manager developing a body of KNOWL-EDGE about the context within which the plan has to function. Knowledge was distinguished from information. The next section examined the importance of using knowledge to develop ORGANIZATIONAL CAPABILITIES. Section 15.4 dealt with systems for successful implementation, and paid particular attention to the importance of effective COMMUNICATION and the development of systems that take into account the different categories involved in giving the strategic plan a practical realization. Section 15.5 discussed the functions of MERGERS AND ACQUISITIONS as systems for implementing the strategic plan, and Section 15.6 dealt with problems that can arise in TRANSFERRING THE IMPLEMENTATION SYSTEM to some other national culture than that of headquarters.

15.9 EXERCISE

This case exemplifies the advantages and disadvantages of using SWOT analysis.

The ThaiSure insurance company, based in Bangkok, has the strategic goal of becoming market leader in the Thai and Southeast Asian marine insurance industry. It has one extraordinary asset. A senior manager, Mr Charnvit, is generally reckoned to be an expert in marine reinsurance, and one of the best anywhere. He has worked in leading firms across the world, has developed a unique body of experience and contacts, and has kept abreast of all recent developments in the field. He advises governments across the world.

However, he is growing old and close to retirement. Every time the CEO suggests that it is now time that he passes on his specialized skills and understanding of client needs to other managers in the company, he hesitates. He prides himself on this knowledge and the reputation that it gives him, and is increasingly unwilling to share it. Top management is increasingly concerned. If Mr Charnvit can be persuaded to pass on his secrets, the company will move closer to achieving its strategic goal. But if he is incapacitated or dies before training his successors, the company will have lost a prized asset. Many of his clients will move their business to other firms and the company is bound to lose competitive position.

QUESTIONS

(a) Why might Mr Charnvit's knowledge be included as a company asset, of value in implementing the strategic goal?

(b) Why might Mr Charnvit's knowledge NOT be included as a company asset?

(c) From ThaiSure's perspective, how far does his possession of knowledge PRESENTLY constitute

- a strength?
- a weakness?
- an opportunity?
- a threat?
- none of the above?

(d) Twenty years ago, a business magazine published a story celebrating Mr Charnvit's unusual expertise. For the first time he and the company became well known. AT THAT POINT do you think his possession of knowledge constituted

- a strength?
- a weakness?
- an opportunity?
- a threat?
- none of the above?

(e) NEXT WEEK, a giant Anglo-American insurance company, AngAmSure, will announce plans to open a Southeast Asian branch, to be located in Bangkok. It is expected that the expatriate staff will include the only serious rival to Mr Charnvit. Indeed, many experts consider that Professor Jones is Mr Charnvit's better. In this new situation, do you think that Mr Charnvit's knowledge gives ThaiSure

- a strength?
- a weakness?
- an opportunity?
- a threat?
- none of the above?

(f) As it happens, Professor Jones decides to retire and AngAmSure will not open a Southeast Asian branch. But unhappily, Mr Charnvit is run over by a bus and killed – without passing on his knowledge. In this new situation, does Mr Charnvit's one-time possession of knowledge constitute

- a strength?
- a weakness?
- an opportunity?
- a threat?
- none of the above?

(g) Applying your answers to (a)–(f), decide what factors constrain the value of knowledge as a means by which to implement a strategic plan?

(h) What do your answers tell you about the uses of SWOT analysis?

Notes

1 Letter to the Editor. *Daily Telegraph*, January 29, 2005.

2 Tom Lester. Accounting for knowledge assets. *Financial Times*, February 21, 1996.

3 Merger would reshape market analysis field. *International Herald Tribune*, April 30, 2008.

E-Communication

16.1   Introduction

In Thailand, an expatriate country manager reported:

> The people here took to using email very quickly and very easily. . . . [so] the issue here hasn't
> been implementation per se, in fact I'd say email's being *over*-used . . . the problem we've got
> here is the way in which email is being used, something that's now starting to hit our bottom
> line.

Chapter 6 explored how cultural differences influence traditional communication methods. This chapter focuses on an increasingly common form of workplace interaction with
which the international manager needs to contend, specifically computer-mediated communication, usually referred to as *e-communication*. E-communication – with email as
its lifeblood – has emerged as the primary conduit for disseminating organizational data,
information and opinion. For the cross-national management of business corporations
this is important because global teams rely on email for an estimated 70 to 80 percent of
their communication

The main advantages of e-communication over traditional methods of communication are

- economies of *time*; and
- economies of *cost*.

Freed from the constraints of time and space, e-communication accelerates the spread of information, speeding up the flow of company data whether across an open plan office in London or from London to Beijing. Transmission is almost instantaneous, greatly reducing the time taken in sending messages. As one executive put it "email means I can contact fifty people simultaneously anywhere in the world. That means one email compared to the 50 telephone calls I would otherwise have to make. There's no choice to make . . .".

In much the same way email saves the *costs* otherwise associated with traditional communication methods, including postal mail, telephone calls and face to face (FtF) meetings – particularly where the latter involves domestic or international travel. Email is supported by the full range of computer-based tools and applications and can be amended, filed and updated with ease.

Used efficiently, e-technology enhances cross-national communication, connecting company employees separated in time and place at any time of the day or night, regardless of language and cultural differences.

16.2 Controlling by E-Communication

Companies control and manage their international operations using a range of bureaucratic and cultural methods. Bureaucratic control involves an emphasis on formal rules and regulations – usually emanating from the corporate center. Conversely, cultural control tends to stress the informal, psychological contract between employer and employee negotiated through loyalty, shared values and commitment.

E-communication effectively bridges these two methods, integrating essential characteristics of both. On the one hand email – as a formal system of data transfer – facilitates bureaucratic control through inherent and continuous vigilance of information traffic regardless of time or origin, recording permanently all messages sent and received in the process.

In addition e-communication is *value infused*, laden with the unwritten rules and expectations of the cultural context in which the technology was created. In this way the successful implementation and usage of corporate e-communication is determined not just by the transferability of knowledge but also by the successful assimilation of the underlying Western values of *transparency, accountability, participation* and *accessibility* in which email is inherently grounded.

E-communication exemplifies what Kostova and her colleagues term a "strategic organizational practice" in a series of influential papers on corporate subsidiary control (e.g. Kostova, 1999; Kostova and Roth, 2002). A strategic organizational prac-tice is more than a mere technology or product innovation in the same way that e-communication is more than an aggregate of machines and systems (Kambayashi, 2003). E-communication encapsulates a particular way of conducting organizational functions, functions which have evolved under the influence of an organization's societal context and have become institutionalized as integral tools for achieving the strategic mission of the firm.

16.2.1   Email versus face-to-face communication

The process of communicating by email comprises moving text from one computer mail-box to another. Yet this apparently simple phenomenon embodies two distinct character-istics that serve to distinguish email from other modes of workplace interaction:

- First, email is *asynchronous* or non-simultaneous. Like memos or postal mail but unlike face-to-face (FtF) conversations, email does not require coordination between sender and receiver. In this way telephone tag – the great problem of workplace communication, where up to 70 percent of initial calls fail to make contact – is almost completely avoided.
- Second, email is *text based*. It has no picture or sound components. In contrast to traditional communication, where communicators depend on the social context of a communication for up to 75 percent of all meaning, the "social cues" in email are almost entirely absent.

On the other hand, successful FtF communication depends on the use of social cues, and these fall into three types:

- *Static* cues emanate from the social and personal characteristics of the individual, for example gender, physical appearance, age and status as well as artifacts such as size of office, awards, prizes and so forth.
- *Dynamic* cues emanate from people's non-verbal behaviors, such as facial expres-sions, body gestures and posture, all of which typically change over the course of an interaction.
- *Verbal* cues are given by tone, quality and modulation of voice.

Because e-communication suppresses these social cues, it has been described as the "lean-est of all communication methods expressing the lowest capacity to facilitate shared meaning" (Kabasakal et al., 2006), see figure 16.1. Conversely, traditional face-to-face (FtF) communication is described as the "richest", because it benefits from instant feed-back, body language, language variety and personal delivery.

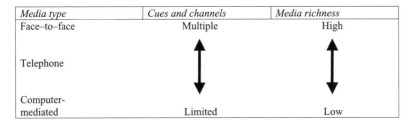

Media type	Cues and channels	Media richness
Face–to–face	Multiple	High
Telephone		
Computer-mediated	Limited	Low

Figure 16.1 Information richness
Source: Adapted from Kabasakal et al. (2006)

16.2.2   Richness in media

Effective communication relies on correctly matching the informational demands of a message (its equivocality) to the capabilities of the media used, its richness.

In general, speaking-rich media are appropriate for complex, ambiguous interaction, relationship building and discussion. By contrast, lean media are a poor substitute for FtF communication, and are best suited for transferring only the simpler, most direct forms of data (Abdul-Gader, 1996; Raman and Watson, 1994).

As Leamer and Storper (2001) note, one can have a conversation through a computer but not a handshake. On the other hand, the US Motorola top management discovered that countless email exchanges might still fail to achieve their intended outcomes; and only when they had sat down with staff and talked the issues through in the traditional manner did "anything got sorted out" (Andrews et al., 2003).

16.2.3   Organizational implications

Although email cannot guarantee shared meaning, business is increasingly dependent on it. It not only supplements other communication modes, it has supplanted them. A study by Sarbaugh-Thompson and Feldman (1988) (cited in Byron (2008)) suggests that the total volume of all other forms of communication will decrease as a direct consequence of email usage – in particular because it employs fewer "greetings" and other informal interactions traditionally used among coworkers. As a consequence of this continued increase in email, employees are reported to feel "less connected" and "more distant" from their colleagues and coworkers (Byron, 2008)

Of course, such studies express broad generalizations, most obviously because email usage across both companies and industries varies considerably. In different companies, variations occur because of industry and sector demographics. At the individual level, differences may be due to experience, personality characteristics and managerial attitudes.

Taken as a whole, the overuse of email presents a potential problem in terms of relationship development, team building and trust. When participants are communicating face to face, they employ rapid feedback and the social cues listed in 16.2.1 to identify and repair misunderstandings with relative ease.

A recent review by Kristin Byron (2008) suggests that the "lean" features of email can contribute to the miscommunication of emotion between employees, and therefore increase the likelihood of misunderstandings, resentment, and conflict, These behaviors may have the effect of slowing communication rather than speeding it – which is one intended outcome of using email. Attempts to reduce such problems by using "emoticons" in email messages (e.g. smiley faces) has produced mixed results. Byron (2008) suggests that these emoticons are not always interpreted in the same way, even within the same social context.

16.3   Cross-national Implementation

When MNCs seek to extend their corporate e-communication systems across borders, the problems outlined above may be made worse by contextual variations. These include variations in the cultural, political, legal, technological, and economic environments in which the MNC is operating.

MNCs may find that the availability of e-communication does not necessarily guarantee that it can be used to its full potential – and in this respect, e-communication is like many other innovations. Messaging systems may be used with varying regularity or not at all. E-communication may be adopted but then used in a different manner or for purposes other than intended by corporate headquarters. Even where e-communication is being utilized as intended, MNCs may find it leads to higher productivity in one setting while reducing productivity in another.

Anecdotal evidence suggests that learning how to manage the technology across different cultural contexts poses the biggest challenge. This section first briefly explores the infrastructural concerns, and then focuses on the impact of cultural variations.

16.3.1   Development

Western companies have been developing their e-communication systems for nearly three decades. Email has emerged as the everyday heart of the system since the early 1990s.

However, at the international level the implementation of email across corporate subsidiary networks has been substantially more rapid and often haphazard. In emerging Asian economies, many e-communication systems were imposed almost overnight after the regional economic crisis of 1997–98. The recipient local subsidiaries of Western headquartered MNCs of the period were collectively described as "Ground Zero" for email assimilation across geographical and cultural borders (Andrews et al., 2003; Yeung, 2000; Legewie and Meyer-Ohle, 2000).

But in general, initial phases of implementing email across borders have been beset by problems that usually arise from the infrastructure. The emerging economies across parts of Africa, the Middle East and Asia have been constrained in using e-communication by a lack of technical infrastructure (e.g. stable electricity supplies) and in particular a lack of skilled operational manpower (Furuholt and Orvik, 2006; Abdul-Gader, 1996). Implementing the use of the new technology through subsidiaries was also hampered initially by the unwillingness and inability of senior local managers to actually *use* the new computers on their desks – despite being happy to have them there as status symbols.

Initial fears of the new technology focused on issues of privacy, security and authentication of messages. Recently, however, that aspect of e-communication that has emerged as the most disliked is the excessive volume of unnecessary and unwanted emails. And this is the same problem in the West.

Over time email use has increased across corporate subsidiary networks across the globe and is now, in certain cases, positively welcomed among virtual teams from different cultural and linguistic backgrounds. The email format and the time it allows both sender and receiver to construct meaning helps the non-native speaker of English to communicate more effectively. A participant in a study by Grosse (2002) opines that whereas on the telephone it is difficult to communicate with limited vocabulary across a cultural divide, with email one has the time to compose one's words and look something up if one doesn't know what to say.

16.3.2   *The culture factor*

Beyond the technical and linguistic challenges outlined above it is the subtle but often deeply entrenched effect of *cultural* variations that can play a pervasive but often invisible role in cross-border email utilization. A landmark study by Sproull and Kiesler (1986) noted that the context within which senders and receivers are situated regulates and moderates both communication *contact* (i.e. who exchanges information with whom) and communication *content* (i.e. the nature of information to be communicated).

Strongly shared cultural norms promote the quick and accurate use of computer-mediated communication (CMC), reducing the risk of miscommunication. However, it is when strongly shared norms within one context meet with strongly shared norms from another that the culturally derived difficulties begin to emerge. Specifically, in spite of the increasing prevalence of electronically connected virtual teams, such functional groups have consistently failed to create the value expected when made operational across cultural borders.

Part of the problem appears to stem from the fact that the subsequent use of e-communication *as intended* hinges on the acceptance of a culturally specific set of assumptions, specifically those of the Anglo-US societal context from which email was created. International management theorists have consistently positioned the Anglo-US context at one extreme of the major cultural distance continuums – i.e. highly individualist, direct, overt, egalitarian and task based. The key question then – by implication – is to what extent the norms and values of *different* cultures (e.g. highly collectivist, indirect, implicit, hierarchical and relations based) influence the subsequent adoption and usage of Western corporate email systems.

On the one hand, the assumption is that such particularities are of minimal consequence, primarily because the lack of social cues in email eliminates contextual biases and allows for more accurate perceptions of messages across cultural and linguistic divides (Byron, 2008). Ma's (1996) research, for example, found that when using CMC East Asians became more direct in their communication behavior than in traditional FtF interaction.

Anecdotal evidence also suggests that the individualist nature of computer-mediated interaction is also adopted in e-communication by those from traditionally collectivist Asian contexts. It is also important to note that the new generation of global subsidiary managers are generally younger, often Western educated and thus far more likely to have more positive attitudes towards e-communication than their indigenous predecessors.

However, there is also evidence to suggest that even as the boundaries between societal cultures become increasingly blurred, the adoption and usage of email does not occur in a cultural vacuum. Martinson and Westwood's 1997 study, for example, indicates that many of the larger Sino-foreign joint ventures have simply grafted Western CMC technology onto the existing management system – retaining the dominant societal values and orientations. Martinsons and Hempel note that "beneath a business veneer which resembles that found in the West [the Chinese have] a deeply-rooted and different social culture [which] has led to unique patterns of intra- and inter-organizational behavior..." (quoted in Martinsons and Westwood, 1997, p. 224).

Perhaps more relevant still is the small but growing evidence from practitioners suggesting that e-communication and cultural values exert a reciprocal, continually evolving influence on one another. On the one hand, computer mediation necessitates the adaptation of communication style by members of high-context cultures towards the more overt, direct norms of the West. However, distinct cultural facets moderate not just the degree to which people adopt e-communication at the workplace but the degree to which they then utilize such communication *as intended*.

16.4   Email Utilization: Exploring Culture's Consequences

The two main dimensions of cultural variance held to moderate e-communication are: (i) the high-context versus low-context scale developed by Edward Hall (1976) and (ii) the hierarchy/power distance dimension developed from – among others – Hofstede (1980) and Trompenaars (1993).

16.4.1   The context continuum

Hall's scale of high-context/low-context variations (discussed in Chapter 6) denotes the degree to which information in a culture is explicit, direct, vested in words and unambiguous. A high degree of direct communication typifies the low-context (LC) cultures of the Western (Anglo-European) world, where the belief is that the intended meaning of a message can be almost entirely conveyed by overt cues and elaborate codes (primarily words and numbers). This tends to promote the use of direct speech and formal communications systems – such as email – as being both natural and almost entirely adequate for everyday working use.

By contrast, traditional communication across the high-context (HC) cultures of the Far East is predominantly implicit. As noted by Andersen (2000), "Asians are reluctant to arbitrarily advance personal opinions or attitudes [and] will draw on the situational context and attempt to instinctively discern what the other person is thinking". To the outsider HC communication can be disarmingly indirect as so much of the explicit, verbal content is replaced by this emphasis on tacit, non-verbal cues. In an HC context social cues *need* to be perceived and interpreted face to face in order to accurately understand the message being conveyed. HC cultures are above all "relationship cultures" where organizational coordination and control are achieved using subtle, personalized codes and networks

In such an environment there is little perceived value in codifying traditional communication into the formal, impersonal, standardized format that email epitomizes. Nonetheless, given the strategic importance of MNC global integration, subsidiary organizations across a variety of ostensibly HC contexts have had little choice but to adopt the technology imposed. What are the consequences of this apparent dissonance? The following examples – drawn from a host of conversations with subsidiary employees across East Asia – will serve to illustrate the potential dangers and pitfalls to avoid.

The first of these focuses on what Kostova and colleagues have termed "ceremonial adoption". This is where a corporate practice is *implemented* but remains to be *internalized* by indigenous personnel. In other words, subsidiary managers will have adopted email solely in acquiescence to coercive corporate pressure. However, due to the perceived incongruence of e-communication (and the values on which it rests) in the host context the practice is simply not *valued*.

The *cumulative* dislike of email interaction is still common across emerging Asia – particularly among older, senior-level managers – due to the way it has supplanted much of the traditional communication methods. The lack of team meetings, in particular, is held to damage group feeling, harmony and motivation as a result. In HC cultures one is first and foremost a member of a collective, the HC–LC scale being largely synonymous with Hofstede's Individualism–Collectivism continuum. For this reason email is practiced but often grudgingly so at best.

Another example of ceremonial adoption concerns the *way* in which the new technology is being used. Due again to its perceived cultural incongruence email tends to be used solely to convey bland, unimportant and/or uncontroversial information simply to conform to the usage-frequency expectations of Western corporate headquarters. Much of the information of real consequence locally, however, is kept away from the computer and is conferred only by FtF among trusted "in-groups" (another facet of HC cultural contexts). As a consequence many foreign expatriates suffer a persistent and frustrating gap between reality and the information he or she receives about that reality.

In addition to ceremonial adoption it is also interesting to look at customized adoption, where email has been both implemented and internalized but in a way that counters corporate intentions. This involves indigenous employees shaping e-communication technology for use in ways that are fundamentally congruent with prevailing HC communication norms. The need to maintain face and harmony and to avoid confrontation wherever possible gives rise to a number of examples.

First, email traffic is being used in order to *delay* any potential meeting and resultant conflagration with the recipient – whether a supplier, customer or simply a departmental colleague. The second example concerns the way email is being used in preference to FtF communication in order to defuse expected anger or emotion prior to the imminent FtF meeting.

Anecdotal evidence suggests that there is a much higher frequency in HC contexts for both these forms of usage than per headquarters norms. However, the results of this from the corporate perspective are at best mixed. Concerning the diffusion of anger/emotion the reaction from Western expatriates has been largely positive. However, where email is being used to delay an uncomfortable meeting the problem is that this can delay the resolution of problems, and therefore acts to slow the communication process rather than accelerating it.

16.4.2   Hierarchy

Generally speaking, high context cultures are characterized by relatively hierarchical, status-oriented organizational relationships. This contrasts with the egalitarian tradition on which e-communication was first created. In Western contexts email is viewed – and often lauded – as a democratizer, a force for status equalization and participation, used as an integral tool in the quest for flatter organizational structures predominant since the late 1980s (Owens et al., 2001).

Email democratizes intra-corporate communication in two ways. First, it erodes status-based hierarchies by diminishing the social context and dynamic communication cues (as outlined above). Second, email facilitates organizational accessibility and participation, allowing employees to communicate directly with any corporate actor regardless of rank or position.

Email accessibility is designed to expedite the speed of information flow, encouraging improved efficiency and intra-corporate integration. However, in socially hierarchical contexts where relationships and networks are sustained and nurtured through status differentials, the impetus to democratize communication is considerably weakened, employees responding negatively to closer relationships between superiors and subordinates.

This has been observed in locations as far apart as Bulgaria (e.g. Griffith, 1996), China (Martinsons and Westwood, 1997) and Japan (Kambayashi, 2003). However, by far the most hierarchically oriented societal contexts are those of Eastern Asia. The power structures of traditional Asian organizations resemble a series of concentric circles. Open communications systems are thus viewed with suspicion as a threat to the control of information among privileged in-groups.

For subsidiary managers raised in hierarchical social contexts the big boss is the central node for external communications. In this way accessing external colleagues – whether from a different department or a different country – without first obtaining the boss's approval has often been met with discomfort and confusion. As a consequence the tendency is for this function of email to be ceremonially utilized, without conviction and with less frequency than intended by corporate headquarters.

Again this illustrates the case of ceremonial adoption, at least initially – where the functions is practiced at best mechanically but without conviction. Over time, as utilization has increased, it has often been done on the basis of subsequent adaptation towards indigenous cultural norms. For example, emails written for external recipients are sent initially to the boss for approval and amendment first before being forwarded outside.

The problem with such infidelity of usage is that, again, instead of expediting information flows within the company as intended, e-communication can actually slow it down. A related example concerns the growing tendency of lower- and middle-ranking employees to follow any action or decision taken with an email to the boss, effectively signing off accountability for the boss to assume all decision-making responsibility. Not only does this manner of email usage run contrary to corporate intentions towards accessibility and participation, it also adds to the inbox overload of senior indigenous executives and again impacts on efficiency and productivity.

One final example of customized usage – in adherence to indigenous cultural norms – concerns the relatively frequent use of email across Southeast Asia to convey news or requests to one's superior or peer in favor of face-to-face or telephone communication. In hierarchical contexts email is perceived as being suitably non-intrusive, obviating the need to disturb those of a superior status (e.g. through a telephone call or a knock on the office door). The Thai concept of *kreng jai* (or "reticence to disturb" – particularly an elder or superior) typically expresses this norm across hierarchical cultures in the region. Unfortunately, where email is concerned excessive use in this manner may again slow down speed of information flow in that news – particularly negative news – that may need urgent attention is unnecessarily delayed.

Writing about Thai business culture at the advent of email implementation in 1995, the following quote from Holmes and Tangtongtavy now seems almost prophetic:

> Bringing egalitarian systems and values to socially hierarchical Thailand can create a myriad of problems, most prominently in the areas of communication [and] sharing of information ... both verbal and non-verbal. *(p. 33)*

16.5 Implications for the Manager

(a) The cross-national implementation of corporate e-communication forces individuals to adopt new communication behaviors.

(b) Given that this requires the use of cognitive and emotional effort on their part it is especially important to gain both their cooperation and commitment to the new technology.

(c) The examples presented in the previous section illustrate how a lack of such commitment in the value of corporate CMC programs can effectively circumvent the benefits.

(d) Obviously they are extreme cases. The response of individual company subsidiaries may be mitigated by factors such as the extent to which the organization interacts with foreign counterparts and/or deals with foreign customers.

(e) Nonetheless this has highlighted the fact that unintended, culturally derived usage adaptations compromise corporate control and organizational productivity.

(f) Increased awareness of how e-technology and cultural norms and values interact to shape the use of organizational e-communication can help MNCs to maximize the benefits of the technology in any given context while minimizing the drawbacks – which may be difficult to foresee.

(g) Understanding the subtle means by which specific cultural dimensions influence subsidiary adoption and subsequent use of corporate CMC systems will also reduce the occurrences and limit the damage of email miscommunication.

(h) In addition, MNCs should consider offering training in the cross-cultural use of email across the corporate fold.

(i) Despite the many advantages of email communication, managers must be wary of supplanting FtF communication and the specific benefits it affords. This is especially important for virtual teams, for example at the beginning of a project in order to establish working relationships and build trust.

(j) FtF meetings also make up for the deficit of visual cues in e-communication and provide an opportunity to resolve any misunderstandings and ambiguity caused by cultural differences. Bargiela-Chiappini and Nickerson (2003) suggest that it is "no accident that corporate meetings should continue to dominate much of the research in business communication ... [for] ... the technological advances that accelerated internationalization in business have not and, arguably, never will, quite replace FTF encounters".

(k) Information richness theory points to the need to optimize communication effectiveness by matching the purpose of the communication with the communication media being used. However, during the rapid imposition of corporate email systems overseas the cross-cultural implications of this theory have been underexplored.

(l) A more sensitive examination of cultural context points to the need for MNCs to adopt a portfolio approach among differing communication methods in order to manage effectively organizational interaction across borders

16.6 SUMMARY

Communicating across borders has always presented managers with special challenges. E-communication alleviates many of the practical constraints, allowing instantaneous communication between corporate employees right across the globe. From its inception, however, email was designed primarily for the transmission of relatively short, simple, unambiguous types of data.

Section 16.2 looked at the use of EMAIL versus FACE-TO-FACE COMMUNICATION. Email filters out the non-verbal cues that are essential in FtF discussion and opinion exchange and so can lead to miscommunication if not utilized with care. Section 16.3 dealt with CROSS-NATIONAL IMPLEMENTATION and saw that the use of corporate email across geographical and cultural boundaries involves additional complexities of both a social and an infrastructural nature. The latter were mostly due to developmental differentials, particularly across the emerging markets of Asia and Africa.

Over time, however, it is the influence of CULTURAL differences that have become most important – discussed in Section 16.4. They moderate both the extent and, increasingly, the way in which email is used. Customized adoption of email poses a particular challenge because where email is being used in ways that circumvent original corporate intentions the result may be slower information flows and decreased productivity. Extrapolating corporate e-communication systems effectively across different societal contexts therefore necessitates a closer examination of the dominant values of employees and culture in which the corporate subsidiary functions.

Finally, MNCs should view their intra-organizational communication systems as a portfolio of complementary methods, using email *where possible* but investing in FtF *where appropriate*.

16.7 EXERCISE

Analyze your own usage of email at the workplace.

How long do you spend reading, writing and responding to emails?

How has this changed in the last five years?

What, after many years of email use, do you still consider to be the major benefits? The major drawbacks?

To what extent, if at all, do the benefits outweigh the drawbacks (a) now and (b) five years ago?

How does your own email "style" (response time, response content, level of formality, etc.) compare with that of your immediate work colleagues?

How do these differences cause misunderstanding?

How does your email style differ when writing/responding to (a) superiors and (b) subordinates both individually and to a group?

How does email use in your present organization compare with that of your previous organization? Why do you think such differences occur? To what extent does an organization's sector (e.g. public versus private) or industry context moderate email usage?

In your experience what are the main differences in email use across your organization's international network? This may include response time, response style and email discipline

Think of a subsidiary with which you are particularly familiar:

- How do the perceived advantages and disadvantages of email compare among indigenous employees with those of your own organization?
- What differences are there within the identified subsidiary?
- How far does role, function, age, education and experience influence email usage?
- What other factors may be involved?

CHAPTER SEVENTEEN

Forming an International Joint Venture

CHAPTER OUTLINE

Introduction

Why Invest in an IJV?

Preparing for Success: The Four
    Compatibilities

Trust and Mistrust

Sharing Control

Implications for the Manager

Summary

Exercise

Notes

17.1   Introduction

An Austrian–Vietnamese international joint venture (IJV) planned to announce a new development to the Asian media. The CEO of the Austrian partner traveled to Ho Chi Minh City to participate in the ceremony. He arrived at the IJV to discover that his opposite number in the Vietnamese partner and the IJV CEO had pre-empted him and had made the announcement a day early, thus taking all the credit for themselves. He was so angry that he withdrew his company from the project.

This shows a breakdown in the relationship between IJV partners and management. It also demonstrates a lack of communication, and perhaps raises the question as to whether the Austrians made a wise choice of partner in the first place. If they had prepared more fully, could they have prevented this situation arising?

This chapter deals with three topics; reasons for investing in an IJV, partner selection, and the practical problems of making the project work.

17.2 Why Invest in an IJV?

In an increasingly globalized world, companies increasingly choose to implement strategic goals by operating abroad and developing a multinational profile. A MULTINATIONAL company is defined as one that has one or more investments located abroad, in countries other than that of its headquarters.

17.2.1 *Options for operating abroad*

Lessassy and Jolibert (2007) describe four strategies for internationalization:

- by franchising;
- by direct acquisition;
- by joint venture;
- by operating a subsidiary.

Franchising involves the least risk; among strategies calling for less investment we might add licensing contracts, turnkey agreements, representation by an agent. Among those calling for far heavier levels of investment, mergers and acquisitions were discussed in 15.5. Problems of operating a subsidiary are discussed in the next chapter and this chapter focuses on investing in an international joint venture (IJV).

17.2.2 *The IJV*

The IJV has limited but tightly defined aims. It expresses an alliance with another company that also needs to satisfy strategic goals. Here is a definition adapted from Shenkar and Zeira (1987):

- the IJV is created by the investments of two or more parent companies;
- the IJV is a separate legal organizational entity, and belongs entirely to neither/none of its parents;
- it is jointly controlled by its parents;
- these parents are legally independent of each other;
- the headquarters of at least one parent is located outside the country in which the IJV operates.

The IJV might focus on one or more of a range of functions, including production, marketing, R&D, sales, etc.

Some IJVs are formed on an equity basis. More flexible arrangements may depend on contracted cooperation without involving the legal commitments of equity.

Some IJVs may have more than two parents. Sometimes, both (or all) parents are located outside the IJV country. Coca-Cola (Vietnam) was started as an IJV between Coca-Cola

(USA) and a Singaporean bottler; originally it did not employ any Vietnamese managers. In general, the more parents, the greater the administrative complexities and the greater the problems of managing the project. This applies in politics as much as in business, and the European Union, comprising 27 members, provides an example.

17.2.3   *IJV profitability*

A company enters an IJV partnership in order to satisfy its strategic goals. However, IJVs are not always immediately profitable, and profitability is sometimes difficult to prove. Figures for market share and sales levels may be interpreted differently by the parents and the IJV management and have to be treated with caution; these "objective" measures may be no more reliable than were subjective assessments of long-term advantage. In the short term, alternative forms of foreign investment often bring greater profits. Kent's (1991) longitudinal analysis of deals made by the seven major oil companies (British, Dutch, and five American) showed that joint ventures produced significantly lower gross yields than did non-joint ventures.

There can be no doubt that many IJVs appear to fail, often because they fail to meet their financial targets. Park and Ungson (1997) review the research and suggest a figure as high as 50 percent. Given that many companies would prefer to hide a failure that might frighten off some other prospective partner, the real figure might be much higher.

Failure is most obviously signaled by early termination. The parents dissolve the project prematurely, or one withdraws. However, early termination or withdrawal does not necessarily mean failure. An IJV might be terminated because it has achieved its aims ahead of schedule – that is, it has been an unexpected success. Or perhaps one parent sees advantage in acquiring the project as a wholly-owned subsidiary and the other in selling out.

Given these difficulties in measuring the success or failure of IJVs and problems in predicting and measuring their profitability, why do so many companies persist in entering them? The answer must lie in the opportunities that the arrangement offers for long-term growth.

17.2.4   *Reasons for making the investment*

The partners may have shared interests in forming an IJV that give them both opportunities to

- create greater market power by combining resources;
- reduce risk by sharing risk. Costs of investment and production are shared;
- reap economies of scale;
- cooperate in order to avoid expensive competing. The IJV is an alliance that restricts your own capacity for independent action, but also restricts that of your partner – who might otherwise be a dangerous competitor.

Here are other examples of interests which may not correspond for the two partners. The IJV offers

- the less technological partner, opportunities to benefit from the transference of technology;
- the less well-managed partner, opportunities to acquire new management systems;
- a failing company, opportunities to regain a competitive edge;
- either partner, symbolic benefits. A project formed with a high-status partner from a more developed economy may give status to a partner from a less developed economy. An Indonesian manager explained:

  > when your company forms an alliance with other companies from other countries, the image that they bring to your company is that [it is] going international. When the local company P T Bimanta Na Telecomunication formed an IJV with AT&T, they suddenly gained the trust of the government. [It seemed] reliable to take projects because of the big name of AT&T.

- either partner, opportunities to acquire experience as the first stage to taking the project over and re-establishing it as a subsidiary.

The IJV offers the foreign partner

- the opportunity to meet the host government's requirements for doing business in the country. For instance, a foreign company is only permitted to operate in the country if ownership is shared with a local company;
- opportunities to learn about local marketing conditions and to develop customer networks;
- opportunities to gain access to local resources, including production facilities, labor, and materials.

The IJV offers the local partner

- opportunities to generate up-stream and down-stream industries. For instance, the development of an IJV pulp mill encourages local entrepreneurs to increase logging facilities and to invest in paper manufacture.

The IJV offers the local government

- opportunities to encourage foreign investment. Governments increasingly recognize the benefits of IJV, and many less developed countries have jettisoned centralized regulations restricting foreign ownership. The foreign partner may be allowed to take only minority ownership, and must fulfill conditions regarding local employment, technology transfer, purchase of local materials, etc.

17.2.5   How partners contribute

Both partners choose to establish an IJV because they see this as the way to achieve their strategic goals. But inevitably their goals differ, in the sense that they share a commitment to the IJV's success for different reasons.

Section 17.2.4 shows why they may have different reasons. It also indicates that they make different contributions. It is in the nature of the arrangement that the foreign partner contributes international inputs and the local partner makes local inputs. More specifically, the foreign partner contributes

- international know-how and access to international connections;
- international reputation;
- access to international product markets;
- access to international labor markets;
- access to international finance;
- access to international technologies;
- access to other international resources;
- international distribution.

The local partner contributes

- access to local connections, including government contacts;
- local reputation;
- knowledge of government regulations;
- knowledge of local culture;
- access to local product services;
- access to local labor markets;
- access to other local resources;
- local distribution.

17.2.6   *Reasons for not investing*

Your company may decide not to invest in an IJV because

- you do not expect to receive the benefits listed in 17.2.4;
- you are not prepared to make the contributions listed in 17.2.5;
- you perceive the risks to be unacceptable;
- you cannot afford to make the necessary investments;
- you lack experience and knowledge of the country of operations;
- you are not prepared to meet the conditions set by the government;
- you do not wish to share control of essential resources – for example, technology, your knowledge of local marketing channels;
- you expect an alternative arrangement to be more profitable – for instance, operating through a wholly owned subsidiary – and you do not wish to share profits;
- the company is already market leader and its primary need is to exploit an existing competitive advantage; in this situation, establishing a wholly owned subsidiary is the better alternative.

17.2.7 *Finding a partner*

Finding an appropriate partner requires investment. Here is an example. An American engineering company recognized that its best and perhaps only hope for long-term survival was to form a strategic alliance in the People's Republic of China. A search team was sent to find a partner.

Alliances with most of the possible partners were not practicable because their interests differed too sharply. The Americans wanted to build a long-term position for growth within the region whereas most of the Chinese were looking for a rapid transfer of technology from which they could benefit immediately before searching out a new partner able to supply the next technology. The Chinese would not commit to a 10-year deal. The search team spent 18 months visiting potential partners before they agreeing on terms with the forty-fourth.

This case shows that choosing the right partner may be a long and expensive process that demands careful research. It also shows the importance of recognizing where fundamental interests coincide and differ. The constraints on developing a successful partnership are discussed below.

17.3 Preparing for Success: The Four Compatibilities

Madhok (1995) shifted discussion of IJV governance away from legal and ownership issues to the question of trust. In order for the project to succeed, the relationship between partners has primarily to be created through a process of cooperation and understanding between the partners. This departure from mechanistic controls calls for a more sophisticated process of governance (Madhok 2006). Insights from comparative sociology, cultural studies and economic geography can serve to clarify causes of success and failure. Svejenova (2006) reviews the discussion since 1995.

An early stage in this process of developing a successful partnership consists of identifying possible partners with whom you have STRATEGIC FIT. In general terms this means that

- your different strategic interests are not in conflict;
- both need the IJV in order to achieve your different strategic goals;
- your goals for the IJV are compatible;
- each can supply necessary resources.

More specifically, you must be compatible on four dimensions.

17.3.1 *Compatibility in interest*

Compatibility in interest does not mean that both partners should be in the same industry. It means that each can learn from the other's interest.

Suppose that you refine petroleum and plan to set up an IJV to develop industrial paints, which of these possible partners might best suit your needs?

- a travel agent;
- a bank;
- a construction company;
- a petroleum refiner.

The travel agent is in an entirely different business, and can probably offer nothing relevant to the development of paint. The bank can provide financing, but no relevant expertise. The construction company belongs in a complementary industry and can offer skills, knowledge, markets and business contacts that you lack.

The petroleum refiner may not offer any technology or business contacts that you cannot supply, and there may seem little advantage in joining with a competitor who has precisely the same interests and brings the same resources to the table. But companies in the same industry do form alliances when they hope to benefit from discrepancies in technology, systems, and markets. Past IJVs formed by the Swiss food firm Nestlé include alliances with Coca-Cola, General Mills, and two companies in the People's Republic of China – a coffee and creamer plant, and an infant formula and milk powder plant.[1]

A partnership in the same industry might be valued if it offers opportunities that arise from its different environment. Such an IJV gives the foreign partner access to a local market, and the local partner access to the international market. In 1997 two securities companies, the Premier Group of Thailand and SBC Warburg, formed a joint venture designed to provide Warburg with local expertise and Premier with international access.

17.3.2   Compatibility in resources

Partners must not only share goals for the IJV; they must also be willing to implement these goals. Each demonstrates its commitment by contributing the organizational and financial resources decided by the agreement. The efforts made by each should complement and not duplicate those efforts made by the other. The application of resources must be complementary. In addition, both must be prepared to invest its reputation and important business contacts.

A project is unlikely to succeed when the supply of resources is not complementary; for example, when both insist on supplying staff but neither is willing to commit the necessary technology.

Resources include knowledge, which may be embedded in social networks; see Parkhe et al. (2006). Despite advances in information technologies, networks of interpersonal relationships may still be crucial in building trust.

17.3.3   Compatibility in size

The parents may be more likely to trust each other when they are of similar size, Difference in size is destructive if one uses its greater resources to dominate the IJV in its own interests alone. Problems arise if managers from the large secure company are unwilling to participate and adapt, and will not share information with the partner and the IJV.

However, the development of business by IT means that businesses expand and contract in a very short time, and the size of staffing complements and physical resources is no longer so accurate a guide to a firm's financial and knowledge power as once it was. In companies that are technology intensive, the numbers on the payroll may be irrelevant. But a difference in size may be important when it causes dispute within the organizational culture.

17.3.4 *Compatibility in time-scales*

The parents need to share a time-scale. Suppose that Parents A and B are both prepared to invest five years' development costs. The project is set fair. But contradictions arise when Parent A aims at reinvesting profits made during the initial period whereas Parent B wants a quick return from its investments.

The Introduction provides an example of a company experiencing difficulties in locating a partner that needed a long-term venture. In that case, the problems arose from needs for technology transfer.

17.4   Trust and Mistrust

The most important factor in choosing a partner is that you feel able to trust them and they trust you. Trusting them means that you understand their needs and interests and feel competent to predict their behavior in routine circumstances. It does not necessarily involve emotional commitment – you may not even like them. Trust is developed when the partners have the compatibilities listed in 17.3, and in addition understand and agree on

- priorities in planning and implementing IJV strategy;
- contractual details;
- development stages;
- the design of management style, structure and systems;
- systems for communicating between the parents, the IJV and parents, within the IJV, and with the environment;
- criteria for evaluating IJV development and success.

A previous history between the partners helps to stabilize the relationship, and an atmosphere of reciprocity and goodwill prolongs it. Hagedoorn (2006) argues that in a successful partnership, the learning process between partners creates positive conditions for future partnerships.

But when these conditions do not apply, trust is harder to achieve. Opportunism and mistrust destroy the relationship, and the IJV parents act less as partners and more as rivals.

17.4.1   Change in the environment and trust

Change in the environment may force the partner to modify its commitment. New opportunities in new markets, new competition, new technologies, new economic and political constraints imposed by the government may all explain why a partner loses interest in the IJV. It may have negotiated the IJV in good faith, fully intending to commit all contracted resources, but for reasons beyond its control, corporate priorities have changed. It no longer needs the venture to succeed in order to achieve its strategic goals, or can no longer afford to invest in it, or no longer values a long-term relationship with its partner.

Both partners operate in volatile environments, and it is in the nature of an international JV that they operate in different environments. Their local markets and competition differ. They are subject to different local political, social and economic pressures. These environmental differences make any alliance inherently unstable.

This factor of environmental uncertainty explains why many companies increasingly prefer short-term alliances with highly specific goals. The partners might use an initial limited alliance in order to test the possibilities for a greater commitment and to build trust.

Changes within the partner may affect its interest in the IJV. For example, it appoints a new CEO with new strategic goals or the IJV champion is replaced in his post. The partner develops new priorities and downgrades the IJV.

The picture is further complicated by the extent to which cultural factors influence how trust is given. When the cultural bases of trust differ in the countries of the partners, they bring with them different motivations and expectations of behavior in the venture; see Zaheer and Zaheer (2006).

17.4.2   Mistrust between the partners

Mistrust between partners is expensive, and involves costs in policing the agreement (Madhok, 2006). Mistrust arises when there is a lack of understanding of the degree of commitment required.

Perhaps a partner has failed to prepare sufficiently; the foreign partner lacks understanding of the local environment. Or the negotiations and contractual documents are confused and fail to spell out the IJV goals and each side's rights and obligations. Or the partners conflict over their interpretations of strategic goals, commitments to resourcing, sharing of costs and benefits. A study made of Canadian high-technology alliances emphasized that the first year of operations is particularly fraught with difficulties, particularly those associated with partner selection, communication, and reconciliation (Kelly et al., 2002). The implication is that first year operations demand the wholehearted attention of headquarters, who must be prepared to renegotiate aspects of the agreement. Renegotiation is discussed in 8.5.9. Or one partner has learned faster from the IJV and so is able to dominate the relationship, and no longer needs the other.

17.4.3   Mistrust within the IJV

The success of the IJV hangs not only on relationships between the partners. It also depends on trust and mistrust within the IJV, between staff posted to the IJV and their headquarters, and between the IJV and its environment.

An IJV succeeds when project staff trust each other and when persons posted from the two parents develop productive relationships. Before project operations start, a shared project culture is fostered by mixing staff from the parents in groups, where they work together on project planning. They exchange non-critical technological and business data.

Mistrust arises when

- staff from the two partners interpret the goals of the IJV differently;
- staff join the IJV ignorant of the needs and interests of their colleagues from the other partner;
- local staff feel threatened by a stronger foreign parent;
- conflicts arise from human resource and technology transfer policies. Staff from one partner cannot supply the skills and other resources to which they are committed;
- differences in the partners' organizational cultures, structures and systems lead to misunderstandings;
- differences in the partners' national cultures lead to misunderstandings.

17.4.4   Trust and mistrust between staff posted to the IJV and their headquarters

An IJV is more likely to succeed when staff posted to it feel confident of the support of their headquarters. Mistrust arises when

- support promised by headquarters fails to materialize;
- staff feel that their long-term career prospects with headquarters are in jeopardy;
- staff are not adequately compensated for taking part in the IJV;
- the partner fails to communicate its goals effectively within headquarters;
- subordinate levels responsible for servicing the IJV perceive it as a drain on their resources, and give it a minimum of attention.

17.4.5   Trust between the IJV and its local environment

The IJV needs to secure trusting relationships with a range of organizations in the local environment. They include

- professional associations and trade unions;
- consumers and consumer associations;
- stockholders;
- environmental agencies;

- suppliers, distributors, agents;
- analysts and the media;
- religious groups;
- the government and bureaucracy at national, provincial and municipal levels.

17.4.6   Fit between organizational cultures

When talks designed to lead to a strategic alliance between Mitsubishi of Japan and Daimler-Benz of Germany broke down,

> analysts say the match has been strained from the beginning because the companies have fundamentally different structures. Daimler-Benz, a much smaller company than Mitsubishi, has traditionally had a close-knit management structure that has tended to set out clear strategic goals and forge ahead. Mitsubishi, an amorphous conglomerate of several large companies, has moved much more cautiously with internal factions often disagreeing over broader policy, analysts said.[2]

The companies were unable to overcome differences in their strategies, structures and organizational cultures.

Staff posted to the project from the two parents are more likely to work well together when their organizational cultures are similar. This does not mean that they should be identical – an impossible condition. Rather, a sense of comfort about how the other does business, a willingness to work together and learn, and a need for shared solutions generates a willingness to communicate and to avoid misunderstandings.

Staff posted by their headquarters are more likely to feel loyalty to their parent company – which is responsible for their long-term career development and may eventually pay their pensions – than to the IJV, to which they are seconded for a short time.

17.4.7   Fit between national cultures

Jolly's (2002) study of Sino-foreign IJVs found that cultural differences and language differences constituted the two most significant barriers to knowledge transfer between the partners. Perceptions of cultural distance can be fatal, particularly when the partner headquarters use different first languages. On the other hand, an IJV is more likely to succeed when their cultures fit. CULTURAL FIT occurs when barriers to knowledge flows are low and communication is accurate. In such circumstances, trust increases and technologies are transferred efficiently with a minimum of misunderstanding.

Your culture influences how willing you are to trust a possible joint venture partner. Shane (1993) studied perceptions of transaction costs in American affiliates across 38 countries. He found evidence that members of low-power distance cultures are more likely to trust in joint venture partnerships. But where power distances are high and trust is low, people need greater control, fear paying greater transaction costs, and prefer sole ownership.

Your culture also influences your perception of whether your business interests and IJV goals are compatible, whether differences in size are important, what timescale should apply. In theory, you and your partner are more likely to agree on these points when your cultures are close. That is, a venture formed by parents of similar cultures stands a greater chance of succeeding than does one between dissimilar cultures.

Hofstede (1985) hypothesized that synergy between organizations took place when cultures were balanced around the masculine and feminine mean and were close on the "organizational" dimensions of power distance and uncertainty avoidance (pp. 355–356). He cited the examples of British and Dutch cultures (more masculine, more feminine; otherwise similar). Most problems would be experienced by cultures that differed on the organizational dimensions. Hence, a typical company in a full-bureaucracy culture (for instance, France or Belgium) could expect greater problems cooperating with a company in a personnel-bureaucracy culture (Denmark, New Zealand, United Kingdom) than with a company from, say, Korea or Salvador. These two cultures are very close to France and Belgium in terms of both power distance and need to avoid uncertainty although in other respects they are far apart.

17.4.8   The IJV organizational culture is inherently unstable

Most IJVs are inherently unstable arrangements, for a number of reasons. First, both because their parents exist in different, rapidly changing environments. Second, the partners need control and the IJV needs independence. Third, the partners join together (partly) in order to learn from each and this learning reduces the level of mutual need between them, thus reducing the need for cooperation – which may have been one reason for their establishing the IJV in the first place. Fourth, there is an inherent structural weakness; not one but three different management hierarchies (in the partners, and the IJV) are involved in decision-making. The overlaps in authority are always likely to cause misunderstandings and give rise to factionalism. Fifth, as partners learn to work with each other, differences in their national and organizational cultures may become less important. These factors mean that the influence of the partner's cultures is mutable and their fit is continually changing.

17.5   Sharing Control

The models discussed in this section deal with the practical problems of making the venture work. First, Fedor and Werther (1996) proposed eight stages for developing a "culturally responsive alliance" by which they meant an alliance

> that takes advantage of the partners' complementary strengths to exploit the opportunities
> available in its operating environment.   *(p. 46)*

Thus the IJV draws on the strengths of its two parents to create a new culture.

In summary, the eight stages are

1 Each partner identifies its own cultural profile.
2 Negotiating teams compare profiles and identify areas of cultural compatibility and incompatibility.
3 Teams develop a joint business plan. This shows both partners where they converge or diverge in their plans for the IJV.
4 The teams plan the degree of operational independence permitted in the IJV by the partners.
5 The formal structure of the IJV is agreed.
6 The management systems of the IJV are planned to reflect those functions and structures in which it is dependent on its parents and those in which it is independent.
7 The selection of the managing director and key staff is agreed.
8 In the IJV that continues to depend on the parents for critical inputs, its development may require changes in these inputs. These are assessed.

This model recognizes that each partner hopes to exercise the level of control needed in order to achieve its own strategic goals while still retaining the trust of its partner. The model links problems of building an organizational culture, the design of structures between headquarters and subsidiary and within the subsidiary, to the selection of senior staff. (Chapter 20 sees how the MNC headquarters used staffing as a control mechanism.) What the model does not do is show how the partners balance their control over the IJV and manage senior staffing in order to achieve this balance.

Partners agree on a balance of management responsibilities. Each takes responsibility for those functions in which it is the stronger. For instance, an American manager working in a Swiss–United States joint venture reported that his IJV had

> been fortunate that [the Swiss parent] ... has assumed a subordinate role and that [the American parent] has been willing and capable of fulfilling the dominant role. The affect on [the IJV] is that all ordering, invoicing, inventory, distribution, tax obligations, and financial reporting is done through [the American parent] systems. [The Swiss parent] influence comes mainly from product-oriented issues.

17.5.1 Building trust

Integrative mechanisms are developed to build trust between staff in the partners and the IJV (see Kumar and Seth (1998, p. 580). These aim to

- socialize of IJV managers in training sessions and meetings with the parents;
- motivate IJV managers to align their interests with those of the partners;
- staff top management of the IJV with parents' representatives;
- develop an IJV board of directors who participate in strategic planning and performance monitoring.

These systems aim to enable the partners to express their needs for appropriate control and at the same time the IJV to express its needs for independence. In practice, the balance between these forces is being continually renegotiated, and the mechanisms provide opportunities for the parties to communicate and resolve problems. They express an understanding that negotiations between the partners are not completed merely by signing contracts, but continue throughout the implementation of the project. However, building them is not straightforward when trust is based on different conditions in their cultures; see Zaheer and Zaheer (2006).

17.5.2 Communicating between the parents and the IJV

The sections above argue that good relationships between the partners and other parties involved are important in order to improve the odds on success. The integrative mechanisms listed above are augmented by systems designed to prevent misunderstandings occurring in communications. The example given in the Introduction showed that a failure to communicate vital information can damage trust between the different parties and have serious consequences.

Communications need to be managed

- between the parents;
- between each parent and the IJV;
- within the IJV;
- between the parents or IJV and audiences within the environment.

Communication is always most efficient when it is selective. This means, first, that the parties concerned avoid

- undercommunication;
- overcommunication.

Problems also arise when the various parties overcommunicate, and communications are not prioritized. In many projects, quantity of information flow is achieved at the expense of quality. The greater the quantity of unimportant messages that flow in, the less easily can the manager identify and act decisively upon those that matter – particularly if the communications is not in his/her native language. And the process is expensive; both direct and indirect (time, energy) communication costs are incurred.

17.5.3 An IJV communications strategy

An IJV communications plan defines responsibilities between

- the partners;
- IJV management;
- the external environment – including the media, agents, analysts, suppliers, customers, etc.

Table 17.1   The IJV communications plan

WHO (in each partner, the IJV) should be responsible for communicating, given a
    particular addressee and topic?
TO WHOM (in each partner, the IJV, the environment) should different messages
    be communicated?
WHAT messages should be communicated?
HOW should messages be communicated? The plan indicates the appropriate style
    and medium. These may change at different stages of the project. Electronic
    mail works best after the initial relationship has been established.
WHEN should messages be communicated?
WHERE should messages be communicated?

These parameters are adapted from the context of communications, Table 6.1.

17.5.4   *How the IJV affects the organizational cultures of the partners*

Parenting an IJV project influences the culture of the partner headquarters by fostering a
culture of internationalism.

This is ADVANTAGEOUS when the headquarters benefit from an inflow of new ideas
and technologies, and develop new knowledge. It is DISADVANTAGEOUS when the out-
flow of staff to the IJV (and inflow of replacements) impairs internal cohesion. A positive
culture is weakened when staff feel pressured by responsibilities for which they have no
training and experience. Supporters of the project are isolated.

In order to respond to problems and opportunities arising from parenting the project,
headquarters streamlines and reorganizes its structures. This may involve

- rethinking roles and relationships between headquarters and investments abroad;
- flattening hierarchies;
- breaking down boundaries between units.

International commitments may force the company to decentralize and develop structures in which ease of access to units and individuals with knowledge is treated as an
organizational priority.

17.6   Implications for the Manager

In your experience, what factors influence the decision to form an IJV? What factors
influence failure? Base your answers on any knowledge you may have of a current or
terminated IJV project.

1 Why did the parents decide to establish the IJV in partnership?
   • what advantages and disadvantaged did the IJV partnership offer the local parent?
   • what advantages and disadvantages did the IJV partnership offer the foreign parent?
2 Why did the IJV project succeed, or fail?
   • what factors influenced the success or failure of the IJV, from the local partner's point of view?
   • what factors influenced the success or failure of the IJV, from the foreign partner's point of view?
   • If you think the IJV failed, what factors might have prevented this? Consider these:
     (a) preparation;
     (b) choice of partner;
     (c) trust between the partners;
     (d) trust within the IJV;
     (e) the contract and other documentation;
     (f) fit between national cultures;
     (g) fit between organizational cultures;
     (h) planning for control;
     (i) how control was exercised.
3 Describe communications
   (a) between the partners;
   (b) within the project;
   (c) between the partners and the project;
   (d) with the environment.

17.7 SUMMARY

This chapter has examined factors that influence the planning and implementation of an IJV.

Section 17.2 asked WHY companies INVEST IN AN IJV – despite the uncertainties over immediate profitability. It looked at the benefits that each partner can hope for and the contributions that it must expect to make. Section 17.3 examined factors needed for SUCCESS, and focused on partner selection and the importance of COMPATIBILITY. Section 17.4 argued that TRUST between the various parties involved in planning and implementing the venture is of supreme importance. This can be badly damaged when changes in either's business environment leads to a revision of interests and a new attitude towards the IJV.

Section 17.5 dealt with the problems that partners face in SHARING CONTROL. Questions as to which partner provides the CEO and senior managers is usually decided by the investments made and interests in particular functions. Integrative structures, including a communications plan, are established in order to build trust between partners and the IJV.

17.8 EXERCISE

This exercise gives practice in preparing a communications plan.

1 Review your answers to Exercise 8.8 – the negotiation between the business college and Acme Hotels.
2 Assume that the IJV is implemented as you have planned it.
3 What are the implications for communicating

- within the project?
- between the parents?
- between the project and each parent?
- with the environment?

What communication needs might each party have? What problems can you foresee?

4 Prepare a communications plan that can resolve the problems that you predict.

Notes

1 John Templeman et al. Nestlé: a giant in a hurry. *Business Week*, March 22, 1993.

2 Richard E. Smith. Daimler-Mitsubishi Divorce? *International Herald Tribune*, March 7, 1991.

CHAPTER EIGHTEEN

Risk and Control: Headquarters and Subsidiary

CHAPTER OUTLINE

Introduction	Summary
Risk for the Subsidiary	Exercise
Control	Note
Implications for the Manager	

18.1 Introduction

Two short cases illustrate different relationships between headquarters and the subsidiary.

Coca-Cola is still a highly centralized company – and before 2000, even more so. All important strategic decisions are taken in headquarters in the United States. Regional and national subsidiaries are managed by staff appointed by headquarters, and they adjust headquarters strategy to their particular circumstances only when absolutely necessary. There is a good reason for this degree of centralization. The company is selling a global product, a unique soft drink and the universal cultural values associated with that drink. It cannot risk confusing the market by local managers developing products that appeal only to local tastes.

Here is an example of the opposite case. Some years ago a locally owned steel company in Korea established a guesthouse for the use of its business visitors. The guesthouse manager had been trained by a top hotel in Seoul and his guesthouse was an immense success. The company decided to expand it and open it to the general public. The management team in the new hotel were local and perfectly understood the local market, and they made increasing profits. But unhappily, the steel business went into decline, and the company was purchased by an American steel manufacturer based in Minnesota. The purchase included the failing steel works and the successful hotel. But after a few years, the new owners decided that problems in the steel works were insuperable. They sold that failing part of the company, but retained the highly profitable hotel.

The Minnesota company now owned one of the best hotels outside Seoul. But top management decided that there was no point incurring the cost of expatriating anyone from headquarters to manage it. Their managers understood how to make and sell steel, not the hospitality industry. And the Korean team were so successful that they did not need advice from outside. So the American owners decided that the minimum of direct control was needed, and so long as the Koreans met the financial goals negotiated every year, they were empowered to run their business as they thought best.

These two cases show two relationships between headquarters and subsidiary, one highly centralized and one highly decentralized. In both cases, this reflected the nature of the company and its business. In general, there is no one best relationship. In any one case, the relationship is decided by a range of factors; these include factors internal to the headquarters and its subsidiary, and those external, associated with the product and its market.

The relationship between headquarters and its subsidiary has a range of dimensions, including structural, cultural, budgetary, technological and human resource dimensions. These are dealt with here and in subsequent chapters in terms of

- RISK. Factors that cause management risk to the investment;
- CONTROL. Controls that are established in order to protect the investment against management risk and to take advantage of opportunities.

18.2   Risk for the Subsidiary

The company looks at those options for investing abroad that maximize opportunity and minimize risk in its investments made abroad. This section deals with risks arising in their management and productivity; financial risk is not addressed here.

The headquarters chooses between different possible arrangements when deciding how to operate abroad, and 17.2.1 included agency agreements, licensing agreements, establishing an IJV, establishing a subsidiary, possibly as a result of an M&A.

A company may make different arrangements in different countries, for different reasons. For example, Acme Company based in the United Kingdom decides to sell its products in Country A, where it has no previous experience. It first contracts sales to a local company under license, and plans that when headquarters managers have learned something about local market conditions, to make an investment that will be more rewarding. The company also wishes to develop a new product in Country B. Managers have experience of the country and realize that needs for local knowledge and contacts with the government are essential; therefore they negotiate an R&D/production joint venture with a local partner that has the necessary expertise. The company has considerable experience of working in Country C and has no concerns about operating in that environment. The preferred option is to establish a 100 percent owned subsidiary – but first it needs local plant, and so a turnkey agreement is contracted with a local property developer to build the factory.

Any operation conducted made in some other country exposes itself to types of risk that might not arise in its own local environment. An inappropriate investment raises the level of risk. In the example above, when Acme Company moves into Country A, it selects a licensing agreement, because this provides an opportunity to learn about the environment, and thus reduces the level of risk in future dealings. Given the company's lack of experience in Country A, the immediate establishment of a subsidiary might be counted risky. Whether or not the degree of risk is justified depends on the expected earnings.

When selecting the location for a new investment, the company looks for basic infrastructure and a potential for economic development. It chooses NOT to invest in a country which

- lacks an attractive investment climate;
- has skilled human resources at attractive prices;
- is perceived as unacceptably RISKY.

18.2.1 Environmental risks

The concept of risk is difficult to objectify and quantify. Organizations that have a culture of risk aversion will perceive risk where some other might not. An apparently risky location, which frightens away its competitors, may offer commercial advantages to an entrepreneurial company that has a relatively higher tolerance of risk. For example, a company gambles on maintaining its investment in a risk spot because it hopes that this gesture will win government support and favored treatment in the future.

Factors in the environment are often perceived as a major source of risk. Knight and Pretty (2003) calculate that risks from the business environment account for 46 percent of all risk (other risks arise from transactions – 17 percent; operations – 14 percent; finance – 14 percent; investor relations – 9 percent). This section describes factors associated with competition, the economic context, the political context, and technology.

COMPETITIVE RISK arises where

- competitive structures are unstable;
- new entrants threaten to break into the market;
- new and substitute products threaten;
- new technologies threaten;
- changes arise in structures of supply and demand.

ECONOMIC RISK arises where

- public resources suffer waste, corruption, and mismanagement;
- economic and financial conditions are unsatisfactory;

- potential markets and their proximity are poor;
- natural resources are not locally available, and are expensive;
- tariffs, import and export controls are punitive;
- payments cannot be enforced;
- unfair local competition is protected by local officials;
- repatriation of earnings is restricted;
- infrastructure systems are poor;
- local labor is inadequately skilled;
- inducements offered to invest are poor;
- taxation is discriminatory.

POLITICAL RISK arises when

- industrial and legal disputes are given official support;
- war, revolution and terror occurs or threatens;
- the subsidiary's assets are confiscated. Forced divestment is termed expropriation when one (or a few) firms are affected, and
- nationalization when all firms in an industry (or industries) are affected.

TECHNOLOGY RISK arises when

- product technology, including patents, may be stolen;
- the skills and technical knowledge needed to operate the product technology are absent;
- the skills and technical knowledge needed to maintain and repair the product technology are absent;
- the systems needed to manage the technologists are absent.

In sum, headquarters feels needs to safeguard its product technologies and control their use when there is a possibility that the technology will be stolen. Headquarters also wants to be confident that the product technology is being properly operated and that skilled technicians are on hand to repair it efficiently if it should break down.

An international food company operating in Indonesia expatriated only production staff and engineers. Indonesians staffed all other posts – the general manager, finance manager, marketing manager, and so on. Headquarters had prioritized this function because it realized the importance of maintaining continuous production. If production was interrupted and the schedule of weekly or even daily deliveries to its many outlets across the country broke down, the company would lose its competitive advantage over other food producers who were not able to promise regular deliveries. Hence it was essential that the plant be properly operated and kept in good condition. Headquarters did not necessarily doubt the qualifications of its local production staff; but the expatriates were bound to the company for their continuing careers and pensions, and so were highly motivated to maintain standards.

18.2.2   Risk in the industry

Some industries are more exposed to risk than others. High risk industries include banking, security and commodity brokers, and highly technical industries such as telecommunications. Any breach of security is bound to be more expensive than a breach in a relatively low-tech industry such as rubber production or textile manufacture. When the perception of risk is high, headquarters expatriates more staff to control procedures and protect company interests. Thus the number of expatriates gives one (not the only) indication of how seriously the headquarters perceives the risks of doing business in that environment.

Harzing (2001) looked at numbers of headquarters nationals expatriated to top management posts in subsidiaries around the world. Her results reflected Hofstede's rankings for uncertainty avoidance. The Scandinavian countries, which have high toleration of uncertainty, had the lowest numbers of expatriates and the Far East and Middle East the highest. With regards to service industry, the lowest numbers were found in business and management services (12.7 percent) and the highest in banking (76.1 percent) and security and commodity brokers (84.8 percent). In manufacturing industry, she found the lowest expatriate staffing levels in commodity-based and usually low technology industries such as rubber (20 percent) and stone, clay and glass products (23.6 percent). The highest were in the relatively higher technology industries of telecommunications equipment (53.2 percent) and motor vehicles and parts (62.2 percent).

In sum, headquarters expatriates were more common in a subsidiary whose headquarters was in a country with relatively high needs to avoid uncertainty; in a large MNC, where there is perceived to be a wide cultural distance between the national cultures of headquarters and subsidiary.

18.2.3   Risk in the culture

Headquarters is more likely to perceive the national culture expressed in the foreign subsidiary as a source of risk when its own national culture has high needs to avoid uncertainty and the cultural distance is perceived to be wide. That is, when the national culture of the headquarters has high needs to avoid uncertainty, the greater is headquarters insecurity over subsidiary independence and the greater the tendency to centralize subsidiary structures under headquarters control.

Rosenzweig and Singh (1991) assumed the notion of cultural distance and developed a number of hypotheses based on earlier version of Hofstede's model; for instance, that

- the cultural similarity of a multinational subsidiary to other firms in the host country is positively related to the tolerance for uncertainty in the headquarters country culture;
- reliance on formal mechanisms of control is positively related to the distance between the national cultures of headquarters and subsidiary.

So when the culture of the headquarters country is tolerant of ambiguity, the subsidiary is permitted greater autonomy. When the subsidiary exercises its freedom to respond to local conditions, it develops management and market systems that express local priorities rather than headquarters-culture priorities. It responds in much the same way as do locally owned companies. But when the headquarters culture reflects high needs to avoid uncertainty, higher levels of control are imposed.

How headquarters perceives its need to control its subsidiary may be reflected in its language policy. Questions arise as to how far the MNC should harmonize their entire communications systems using a single functional language (that of the headquarters country) across all units; and how far it can permit the use of local language in the subsidiary. These issues are discussed in Luo and Shenkar (2006).

18.2.4   The government's perception of risk

A government usually welcomes multinational investment, in particular when it leads to the transfer of technology and the growth of labor skills. Investors who demonstrate commitment to local development and are less likely to suddenly quit or go out of business leaving debts may be given preferential treatment. However, under some circumstances the government may feel itself at risk from the activities of an MNC. This occurs when the activities of the subsidiary are perceived to

- threaten the country's growth or defense;
- develop a monopoly position that stifles local competition;
- attack a powerful local monopoly;
- improperly move profits out of the country;
- hire talented locals away from local companies;
- fail to meet agreements for the transfer of technology;
- exert unfair influence in local politics and legislation;
- damage the environment, and fail to show corporate responsibility.

18.2.5   Risk in transferring competitive advantage

Competitive advantage secured in headquarters or in one subsidiary cannot be automatically transferred to another subsidiary. What has advantage in the first market may have less in another if customers there prefer a competing product. Sustained investment is needed to secure that advantage in the new market. The company may be forced to invest heavily in developing the complementary assets that help secure the advantage – including staffing the subsidiary, training new employees, and transferring technologies.

18.3   Control

All control costs money; insufficient control can result in a loss of profits and over-control can result in costs in terms of expatriation. How does the firm find the optimal balance? The company control style may have to be modified for each overseas investment. Each exists in a different environment, and has different resourcing and staffing capacities.

Decisions have to be made about

- what sort of control is needed;
- how the appropriate control is enforced.

The instruments for control from which the company selects include

- the structural relationship – see 18.3.1–18.3.8;
- technology may be used to both tighten or weaken headquarters control – see 18.3.9;
- budgets and other financial instruments. This is discussed briefly in 18.3.10;
- staffing policy. Chapters 20 and 21 deal with the topic in detail;
- organizational culture. This is discussed in 20.3 and throughout Chapter 23.

18.3.1   *Controlling through the structural relationship*

Bartlett and Goshal (1989, 1998) classified four models of companies operating foreign interests: global, multinational, international, and transnational companies. Each of these expresses a different structural relationship between headquarters and subsidiary. The particular relationship in any one company is determined by such factors as the industry, product type, and market forces:

- The GLOBAL company centralizes its key functions – including marketing and finance. Headquarters produces the new technology and disseminates it to subsidiaries. Cost advantages are achieved through economies of scale and global-scale operations. The need for efficiency and economies of scale means that products are developed that exploit needs felt across the range of countries. Specific local needs tend to be ignored.
- The headquarters of the MULTINATIONAL company decides financial policy but otherwise permits subsidiaries considerable autonomy in determining management style and responding to local product needs and markets.
- The headquarters of the INTERNATIONAL company retains considerable control over the subsidiary's management systems and marketing policy, but less so than in the global company. Products and technologies are developed for the home market, extended to other countries with similar market characteristics, then diffused elsewhere. The developmental sequence is decided on the basis of managing the product lifecycle as efficiently and flexibly as possible.
- The headquarters of the TRANSNATIONAL company evolved in the 1980s in response to environmental change and demands for global efficiency, national responsiveness, and worldwide learning. The transnational model combines features of multinational, global, and international models. A product is designed to be globally competitive, and is differentiated and adapted by local subsidiaries to meet local market demands. Whereas the international company originates the product in the headquarters country and then transfers it to the subsidiary, the transnational might reverse this process. Resources, including technology and managerial talent, might be distributed among subsidiaries and integrated between them through strong interdependencies.

A variant model was designed by Griffin and Pustay (1999) who distinguished three types, the multidomestic, global and transnational:

- The MULTIDOMESTIC company views all country markets as different. It encourages independence for its subsidiaries in marketing and operations.
- The GLOBAL company views the world as a single marketplace. It standardizes all marketing and production facilities.
- The TRANSNATIONAL company is structured so that its operating Units can operate independently. It tries to combine the benefits of global scale with the benefits of local responsiveness.

Complex organizational structures are established to coordinate two-way communications between parent and subsidiaries. What happens in practice is that the headquarters takes decisions for some functions such as production and R&D, whereas functions such as marketing and human resource management are adopted to its local culture by the subsidiary.

18.3.2   The transnational and its environment

The TRANSNATIONAL evolves in response to constant change in the environment. For example, management recognizes that in a particular culture, customers greatly value their person-to-person relationships with members of the sales and marketing teams, and that local staff are far better equipped to develop these relationships than are expatriates.

Andrews et al. (2003) discuss this point in the context of Southeast Asia, and argue that many Western-based companies rely overmuch on systems and strategies developed at headquarters. For example, Castrol modeled its Equipment Services Division in Thailand on a parallel unit that had been highly successful in the United Kingdom and in Malaysia. But the Thai team rejected it, partly because local market segmentations differed significantly, and partly because the great majority of their research informants believed that the working processes assumed by the ESD unit were culturally misaligned.

> The formality, professional and official nature of the ESD setup – deemed in the West to be its strong point – was branded "useless," "unsuitable" and "damaging" in an environment where customers were gained and held almost purely on the basis of personal relationships. *(p. 211)*

The transnational aims to develop subsidiaries that are BOTH highly flexible in their own locations AND also closely integrated with other subsidiaries. Blumen (2002) says that in this new "age of connective leadership" managers "learn to integrate interdependence and diversity" (p. 90). He/she learns from its environment and then makes the acquired knowledge accessible throughout the company; and so is also responsible for applying the lessons learned by others. They share not only flows of parts, finished goods, and capital, but also locally acquired skills and knowledge. That is, developments in the subsidiary influences developments in the whole.

At least, that is the theory. Despite the use of IT, face-to-face interactions are still crucial in knowledge transfer. That is, managers at greater distance from each other are less likely to influence each other than managers nearer to one another and in regular face-to-face contact. In their study of MNCs headquartered in the US, the UK, Europe and Japan, Harzing and Noorderhaven (2006) discovered that the most isolated subsidiaries, in Australia and New Zealand, are the more likely to be local R&D innovators only, and the least likely to be global R&D innovators.

18.3.3 The structural models have to be flexible

In its ideal form the transnational is able to respond and adapt to its environment as though it were an organism. In Allee's (2003) words, nowadays

> we are fascinated with networks, systems and complexity. We are beginning to view organizations as living systems. *(p. 34)*

But the Bartlett and Ghoshal and Griffin and Pustay frameworks are ideal, and very few companies fit precisely into any one category. The former was tested among 131 senior executives in Leong and Tan (1993). Results provided partial support. The hypothesized practices associated with multinational and global organizations were more consistent with the typology's predictions relative to those of the international and transnational types.

The Swedish telecommunications giant Ericsson is frequently cited as an example of a transnational. Ericsson learned from the Australian telecommunications market, transferred the knowledge back home, then applied it worldwide. The company developed

- an interdependence of resources and responsibilities among organizational units;
- a set of strong cross-unit integrating devices;
- a strong corporate identification and a worldwide management perspective.

However, Ericsson does not entirely fit the transnational model. The majority of local managers are Swedes, appointed from their pool of career international managers based in Stockholm. It is true that their products are varied for different regional markets but these variations are dictated by local production and licensing requirements rather than by taste.

18.3.4 The case of Coca-Cola

Every successful company evolves over time in response to commercial and competitive pressures, and may move between categories. For many years, Coca-Cola was highly globalized. The main product sold everywhere, and all aspects of marketing and production are still controlled from Atlanta. For example, the Middle East and North Africa division was headquartered far outside the region, in the United Kingdom.

However, the end of 1999, Coca-Cola profits were falling. A range of problems had emerged, and the company responded by appointing a new CEO, Douglas Daft. He aimed at a major restructuring and introduced a strategy designed to eliminate 6,000 jobs – that is, about a fifth of the total workforce:

> The cuts affects 2,500 positions at the company's Atlanta headquarters, 2,700 outside the US, and 800 jobs elsewhere in the US. . . . [Mr Daft] was trying to decentralize Coca-Cola's operations so the company can react more quickly to local conditions.[1]

An immediate example of this decentralization was that the Middle East and North Africa headquarters was moved from London to Manama in Bahrain. This transfer represented a modification to the original structural relationship between headquarters and subsidiary. Coca-Cola no longer exemplifies the category of global company as precisely as it had done before 2000. In terms of the Bartlett and Ghoshal framework, it has moved towards the international model, and of the Griffin and Pustay framework, a modified global–multidomestic model.

18.3.5   Strategic human resources in the transnational

Human resource management contributes to strategy when it influences what corporate goals are planned and implemented.

The human resource manager advises top management on the skills and knowledge that the company has at its disposal and can expect to acquire in the future. At a time when the importance of knowledge creation is recognized, the old question asked by the human resource manager, "where can we find the labor to perform operation X?" gives way to questions of "what strategic advantages do our labor resources give us?" and "what operations should we be planning in order to apply them most effectively?" This reflects the resource-based theory of the firm, which perceives the MNC as a network of resources transacted among subsidiaries. In practice, the "strategy will determine how these resource transactions are structured among the various subunits" (Taylor et al., 1996, p. 967).

The transnational has to learn from its different environments and the experience of its various other branches in order to become effective. It needs managers capable of this learning, and this places a responsibility on the HR department to select and train managers capable of creating and using knowledge. These managers must be flexible. They will be keen to take part in planning their careers across the range of units.

18.3.6   The international manager

In practice, an awareness of the importance of developing capabilities and new areas of knowledge should subfuse all management activities, not merely formal activities associated with the HR department. And the logic of strategic HR is that the entire company becomes HR oriented, so that questions of defining strategic goals in reference to likely future capabilities become the concern of all units. All managers acquire international interests, and those bound for expatriate postings should be capable of taking assignments wherever the company decides to use them.

How far is this practical? Morgan et al. (2003) examine the internationalization of Japanese banks in the 1980s and examine how Japanese bankers are developing new international social relationships, and how these influence how their firms operate. They propose that a concept of social space can connect the fates of individuals and communities in local contexts to the dynamics of the global political economy (p. 405). On the other hand, Forster (2000) makes the point that although business operations may be increasingly international, this doesn't mean that managers are.

In sum, the notion of the "pure" international manager is vague. The individual has his/her preferences for culture and may not operate at the same level of efficiency elsewhere. He/she has personal interests and plans, and may have limited tolerance to the dislocation and upheaval that accompanies continually relocating to new assignments. Perhaps many managers are capable of maintaining this routine for a few years, but very few throughout a career.

18.3.7   Empowering the subsidiary

Models of organizational empowerment are designed to reduce centralized controls over the subsidiary and give it greater control over its own affairs.

Advocates argue that empowering the subsidiary brings long-term economic benefits to the company. Feedback from the market is rapid, and subsidiary managers have greater freedom to develop their objectives. They have the opportunities to make decisions that previously belonged to headquarters. They are encouraged to develop equivalent expertise – and more, because they are able to apply their local knowledge which may not be so accessible to headquarters managers. Empowerment motivates staff, releases energy, builds commitment, and develops new skills. They feel a far greater sense of control over operations and the outcomes.

The move to self-management benefits the individual, the subsidiary, and the company. When an empowered subsidiary is making decisions, it builds closer links with the local environment and can respond more quickly to local needs.

Malone (1997) claims that the new emphasis on empowerment responds to fundamental changes in the economics of decision-making. The ability to respond quickly to changes in a globalized market is essential, and even a traditional centralized company must increasingly recognize local needs – as the Coca-Cola example (18.3.4) shows. The development of information technologies and falling communication costs enable the company both to decentralize and to maintain a strong corporate identification and to decentralize in response to local needs that can be addressed faster than when decision-making is heavily centralized. A policy of empowerment moves the company towards transnationalism.

Empowerment describes a localization of control, and does not necessarily indicate that all staffing is local. Expatriates might serve in an empowered subsidiary reporting only to subsidiary managers. On the other hand, a unit that is entirely staffed by locals might be controlled by strategies, policies and systems made in headquarters. However, there must be a tendency for empowered subsidiaries to depend on only locally recruited staff.

18.3.8   Questions about empowerment

Empowerment entails risk to the extent that the personalities and skills of the new managers are unknown to headquarters. Empowerment protects against risk to the extent that it gives the subsidiary greater flexibility in response to local competition.

Before top management decide whether or not to take a risk and how far to empower a subsidiary, it finds answers to these questions:

- Do subsidiary staff have the necessary skills, and if not, can they acquire them?
- Do subsidiary staff have the information needed? If not, where can this be acquired?
- Do headquarters staff trust subsidiary staff?
- Are subsidiary staff likely to be more or less motivated by the opportunities presented by empowerment?
- What might be the economic benefits and costs of empowering the subsidiary?
- What might be the economic benefits and costs of NOT empowering the subsidiary?

Empowerment may not always be advantageous. The subsidiary can never be entirely autonomous and headquarters always holds some autonomous control – it needs to retain control of financial operations. Other units may be given different degrees of empowerment – for example, sales might be entirely localized while headquarters retains some influence on marketing. These differences create internal tensions. Successful local managers are likely to be in greater demand on the local labor market, and so the company has to pay more to keep their services. Problems arise if the environment changes and headquarters claws back control over operations that seem in particular difficulty; disempowered local managers are demoralized.

Empowerment assumes a tolerance of uncertainty among headquarters staff. Stewart (1995) quotes the CEO of a Canadian subsidiary:

> The problem is that decentralized, empowering relationships demand an enormous level of self-confidence on the part of the home management and a certain mindset. Empowerment is not a style of management – it's a philosophy.   *(p. 69)*

Where this self-confidence is lacking, empowerment is not feasible.

Finally, empowerment should not be thought of as synonymous with localizing the staff and reducing expatriate numbers. In an age of rapid communications an entirely local staff may still be highly dependent on headquarters for decision-making, and an expatriate staff may be licensed to make their own decisions. Empowerment is primarily a structural issue rather than a human resources issue.

18.3.9 Controlling through technology

When headquarters centralizes policies for the use of technology by the subsidiary, it increases its control. When it decentralizes technology policies. it reduces control.

Traditionally in highly global companies, new technologies were developed at headquarters, adapted for local consumption, and disseminated to the subsidiary. The company aimed to gain maximum protection against the theft and misuse of technology by centralizing control.

Now the situation is changing. In industries where streams of competitors are entering and leaving the market and fast responses are essential, the subsidiary cannot afford to wait for headquarters to approve every decision. Increasing numbers of MNCs are setting up foreign units with a main responsibility to produce research, and these function as technology-focused profit centers. The subsidiary evaluates local demand and responds more rapidly than headquarters could. For example, European and Japanese telecommunications companies have located their units for software development and engineering as near as possible to their major customers in the USA. Thus the companies save the expense of time lost in adaptation.

Theft is now less of a concern. Technology lifecycles have now shortened so much that the potential value of the new technology may be less and hence the potential cost of its theft is less. This cost may be less than the cost of not delivering the technology to the market at the earliest possible time. Thus market pressures drive decentralization.

Decentralizing the production of technology has the effect of empowering the subsidiary to decide on its own policies, possibly up to the level of strategic planning, and so decentralizes organizational structures. This new technology may feed back to headquarters – that is, the traditional pattern is reversed.

The creation of technology depends, first, on finding an appropriate site – perhaps clustering with other technology producers near a university campus; and second, finding a pool of technologists or persons who can be trained to the necessary standards. Where there are insufficient numbers of skilled persons, the development of subsidiary-based technology is fraught with difficulty. However, where there is an abundance of locally skilled persons – or persons with sufficient educational grounding to be trained further – a policy of decentralization provides work and experience. When the subsidiary is located in a less developed economy, this gives a powerful stimulus to the growth of local talent.

18.3.10 Controlling through budget

The more dependent the subsidiary on headquarters' budgetary policy, the more immediate the control that headquarters exerts. But when decisions over expenditure are relaxed, control is pushed down to subsidiary management. For example, if headquarters demands that the subsidiary explain and seek permission for all expenditure over $100,000, control is centralized within headquarters. But if headquarters allows the subsidiary discretion for all expenditure up to the limit of $10 million, control is looser.

18.4   Implications for the Manager

Analyze your own MNC or some other to which you have access. Analyze relations between headquarters and units abroad.

1   What opportunities does each unit offer the company?
2   What environmental risks does each run? Categorize these in terms of
    • competitive risks;
    • economic risks;
    • political risks;
    • risks associated with technology;
    • risks associated with the industry;
    • risks associated with the national culture.
3   How does headquarters try to control each unit against risk?
    • By using the structural relationships?
    • By using budgets and other financial instruments?
    • By using its technology policy?
    • By using organizational culture?
4   How can structural relationships between headquarters and each unit be described? In what respects is the structure of the MNC
    • global?
    • multinational?
    • international?
    • transnational?

18.5   SUMMARY

This chapter described the relationship between headquarters and subsidiary in terms of the headquarters' perception of the risks it incurs in operating the subsidiary, and the types of control it imposes in order to protect itself and the subsidiary against these risks.

Section 18.2 discussed categories of environmental RISK; these include competitive, economic, and political risks; and risks associated with technology, the industry, and the national culture. The possibilities of risk in the eyes of the local government were also noted.

Section 18.3 listed the options for imposing CONTROL as a means of ensuring that strategic goals are met and risks guarded against. It focused on the structural options, and the advantages and disadvantages of empowering the subsidiary were examined.

18.6 EXERCISE

You are CEO of Croyden Forest Foods USA. In Ruritania, your subsidiary harvests and crushes different seeds and nuts, from which it extracts valuable oils. Fifty percent of your earnings come from sales of analonin oil.

Your company owns the technology of the crushing plant, which is programmed by your patented software. A computer programmer expatriated from headquarters writes the software at post. The crushing process imposes great pressures on the hardware which is continually breaking down. At present, a further two production engineers have been expatriated to operate and maintain it. Your board are worried about the security implications of withdrawing all expatriates from posts involving valuable technology. All other staff, including the general manager, are Ruritanian.

Over the past three years costs have grown and profits have fallen. Last year this subsidiary earned profits of $3 million, but you expect a decline of 15 percent per annum in the next two years. Given the ENVIRONMENTAL FACTORS below, you now have to consider the future direction of the subsidiary.

ENVIRONMENTAL FACTORS

1 The industry is experiencing a period of great turbulence.
2 No foreign MNC has ever won a case against a local company in Ruritanian courts.
3 Your software is protected, and cannot be easily copied.
4 You have been invited to form a joint venture with a French company planning to harvest forest foods in Indonesia. If you enter this venture, your technologies will make a major contribution.
5 A Japanese company is manufacturing similar hardware, for sale on the open market.
6 A powerful local company has recently announced plans to enter the seed-and-nut crushing industry.
7 Rumors are circulating that a Taiwanese competitor, TPF Products, has patented a synthetic substitute for analonin oil. TPF Products is not competing in Ruritania.
8 Weather conditions in Ruritania have been excellent this year, and you expect a bumper crop of seeds and nuts at low prices.
9 World demand for analonin oil has been in decline over the past five years, but you expect a major increase over the next three years.

Further than that you cannot predict.

Given the limited data available, which of these options seem sensible?

What further data do you need before making your final decision?

OPTIONS

(a) Continue as at present.
(b) Withdraw from Ruritania immediately; sell the subsidiary.
(c) Withdraw all expatriates, and turn over their jobs to Ruritanian staff.

(d) Withdraw only your computer programmer, and license the production of software to a local firm.
(e) Withdraw only your production engineers, and employ local staff to operate and maintain your hardware.
(f) Withdraw the present expatriate staff, sack the Ruritanian general manager, and expatriate a general manager from headquarters.

(g) Purchase a stake in TPF Products.
(h) Empower your Ruritanian subsidiary to decide on expatriation and technology policies.
(i) Centralize your control. Sack the Ruritanian general manager and all functional managers; replace them with headquarters expatriates.
(j) (Any other options. Please add ....)

Note

1 Coca-Cola to cut 21% of its work force. *Asian Wall Street Journal*, January 27, 2000.

CHAPTER NINETEEN
Managing Human Resources

CHAPTER OUTLINE

19.1   Introduction

At a management conference, a Western-based consultant on human resource management (HRM) compared notes with a colleague working in China. The Western expert commented that he was chiefly concerned with interpreting the law in regards to redundancy, and planning packages for employees whose skills were no longer required. The China expert consultant said that in his companies, this was a low priority; managements hoped to retain their skilled and experienced employees for as long as possible. Rather, his main occupation was training local Chinese staff to work with the constant stream of expatriated Westerners visiting on short-term contracts. The Western expert commented that in his experience, training locals to work with expatriates had never been an issue.

In different contexts, different HR issues arise. In this example, different stages of economic development were significant. Companies in rapidly developing China had adopted growth strategies that meant acquiring a transfer of skills from developed economies.

This chapter sees how the implementation of HR principles is influenced by local factors. It also examines the need of MNCs to adopt headquarters HR policy to conditions in the subsidiary.

19.2   Applying Concepts of HRM

Training in HRM typically covers a range of skills. Those covered in one standard textbook (Torrington et al., 2004) include:

planning: jobs and people
recruitment
selection methods and decisions
staff retention
diversity: the legal framework
health, safety and welfare
job evaluation
incentives
pensions and benefits.

Torrington et al. are all UK based, and their book reflects British and American perceptions. Some of their topics are widely applicable, but others may have limited value elsewhere. For example, an understanding of British employment law may have no direct relevance elsewhere.

This chapter focuses on four aspects of HRM theory developed in the US and the UK. It examines them in terms of their own logic, and then asks how far they can be applied in other cultural contexts. It discusses their implications for the MNC employing local staff. The MNC needs to understand how the meaning and importance of an HR activity is influenced by the local context. HRM techniques developed in one context are not necessarily appropriate in some other. HRM practice is everywhere influenced by historical, political, cultural and economic factors. Expatriate HRM is discussed in the next two chapters.

19.2.1   Economic development and interest in HRM

In many developing and newly developed economies, companies have only recently begun to invest in specialist HR managers and in applying Anglo models for managing human resources. There are many possible reasons. Possibly, this expertise was thought to be of marginal relevance, and unlikely to justify its cost. Or unskilled labor was cheap, and many companies competed only in relatively unsophisticated local markets. Family businesses might have had little need to employ non-family members in other than subordinate roles, and family loyalties were expected to take precedence over bureaucratic arrangements in governing employment relationships.

In the last three decades, that situation has changed. As the world economy becomes global, even small companies in developing economies find that they have to operate internationally. They need skills to compete not only with their neighbor down the road but with a company based thousands of miles away. To survive, they may have to move upscale and apply new technologies, which may mean hiring expertise from outside the family. Employers need to use their labor more efficiently, and emphasis is placed on recruiting, training, appraising and rewarding those who contribute most.

In addition, new managerial techniques have been introduced by multinational parents, joint venture partners and competitors from the more developed economies. These models of how to achieve most from limited resources are augmented by management training offered in specialist seminars and MBA programs taught locally, abroad, and at a distance by new technologies.

New ease of social and occupational mobility means that family units are less cohesive. Rather than living and working together in one compound, family members increasingly live at a distance from each other. As family bonds weaken and companies decentralize, family commitment is less predictable than before. Workforces are less homogeneous, and less reliance can be placed on shared attitudes.

For these and other reasons, there is increasing emphasis on HRM in developing countries. The question is, though, how far can the HRM theories and practices aimed at serving the needs of developed economies (initially the US and the UK) be applied in other contexts, where other relationships apply between employer and employee?

19.2.2 *Personnel management and human resource management*

In the developed economies, HRM functions have developed from the less sophisticated practices of traditional PERSONNEL MANAGEMENT (PM). PM focused on administering the contract of employment and emphasizing correct performance. It aimed to enforce employee compliance with company policies, the minimization of costs associated with staff, and the achievement of short-term objectives. PM still serves necessary functions in many industries and companies, but is usually no longer sufficient in global operations. Its narrow concerns do not facilitate long-term planning in rapidly changing market conditions.

HRM is far broader in that it

- embraces a wider range of functions;
- has to be increasingly long term and strategic in its approach;
- has to be more flexible;
- is resource centered, and focuses on enhanced performance.

This development has been propelled by experience of the changes discussed above and new insights gained into the nature of the workforce. The need for increased sophistication in maximizing staff potentials is reflected in the increased status and seniority of the HR manager.

How far have management cultures in developing economies evolved from PM to HRM? Chan and Lui (2004) review the evidence in Hong Kong, and conclude that the evidence is contradictory. However, this does not mean that no HR functions have developed there. In 1997 the local branch of the headhunters Korn/Ferry International reported that Asian family companies in Hong Kong, Singapore, Malaysia and Indonesia were beginning to call on its services to hire outsiders as CEOs or chief financial officers. The implication is that in any one management culture the balance between PM and HRM is bound to vary in different industries and organizational structures, taking account of the value of the labor in question and the needs of the parties involved.

19.3   The General Functions of HRM

HRM consists of a set of interrelated activities which enable the organization and employees to agree about their relationship. They serve the organization insofar as they enable it to meet its strategic goals, and the individual employee to the extent that he/she achieves satisfaction from his/her work and meets his/her financial goals. The HR department has the following general functions:

1 Setting PERFORMANCE OBJECTIVES. Given the organizational goals and strategy, performance objectives are negotiated and set.
2 STAFFING. Given the agreed performance objectives, job descriptions are designed; competitive employment packages are designed; staff are recruited:
   • training and development is provided;
   • incentive schemes to motivate employees are designed;
   performance is appraised and evaluated;
   promotion structures are established; and
   systems are set up for making dismissals and retirements, when employees can no longer contribute to achieving company goals.
3 ADMINISTRATION. HRM has inherited certain functions from traditional personnel management. These are essentially bureaucratic and regulatory, and facilitate the smooth running of the organization. The department
   • handles paperwork involved in hiring, promotions, dismissals and retirements;
   • administers pay, benefit and compensation systems;
   • collects data on personal interests and objectives of employees;
   • ensures that all aspects of operations comply with labor law;
   • administers tax, national insurance, sick pay, etc.;
   • develops and manages a knowledge bank.
4 Planning and implementing CHANGE. The organization needs to keep adapting its structures and organizational culture to meet changing strategic goals, the needs of the workforce and conditions in the wider environment. The HR department shapes processes and culture to improve the organization's capacity for further change. Issues

associated with the organizational culture and planning change have been discussed in Chapters 5, 14 and 15, and are not discussed further here.

19.3.1   The HRM focus

The focus adopted by any particular organization depends on internal circumstances. In a smaller company, the HR manager may be involved in all these areas, but in a large company roles become increasingly specialized. For example, a training officer may have no administrative responsibilities other than administering the programs.

The economic facts of life may decide the emphasis. The company is not going to invest more in any one function than it needs to, either to ward off threats or to take advantage of opportunities. For example, it will only invest in developing an incentive system to the extent that this promises benefits that outweigh the costs. The emphasis taken by the HR department and its staff is also influenced by such factors as the industry, the market, the organizational culture and the national culture.

HRM that creates unnecessary bureaucracy and entangles productive workers in red tape is counterproductive. The only justification for investing in the various HR functions is that it helps develop excellence, to the advantage of all. Successful HRM is perceived as fair by all members, and is able to champion employees and to represent their interests to top management. This is radical. In most companies, HR still plays the police role and its necessary administrative activities are paramount. The new agenda means spreading the emphasis so that customers and employees benefit.

19.3.2   The long-term focus: strategic HRM

Strategic HRM is expressed in practices that show a long-term approach to staffing opportunities and threats. These practices are developed in response to factors within the organization, and trends in the environment.

These long-term practices reflect the corporate strategy. They contribute to implementing those aspects of the strategic plan that need an HR response, and can play an important part in achieving corporate goals. However, this may only be possible in organizations which depend on having long-term staffing plans in place. Top management have to recognize this priority, and HR managers need the skills to champion it and persuade others of its importance.

An aggressive approach by HR strategists is that staffing strategies should be decisive in determining the choice that the organization makes of plans for the future. This argues that people give the key to competitive advantage, and that the success of different marketing, production and other strategies can only be achieved when the skills and knowledge of those who work in these fields are treated as paramount. In cases where the skills are not yet in place, policies are designed to identify, secure and develop them.

19.4   HRM Activities in Context

This section examines a number of HR functions and sees how their implementation may be influenced by factors in the local context.

The MNC needs to understand how the meaning and importance of an HR activity is influenced by the local context.

Everywhere, the labor relationship between employer and employee assumes a degree of expectancy. The employer expects that the employee perform the task assigned him as well as he is able, and the employee expects to be treated and recompensed as agreed, usually by payment. But the international manager cannot take for granted that the relationship applying in headquarters applies similarly in the subsidiary. On what is it based?

In ASSOCIATION contexts, the relationship is based on a sense of trust and mutual obligation between employer and employee, and the personal knowledge that each side has of the other. This entails learning as much about the other person as possible, and there are obvious benefits in hiring a family member or friend, particularly for a position of responsibility. This may override the contract, as when the employer needs extra work done by the employee who does not expect overtime payment. The employer continues to hire a trusted employee after the normal retirement age, even though that person is no longer as productive as in the past. The family-based cultures of East Asia and Latin America exemplify this.

In CONTRACT contexts, the labor relationship between employer and employee is more legal and bureaucratic. The expected relationship is based on a formal written contract, and if either side fails to perform his contracted obligations he may be liable in law. The employee is at fault if he does not perform his specified duties, or performs them inadequately, or does not work the agreed time; and the employer is at fault if he does not pay the agreed wage or salary, or provide adequate facilities. The Anglo cultures tend to fit this pattern. Jackson (2003, p. 26) comments that there appears to be a tradition within Western studies of HRM and organizations of underestimating the value of "trust" while simultaneously overemphasizing the value of "control".

In all contexts, the employee is expected to perform a certain job, which may be specified more or less tightly by the job design.

19.4.1   Job design

All organizations consist of networks of jobs, which are interrelated in order to meet organizational needs and achieve the strategic goals. The job design makes clear

* the title and description of a particular job, setting out its content and boundaries;
* what activities are involved;
* what targets have to be achieved;
* what inputs are needed;
* how the job relates to other jobs.

Job designs are RIGID when the design in tightly controlled. There is tight specification of

- job targets; what the job holder should do in order to achieve her target, and what she should not do;
- ways of doing the job;
- inputs;
- assessment of criteria that focuses on what is good and bad performance in terms of the design;
- the control of relationships. The job can be performed independently from other jobs, and individuals reach their objectives in relative isolation.

Job designs are FLEXIBLE to the extent that targets are loosely specified and individuals have to coordinate their efforts with others, perhaps forming temporary alliances across the department or across the organization. They have the power to make changes in order to accommodate change in the workplace and market. Assessment criteria focus more on the outcomes rather than on how far the design has been followed.

In practice, both rigidity and flexibility can give rise to problems when it is inappropriate in context. Too much rigidity does not allow for change in response to the context. It restricts possibilities of cooperating with other jobs and may restrict opportunities for learning. On the other hand, too much flexibility becomes a problem when different people's responsibilities overlap, and this gives rise to ambiguity and even to conflict. Individuals may find it harder to identify with their jobs.

The specific task is not the only factor which determines how far the design should be rigid or flexible. When the skills required are scarce in the job market, the individual has greater power to define his own work. In some industries (e.g. banking) jobs always need to be tightly identified. The structures of large companies may impose greater degrees of bureaucracy than of small companies, where everyone should be prepared to take on a range of jobs. An entrepreneurial culture may demand greater flexibility.

Elements of the national culture influence tolerances of discipline in a rigid job design, and tolerances of uncertainty in a fluid design. The implication is that a design that works well in headquarters may need modification when transferred to a subsidiary or IJV in some other cultural context. This condition applies both to local staff and expatriates, and job design is a very important factor when an expatriate assignment is being made. We will see that questions of who designs the job (HQ or the subsidiary) and who evaluates it can be an important influence on the success of the mission.

The next four sections examine four HR activities, and show how they can be influenced by local factors. These activities are

- recruitment;
- performance appraisal;
- training;
- retention.

19.5   Recruitment

In contract contexts, when there appears to be a gap in the range of skills needed to achieve strategic goals, the HR department first makes a JOB ANALYSIS. This spells out the frequent and occasional duties, and what skills and experiences are needed. The obvious option is to recruit a person from the external job market who can fill this gap.

But this option is not chosen automatically, and can have disadvantages. The process of searching job markets and making a selection from the candidates is often costly. Further, recruitment usually obliges the organization to a continuing commitment to the employee. This commitment can extend for years. The longer the commitment, the greater the loss to the company in terms of flexibility and its capacity to adjust to changing markets.

In contexts where it is taken for granted that the relationship is based on contract rather than association, the employer may have little or no prior knowledge of the new recruit's personal qualities – as opposed to professional qualities and experience, which the bureaucratic procedures elicit. This brings a degree of uncertainty to the new appointment and to the existing organizational culture.

The alternatives to recruiting from the external job market include:

- recruiting from the internal job market, within the organization;
- training an existing employee to switch to this new role;
- requesting existing employees to work overtime in order to cover the additional work. But even if this is agreed, it can lead to inefficiencies, for example when staff are tired from their normal working hours;
- using technologies to cover the deficit. This assumes that the technologies are available at an economic price and that staff have the skills to operate them;
- making the job part-time;
- subcontracting the work.

19.5.1   The search

If none of these alternatives is feasible, recruitment may be the only option. The first stage is to decide which channels will be most efficient in attracting applications with the desired skills and experiences.

In contract contexts, the most common channel is advertising in the media. At one extreme, the job advertisement gives a minimum of information, perhaps to attract a wide range of applications, and only an outline of the job and the skills needed. At the opposite extreme, the information on the organization, job, skills, salary and other rewards is exhaustive. The advantage of giving more information is that it places more hurdles in the path of inappropriate applicants. The disadvantage is that it may inhibit applications from persons with unorthodox experience.

The job analysis carried out by the HR department influences the choice of medium. A senior executive post in a major international organization is advertised in a prestigious newspaper or journal and not in a free newspaper – read by the sort of persons the company hopes will apply. At the opposite extreme a low status job stacking shelves is advertised in a free or local newspaper, not in the *Wall Street Journal*. The range of alternatives also includes daily newspapers, weekly and monthly periodicals, international newspapers, the technical and specialist press.

E-advertising is becoming more significant in recruiting for some jobs, and has the advantages of cheapness, speed and the ease with which it can reach a wide audience. But this also carries disadvantages; responding is similarly easy and the e-advertisement may attract a massive number of responses, all of which need to be processed. Also, it may involve a relative lack of security. Jobs are also announced by public advertising and notices, job centers and job agencies, careers services and fairs, and headhunters.

In association contexts, Western recruitment practices may be increasingly common in the state sector, although in state sectors their use may be limited by managerial know-how – in China, for example. But in private sectors, personal knowledge of the candidate may still be more important. In Egypt, labor laws (137/1981 and 91/1959) provided for recruitment in the public sector which was made according to set rules and procedures, and promotion was decided by seniority in the company. Different procedures were observed in companies in the private sector, 99 percent of which could be classified as small or medium sized. Recruitment was

> mainly based upon word of mouth, and to gain more flexibility, avoid taxes and other insurance obligations, private business employers got round restrictions of these laws by not providing their workers with employment contracts or insurance or by making them sign undated resignation letters before taking on the job.   *(Hatem, 2006, p. 202)*

This dependence on relationship may not produce the most competent candidate, but can often be counted on to produce someone trustworthy.

19.5.2   *Discrimination in recruitment practices*

Across cultures, recruitment practices differ widely. In Japan, female applicants for management positions continue to suffer discrimination Jackson and Tomioka (2004) cite examples; females may be sent less information than are male applicants, and what they do receive may be male oriented. The authors refer to one instance and wonder

> What was the company thinking about? They send a recruitment mail-shot trying to attract a talented women recruit, but in their prospectus they only show upwardly mobile men. Did they choose to ignore the obvious irony? Or did they not even realize it?   *(p. 104)*

In the UK, the obsession with youth often means that those of advancing years are ignored by recruitment officers. In 2008, although a million people were working beyond

65, another 2.4 million were seeking but had been denied paid employment. Ageism was technically illegal, but many employers were exploiting legal loopholes. This discrimination is self-defeating. Research indicates that if one-third of Britons in their fifties returned to the labor market, they would contribute more than $55 billion to the local economy.

Other countries are less likely to squander their most valuable asset, their older and more experienced workers. In the US, the cult of the senior citizen is booming. In 2008, film stars Harrison Ford (aged 65) and Sylvester Stallone (at 61) reprised action roles that made them famous when they were much younger; Indiana Jones in the case of Ford and Rambo and Rocky Balboa in the case of Stallone. In the boardrooms of Wall Street, the average age was nudging 57, compared to 44 in the UK.

19.5.3   Searching local labor markets

The MNC has difficulty in recruiting good local managers if it depends solely on techniques that are appropriate in the country of the headquarters but are inappropriate in the local culture. For instance, it

- searches inappropriate labor pools;
- applies inappropriate search techniques. Newspaper advertising is not effective in all contexts;
- applies inappropriate selection techniques. A personality test designed for one culture may be inappropriate elsewhere. A Chinese manager considered "overly aggressive" in her Taiwanese company was assessed as "overly passive" by a test administered in a British business school;
- applies incomplete criteria. Priority is given to behavior that fits a headquarters profile only;
- offers salaries and other rewards that are not competitive with those offered by local firms.

The MNC tries not to depend solely on recruitment criteria usual in the local labor market, particularly when these discriminate against women and minorities who may provide a pool of underutilized talent. In the late 1980s, Western companies moving into Japan recognized that Japanese female graduates were in general denied management positions in local firms. They were easily attracted by Western MNCs, in which sexual discrimination was less. The example above suggests that an MNC investing in the UK might usefully target older and more experienced applicants.

19.6   Performance Appraisal

The notion and practice of performance appraisal (PA) has a wide scope. In general, it may be defined as the process of identifying, observing, measuring and developing human performance in organizations, and the basket of activities that it encompasses may be related to the general functions listed in 20.3:

- Setting PERFORMANCE OBJECTIVES. PA measures the results of performance against objectives. Is performance satisfactory? Or should the objectives be changed?
- STAFFING. PA evaluates performance. It helps the organization decide on who should be retained and who should be made redundant, and what further training and development may be needed.
- ADMINISTRATION. PA may lead to a review of pay and benefits.
- CHANGE. In terms of the individual, how might his career develop, and be planned to his and the organization's advantage? Feedback from a number of employees over time tells the organization what changes might be made to jobs and reward systems.

However, all these activities are unlikely to be of equal importance in any one organization, and different organizations may choose very different emphases, and perhaps different emphases in appraising different groups of employees. It follows that they may also follow different approaches in securing the information needed.

For example, a focus on the RESULTS of performance measures success against such criteria as quantity, quality, time and cost, and might examine the individual's profitability, sales, achievement of delivery dates, and so on. A PROBLEM-SOLVING approach involves the appraiser and employee identifying problem areas and then considering solutions. The evaluation of performance thus emerges from discussion, rather than being imposed by the appraiser. A PERSON-ORIENTED approach examines the employee's personal qualities (of leadership, judgment, initiative and so on) and technical attributes rather than his success in achieving the expected results. A DEVELOPMENTAL approach challenges the individual to evaluate his performance and to suggest how he can improve his performance.

360-DEGREE FEEDBACK is used to pursue the developmental approach. Feedback is collected from the range of persons with whom the individual interacts in doing his job; senior managers, department managers, peers, subordinates, internal and external customers, and so on. The aim is to produce insights which can be linked to specific development goals. However, unless resources are available to provide the necessary support – such as training – this can be demotivating. This technique is not suitable for assessing pay.

Successful 360-degree feedback aims to develop cooperation between appraiser and appraisee in a problem-solving activity, but a range of problems arise. It depends upon a relationship of trust and loyalty between the appraiser and employee. Where this does not exist and the employee has no guarantee of confidentiality or an unbiased evaluation, she is unlikely to participate with enthusiasm. The importance of the relationship makes it difficult to impose management control, and so the technique is not favored in a highly bureaucratic culture. It would appear to be an ideal way of appraising performance in the association cultures where the importance of trust is accepted. But the process is meaningless in cases where the relationship is so close as to make collusion inevitable.

These problems are generally indicative of the difficulties that arise in making appraisal. Unless, at one extreme, the process is entirely mechanistic and based solely on quantitative data or, at the opposite extreme, appraiser and employee develop the ideal relationship of mutual loyalty balanced by objectivity, there are bound to be disagreements over credibility and reliability.

Surveys regularly report that performance appraisal is the most contentious and least popular of all HR activities. Keeping a balance between objective assessment and sympathetic engagement tests all but the most mature employee and the most sensitive manager. Nevertheless, at least in the contract cultures most organizations use some form of it.

The points made above refer to appraisal in the US and the UK, where it is normal that employees are appraised on an individual rather than a group basis. This is to be expected in individualist cultures; most persons would prefer not to be given an evaluation influenced by others' performance. However, this does not apply everywhere.

In collectivist Japan the emphasis is placed on efficiency rather than performance, and group appraisals are usual. Abu-Doleh and Weir's (2007) study of the use of performance appraisal in Jordan showed that data gathered in private organizations had far greater impact on deciding promotion, retention, and identifying training needs (etc.) than in public organizations. Research among Western-owned, Japanese-owned and Taiwanese-owned companies in Taiwan showed that Taiwanese owned were even more reluctant to offer feedback to their employees. The problems of "protecting face" and "establishing a good relationship with employees" were of paramount importance (Wu, 2006).

19.7 Training

Like all HRM, questions about training must be set in an economic framework. How much can the organization expect to profit from investing in training its employees? At what level of investment is training no longer profitable? No organization can be expected to provide training when there is little likelihood of this producing a profit, either in the short or long term.

Reasons for NOT training include the following:

- training is expensive. Expenses include direct training costs (e.g. paying for trainers, training materials, facilities, and so on) and indirect training costs (the time lost hiring staff to cover for those being trained);
- staff already trained in the target skills can be recruited;
- work can be contracted out;
- trained staff may be lured away by competitors;
- potential trainees lack motivation;
- administrative difficulties (e.g. finding trainers, problems of covering for staff while they are being trained, and so on).

Reasons FOR training include:

- the value expected from training is greater than the cost;
- all recruits are given training as a matter of routine;
- changes – for example, new technology – demand new skills;
- the implementation of a new strategy calls for new skills;
- as a proactive move to influence the formation of future strategy;
- valued employees are motivated by training which leads to promotion;
- the state education system does not prepare students adequately to enter the labor market – as in most Middle Eastern countries (see papers in Budhwar and Mellahi, 2006, and p. 294).

These deficiencies have to be overcome within the organization. An alternative is to hire from some other country where the state education system is more successful. In the UK

> In a survey of 217 of the biggest companies by the Association of Graduate Recruiters, more than 43 per cent said positions remained unfilled because students lacked basic skills or the necessary expertise. . . .
> Many companies said that increasingly they had to recruit from overseas.[2]

HR managers commonly have problems in justifying the immediate costs of mounting a training programme, and demonstrating that this is an investment, not a cost. They need to show how development affects performance.

19.7.1   *Training local employees*

In cultural contexts which are less optimistic about the possibilities for changing human nature, the reasons for training may be less persuasive. On the other hand, the increased globalization of management means that training courses and workshops given to managers in the Western developed countries become increasingly popular elsewhere. Popular management topics include:

- leadership/motivation/communication;
- general management;
- human resource management;
- organizational change and development;
- strategy development;
- negotiation skills.

However, these topics may reflect different values in different contexts, and management styles appropriate in Country A may not be appropriate in Country B. Any program of training needs to take the differences into account. When the countries have different experiences of economic development, the problems of transferring management know-how may be complex.

Many traditional societies are still characterized by notions of exclusive authority which inhibit the sharing of managerial power and information across the organization. Where information is hoarded, its owner enjoys respect, and is only likely to share it out when absolutely necessary, and perhaps at the last possible moment. In this situation, training materials reflecting traditional Anglo concepts of informational flexibility are unlikely to be immediately accepted.

19.7.2   *Training local managers in headquarters culture*

Local managers who choose to work for the subsidiary are predisposed to the headquarters values that it reflects. Those who are not so predisposed, and cannot make the adjustment, soon quit.

The headquarters planning to teach its own values to local staff – and so adopt a style of cultural control – has a range of options that include

- expatriating headquarters managers to the subsidiary;
- sending subsidiary managers for short-term attachments to headquarters. This serves to develop local managers' international experience, and to expose them to other aspects of the company's work. It may also deepen their commitment to the organization and reward them.

However, this process has to be carefully handled. Intensive training of local managers in headquarters values carries the risk that they overidentify with headquarters and lose their commitment to local values and hence their local power bases. When local managers become headquarters clones, they accept its values uncritically, which can reinforce ethnocentric orientations in headquarters and centralize headquarters control, whether desired or not. The clone loses his capacity to interpret between headquarters and local cultures. This alienates subordinates in the subsidiary who need effective representation, and can create a morale problem.

19.8   Retention

This section discusses cases in which the employee makes the decision to quit. We are NOT concerned with cases in which he is dismissed (for bad performance, absenteeism, dishonesty, violence, and so on); or when he is made redundant (the skills he has are no longer required); or has reached the end of his contract, or normal retirement age.

In contract contexts, attitudes towards questions of why and how employees are re-tained (or made redundant), and who is retained, are largely decided on the basis of the labor contract and calculation of market factors. In times of full national employment and a shortage of skilled labor, the company is eager to retain its skilled workforce. When there is no shortage, a greater turnover may be tolerated, or even encouraged.

Arguments AGAINST turnover are that

- costs of replacement are avoided;
- the investment made in training and supporting the employee is lost;
- good people move to competitors;
- a high turnover rate may be symptomatic of a poorly managed organization and suggests that members are dissatisfied. This demoralizes continuing members and sends a negative message to the environment.

Arguments FOR turnover are that

- turnover rejuvenates the organization;
- turnover helps managers keep tighter control over labor costs. In a weak business environment, the organization can more easily respond to a loss of business by not replacing leavers until conditions improve;
- voluntary departures save the cost of making redundancies.

In practice, acceptable turnover rates vary across industries and organizations. But in general, an annual rate of more than 10 percent is likely to cause damage. And organizations that maintain rates below the industry average signal their relative health to the environment.

The organization hopes to manage its turnover rate, and the first stage is to discover why employees choose to exit. Attitude surveys, comparisons of rates between different departments, and exit interviews, provide some information. The organization needs to distinguish

- internal PUSH factors. These include boredom, frustration, dissatisfaction with conditions, bad management;
- external PULL factors. The employee is lured away by rival employers, opportunities to earn more elsewhere, or to start his/her own business.

Turnover is reduced by

- adjusting pay and benefits;
- managing employee expectations, for example by communicating prospects for promotion in the company in realistic terms;
- creating a psychological contract with the individual – for example, by using induction processes to introduce the new recruit to the organization's history and goals, and to his/her group;
- giving appropriate training and development;
- in general, creating a positive culture.

19.8.1 Retaining the loyalty of local staff

In an MNC subsidiary, tensions set in between expatriate and local staff when the local staff perceive that expatriate staff are rewarded at higher rates for the same work, or –

worse still — lower performance. Morale plummets, production suffers and expatriates become isolated from their local colleagues.

Headquarters retains the loyalty of local managers by

- showing that it trusts their judgment, particularly about local conditions;
- appraising and promoting them by criteria that recognize both their contributions to the global organization and their local expertise;
- giving them responsibilities appropriate to their level in the MNC;
- compensating them at rates that are fair, if not equivalent to expatriate rates, and providing appropriate benefits;
- providing opportunities to rotate to headquarters and other subsidiaries;
- having HR officers devote equivalent time to both locals and expatriates when planning their careers;
- providing appropriate training. Giving equivalent consideration to both locals and expatriates when training budgets are designed.

19.9   Implications for the Manager

A. In general in your country, how far is the relationship of trust between employer and employee based on
- ASSOCIATION?
- CONTRACT?

B. In your opinion how far does the relationship of trust within your organization typify what is generally true in your country?

Now research these questions for an MNC that you know well. Compare conditions in the headquarters, and in a subsidiary in some other country.

1 In headquarters, what problems arise in each of the following HR activities?
- recruitment;
- job appraisal;
- training;
- retention.

Explain why these problems occur.

2 In the subsidiary, what problems arise in each of the following HR activities?
- recruitment;
- job appraisal;
- training;
- retention.

Explain why these problems occur.

3 Compare your answers to 1 and 2. Explain any differences.

19.10 SUMMARY

The field of HRM is wide, and this chapter has limited itself to two themes of interest to the international manager; how far the implementation of general principles is influenced by local factors, and the need to adapt headquarters HR policy when applying it in the subsidiary.

Section 19.2 asked how far CONCEPTS OF HRM can be APPLIED. Concepts taught in business schools in the US and the the UK may have limited or different value elsewhere. The section also discussed the emergence of HRM from traditional personnel management, and its growing significance in a globalized world. The next section examined the GENERAL FUNCTIONS – setting performance objectives, staffing, administration, and planning and implementing change. A range of factors influence the balance found within any one HRM department. The notion of strategic HRM was examined.

Section 19.4 dealt generally with the importance of CONTEXT as a constraint on HRM ACTIVITIES. The labor relationship depends on the expected relationship between employer and employee; at one extreme this is based on trust through association, and at the opposite extreme on contract. The relationship is specified within a job design. The next four sections briefly discussed RECRUITMENT, PERFORMANCE APPRAISAL, TRAINING and RETENTION. They showed that their significance within a contract context might not apply elsewhere, and indicated what problems any lack of correspondence might pose for an MNC.

19.11 EXERCISE

In Vietnam, the Hanoi Hat Company made hats and caps. At first, it focused on producing a limited range of basic models. The organizational structure was simple, and there was no need for sophisticated HRM. Issues of recruitment, pay and dismissal were handled by the administration office, and any other personal problems were dealt with by the employee's functional manager.

Cutters were paid on a piece-rate basis, and developed skills to produce indefinite numbers of these models – and hence to earn good wages. Then, as the company became more successful, it was contracted by an international sportswear company to produce short runs of special models for particular events – for example, the South East Asian Games. This contract was highly profitable. However, each of the special models might be designed differently, and so the cutters had to develop different skills to produce each order. This training had the effect of reducing their production rate, and hence each individual earned less. This led to considerable dissatisfaction, although the external labor market offered few comparable opportunities.

Alone among the managers, the General manager had an MBA earned in a Western business school and was aware of the problem. She argued that the first step to overcoming this difficulty was to appoint a specialist HR manager.

However, the functional managers resisted this, which they saw as an unnecessary expense and likely to weaken their own influence. The GM was not a member of the owning family – whereas several of the functional managers were – and so was unable to persuade the owners to her way of thinking.

QUESTIONS

1 What is the problem?
2 What – if any – changes should be made?

Notes

1 Erik Guyot. Headhunters in Asia try to help companies owned by families. *Wall Street Journal*, February 24, 1997.

2 Graeme Paton. Graduates lacking skills to win jobs. *Daily Telegraph*, January 31, 2008.

CHAPTER TWENTY
Controlling by Staffing

20.1   Introduction

Previous chapters examined a range of techniques by which headquarters applies appropriate controls in its investments abroad, but did not touch on staffing. Chapter 19 discussed HR topics associated with the employment of local staff, and here we deal with appropriate control styles in the investment.

In 1930, one Anglo oil company employed 60 expatriates in Taiwan. By 2000, this number had fallen to a single individual. This decline is not unusual. Established MNCs that once sent dozens of managers to an important investment abroad may now depend entirely on local staff. But this does not mean that different headquarters enjoy less control over their investments, or that fewer managers are working expatriate, for at least some of their career. In a globalizing world, many more companies are sending staff abroad than previously.

This chapter focuses on local and expatriate staffing in IJVs and subsidiaries. Which gives greater opportunities for control in different circumstances? It deals with three areas:

- problems of control in the IJV;
- what control style to use in the subsidiary;
- whether to use local or expatriate top management in a subsidiary.

20.2   Staffing to Control the IJV

Chapter 17 saw that when planning their participation in the IJV, each partner hopes to exercise as much control as is necessary to protect its interests and achieve its goals. Here we see how they translate their different needs for control into staffing policy.

20.2.1   Who manages the IJV?

Which partner contributes to management? The partner who contributes most resources has a prime claim on the post of CEO. Factors determining allocation of other senior positions include

- the availability of MANAGEMENT TALENT in the partners and in external labor markets;
- the GOALS of the IJV. An IJV dedicated to marketing may be headed by a marketer, one dedicated to production by an engineer;
- needs to safeguard proprietary TECHNOLOGY. A partner that makes significant technological inputs may demand control in order to protect itself against theft and guarantee efficient operations and maintenance;
- needs to safeguard MARKETING expertise. For example, the local parent balances the technological parent's inputs with knowledge of local markets and customers.

These allocations, made at the early stages of IJV planning, can lead to disagreements between the partners at a later stage if they are not properly planned. For example, the non-technological partner begins to claim that the inputs made by its partner are out of date or overvalued, and do not justify the scope of control which the technological partner had initially claimed. Or, over time, the foreign parent develops its own knowledge of markets and customers, establishes its own database, and so weakens the local monopoly.

20.2.2   The project staff are heterogeneous

IJV staff may be selected from a number of labor pools. Figure 20.1 gives an illustration. The foreign Partner X is based in Country P; the local Partner Y, and the IJV project, are

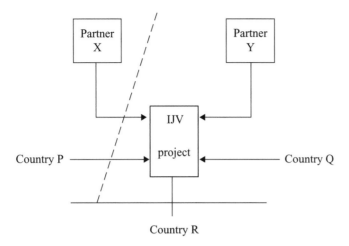

Figure 20.1   Staffing the IJV

based in Country Q. Staff may also be recruited from third country, Country R, and other third countries. Assume that the project has a planned lifespan of five years.

IJV staff are recruited from these labor pools:

1 Partner X. When the project ends in five years' time, these project staff return to Partner X;
2 Partner Y. When the project ends in five years' time, these project staff return to Partner Y;
3 Country P. These project staff are recruited EITHER by the project OR by Partner X. They are contracted for the life of the project only;
4 Country Q. These project staff are recruited EITHER by the project OR by Partner Y. They are contracted for the life of the project only;
5 Country R and other third countries. These project staff are recruited EITHER by the project OR by Partner X OR by Partner Y. They are contracted for the life of the project only.

The wider the range of labor pools, the more diverse the workforce and the wider should be the possibilities for creative learning. However, the possibilities for misunderstandings and dispute are also wider.

20.2.3   *When loyalties clash*

Staff from a range of labor pools have different interests. Their different organizational and cultural loyalties can lead to misunderstanding and conflict.

For example, if there should be a dispute between the partners, or between, say, Partner X and the IJV management, staff posted from Partner X are naturally inclined to place its interests above those of the project. They hope to return to Partner X when the project ends, and depend on it for continued employment and promotion and possibly pension rights. They have the experience of its organizational culture, and assuming that they are nationals of Country P, Country P culture. Similarly, staff on temporary secondment from Partner Y take their company's side.

In the event of a partner–project dispute, staff posted by the partner may start operating informal matrix structures, reporting to managers in both the IJV and their partner. This informal dual-reporting undermines the authority of the project CEO and complicates problems of control.

Staff recruited directly to the IJV from Countries P, Q, and R depend on the IJV during its life and have no loyalties to either partner (unless they hope to be recruited by one). Their performance is heavily influenced by their career needs, their national culture and the evolving culture of the IJV.

The different interests of these groups may be creative when managed appropriately but dispute always threatens. Their different organizational loyalties are complicated by professional, hierarchical, and cultural factors. Competing organizational and cultural loyalties are reflected in

- relations with each other and with IJV management;
- competing interpretations of IJV goals;
- competing expectations of IJV outcomes;
- competing perceptions of appropriate structure, management systems and style, work norms, organizational culture.

IJV staff also belong to different professional groups. If one profession is associated with one cultural group, competition between professions might be interpreted as a clash between cultures.

20.2.4   *Third-country nationals*

Why might the IJV employ a third-country national from Country R, who is not employed by either partner? Possibly neither, nor their country labor markets, can supply the skills needed at an economic price. For example, Scandinavian countries have a limited pool of experienced international managers, and their companies regularly employ third-country nationals.

Third-country nationals who are knowledgeable of the cultures of both parents play a useful role in bridging the cultural divide and in acting as informal mediators.

20.2.5   *The one-culture solution*

The danger of misunderstandings is reduced when all IJV staff are drawn from a single labor pool. When ALL are transferred from the local partner, or are ALL transferred from the foreign partner (supposing that the government of the local partner permits this), their cultural values and experiences correspond. This solution may attract a partner that cannot spare staff from its routine operations.

However, this foregoes opportunities to learn from cooperation, and means that the absent partner has to exert its share of control through some other means. For example, its inputs of finance or technology are sufficient to dominate. It also implies considerable trust. This may only be realistic in the case of two partners who have built up trust from a history of cooperating on similar projects.

20.2.6   Balance in project staffing

A balance in staffing does NOT mean that a marketing manager posted from Partner X has to be balanced by a marketing manager from Partner Y. Instead, it might mean that the appointment of a Parent X marketing manager (reflecting a concern to safeguard its marketing expertise) is balanced by a technology manager posted from Partner Y (which reflects Parent Y's interest in developing marketing expertise).

Balanced recruitment meeting the needs of partners, IJV, and IJV staff is sometimes difficult to achieve. Here are situations in which a failure to provide balance creates disputes between partner and within the IJV:

- One partner tries to dominate by placing its own staff in all key positions;
- One partner withholds its best staff and throws on to the other the responsibility for contributing expertise;
- One partner uses the project to rid itself of "deadwood" and troublemakers, or to secure posts for technically unqualified persons. For instance, the CEO of the partner appoints his unqualified son-in-law to a senior post;
- One partner is unable to fulfill its contracted obligations to supply certain skills, either because of internal deficiencies or because of differences in the technical and economic developments of the two countries of the partners.

Imbalances in skill levels can often be corrected by transferring skills technologies. Staff from the less-developed partner may be employed in the IJV as trainees or "shadows" of their experienced colleagues from the stronger partner. Over time, the staff-in-training play increasingly proactive roles. This arrangement works well, so long as all parties (the partners, the IJV management, and the staff concerned)

- adequately plan how the technology transfer and training activities should be implemented;
- are satisfied with the implementation process;
- are motivated to participate. Questions of motivation are discussed below.

20.2.7 Motivating staff to work for the IJV

Staff may be unwilling to leave the security of their regular work and their work groups at headquarters to move to the IJV. This is a problem in collectivist cultures, where members may interpret the move as punishment and "exile" – even when the IJV is in the same country – rather than as promotion.

Staff transferred from a parent to work in the project are motivated when they

- are given a free choice of whether or not to join the IJV;
- recognize that working for the IJV is in their career interests;
- are adequately compensated. Resentment over inequalities in pay is damaging. In many countries it is a matter of pride that local managers receive salaries equivalent to expatriate managers for similar positions. Partners in developing economies may find it hard to understand why generous packages have to be paid to attract experienced expatriates. Two possible solutions are that expatriates are paid on a separate basis, which avoids putting them on the IJV payroll; or having the foreign partner pay their benefits and bonuses;
- are trained. But training can be a sensitive issue. Staff from the weaker parent are NOT motivated if trainee status is perceived to diminish their status, and if they have no professional reasons for making the commitment. For instance, staff transferred from a public sector organization, whose jobs are guaranteed and protected from competitive forces, may have no need to upgrade their skills. In this situation, skills are not transferred.

20.3   National Culture and Control

What options does headquarters have when deciding how to manage its human resources in a foreign operation? At one extreme it might depend heavily on rules and regulations. This emphasis reflects the notion that the relationship between company and employee is essentially contractual and can be measured in job performance. At the opposite extreme, control is negotiated through mutual respect, loyalty and trust and the relationship is perceived to be based on a psychological contract – which is continually renegotiated. This point is developed here and throughout Chapter 23.

Jaeger (1983) described these two approaches in terms of

- bureaucratic control of the subsidiary;
- cultural control of the subsidiary.

Each of these is expressed in a philosophy of how managerial staff can be used most efficiently.

20.3.1 Staffing for bureaucratic control

In Jaeger's (1983) model the aim of BUREAUCRATIC CONTROL is that the subsidiary should develop a culture of impersonal and bureaucratic efficiency. Headquarters encourages these values by enforcing impersonal rules that govern selection, recruitment, training, rewards, and that regulate the individual's behavior and output:

- The CONTROL OF BEHAVIOR focuses on the monitoring and evaluation of activities. This control is exercised by headquarters staff, headquarters expatriates, or local managers, using regulations, rules, text and electronic instructions, manuals, and reports. Training focuses on developing specific technical competences.
- OUTPUT CONTROL means developing reporting and monitoring systems by which the subsidiary reports on its activities to the headquarters, and assessing subsidiary performance on the bases of data submitted.

When bureaucratic control succeeds, the subsidiary grows into an efficient operating unit that can build its own culture. The expenses involved may be light. The weakness is that loyalties to headquarters are weak. Relationships conducted through emails do not win loyalty when the subsidiary is in a collectivist culture, where personal relationships between superior and subordinates are all-important. Headquarters may be unaware of organizational developments that could threaten company interests.

20.3.2 Controlling through the organizational culture: cultural control

The aim of CULTURAL CONTROL is to develop loyalty to the company and to headquarters managers, so that the subsidiary culture eventually replicates headquarters culture. Cultural control is created through implicit norms that persuade members to make a moral commitment to the company. Manuals are used as training tools, but at least as much emphasis is laid on developing an awareness of the organization's norms and values and integrating a newcomer into the shared culture by structuring his/her personal interactions with established members of staff.

Cultural control companies aim to induce headquarter values at a much deeper cultural and psychological level than do bureaucratic control companies. Techniques used to induce cultural control are most intense in the subsidiary's early years, and include

- staffing with large numbers of expatriates who act as role models;
- employee socialization programs;
- frequent visits between the subsidiary and headquarters. For example, headquarters staff make consultancy and advisory visits, and subsidiary staff are given training
- company seminars; visits to headquarters;
- social events. These include activities such as dining and drinking together, picnics, group travel, and group sports.

The strengths of cultural control are that it can develop powerful commitments between headquarters and subsidiary. However, the costs of maintaining high expatriate levels and constant visiting between headquarters and subsidiary are bound to be high. But this can alienate local staff when the headquarters holds values do not fit with the local culture – or when locals suspect that it does:

> In 2001, McDonald's faced furious protests in India over allegations, which it denied, that it had laced its French fries with beef fat. The Indian Mutiny of 1857 was sparked in part when Indian soldiers employed by the British East India Company heard rumors that their cartridges had been greased with animal fat. Few companies learn from history.[1]

Any conflict between the interests of the headquarters and of local society may cause low morale among local employees, whose loyalties are divided. Bureaucratic control does not place their employees under this psychological constraint.

20.3.3   *National culture and the choice of control style*

Bureaucratic control reflects a tolerance of ambiguity by headquarters staff. The organizational culture of the subsidiary is allowed to develop its own characteristics, which are bound to reflect values in the local national culture. On the other hand, controlling through the growth of a positive organizational culture reflects relatively high needs to avoid uncertainty. Bureaucratic structures are applied but are considered insufficient to generate the trust needed between management – which may be largely expatriate – and local workforce when the subsidiary is abroad, and located in a foreign culture. And so trust must also be developed on a personal level through personal relationships.

The extremes of bureaucratic control are more likely when the national culture of headquarters has relatively low needs to avoid uncertainty and an expectation of individualist decision-making – in the Anglo and Scandinavian cultures, for example. Cultural control occurs in collectivist cultures where ambiguities are high – in Japan and Korea, for example.

The two models of bureaucratic and cultural controls are "ideal"; there may be no companies that entirely fit either one. In practice, all companies fit at various points on a continuum between the extremes, and may move between them depending on circumstances in the company and the wider environment. For example, when the subsidiary is new, headquarters might invest in more cultural control; and when local managers have shown their competence, the headquarters withdraws expatriates and moves towards bureaucratic techniques. When the business environment is stable, headquarters might reduce personal controls, but when new competitors enter the market and conditions become uncertain, the company might decide that personal interventions are in order to develop a sense of common purpose and identity.

Anglo companies are more likely to exercise bureaucratic controls over their subsidiaries abroad, and Japanese and Korean companies use cultural control ALL OTHER THINGS BEING EQUAL. But often, all other things are not equal. There may always be special factors that lead an Anglo company into adopting a more cultural style, or, say, a Japanese company into applying cultural controls.

For example, an Anglo company worries about the security of its technology, and decides to invest in motivating personal loyalties between local subsidiary technologists and their counterparts in headquarters. Alternatively, a Japanese company buys a foreign business for its investment value only, decides that headquarters staff are not needed to control the use of technology or are less competent to do so than are local managers, and that bureaucratic structures are sufficient to guarantee the stream of profits.

When headquarters controls the technology and expertise, resources are needed to guarantee effective use and protect its intellectual rights. The reverse also applies; when one partner has no interest in a particular technology it normally has no need to control it – unless this managerial control provides an opportunity to acquire expertise from its partner.

The location of the subsidiary and the availability of local staff also influence the decision as to what style of control is needed. Japanese companies tend to rely more on cultural controls in Asia than in Europe. Delios and Björkman (2000) found that Japanese companies used expatriates with a control function in their Chinese subsidiaries to a greater degree than in their US subsidiaries.

Harzing (1999) re-examined Jaeger's categories. She distinguished

- bureaucratic formalized control;
- personalized centralized control;
- control by socialization and networks;
- output control.

Bureaucratic controls exploit the use of artifacts, and are more direct, formalized and explicit. Personalized controls are based on culture and social interactions and networks, and tend to be indirect and implicit.

20.4   Local or Expatriate Top Management?

This section deals with the factors that influence the decision on whether senior posts in the subsidiary should be taken by local or expatriate staff (at levels of CEO, managing director, functional managers, senior technicians). The claims of two groups are discussed:

- LOCAL managers belong on the staff of the foreign investment or are hired in the country of the investment.
- EXPATRIATE managers are transferred to the investment by headquarters. They may have previous experience in the country of headquarters, or have been especially hired for this assignment. Expatriates include employees hired from a third country by headquarters.

Tharenou and Harvey (2006) found that local managers protect the MNC from risks that arise from not being responsive to the local environment, and expatriates can provide skills and sometimes develop local managers for future promotions in the company.

20.4.1   The advantages and disadvantages of local staffing

What are the advantages and disadvantages of employing a LOCAL MANAGER to run your foreign subsidiary?

Possible ADVANTAGES are that

- the multinational is "internationalized", particularly if subsidiary managers are rotated back to headquarters;
- the subsidiary can be empowered;
- the local manager is developed and given opportunities to manage;
- the local manager is better connected in local markets and has a keener sense of local needs;
- political risk is reduced when the local manager deals with government officials;
- the local manager has more experience of managing local staff;
- there is no demand for expatriate training;
- expatriation costs are avoided;
- the local manager may cost less to reward;
- ill-feeling arising from disparities in expatriate and local rewards are avoided.

Possible DISADVANTAGES are that

- headquarters control is weakened;
- the subsidiary is more likely to develop an organizational culture at variance to that of headquarters;
- headquarters staff do not have opportunities to work abroad. The organizational culture is in danger of growing parochial;
- headquarters is less sensitized to subsidiary needs;
- headquarters is less able to control local managerial and technical skill levels;
- headquarters is less able to protect its proprietary technology, and operating and maintenance standards;
- headquarters and the manager do not share a common culture, and their cultural differences can give rise to misunderstandings;
- communication between subsidiaries (each managed by a local manager) may be harder to maintain;
- communication between headquarters and subsidiary is weaker. Local managers may have less understanding of the worldwide organization and identify less with its strategic goals;
- headquarters is less able to influence operations at critical times.

By expatriating its managers, headquarters is apparently able to exert greater control, but at a cost. There may be greater advantages associated with local management. For any one company, the choice between expatriate and local staffing depends on its circumstances and the particular opportunities and threats, strengths and weaknesses that influence its operations.

20.4.2   *The advantages and disadvantages of expatriate staffing*

The advantages and disadvantages of appointing an EXPATRIATE MANAGER to run the subsidiary mirror the disadvantages and advantages of the local appointment.

The ADVANTAGES include the following:

- headquarters control is greater;
- headquarters organizational culture is more easily spread to the subsidiary;
- headquarters staff gain experience abroad. Managers gain understanding of international business through expatriate assignments, and the organizational culture of headquarters becomes internationalized;
- headquarters becomes more sensitized to subsidiary needs;
- headquarters is more able to control local managerial and technical skill levels;
- headquarters is better able to protect proprietary technology, and operating and maintenance standards;
- headquarters and the manager share a common national culture, and at this level, cultural differences and misunderstandings do not arise;
- communications between headquarters and subsidiary are stronger;
- headquarters is better able to influence operations at critical times – for example, when the subsidiary market grows unstable, when the subsidiary is ailing, in a start-up;
- closer links are made with other subsidiaries that are managed by headquarters staff.

Expatriate headquarters management also carries DISADVANTAGES. They are that

- local staff get fewer opportunities to manage;
- political risk is increased when the expatriate does not understand the local political situation;
- the expatriate takes time to develop local connections;
- the expatriate has less sensitivity to local market demands;
- the expatriate may not know the local language;
- the expatriate has less experience of managing local staff;
- training for the expatriate assignment has to be provided;
- expatriation costs are incurred;
- the expatriate may cost more to reward;
- disparities in rewards between the expatriate and local staff create ill-feeling among local staff.

20.4.3   *What factors decide whether local or expatriate local staffing is better?*

Assuming that the company has a free choice (for example, when it is not subject to government controls) when should it look for the advantages of a local appointment, and when for the advantages of an expatriate appointment? No one answer holds true for every situation. The lists above make clear that the decision must depend on factors particular to the company in its context.

For example, if the headquarters of a company marketing a global product sets a high priority on uniform, centralized control, has staff available and can afford the costs, expatriate postings are a priority. If headquarters needs close control, it must be prepared to invest more. On the other hand, if headquarters wishes to decentralize control and focus on meeting local demand, it may decide not to incur the costs of an expatriate appointment and instead appoint a local manager.

Some of the factors are discussed below:

(a)   STRUCTURE OF THE MNC. Section 18.3.1 saw that the MNC chooses between different structures in order to obtain the most appropriate degree of control over its operations in the subsidiary. The choice of structure may influence staffing policy. A decentralized relationship may provide greater opportunities for local managers; a highly centralized relationship may call for a manager expatriated from headquarters. However, there is no automatic correlation between structure and staffing arrangements.

(b)   INDUSTRY. An industry that depends on legal precision and reliability demands has greater needs for headquarters controls, and this often means an expatriate top management. For instance, banking procedures are highly standardized and experience acquired in one branch can be applied elsewhere. On the other hand, retail trade practices are localized and experience of managing a department store in Dallas is of limited value in Seoul;

(c)   STRATEGY. If the subsidiary serves local markets a local appointment may be appropriate. If it serves international markets and is integrated with other subsidiaries a headquarters manager may be suited. A decentralizing strategy points to appointing a local; a centralizing strategy, to expatriating a headquarters manager. A transnational alternative is to select from a third-country subsidiary.

(d)   TECHNOLOGY. When headquarters has strong needs to safeguard headquarters technology, it expatriates expatriating technical staff. Needs for reliable operations and maintenance may also sway the issue.

(e)   AGE AND CONDITION. A subsidiary may require control from headquarters when it is starting up, or is ailing, or when the business environment is particularly unstable.

(f)   HEADQUARTERS AVAILABILITY. Is there a headquarters manager qualified to take the post? And, if so, is there another manager qualified to replace him at headquarters? If expatriate postings are necessary for internal promotion, the headquarters manager welcomes the opportunity. If these conditions do not apply, the company may choose the local solution.

(g) LOCAL AVAILABILITY. Is there a local manager qualified to take the post – and can the company benefit from his appointment? Qualifications may include an ability to speak the headquarters language.

(h) FEAR OF LOSING LOCAL MANAGERS. Headquarters may be deterred from promoting a local manager if it seems likely he will be poached by a local competitor or will set up on his own.

(i) QUALITY OF LOCAL STAFF. In a rapidly developing economy, local staff may be frustrated and demoralized by expatriate employment when they do not perceive the expatriates to be any better qualified than they are. To add insult to injury, expatriate managers from developed economies working in less-developed economies are usually paid far more than local managers, especially when travel and relocation allowances have to be paid.

(j) NATIONAL CULTURE. When the national culture of the headquarters country is risk averse, more expatriates may be posted out to manage investments abroad. Thus the advantages of expatriate appointment are taken, and the advantages of local appointment discounted. When the culture is more tolerant of risk, the reverse applies; there may be relatively greater willingness to appoint a local. In 1982, Tung found that Japanese MNCs were more likely to staff senior levels in their foreign subsidiaries with their headquarters-country nationals (Japanese) than were European or American firms.

In addition, the personalities and experiences of the candidates for the post (whether locally or headquarters based) influence the decision, sometimes crucially. The question is complex, and there is no absolutely right or wrong answer that fits all situations.

20.4.4   *Senior local management one level down*

Senior managers in a subsidiary managed at the top level by expatriates exert enormous influence. They understand

- headquarters' perceptions of goals, internal resources, external environment, strategic priorities;
- subsidiary's perceptions of goals, internal resources, external environment, strategic priorities;

and communicate these between subsidiary and headquarters.

This role of communicating – or negotiating – between two interests that are at times bound to be in dispute and may even have different first languages can be stressful. The local manager who identifies himself too strongly with local interests may lose internal legitimacy within the MNC. The manager who is perceived as entirely representing the voice of expatriate top management may lose legitimacy in the eyes of the local environment (Geppert and Williams, 2006). A delicate balancing act is required.

Local managers also have access to informal networks to which the expatriate may never belong. The local culture may have expectations of patronage obligation that do not conform to the perceptions held by top-level expatriates from the headquarters country. The success of the subsidiary depends heavily upon the senior locals being able to move between the two cultures.

20.5 Implications for the Manager

Analyze how staffing is used to control your IJV, subsidiary, or some other organization to which you have access.

How important is staffing in controlling the company's foreign investments? Make a survey of each investment, and compare them.

1   In each IJV, describe staffing:
    (a)   staff transferred from the foreign partner;
    (b)   staff transferred from the local partner;
    (c)   staff recruited from the country of the foreign partner;
    (d)   staff recruited from the country of the local partner;
    (e)   staff recruited from third countries.
2   What advantages and disadvantages arise from this staffing mix? What disputes arise between these groups? What factors cause these disputes? How are they typically resolved?
3   What policy does your MNC apply when staffing senior positions in its subsidiaries?
    •   In what respects is staffing policy uniform across all subsidiaries?
    •   In what respects does staffing policy take account of differences between subsidiaries, their local business/economic contexts and markets?
    •   In what respects does the national culture of headquarters influence staffing policy?
    •   In what respects do the national cultures of the subsidiaries influence the staffing policy?
    •   In what respects do organizational cultures in headquarters and subsidiaries influence the staffing policy?
4   In each subsidiary, is top management expatriate or local?
    •   In each case, why?
    •   In each case, how does this satisfy headquarters' needs for control?
    •   In each case, what control does top management apply?
    •   In each case, how does the subsidiary benefit from this staffing decision?
    •   In each case, how does the subsidiary lose from this staffing decision?

20.6 SUMMARY

This chapter has examined how the MNC headquarters uses staffing policies to enforce its control in an investment abroad. The specific implications for expatriate selection, training and support are dealt with in the next chapter.

Section 20.2 examined problems of STAFFING TO CONTROL THE IJV, first dealing with the role of the top manager. Then it turned to project staff at lower levels, noting that these may be drawn from a range of labor pools. This heterogeneity gives rise to both opportunities and problems. The next section examined styles of management appropriate in a subsidiary abroad, and looked at two extremes, BUREAUCRATIC control and CULTURAL control. Cultural control involves constant interaction between headquarters and subsidiary, and this demands an expatriate presence.

Section 20.4 dealt with the identity of the top manager, whether a LOCAL OR EX-PATRIATE posted from headquarters. Each choice presents a number of advantages and disadvantages, depending on the needs of the organization. The section also dealt with the various factors that influence the choice.

20.7 EXERCISE

This exercise asks you to decide whether to employ expatriate or local managers in a subsidiary. Students can work on their own or in pairs.

Upanattem Universal (UU) is an MNC headquartered in Ruritania. It develops and manufactures children's products ranging from baby food to toys and clothing. The subsidiary in Darana, Upanattem Darana, employs 500 people and management is structured as shown in Figure 20.2. (E indicates that the post is currently held by a Ruritanian expatriate and L by a Daranese local. Numbers indicate how

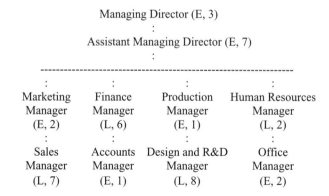

Figure 20.2 Management structure at Upanattem Darana

many years that person has been in post.)
The costs involved in maintaining current
expatriate staffing levels are increasing
and some board members have queried
human resource policies followed in UD.
You have been hired as an external consultant to advise on the HR implications
of the alternative situations listed in (4).

1   Each of (a) − (d) lists four factors.
    Decide which factors affect the deci-
    sion to employ expatriates or locals,
    then for each set (a, b, c, d), decide
    who should be repatriated, promoted,
    or continued, and on criteria for re-
    cruiting where necessary.
2   Decide which factors can be ignored,
    and explain why.
3   No one need suffer! Assume that all
    staff have been performing satisfacto-
    rily. Any expatriates recalled to head-
    quarters will be promoted. Any local
    staff that are replaced will be moved
    to a new, highly prestigious, joint ven-
    ture project.
4   THE ALTERNATIVE SITUATIONS

Situation (a)

(ai)   Ruritanian culture has low needs
       to avoid uncertainty;
(aii) UD has recently introduced a new
       baby food product, produced by
       the design and R&D department;
(aiii) Local market conditions are sta-
       ble. UD dominates the local mar-
       ket, and has no significant com-
       petitors;
(aiv) The Daranese economy is devel-
       oping. Trained managerial and
       technical staff are in short sup-
       ply.

Situation (b)

(bi)   Ruritanian culture has high needs
       to avoid uncertainty;
(bii) Local market conditions are very
       changeable. Until now, UD has
       dominated the local market, but
       now a major foreign MNC is com-
       peting for market share;
(biii) The human resources manager
       has recently proposed a new
       HR strategy, designed to recruit
       and train the next generation
       of Daranese local managers. The
       board support this initiative;
(biv) UU will benefit from greater com-
       munication and transfer of re-
       sources between UD and sub-
       sidiaries in other countries.

Situation (c)

(ci)   Relations between expatriate and
       local staff members are un-
       friendly, and communication
       within UD is bad;
(cii) Communication between the top
       management of UD and head-
       quarters is good;
(ciii) The Daranese economy is devel-
       oped. There is no shortage of
       trained managerial and technical
       staff;
(civ) Back in UU headquarters, a new
       CEO has been appointed. He pro-
       poses that all managerial pro-
       motions take the number of ex-
       patriate years into account. A
       manager who has no expatriate
       experience cannot hope for fast-
       track promotion.

Situation (d)

(di) The market for UD products in the Daranese middle classes is expanding rapidly;

(dii) UU headquarters staff consider that the current UU policies do not reward headquarters staff who take expatriate assignments;

(diii) New Daranese laws offer tax incentives to multinationals that employ locals in management positions; if UD replaces one of its current expatriates with a local, it will receive a 10 percent tax break, if two, a 20 percent tax break, and so on;

(div) Daranese culture has lower needs to avoid uncertainty than does Ruritanian culture.

Note

1 Michael Skapinder. Empires of ignorance: companies should look to history for lessons in how to operate in foreign cultures. *Financial Times*, January 15, 2003.

CHAPTER TWENTY ONE
Managing Expatriate Assignments

CHAPTER OUTLINE

Introduction	Expatriate Support
What Expatriates Do	Implications for the Manager
Expatriate Success and Failure	Summary
Expatriate Selection	Exercise
Expatriate Training	Note

21.1 Introduction

In 1966, an American food producer expatriated 12 headquarters' managers to its operations around the world on assignments lasting at least 18 months. By 2006, this number had fallen to three, but 15 managers were being regularly posted on short-term assignments lasting no more than three months.

This chapter examines changing patterns of expatriation, and sees how these influence functions of selecting, training and supporting expatriates. The text refers to the expatriate in the subsidiary, but the same points apply in an IJV or some other investment abroad.

21.2 What Expatriates Do

Traditional expatriate assignments tended to be long term. The expatriate might be sent abroad for several years – and some stayed for all their careers. Typically, expatriates were posted to senior posts in the subsidiary; CEO, finance director, and so on. Local supplies of management talent might be sparse – as the Introductory case suggests.

At least in MNCs headquartered in the Anglo countries, this pattern has changed, and long-term postings are no longer typical. (Japanese and East Asian MNCs still tend to maintain longer expatriate postings than do their Anglo counterparts.)

The factors that explain reductions in Anglo expatriate complements include

- expense. The cost of expatriation is increasingly prohibitive;
- new information technologies, which often reduce needs for the physical presence of headquarters staff;
- increasing numbers of well-trained and experienced local staff;
- increasing opportunities to empower local operations;
- government policies to reduce expatriation levels and encourage the development of local managerial talent. For example, governments impose visa controls limiting the MNC to an expatriate workforce in proportion to its investment. The subsidiary might be permitted one expatriate visa for, say, every $300,000 invested.

However, this does not mean that worldwide, or in any one country, the *total* number of expatriates is falling. On the contrary, more companies than ever have international commitments, and are making expatriate assignments.

The increase in globalization means that young managers now entering the workforce must expect to work abroad at some point in their careers, and be rotated between posts.

21.2.1 Short-term assignments

Increasing numbers of managers work abroad on short-term expatriate assignments, perhaps for a few months or even only weeks. These may be associated with both CONTROL and KNOWLEDGE – for instance, transferring knowledge between subsidiary and headquarters. The pace of change is now so rapid that MNCs need short-term projects in order to continually update their foreign operations, and to learn from them. Related to this, it becomes increasingly difficult to estimate benefits and control expenses with any certainty.

These short-term expatriate projects include

- conducting an internal consultancy;
- establishing a new system;
- explaining headquarters strategy;
- inspection and evaluation;
- training;
- mentoring.

The advantages of short assignments are that objectives are precisely defined and activities can be tightly controlled. The disadvantages are that the expatriate has fewer opportunities to learn from mistakes and to increase his sum of knowledge.

The increased use of short-term assignments means that the manager must develop skills to adjust to a range of new countries, organizations, and professional roles. This may mean working in several languages.

21.3   Expatriate Success and Failure

There is little agreement on what constitutes success in an expatriate assignment, but here are some of the common benchmarks. Success is measured relative to

- the expatriate's performance in headquarters;
- the expatriate's performance in his previous assignment abroad;
- the job description;
- the environment. What counts as a successful assignment in this situation?
- the circumstances. For example, given that a country is suffering an economic recession, the expatriate is perceived to be performing well.

Success may be rewarded by promotion. The expatriate's return to headquarters, or his departure from the company, may signal failure; but not necessarily. Eschbach et al. (2001) cite data indicating that between 10–50 percent of American managers choose to curtail their assignments early. That is, the manager who succeeds abroad may decide to move to a new employer who will reward his success more generously. And the manager who performs below expectations may be continued at post in order to avoid embarrassing those responsible for his appointment or because no one is available to substitute. In sum, apparent indicators of success or failure may be ambiguous.

The vast majority of assignments achieve success, but the expense involved in failure explains why this attracts most attention. Taking into account the cost of expatriate salary, accommodation, moving expenses, schooling and other allowances, the expense to the firm may be in excess of $1 million, and in addition there are the personal costs to the individual in terms of loss of earnings, loss of reputation, and possibly psychological and domestic disruption.

The ambiguity surrounding success and failure is compounded by the lack of agreement on how failure should be estimated and what factors have to be taken into account.

21.3.1   Why problems arise in identifying failure

Here are some of the problems that arise:

- A COMPARISON TO PERFORMANCE back home is unrealistic if the expatriate is working in new and unfamiliar surroundings, or has never been expatriate before.
- A failure to fulfill the JOB DESCRIPTION begs the question, who wrote it? Headquarters and subsidiary may be operating different criteria, and headquarters may be out of date in regards to conditions in the subsidiary and its environment.

- The relevance of CULTURE an as explanatory factor. An early report on Japanese managers failing in the United States identified as an important cause insecurities resulting from being cut off from their *dou-ki-kai*, or fraternity of co-workers.[1] In this particular collectivist culture, the manager identifies strongly with those who joined the company at the same time. This is far less of an issue elsewhere.

The national culture of the headquarters influences how the expatriate operates; it also influences the attitudes of headquarters managers to his operations:

- TIME. At what point should success and failure be evaluated? A manager who is failing after three months may be suffering from culture shock and may succeed later. American companies have a reputation of pulling managers at the first sign of failure; at the opposite extreme, Japanese companies sometimes keep an initially unsuccessful manager in place for years, trusting that eventually he will learn and turn his experience to good account. The tolerance of initial failure shown by headquarters inevitably influences the figures.

A major Japanese pharmaceuticals firm did not evaluate its expatriates until after their first six months at post. The performance of the manager's unit during this period was attributed to his predecessor. This had the effects that

- the predecessor maintained his performance level up to the end of the posting;
- the predecessor fully briefed his replacement and eased his entry into the unit;
- the replacement had several months in which to learn the job without worrying unduly about evaluation;
- perceptions of CULTURAL DISTANCE. It is sometimes argued that some cultures are intrinsically harder for managers and their dependents. In practice though, intrinsic difficulty cannot be measured. But what these claims often boil down to is that managers from Culture X may have greater difficulty acclimatizing to Culture A than do managers from Culture Y. For instance, Americans have greater difficulty acclimatizing to Japan than do Koreans.

    These perceptions should not be dismissed as unimportant. The manager who worries about his ability to adjust to a particular culture is likely to be inhibited when working and living there. The implications for management are either that it should invest in the necessary cultural training or – in the example above – post a Korean not an American to Japan;
- the IDENTITIES and INTERESTS of those identifying and explaining failure. When different persons submit explanations, these are bound to differ. A study of American expatriates failing identified the manager's personality or emotional im-maturity, and the manager's inability to cope with responsibilities posed by work abroad (Tung, 1987). Internal features suggest that these judgments were made by human resource departments. On the other hand, a British study (Hamill, 1989) identified inadequate pre-post briefing, poorly designed compensation packages, and lack of advanced planning for re-entry. These explanations are more likely to have come

from the expatriate managers themselves than from the headquarters HR departments, who are responsible for managing the briefings and the compensation packages. In sum, explanations for failure depend on who is explaining. The persons with interests in the expatriate's performance include

- managers to whom he reports at headquarters;
- managers to whom he reports in the post abroad;
- colleagues;
- subordinates;
- trainers;
- the expatriate himself;
- the expatriate's dependents.

21.3.2   Dependents

The significance of the last item, dependents, is discussed in the sections below. One point agreed by the three studies cited in 21.3.1 and elsewhere is that the manager is far more likely to adjust happily to living and working at post if his dependents adjust. Tung (1987) lists family-related problems, including an inability of dependents to adjust as the main cause of expatriate failure in American MNCs.

This book refers to the expatriate as "he" and the main dependent as "she". In practice of course, this stereotype does not always apply. But it is still the case that many companies are still biased against expatriating their female managers. In the past, dependents have been the manager's spouse and children. But increasingly, the manager may ask to be accompanied by a partner, sibling, or parent. If the assignment is sufficiently important, the company accedes.

The company may decide that the post is for a single person only and that the manager should be unaccompanied. This may be influenced by a perception that

- a domestic relationship is unlikely to survive the rigors of the environment, and the stresses arising from a failed relationship should be avoided; or that
- the assignment is relatively unimportant and does not justify the cost of expatriating dependents; or that
- the assignment is far too short a period to justify the cost.

Ideally, dependents are involved as early as possible in planning for relocation to the expatriate post. They are given any necessary training, opportunities to work in the new culture, and support at post and on return home. These issues are explored further in 21.6.

21.3.3   *Expatriate assignments and the organizational culture*

The company that foresees a continued dependence on expatriated staff tries to develop the conditions for expatriate success as opportunities for optimization. In part this means developing an organizational culture which is positive towards expatriate work. Members welcome interesting work in investments abroad, and there are always willing volunteers for assignments abroad.

The culture is developed first by recruiting persons motivated to work abroad. They are guaranteed being given the relevant training and pre-post briefing, rewarded fairly, and supported at post. Promotion is guaranteed. The importance of expatriate programs is underlined in strategic documents and mission statements, and top management are involved in their planning and implementation.

Expatriates are confident that their dependents at post will also be encouraged to adjust, and will be given any necessary support and training.

At the opposite extreme, the culture is NOT supportive when these conditions are not present; that is, when training, pre-post briefing, and rewards are inadequate. No support is given. Promotion on return is unlikely and even continued employment cannot be guaranteed. Top management take no interest in expatriate assignments, and the expatriate very quickly has the sense that he has been abandoned and forgotten by head-quarters. In such conditions, few will volunteer to work abroad and those who do cannot be expected to show much motivation. The expatriate failure rate is bound to be high.

21.4   Expatriate Selection

Headquarters and subsidiary managements need to protect and develop their investment in the expatriate, and this has implications for three functions associated with expatriate management:

- selection;
- training;
- support.

These functions focus on developing the manager and dependents to both

- WORK in the culture; and to
- LIVE in the culture.

21.4.1   The job description

The job description specifies

- the tasks that the expatriate is expected to perform in the assignment;
- the target standards of performance;
- reporting procedures. Who the expatriate reports to in the subsidiary and headquarters, and who takes precedence;
- what activities are evaluated, and how;
- who evaluates.

The expatriate, his reports in headquarters and in the subsidiary, and all other persons with an interest should be left in no doubt as to his priorities in reporting. The success of any assignment is placed in doubt when he and his managers are confused over his role and status. These ambiguities quickly lead to misunderstandings and conflicts.

The job description influences criteria for selection, and the analysis of training needs.

21.4.2   Criteria for selection

The expatriate needs the necessary technical and managerial skills, but these alone are not enough. Technical incompetence is seldom the major cause of failure, and he and his dependents need a range of personal qualities. They are most likely to succeed when they also possess

- a realistic understanding of the positives and negatives of the assignment;
- *but also* positive expectations about living in the host culture. Those who expect adjustment problems are likely to suffer them;
- the ability to adjust;
- negotiation skills;
- skills to recognize and solve problems;
- communication skills;
- the emotional maturity to tolerate uncertainty;
- capacity to learn from experience;
- skills to integrate with other expatriates and locals;
- motivation to work and live in the new culture.

21.4.3   What the expatriate expects

In sum, the expatriate expects a reliable contract that makes clear the job description, conditions of work, and reporting priorities. In addition, he expects

- fair compensation, including salary, allowances and other benefits;
- adequate time to prepare for the expatriate posting;
- any necessary training;
- support at post and on return to headquarters;
- career planning;
- the opportunity to continue work on return – or at least an honest appraisal of whether this is an option;
- enhanced promotion prospects;
- training and support for dependents.

21.5   Expatriate Training

Training takes place before and during the expatriate assignment, and serves general functions of preparing the expatriate to both

- work in the local culture; and
- live in the local culture.

Training is given both to the manager and to dependents, although the contents of their training programs differ.

Preparation before posting includes teaching the skills needed and developing the trainee's expectations of the job and living in' the culture. Research by Caligiuri et al. (2001) shows that the more tailored and relevant the pre-departure cross-cultural training, the more expectations were met or positively exceeded. Expatriates who have no idea of what to expect are more likely to be frustrated.

21.5.1   Needs analysis

A needs analysis provides the data on which the training syllabus is based. The FIRST step is to make an analysis of the trainee's needs in order to operate successfully at post. This specifies the target behavior of the manager and dependents, in terms of

- roles;
- technical areas (see 21.5.2);
- skill sets, including both
  PRESCRIPTIVE skills (that the trainee should perform); and
  DESCRIPTIVE skills (that the trainee actually performs).

For example, the expatriate is posted as consultant to a joint venture, with a role to advise and train – a prescriptive norm. In practice, the lack of local staff means that he has to manage certain points of the production process. This management role is not included in the job description and is covert. Two descriptive norms apply; the consultant-as-manager, and the consultant-as-diplomat – handling the difficult issues arising from the role confusion.

The SECOND step is to decide on levels of expertise needed, and which may be taught given the constraints (funding, time available, training expertise, etc.).

The THIRD step is to distinguish those skills that the manager and dependents can already perform from those that must be acquired. This avoids re-teaching what is already known.

The FOURTH step is to decide on the practical aspects of delivery. This decides

- WHEN training is given – before starting the assignment or during the assignment;
- WHERE training is given. For example, at headquarters, at post, on company premises, in a training school, etc.;
- WHO gives the training. For example, company trainers, outside experts, etc.;
- WHAT materials are to be used in training, including distance media.

The expatriate may be given focused training in four areas, relating to technology, management, culture, and language.

21.5.2   Technical training

Technical training focuses on technologies used by the subsidiary with which he is unfamiliar, including alternative technologies, and opportunities for and constraints on technology transfer and innovation.

21.5.3   Management briefing

The expatriate is briefed on management issues particular to the subsidiary, its relations with headquarters and with the environment. This is targeted, which means that a person assigned to a general management role at the top level probably needs understanding of a wider range of topics than does a functional specialist. It includes

- training in subsidiary strategy;
- the responsibilities of the post;
- the structure;
- formal systems and culture of the subsidiary;
- informal systems, including communications;
- systems for communicating with headquarters;
- systems for communicating with the business environment;
- local risk factors;
- HRM issues, including labor markets and recruitment, labor relations, salary and reward structures; training resources and policies, ethical policies, etc.;
- investment and treasury factors (including accounting and auditing procedures, financial sources, investment commitments, etc.).

21.5.4   Cross-cultural training

Cross-cultural training aims to teach

- about the other culture;
- how to live and work effectively in the other culture.

21.5.5   *Language training*

A language training syllabus varies depending on whether it aims to teach

- at beginner's level; at intermediate level; at advanced level;
- reading and/or writing and/or listening and/or speaking;
- social varieties; business/work varieties; any other varieties;
- up to near-native speaker fluency; polite openers; all levels between.

The mix of these categories determines the syllabus in terms of

- content; grammar, vocabulary, communicative discourse;
- teaching techniques used;
- materials needed.

21.5.6   *Reasons for not giving cross-cultural and language training*

Many companies still doubt the value of training their expatriates in cross-cultural skills. The reasons given for NOT giving cross-cultural training include the following:

- Training is unnecessary because the manager is already EXPERT. It is assumed that the manager has a good domestic track record. However, a good record in New York, say, is not a good predictor of achievement in Tokyo or Taipei.
- Time is insufficient; the expatriate's schedule before posting does not allow opportunities for training. This is an argument for planning the assignment as long as possible before the expatriate takes up the post in order to give greater opportunities for effective training.
- The assignment is short term, and not long enough to justify the investment in training. But against this the responsibilities of the post rather than length of tenure should be taken into account.
- Content cannot be identified accurately. Training is often misdirected when planned by headquarters staff who have no direct experience of the country of posting. Those responsible often underestimate the importance of language training, and do not take advantage of consultants and specialists.
- The effectiveness of cross-cultural training programs is disputed. These doubts may reflect experiences with poorly planned and delivered programs in the past.
- Training is unnecessary because the expatriate will have no cross-cultural responsibilities. This may be the case when the assignment is short term and in some functional fields.
- The cost is too great. The economic argument for not training may be decisive, and this is discussed below.

21.5.7   The costs of training

In addition to direct training costs, indirect costs must be included – for example, the loss of the manager's labor and the cost of replacement labor.

Further indirect costs may be incurred in the labor market. The more highly a company trains its staff, the higher the price they can command on the market. In order to keep a skilled manager from moving to competitors, the company may need to better reward him. If he does move, the company has to pay search and recruitment costs in finding a replacement. Thus the company faces a decision:

- train staff to be more productive and pay more for their labor, OR
- do not train and cope with less productive staff; OR
- focus training on skills that cannot be easily transferred.

The company calculates the investment against the expected value. If the value is less, then obviously training may be money wasted.

21.5.8   Training dependents

How far the manager's spouse and other dependents adjust to living in the new culture is a major influence on his performance. An increasingly popular solution to problems of dependents' adjustment is to train them in the culture and language of the new situation. Many companies routinely invite the spouse to cross-cultural briefings.

In some cases, the spouse has greater needs for cross-cultural training than the manager. In a centralized global company, the manager follows routines influenced by headquarters, and works primarily with other expatriates or local employees who have learned the organizational culture. The language used in the office is that of headquarters. These routines restrict the manager's contacts with the local culture. On the other hand, a spouse at home, responsible for dealing with domestic servants and trades people, is forced into a wide range of contacts with the general culture.

The spouse may also need to understand something of the scope of operations in the joint venture or subsidiary, and the manager's general area of responsibility for this; how much is influenced by the degree of business entertainment that she is willing to undertake?

21.5.9   Program evaluation

Whether or not a training program achieves its goals and represents a good investment is decided by evaluation. This tells the company whether it is using its training resources to optimal advantage and indicates areas of improvement and resolves uncertainties. It has functions of

- specifying and comparing program goals and achievement;
- showing how far achievement has met program goals;

- assessing the performance of trainees, trainers, and others involved;
- showing how far the program has given value for money;
- providing feedback, which can be applied in developing future programs.

Evaluation is conducted by headquarters, the subsidiary, or outside consultants. Internal evaluators might include HR staff, program developers and trainers, subsidiary managers, and trainees. Accounting staff evaluate training for cost benefits.

Evaluation can be conducted at every stage of training. At each stage, the costs are assessed against expected benefits:

- In the PREPARATION phase, evaluation focuses on program goals, program development, an inventory of resources needed and available;
- DURING TRAINING, evaluation focuses on what learning is taking place. It checks how far the training corresponds to the original plan, demonstrates ongoing progress to trainees and trainers, and motivates;
- IMMEDIATELY AFTER TRAINING evaluation gives immediate feedback on how far achievement has met the program goals;
- evaluation made at PERIODIC INTERVALS AFTER IMPLEMENTATION and when the trainees are at post gives long-term feedback on how far achievement has met goals. It shows how much learning has been short term and how much long term.

Evaluation is conducted by tests, surveys, interviews, observation, control group testing, accounting and financial data.

21.6 Expatriate Support

The company helps the expatriate and any dependents succeed by supporting them to

- work in the new culture;
- live in the new culture;
- return to headquarters.

Support is given at post and when the expatriate returns to headquarters.

21.6.1 *Support for working*

Support for working aims to motivate the expatriate and reduce stress levels. It aims to make him confident that his professional interests are being protected, and that the assignment contributes towards a continuing career. This means giving him information and guarantees on

- the duration of the post;
- career planning;

- career security on return to headquarters;
- promotion prospects on return;
- training for return.

Career counseling and repatriation training may be planned for either before or immediately after return.

21.6.2   *Mentoring*

Some companies support their expatriates by appointing a shepherd or MENTOR. Mentors can operate at home, in headquarters, and at post. The mentor is in a position to give impartial advice, and is not connected to the mentee within a management structure. (For a practical guide, see Kay and Hinds, 2002.)

The HEADQUARTERS MENTOR may be an older manager who gives advice and help based on experience and is responsible for protecting the expatriate's professional and career interests while the expatriate is abroad. This means ensuring that all agreements reached between the expatriate and headquarters are honored, keeping him up to date with changes in headquarters, and reintroducing him to headquarters on return. Reliable headquarters mentoring is difficult to achieve if the expatriate cannot be sure that on his return, the mentor will still be working for the company.

The MENTOR-AT-POST provides support and guidance, and helps the expatriate and dependents adjust to working and living in the new culture.

21.6.3   *Support for living*

The subsidiary organizes support for the expatriate and dependents in the local culture. Support may be needed in

- locating and subsidizing housing;
- arranging medical facilities and other social services;
- finding educational facilities for dependent children at post;
- briefing on shopping facilities and supplies of domestic goods and services;
- briefing on customs regulations and procedures;
- arranging appropriate insurance;
- organizing support groups for newcomers;
- organizing training in the local language and culture;
- arranging and subsidizing regular leave;
- finding part- or full-time employment or study for a dependent spouse who wants this. Given the importance of spouse adjustment this point is crucial.

Support information given before arrival at post must be practical and up to date. The manager and dependents who arrive to discover that their briefing was inaccurate or outdated are immediately demoralized. As is the case with training, the more focused the support program the better.

The company might send the manager and dependents on an information trip to the local country before they take up the assignment. This gives them opportunities to inspect the local organization and to review their needs for information.

21.6.4 Defining culture shock

The expatriates and dependents need to be advised on culture shock. This can be seriously unsettling, particularly in the first few months of the assignment, and can reduce productivity. The company supports the expatriate and dependents by helping them overcome the worst symptoms.

However, the help that the company can give is limited, and some degree of culture shock may be inevitable. It is a natural response to new cultural experiences, and may be defined as a sense of psychological disorientation that most people suffer when they move into a culture that is different from their own. The expatriate cannot resort to cues in his home culture when developing a relationship, responding to other people's behavior, and communicating.

Everyone expects culture shock when traveling to a culture that seems very distant from their own. In practice, more severe culture shock can occur when the new culture is superficially like your own. Slight differences are shocking when you expect everything to be the same.

This sense of dislocation occurs when you experience behavior that does not occur in your culture, or behavior that occurs but with some other meaning. You may be equally shaken by the non-occurrence of expected behavior; for instance, the Anglo takes for granted that disagreement is expressed explicitly. A lack of explicit disagreement in Japan can be disconcerting.

21.6.5 Recognizing and coping with culture shock

Culture shock is usually associated with unpleasant effects:

- low energy levels;
- a sense of frustration;
- a sense of alienation and homesickness;
- antagonism towards locals and the culture;
- a need to be alone. Some resort to solitary activities, including drinking;
- depression.

The expatriate overcomes the worst effects of culture shock by

- expecting it. It is a natural reaction to novelty. Treating culture shock as a pathology is negative;
- understanding why it occurs and recognizing the symptoms;

- broadening his range of business and social contacts in the local culture;
- learning about the new culture, and using new contacts as informants. Learning at least a little of the language;
- discovering what communicative forms and behaviors are appropriate. For example, who should be addressed by first name? Who by title? How are invitations made, accepted, and refused? What gifts are appropriate, on what occasions, and how should they be presented? How is agreement and disagreement expressed? What do locals mean when they say "Yes, maybe"? "Tomorrow"?

Experienced travelers develop their own routines for coping with the worst effects. One manager prepares by examining maps of the new city he expects to visit and spends the first days walking the streets in order to turn his theoretical understanding into practical experience. Examine your own reactions to culture shock, and adapt the techniques above to meet your own needs.

21.6.6   Reverse culture shock: return home

Repatriation to headquarters after a long-term assignment abroad is sometimes known as reverse culture shock. The repatriate needs to adjust to differences from the country of the assignment. These include differences in

- financial benefits;
- cost-of-living expenses;
- supplies of domestic help;
- social life;
- less power and excitement;
- job alienation and a sense of being out of touch with changes at headquarters.

For many, the most disturbing aspect of repatriation is the problem of trying to communicate to colleagues, friends and family who have problems understanding the intensity of the expatriate experience.

The company can help overcome these problems by reducing the length of expatriate assignments – but this may reduce the long-term effectiveness of a posting:

- mentoring, and preparing the expatriate for return;
- introducing the repatriate and dependents to support groups of other returnees;
- debriefing the manager – see below.

21.6.7   Debriefing

The expatriate and dependents are debriefed by headquarters staff. They are sources of up-to-date expert knowledge on such topics as

- the expatriate post, its opportunities and constraints;
- the subsidiary;

- the business environment;
- the political and economic environments;
- the cultural context; opportunities and difficulties living there.

Debriefing serves a number of functions. It gives the repatriates an opportunity to review and discuss their experience abroad. It demonstrates that their experience is valued by the company, which helps to overcome any sense of alienation and lack of purpose that they may be experiencing. It adds to headquarters' knowledge of the subsidiary, the country, its culture and politics, and local trading partners and competitors. This new knowledge is applied in analyzing the subsidiary's performance, briefing negotiators and new expatriates. In sum, debriefing adds to the sum of useful knowledge; the creation of knowledge is discussed in 15.2.

21.7 Implications for the Manager

1 Evaluate the TRAINING given by your organization to the following groups, when expatriated.
   (a) the CEO;
   (b) persons on long-term assignments;
   (c) persons on short-term assignments;
   (d) dependents of the above.
2 In which of these is each group trained?
   - technical topics;
   - management topics;
   - cross-cultural topics;
   - language.
3 For each group, how successful is the training? Take into account
   - goals;
   - expense;
   - time;
   - trainers and training facilities;
   - use made of other resources.
4 How might training for each group be improved? Evaluate the SUPPORT given to each of the groups above.
5 How is each group supported before expatriation? During expatriation?
   - at work?
   - outside work?
6 How are expatriates and dependents debriefed on their return to headquarters? How are debriefings applied?
7 How might support for each group be improved?

21.8 SUMMARY

In order to increase the odds on the expatriate and dependents succeeding in the assignment, the company focuses on selecting the best available candidate, then provides training and support packages. However, economic constraints are always important. The company cannot invest more in these functions than it expects to benefit.

Section 21.2 examined WHAT EXPATRIATES DO, and examined changes in the job market. It looked at the problems of identifying and explaining success and failure, and noted the importance of dependents adjusting. Section 21.3 dealt with questions in SELECTING EXPATRIATES. Selection processes aim at identifying the candidate best adapted to both working and living in the new environment. Particularly in posts where the expatriate needs to interact with a wide range of people, technical skills may be less important than communication skills. The company with long-term expatriation policies must foster an organizational culture that is favorable to assignments abroad.

Section 21.4 examined the TRAINING of EXPATRIATES and their dependents. A successful training package is based on a needs analysis that focuses on content areas; technical, management, cross-cultural and language skills. An efficient evaluation system is needed to ensure that the training investment meets company goals. Section 21.5 looked at a related topic, SUPPORTING expatriates, at post and on return to headquarters. Debriefing can help resolve some of the problems associated with repatriation and also add to the company's sum of knowledge about the post.

21.9 EXERCISE

This exercise practices designing a flexible support package.

Assume that you work in your own town for a subsidiary of an MNC headquartered in some foreign country. Headquarters decides to post one of its staff to manage your subsidiary for a two-year assignment. Assume that the manager is 37 years old and male, and will be accompanied by his spouse and two children aged 13 (a boy) and 8 (a girl).

1 Decide on
   • the country of headquarters. Choose

from Japan, Sweden, Taiwan, Australia;
   • the manager's rank and functional specialism;
   • the relationship between headquarters and subsidiary. (How far is the subsidiary empowered to design and implement its own strategy?)

2 Write the manager's job description, taking into account
   • needs for managerial and technical expertise;
   • headquarters' needs to control the subsidiary.

3 Design a support package that will facilitate their adjustment, taking into account that

- the manager previously worked for two years in a culture very different to both the headquarters country and yours;
- the spouse is an accountant, and has no previous expatriate experience.

She wishes to continue working, on a part-time basis;
- the children need schooling;
- at present, no one in the family speaks your language but all are prepared to learn.

Now assume that the organization is headquartered in one of the other countries listed in (1). Revise your answers to (2) and (3) where necessary.

Note

1 Robin Pascoe. Employers forsake expatriate spouses at their own peril. *Asian Wall Street Journal*, February 27, 1992.

CHAPTER TWENTY TWO
The Expatriate Brand Manager

CHAPTER OUTLINE

22.1 Introduction

An expatriate brand manager in China commented:

> The simplest way to think of international brand management is like a thermometer. So far as headquarters is concerned, the core of the brand is frozen, below zero. It may consist of three or five values that are what you want the world to think of the brand, and they must not be changed. If you try to change this frozen core, you're in trouble. You're seen as unreliable and you lose the trust of your customers. The marketer who makes that mistake can lose his job.
>
> Above zero, however, everything is fluid. These are the values or attributes that can be changed, depending on whichever market you happen to be serving ... Mumbai, Madrid, wherever.... Maybe the warmest you'll get is a promotions event, and the decisions for that may all be made locally.

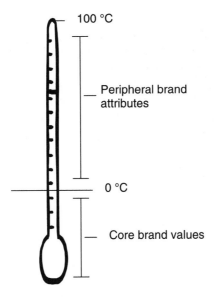

100 °C

Peripheral brand
attributes

0 °C

Core brand values

Figure 22.1   The brand thermometer

The key to successful brand management is how you mix your frozen core – which can't be changed – and the fluid outside, which you make as irresistible as you can to the local market. . . .

It's easy to sit here and talk about it, of course. The difficulty is to make it work in practice.

Figure 22.1 illustrates this notion of a brand thermometer.

This chapter examines the expatriate brand manager (EBM). It focuses on the primary importance of brands to the MNC and shows why expatriate brand management can be a source of tension between headquarters and subsidiary. It examines the rise of brand development as a corporate priority and then shows that the role of the expatriate brand manager is so complex.

22.2   The Emergence of Global Brands

A brand is defined as a name, symbol or design that makes the company's product (good or service) distinct from products sold by other companies.

The purpose of branding is to make the product easily identifiable to consumers; create consumer loyalty to that product, and so increase sales. The company creates brand identity through imaginative use of name, symbol (such as a logo), packaging, and advertising, which cannot be copied.

22.2.1 The development of brands

In the last two decades organizational strategies have focused on the development and management of the brand. This is because

- a well-developed brand is particularly potent in building trust among consumers, and this trust helps prolong and sustain the life of the product. Sir Hector Laing, CEO of United Biscuits, observed:

  > Buildings age and become dilapidated. Machines wear out. People die. But what live on are the brands.[1]

- brand values are now included on corporate balance sheets. Brand valuation began in the mid-1980s when companies like RankHovisMcDougall started registering the value of their brands in order to defend themselves against hostile takeover bids. Now the practice is common.

22.2.2 Brand identity

Companies no longer define themselves by products or services they sell. The brand gives a personality that may be expressed in various ways. Consider these examples:

PROCTOR AND GAMBLE. Rather than being simply the producer of household goods Procter and Gamble has repackaged itself as the solver of household problems. Rather than using its budget on improving its toothpaste tube (as Colgate Palmolive were doing in the same year) P&G focused on practical innovations such as premium priced Whitestrips teeth-widening kits and inexpensive spin toothbrushes.[2]

BMW. Having acquired the Mini, BMW has focused on those aspects of the car that make it unique in consumers' minds. The company emphasizes "the free-spirit" and the "Britishness" in every aspect of its promotional campaigns,[3] and pushed them to the hilt. The flagship Mini showroom in downtown Berlin boasts a range of fashion apparel labeled with the British flag insignia.

CADILLAC. In a recent advertisement for the new Cadillac STS, the front cover of *Business Week* was devoted to communicating a composite of attributes: "Mindset: Independent. Style: Trendsetting. Personality: Passionate" alongside a James Dean type strolling down a city alley. There was no mention of the car's attributes or even a photograph, which only appeared on the inside and back covers. The factors being pushed are intangible characteristics.[4]

IKEA. The IKEA brand represents far more than a company merchandising furniture. It sells a lifestyle that revolves around contemporary design, environmental sensitivity, egalitarianism and low prices. Backed by trademark promotions and "an enthusiasm that few institutions in or out of business can muster" IKEA represents consumer taste across the globe.[5] As a consequence the global awareness of the IKEA brand is much bigger than the size of the company.

22.2.3   Founders and country-of-origin

Two important facets often incorporated into a brand identity are

- the company's founders. For example, Howard Schultz (Starbuck's "brand custodian"), Walt Disney, Richard Branson at Virgin and Ingvar Kamprad from IKEA – described as the world's most influential living tastemaker;[6]
- its country-of-origin. In the chocolate, automotive, watch-making and fashion industries, a company that is, respectively, Belgian, German, Swiss or French has greater credibility.

Anyone familiar with IKEA will appreciate the importance of the brand's Swedish roots. Scandinavia plays well in consumers' minds in both the design- and environmentally-conscious stakes. The blue and yellow colors of the Swedish national flag are highly visible in all brand promotions, in the company's transport vehicles and in the stores themselves. The product names, even the restaurant menu, carries an unmistakably Swedish flavor the world over.

22.2.4   The risk of losing brand identity

Once the company has agreed on the brand identity of its product, the key to success lies in consistently adhering to the core values of the brand. This means that *consistency* and *coherency* are critical in all communications with the public. In competitive markets, this is not easy. But if the company neglects its brand and opts for short-term gain at the expense of the consistency, it may find it difficult or even impossible to win back its position in the market.

These examples show companies that neglected their core brands:

- Pierre Cardin (PC) temporarily lowered the image of their prestigious logo through the decision to chase short-term returns on PC branded saucepans and biro pens. Suspicious as to whether the designer had any hand in the design of such items, consumers lost faith in the integrity of PC and the company faced serious problems winning back their trust.
- The international airline THAI reportedly decided to add second-hand aircraft to its fleet. This may have made financial sense, but consumers' perceptions of the brand may have been damaged. THAI has enjoyed a solid reputation among choosy Western air travelers for many years. Only time will tell whether this has been lost.
- The Ford Motor Company tarnished the image of the luxury British brand Jaguar when it tried to cut short-term costs. Hoping to follow examples set by BMW and Mercedes, Ford wanted to build a starter model which would enable the Jaguar brand to tap into the mass market. BMW and Mercedes seemed to have been relatively successful with their 3-series and C-class cars. But Ford mismanaged Jaguar from the very beginning by basing its X-type on the mass market Ford Mondeo, which served to cheapen the

brand.[7] Diverging from the trademark feline grace of the Jaguar image Ford confused both loyal and aspiring customers of this luxury-niche brand.

22.2.5   *Global brand management*

As the world's markets become increasingly connected, the need for consistency when communicating in international markets grows in importance. Ensuring that core brand attributes are neither neglected nor contradicted is key. Returning to the "thermometer" in the Introduction, it's about making sure that what is frozen remains frozen.

In sum, the major challenge faced by the global brand manager is to maintain the core and keep coherency across all markets while at the same time responding to the specific demands of a particular market. Taking a brand identity grounded in a set of core values and then communicating it successfully in different contexts is a hugely ambitious and problematic task.

22.3   Role of the Expatriate Brand Manager

The expatriate brand manager (or EBM) implements the corporate brand development strategy abroad, and links corporate headquarters and subsidiary. This means managing headquarters pressure for brand consistency and at the same time achieving local performance targets (host pressures) simultaneously; see Figure 22.2.

Trying to manage both these pressures generates enormous tension. Successfully managing this tension requires:

- knowledge of headquarters and subsidiary's aims and objectives, both stated and implicit;
- an understanding of both entities' underlying motivations;
- the ability to converse effectively with both headquarters and subsidiary.

The EBM needs to be able to identify with both headquarters and subsidiary equally.[8]

22.3.1   *The expatriate brand manager's mission*

The EBM faces a two-edged task. On the one hand he is responsible for meeting local performance targets agreed with headquarters. This means working effectively with

Figure 22.2   The expatriate "dual pressure" environment

subsidiary marketing and sales teams, agencies, distributors, suppliers and customers, to ensure the brand is positioned and packaged as attractively as possible. Paradoxically this is probably the easier part of the expatriate's task.

The major challenge comes in meeting and exceeding these targets without compromising the identity of the global brand. All decisions made for the local market must reflect the overarching brand values, no matter what the short-term market consequences may be. This means that the EBM has an overriding role as brand "custodian".

In addition, the EBM needs to consider the implications for production. Should the subsidiary build a local production facility? This may be attractive, depending on the cost of local labor. But the main question will always be: what long-term impact will a decision to produce locally have on consumer perceptions of the brand?

22.3.2   Outcomes for the expatriate brand manager

Responsibilities for a corporate brand offer the EBM both good and bad outcomes. They provide opportunities to achieve instant recognition and credibility in the market concerned. On the other hand, a strict adherence to the "frozen" core of the brand can lead to problems in meeting annual performance targets.

Meeting targets may not be the priority if the EBM is assessed on the extent to which he has made a local-level contribution to the global value of the brand. For this reason ostensibly "successful" expatriate managers – those who have met and exceeded their local targets – may be transferred, demoted or worse. This "punishment" may amaze local staff, but reflect a perception at headquarters that local success has been obtained in a way that has diminished the core brand worth.

22.3.3   Triple pressures

We have seen that the EBM is caught between pressures from corporate headquarters and the local subsidiary. Further pressures stem from local customer groups that can complicate on-the-ground brand management procedures. The EBM will have to deal with the demands of key account representatives both indirectly (e.g. through the sales team) but also *directly* – for example, at meetings, product launches and so forth.

Key customers can be hugely influential in deciding the local success of a brand, especially where they double as distributors. Coping with these additional stakeholders leads to particular problems in local contexts which are markedly different from that of the corporate headquarters in terms of both culture and infrastructural development. Whereas local subsidiary managers may be socialized in headquarters values, local customers are more traditional in their business practice.

By way of example, consider the situation of a US-based marketer of premium motor oils based in an emerging economy in Southeast Asia. The key account representatives are a diverse body with differing needs and agendas – ranging from global customers such as the Premier Automotive Group (recently acquired by the Indian conglomerate

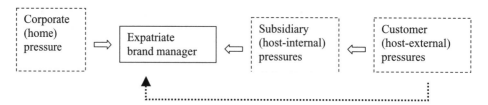

Figure 22.3   Expatriate brand management: triple pressures

TaTa and responsible for a number of premium Western auto brands) on the one hand and the smaller, often family owned non-franchise dealers and oil shop chains on the other. The expatriate may also have to deal with state-owned enterprises (SOEs). In developing the brand the EBM will need to respond to all these additional pressures – modeled in Figure 22.3.

When the headquarters and the subsidiary apply different ethical standards, the EBM has additional problems in operating efficiently while still maintaining the ethical integrity of the brand. This point is elaborated in the concluding chapter, Section 24.3.

22.4   Brand Communication: Managing the Mix

Successful management of the multiple pressures outlined in Section 23.3.2 will necessitate the effective leveraging of the local marketing mix of the "4Ps" through which the brand is communicated to customers. These are

- price;
- product;
- promotion;
- place.

This section explores forms by which these 4Ps are managed and communicated.

22.4.1   Advertising

ADVERTISING is the most visible element of the marketing mix. In a world where increasing numbers of consumers access global media channels, the need for consistency in advertising is paramount. MNCs can no longer afford to portray their range of brands in different ways in different markets for fear of damaging the consistency and coherence of the brand and confusing customers. This means that advertising decisions are increasingly moved away from the subsidiary towards headquarters.

MNCs are increasingly likely to design and execute global campaigns at corporate headquarters and then simply forward them by electronic disk across the global subsidiary

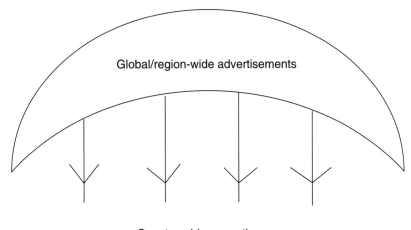

Global/region-wide advertisements

Country-wide promotions

Figure 22.4 Advertising umbrella: illustrative example

network. In this way the amount of fluidity and leeway afforded to local subsidiary teams to adapt and manage their own locally oriented advertisements has been on the decline.

Local staff often resent this loss of independence, which causes serious problems for the EBM. In addition to acting as the brand enforcer, the EBM has to act as a motivating coach, convincing local teams of the correctness of headquarters' decisions and the underlying rationale of the brand:

A global advertising campaign may function as an umbrella under which local subsidiaries plan their promotion campaigns – see Figure 22.4.

22.4.2   *Promotions*

The EBM has the opportunity to strengthen morale among his local team by stressing the importance of local promotions. These complement corporate umbrella advertisements, but also require a local emphasis. They give the team relative autonomy, although the budget for them may be relatively small.

Whether in the guise of an exhibition stand or a trade fair, a product launch or a sponsored cycle ride, all promotional events need intense face-to-face interaction with local customers, actual or potential. The EBM needs to be present, although he may act mainly as a figurehead, as the "face" of the brand, and leave most of the detail to the marketing team. Promotions are thus fluid, the "warm" component of the corporate brand thermometer.

Although the local team have relative freedom in planning the promotion, the EBM ensures that care is taken with the presentation of the brand. In order to avoid any negative associations, MNCs are sensitive to activities which may be perceived as discriminatory, for example concerning race or gender.

An example is given by the increasing concern expressed by Western automotive manufacturers towards the usage of female models and dancing teams at international motorshows. The use of scantily-clad young women is still common in some local contexts, but seems to most Western and many other observers as being dated and sexist. Aware of this concern, the association of motor shows is trying to find compromises between traditional local practices and international best practice.

22.4.3   *Distribution*

Distribution is perhaps both the most challenging and the most underestimated aspect of the communication mix. The effective management of distribution channels across different local contexts is critical, because the branded good or service must be available at the appropriate place with an appropriate level of coverage and at an appropriate time. If distribution is not managed properly then even the best communication campaigns can be for nothing and the brand loses coherence.

The integration of distribution strategy with the rest of the communication mix is, however, difficult to achieve because the channel network of a given territory tends to be just that – a *given*. For the most part it cannot be centrally controlled in the same way as, for instance, an advertising campaign – particularly during the formative years of subsidiary operation. Often the most problematic territories for the EBM are those where differences in infrastructural development on the one hand and cultural norms/values on the other are at their greatest. For Western corporations this can mean, typically, the emerging territories of East Asia.

Where corporate attention is focused on the pre-eminent urban cluster (usually the capital city) of a host environment then distribution challenges can often be overcome without too much difficulty. However, if the share of the host national market is the key – e.g. for mass-market consumer goods manufacturers – then overcoming the infrastructural and cultural challenges inherent in predominantly rural environments becomes critical. The problems brand managers face are that distribution access can often only be secured in the first instance by piggy-backing on existing channels controlled by key indigenous wholesale chains. Such wholesalers represent a major force with which to contend, particularly as they tend to exhibit unique, culturally-driven characteristics in each domestic territory.

The major problem with relying on these key customers/distributors is the price they are able to extract – sometimes barely above cost. This can be an immediate challenge to reaching local performance targets. The problem here also concerns the ensuing lack of control the EBM faces over final price-to-market. In the medium term this can damage positioning objectives and, ultimately, the identity of the brand both in the territory concerned and further afield.

In extreme cases – where customers are buying at bulk discount – the EBM may find that excess quantities of product are being passed off (sometimes illegally) into neighboring markets. This can then undercut either the company's own exported product or that of a sister subsidiary. In either case the value of the brands concerned is likely to be compromised. In short, then, the inability to control brand distribution can have serious detrimental consequences for the two sets of criteria on which the EBM is assessed.

22.4.4 Local distribution

Addressing local distribution challenges requires that the EBM balance a range of possible tactics. One method is to collaborate with other foreign corporations – even with direct competitors. Expatriates generally tend to be in contact with one another across both company and industry boundaries to a far greater extent than their domestic counterparts. This may be through common membership of organizations such as the associated foreign chambers of commerce and trade associations as well as, more informally, the various Rotary clubs, Churches, sports and golf societies, parent–teacher evenings at local international schools, charitable events and national clubs. Meeting regularly in these contexts, expatriate managers discuss their experiences of working in the local environment to which they are forever adjusting.

Because nationwide distribution is a common issue, one finds unlikely alliances developing that may only be utilized in the territory concerned. One example is that of the Shell corporation and Coca-Cola, who shared a product depot using teams of motorcyclists to help distribute product on a cash-on-delivery basis in southern Vietnam.[9] Similarly, the UK motor oils marketer Castrol formed an alliance with the US oil major Conoco in order to make their motor oils available to the rural consumer at the latter's Jet petrol station forecourts[10]

The primary method of securing local distribution access for MNCs is to ensure that this is negotiated as part of the initial market entry decision. For example, companies will sometimes forego the opportunity to open a wholly-owned subsidiary unit for a partnership with a local organization – typically a joint venture – in order to get their "feet under the table" with influential local stakeholders. The *choice* of partner is the most important factor; the EBM must take care to ensure the partner understands what makes the brand distinctive and how he can assist the subsidiary unit in ensuring this is not compromised. The ideal partner provides the "know-*who*" to complement the corporate center's "know-*how*", leaving operational brand control to the EBM.

22.4.5 The right expatriate brand manager

Building relationships with local partners, government officials and other stakeholders involved in distribution requires an EBM who

- understands local cultural values;
- has communication skills. The expatriate who does not understand the local language is dependent on interpreters and translators;
- Is on post for an appropriate length of tenure.

Tenure is important because any agreements and promises made by an expatriate who will be gone in 18 months may be perceived as worthless in societies where long-standing, mutually supportive business relationships are key. Also, an expatriate serving only a two to three-year assignment does not have the time to learn the norms of local business at any depth.

The length of the EBM's assignment is just one of several contentious issues involved. The biggest worry for most MNCs is that an assignment exceeding three to five years will sway the expatriate away from his role as corporate brand enforcer and towards identifying with the more marker-driven priorities of the indigenous team. In other words their *dual* identity would be compromised, the expatriate becoming little more than a mouthpiece for the subsidiary organization – and in this respect a risk.

22.4.6   *Price*

Pricing has traditionally been singled out as the sole revenue component of the 4Ps (the others all representing costs). However, in the contemporary business context price is a just as critical communication tool – the clearest point-of-purchase indication as to the positioning of the brand. In simple terms the price itself is not an issue with the consumer, in that the consumer will either buy the product or service or not. However, from the perspective of local distributors, wholesalers and even local partners price can be a major source of contention.

Of course, each of these participants, in essence, are rent-seeking go-betweens. No matter how carefully chosen by the EBM and his local managers, no matter how well they understand corporate brand priorities, at the end of the day the maximization of their own revenue streams will come first. Accordingly sales and share-of-market will be the principal objectives and "unrealistic" corporate premium pricing will always be a point of conflict. In many emerging markets – especially in Asia – where brand strategy has traditionally been of minor import the "sales mentality" is a powerful legacy.

In this environment the EBM will need to ensure adherence to the corporation's overall – i.e. global/regional – positioning map as opposed to focusing primarily on the host market. In the main an international brand purveyor will not wish to compete downmarket, i.e. directly with the local competition – and certainly not if this means a marked reduction in price. As the Volkswagen CEO insisted following criticisms of its relatively high local prices "we will not get into a price war... market share is important for us but *not at any price...*".[11]

In order to compete in volume terms at all, however, and in order to demonstrate trust in subsidiary management, the EBM may adopt the so-called "bandwidth" approach to pricing. Essentially this involves giving local leeway to adjust prices with set limits, i.e. a floor and a ceiling (to include promotional discounts). When setting prices for an export market – using the host territory as a market platform – the bandwidth approach is also useful to minimize any disruption caused by currency exchange fluctuations. For the

EBM and his team it will also save them the time and resources of having to calculate and expedite a new price list for every minor currency change.

22.4.7 *Product*

In line with the increasing need for brand micro-management the amount of leeway afforded to subsidiary managers to adapt the corporate has also decreased. During the latter half of the 1990s Unilever cut its global product range 10-fold from circa 4,000 products to around 400. Moreover, central control has become increasingly apparent even with those that remain, expressed in the increasing corporate "endorsement" of product brands on all product packaging. The Nestlé corporation from Switzerland provides one of the most visible examples, the corporate logo clearly made visible across its entire family of products.

Of course, this isn't to say that in certain cases local product adaptation is not pivotal to local success. The Chinese automotive market, with its emerging global importance, forms one example. Within this host context the Volkswagen corporation, a long time participant, adapted its Audi A6 for the local customer, creating a China-only version that's 10 cm longer than the standard model in order to make the back seat roomier for executives with drivers.[12]

Given the need for balancing local attractiveness with brand consistency simultaneously, the usual strategy adopted consists of maintaining a core global product/service while promoting an imaginative periphery of market-specific offerings.

The IKEA corporation, for example, retains its Billy bookcases, Lack side tables and Ivar storage systems across the world. The store visit is also kept strictly the same, providing global consumers with the same experience. However, the company is not averse to making locally tailored adjustments, instanced by the 250,000 commemorative placemats it rolled out to celebrate Chinese new year – all of which were quickly sold.[13]

Perhaps the best known example of the core-periphery approach to local adaptation is the McDonald's burger franchise. Central to the McDonald's experience – other than "Americana" – is the concept of fast food. In an attempt to harmonize the speed of service in different locations across the world, timing devices have often been displayed prominently aside the cash registers. Concerning the product itself, wherever possible the Big Mac and fries will be available as the core offering. However, at the secondary level a locally oriented range will be the major focus of day-to-day activity, where dozens – possibly hundreds – of locally designed/tested fast foods will be designed to suit the host context customer.

The other current global franchise heavyweight – Starbucks – is perhaps more standardized in terms of its choice of locally-tailored products. Nonetheless the emphasis on iced-coffee derivatives in certain markets and hot coffee in others makes for logical and highly popular customization. The increasingly important range of foods is also subject to sensible host–context adaptation. More important still is the extent to which the Starbuck's "experience" is the same across the world. Essentially, the Starbuck's visit should encompass the "getaway" environment (or "urban oasis") where people can meet leisurely over premium-quality, ethically traded coffee.

22.4.8 Standardizing brand experience: an example

The EBM for a global hotel chain made these observations about how Starbucks organized its flagship branch in Bangkok.

> In the last few years Starbucks have re-designed the branch. Beforehand almost all of the chairs were hard-backed. Even so, it was packed out with people each and every day – anytime after 9.30am and you'd be struggling to find a seat, it would be take out only from then on.
>
> So what did they do? Increase the seating capacity? No. They *reduced* it. They replaced most of the hard-backed chairs with more comfortable armchairs which took up the whole of the floor space. At first I was thinking they must be crazy because they were effectively turning people away. Then I realized that the problem was the groups of young adults, usually students, who'd buy a frappucino between them and then sit chatting or doing their homework for hours at a time ... so there were never enough chairs in the first place and now there are even less.
>
> Of course they wanted to increase turnover. But the new chairs were much more comfortable that the old ones, and so they merely encourage people to stay longer.
>
> So now the Bangkok branch follows the same priorities as in the States. Starbucks have chosen to align their flagship Bangkok franchise with the global, or at least the US, standard, in preference to building up sales volume. This takes courage.
>
> Recently they've opened up a second branch across the street to absorb the excess demand. It's next to a bank, so at lunchtime bank customers can go next door to grab a coffee.

22.5 Implications for the Manager

In an environment of constant change and ever-shortening product lifecycles the development of unique brands has become increasingly attractive as a means of sustaining competitive advantage.

A crowded marketplace necessitates intelligent differentiation techniques. To create and maintain emotional bonds with consumers a focus on communicating not just the tangible product/service offering but the values behind it is becoming ever more popular. This has encouraged attention towards ethical, cause-related marketing to cushion and surround the product/service brand.

The effective communication of brand attributes and values necessitates consistency, coherency and a long-term approach.

Building brands in your domestic market is a challenge in itself. Communicating your brand effectively across borders, i.e. different cultural and infrastructural contexts, can be far more complex and risky.

The essential role of the expatriate brand manager (EBM) lies in how he balances the often competing demands of maintaining global brand consistency on the one hand and making the brand as attractive as possible locally on the other – *at the same time.*

Although an EBM may hold the requisite skills and knowledge to perform his formal role he may still be relatively unsuccessful in any one host subsidiary environment. The key EBM attributes required often amount to the more informal qualities of sensitivity, understanding and the ability to communicate and motivate in a particular culture.

Expatriating brand managers on a short-term basis (i.e. less than three years) may be counterproductive. Short-term assignments may be adequate for the task of "brand enforcement". Obtaining an optimal balance between global consistency and local responsiveness may take considerably longer.

Promotional effectiveness will often require maintaining advertisements that are global/regional in design and execution. These can then be offset with locally focused promotion campaigns. The EBM may need to motivate and educate the local team, countering any loss of advertising autonomy with increasing corporate "coherence" campaigns – for example, through use of the intranet.

Local product/service distribution should not be underestimated. Effective control may be obtained through choice of local partner (during initial entry) and/or collaboration with appropriate participants – including cross-industry arrangements and even short-term linkages with direct international competitors.

Product/price adaptations need to be made with attention to global positioning and values, retaining the nucleus of the brand while adjusting the periphery to suit local market conditions. Local decisions should always be made keeping the core brand personality in mind.

22.6 SUMMARY

Section 22.2 described the EMERGENCE OF GLOBAL BRANDING, and the importance of creating a unique set of attributes and associations in consumers' minds in the form of the brand. Ensuring that the brand image is then communicated consistently across diverse cultural and developmental contexts is a complex and persistent challenge.

Section 22.3 discusses the pivotal ROLE OF THE EXPATRIATE BRAND MANAGER. The primary task of the EBM is to balance the corporate pressures for global brand consistency on the one hand against local-market pressures to meet pre-set subsidiary sales and profitability targets on the other.

The means of achieving this overarching objective is described in Section 22.4 on BRAND COMMUNICATION. The 4Ps of the marketing MIX – promotion, place (distribution), product and price – are discussed as a set of communication tools through which the brand is coherently and accurately positioned against both subsidiary needs for responsiveness (meeting the demands of the host-market consumer) and corporate needs for integration (meeting the standards of the global brand image).

22.7 EXERCISE

Organize yourselves into groups of 4–6.

1 Each group is an expatriate brand management team for Cesarix Autos, a German manufacturer of luxury saloons with over 100 years of brand reputation for style, class and engineering excellence.

2 You are currently in the second year of your five-year expatriate assignment in Shanghai, China. To date performance has been solid, with sales and profitability figures on the increase. Sales consist exclusively of models imported from the production plant in Germany and demand has continued to outstrip supply.

3 A new wealthy middle class has emerged. Your market research indicates a substantial and increasing customer base for your starter model, as yet unavailable in China but already selling well across the USA and Europe. Your long-standing JV partner is recommending you introduce the model in China crucially through the commencement of a locally-based production plant that would serve not just China but East Asia as a whole.

4 The choice is yours – should you restrict supply to imported models from Germany or should you begin production in China?

5 Outline in detail the potential advantages and disadvantages of the local production option for the short-, medium- and long-term brand development and company performance. Consider the dual pressures you may be under from the local subsidiary organization on the one hand and corporate headquarters on the other:

   • What is your instinctive preference and why?
   • What other extraneous factors/data would you wish to consider before making your decision?

Notes

1 P. Temporal. 2000: *Branding in Asia*. Singapore: Wiley, p. 1.

2 Nanette Byrnes. Branding: Five new lessons. *Business Week*, February 14, 2005, p. 28.

3 Gail Edmonson with Michael Eidam. The Mini just keeps getting mightier. *Business Week*, April 5, 2004, p. 26.

4 *Business Week*, European edition, 2005.

5 IKEA. *Business Week Online*, November 14, 2005.

6 IKEA. *Business Week Online*, November 14, 2005.

7 Kathleen Kerwin. The care and feeding of Jaguar. *Business Week*, October 4, 2004, p. 38.

8 Dutton, Dukerich and Harquail. 1994: Quoted in Vora, D., Kostova, T., Roth, K. et al. 2007: Roles of subsidiary managers in multinational corporations: the effect of dual organizational identification. *Management International Review*, 47 (4): 595–620.

9 Tim G. Andrews, Bryan J. Baldwin and Nartnalin Chompusri. 2003: *The Changing Face*

of Multinationals in Southeast Asia. London: Routledge.

10 Tim G. Andrews, Bryan J. Baldwin and Nartnalin Chompusri. 2003: *The Changing Face of Multinationals in Southeast Asia*. London: Routledge.

11 Dexter Roberts. GM and VW: how not to succeed in China. *Business Week*, May 9, 2005, p. 22 (italics added).

12 Dexter Roberts. GM and VW: how not to succeed in China. *Business Week*, May 9, 2005, page 22.

13 Dexter Roberts. GM and VW: how not to succeed in China. *Business Week*, May 9, 2005, page 22.

CHAPTER THIRTEEN **Globalization and Localization**

CASE THE CALL CENTER REVOLUTION

Read this newspaper story and answer the questions below. Explain your answers.

Indians train UK call center staff
By Tom Peterkin: Ireland Correspondent
DAILY TELEGRAPH August 9, 2006.

The call center revolution has turned full circle with Indian experts now training British workers in how to operate the much-maligned message handling services.

The United Kingdom's first Indian-owned call center has opened in Belfast, reversing the controversial trend of British firms switching to the subcontinent to take advantage of cheap labor.

ICICI OneSource, which has 8,000 staff in Bangalore and Bombay, aims to create 1,000 jobs in Northern Ireland over the next two years.

The first batch of 60 employees in Belfast began a seven-week training course yesterday in which Indian call center experts will put them through their paces. The firm's British clients come mainly from the financial and telecommunication industries.

The idea of Indians training British call center employees could raise the eyebrows of those customers who have complained of frustrating waits and difficulty in understanding accents, when dealing with companies relying on foreign call centers.

Matthew Vallance, the European managing director of ICICI OneSource, said: "This is not about moving work from India to the UK; it is about the growth and expansion of our business. . . ."

QUESTIONS

1 Do you agree with Mr Vallance that this is not about moving work from India to the UK?

2 Should the India-based employees of ICICI OneSource interpret this development as a threat to their jobs?

3 What factors might limit the globalization of labor markets in this industry?

4   What factors might limit the globalization of labor markets in the following industries?

Bio-technology

Fast food

Retail trade in department stores.

CHAPTER FOURTEEN   **Planning Strategy**

CASE   BABY FOOD

You are Japanese, and are marketing manager in a baby food producer. The company is headquartered in Tokyo.

The 1950s and 1960s were baby-boom years, and demand for your products was healthy. But since then, population growth has slowed drastically. In 2007, one in five was aged 65 or older, and demographers estimated that by 2014, one in four will be over 65.

This decline in the birth rate is reflected in your sales figures. Your products are of top quality, but it's become obvious that you need to rethink your strategies in order to save the company from a very uncertain future and possible extinction.

Recently, you reviewed sales figures for all your outlets. Overall, they reinforced your pessimism about the company's hopes of surviving. But then you discovered that in one shop in the small town of Hyuga, in the southern prefecture of Miyazaki, sales were actually rising, against the general trend. You were particularly surprised because Hyuga is known as a retirement destination for pensioners, where the birth rate is low. Puzzled, you decided to visit in person, to find out why.

Mr Nakamura, the store manager, was amused by your questions, and then let you into his secret. He had realized that your products, intended for babies, also provided excellent nutrition for elderly people – who might also lack teeth and could not digest rich food. He had moved your baby foods into a section catering for these senior citizens, and after some persuasion, his regular customers were buying them. The soft, small morsels with low salt that could be easily prepared were proving attractive. But, he regretted, some of his customers were still not prepared to purchase cans labeled "baby food" for fear of losing face.

On your way back to Tokyo, you began to think that the firm could still be saved. You made notes on the strategic implications of this discovery.

DECISIONS

1   *How does this discovery impact upon your old ideas of the scope of your product?*
2   *Supposing that the company decides to serve this new market segment, what are the implications for resourcing and production?*
3   *What changes must be made to your sales techniques, including advertising?*
4   *Who in the company will need retraining?*
5   *How will you sell your new strategy to your colleagues?*

CHAPTER FIFTEEN **Applying Knowledge and Implementing Strategy**

CASE NEW KNOWLEDGE

A Dallas finance company sent a young economist, Mike, out to conduct a two-year development project on its small subsidiary in Singapore. As was typical with this bank, Mike was given a very precise job description. He was managed out of Dallas by a middle manager, Judy. She told him that if he did a good job he could expect promotion on return.

When Mike had settled into the post he quickly realized that he had been badly briefed and that Singaporean markets were more advanced than headquarters supposed. He completed the project within a year and then devoted himself to researching the new regional markets. He developed plans for new instruments.

When he had six months left to run, he reported his proposals to Judy and requested an extension to his assignment. Judy summoned him back to Dallas, and sacked him for exceeding his job description.

QUESTIONS

1 How far does this case illustrate these points? Explain your answers.

Typically, middle managers do not feel threatened when their subordinates develop new knowledge.

The development of new knowledge is usually counted as more important than precise adherence to company rules.

2 How should Mike have proceeded in order to protect his position while also developing his plans as he wished?

DECISION

3 *You are vice president of the bank. You understand Judy's argument that Mike exceeded his job description, and that the bank must not set a bad precedent by rewarding rule-breaking. On the other hand you wish to encourage the development of new knowledge. Make notes for a policy document that will make clear the conditions under which new knowledge can be developed.*

CHAPTER SIXTEEN **E-Communication**

CASE BETAFIELD

Khun Wororat is the commercial sales director for the Thai subsidiary of Betafield,* the Western motor oils corporation. He has mixed feelings about the substitution of email for traditional communication methods, particularly telephone and face-to-face meetings.

He spends up to two hours each day reading and writing emails. He receives only about 20 messages in the course of an average working day. Of these around half are from his sales managers:

"I don't reply to these," he says. "Mostly they just tell me what they have been doing. If they have a question that's important I will call them."

Of the remaining 10 messages five or six will be from corporate headquarters, either from the UK or Hong Kong. Of these two or three will require a reply – on which he may spend 90 minutes in total, mainly to ensure his English is free from grammatical error. His other emails are generally from customers:

I don't reply to these. Unless they come from the foreign customer. For the Thai customers usually it will be their secretaries who email me. For the senior manager it is not suitable to write your own email. Not with the traditional Thai companies with the big bosses. For them email is an admin job. Sometimes I will get my secretary to write for me but it is not company policy to do that. So usually I ask her to call them for me. Or sometimes I see them. Sometimes I ask her to write emails when I am outside the office. I dictate to her on the telephone.

The country manager for Betafield (Thailand) Ltd describes Khun Wororat's usage patterns as "typical."

QUESTIONS

1   In your opinion is the CM using the word "typical" to describe
    (a)   email use at Betafield (Thailand) Ltd?
    (b)   email use in Thailand?
    (c)   email use for a Thai sales director?

Give reasons for your choice(s).

2   If your answer combines some or all of the above explain the role and relevant importance of each characteristic

3   What are the potential problems should email continue to be utilized in this manner across the Thai-based unit? How do you think it differs from the way in which corporate headquarters intends its email system to be used?

DECISIONS

1   You are a consultant assigned with auditing the Betafield e-communication system. What changes would you recommend
    (a)   to be made at Betafield HQ?
    (b)   to be made at Betafield (Thailand) Ltd?

*a pseudonym

CHAPTER SEVENTEEN **Forming an International Joint Venture**

CASE THE INDIAN JOINT VENTURE

You manage a textile sales company in Sydney with an extensive sales network in Australasian and Southeast Asian markets. Now you want to develop high-quality brands targeted at the expanding middle classes across the region. You expect to invest in the latest technology while taking advantage of the relatively low labor costs. Your agent in Mumbai has put you in touch with an Indian textile manufacturer, who are looking for an opportunity to break into Australasia. You have had several meetings with the owner, Mr Ghopal, and together you are planning an exploratory joint venture. This three-year project is important to both of you, and if successful could pave the way to more profitable cooperation in the future. One of his main conditions is that the project should be managed by one of his senior managers.

Your consultants are concerned by the management structure of Ghopal Brothers. They have interviewed the senior managers, and they do not think that any of them have the entrepreneurial skills needed.

Mr Ghopal himself is remarkably experienced and energetic, and some of the second generation are promising – although he has no children of his own. Mr Ghopal's three brothers are reliable but have no experience of international business, and are conservative in their practice. Each has two sons.

The consultants suggest that you propose the appointment of Mr Ghobal's nephew (the son of his sister). Vikram is by far the most intelligent. He has an MBA from an Australian business school, and has three years' experience with a consulting company in the US and Europe, and a fur-

ther two years' with a textile manufacturer in Taiwan.

You agree that Vikram is the rising star in the company. However, he is also younger than any of his cousins. Mr Ghopal says that if he accepts this proposal to appoint your consultant's proposals, he is bound to annoy his brothers who would like the appointment for themselves or for one of their sons. Any appointment to which they do not agree would split the family, and lead to a cancellation of the project.

QUESTION

1 What are the alternatives to appointing Vikram now?

DECISION

2 *Decide on your policy.*

CHAPTER EIGHTEEN **Opportunity and Risk:**
Headquarters and Subsidiary

CASE   GLOBAL PAPER (1)

You are CEO of a multinational company in the paper industry. The company is headquartered in Canada. Your subsidiary in Argentina faces an uncertain future, and you are visiting in order to assess the situation for yourself. You have planned a meeting with the managing director, Gavin, an expatriate Scot.

Gavin has been at post for two years. He has not enjoyed the assignment, and tells you he is looking forward to retiring.

The local industry is in a state of turbulence. Your largest competitor has gone out of business, and an American company is about to enter the market. Supplies of paper pulp cannot be predicted accurately beyond four months, which has strategic implications. You have been warned by your accountants that you may soon be liable to increased corporation tax.

You have met with Gavin to ask his advice on the risks that the company faces, and the controls that may need to be imposed by headquarters. His advice is inconclusive, but he suggests that you meet with his senior management team. He will not attend.

You have reviewed the personnel files for the team, then met them in a group, and asked them to describe, in general terms, how they saw the future. You have written these notes of the contributions made by the five who attended. (The HR manager was not present; you suspect he was absent interviewing for another job. No one was prepared to comment on HR issues, but you have no reason to think that these present serious problems.)

Juan Pablo Ortelli   ENGINEERING
Before joining the company three years ago, Juan Pablo worked in the university as a research chemical engineer. In terms of age and commercial experience, he is the most junior in the team. He

isn't frightened of speaking out, and argued clearly that the subsidiary should be empowered to produce more of its own technology and be less dependent on headquarters. He is convinced that a new R&D unit can be staffed, but has no evidence to support this claim. Only Hector expressed any disagreement. The others kept quiet.

Ulises Bryant   PRODUCTION
Ulises has worked for the company for 22 years and at 47 is the oldest of the team. He understands the local industry better than the others – perhaps more than anyone in the country. Standards in his department are high. He is confident that if standards are maintained throughout the company they should be able to weather the storm. He thinks that the relationship between headquarters and subsidiary can be decentralized. This would reduce costs at a difficult time, and need not weaken communication. His colleagues appear to agree. One of them (you're not sure who) commented "it's time we were managed by one of our own".

Hector Marcos Cima   FINANCE
After graduation, Hector worked for three years in the Ministry of Economics, and was an expert on corporate tax. He then moved to the private sector. Over the next 12 years he worked his way up in a rage of industries, and has been with the company for five years. He disagreed strongly with Juan Pablo. In the present state of economic uncertainty

affecting all parts of the national economy, the company cannot afford to invest in a high-risk venture such as that proposed. Rather, this is the time to consolidate. He endorses the warning given by your accountant.

Silvia Telermann   MARKETING

Silvia comes from an old family, and has valuable social and business links throughout the government. She has a keen instinct for change in the markets. She graduated from Harvard Business School with a good MBA and has experience working for companies in the US and Canada. She joined the subsidiary eight years ago. She agrees that "very normal" problems do arise in the relationship with sales, but appears unwilling to wash this dirty linen in an open meeting.

Marla Luisa Borge   SALES

Marla is locally educated and has no experience abroad. She limited her response to your question about future possibilities to the need to change the relationship between sales and marketing. She explained that marketing is responsible for setting suggested list prices and establishing promotional pricing, but sales decides transactional pricing. This leads to contradictions, exacerbated by the fact that both managers report directly to the managing director. Also, she thinks that marketing is spending far too much on promotions; in her opinion, these sums could be better spent on developing new sales persons.

Maria talks about the general need for increased cross-departmental coordination. She seems to be alone in seeing this as a general problem. You have the impression that the team lack a shared sense of strategic purpose.

QUESTIONS

1   In general, do you think that the subsidiary is equipped to weather the risks it faces in the environment? Explain your answer.

2   What controls need to be imposed?

Please keep your answers. You will need them to work on the Chapter 20 case.

CHAPTER NINETEEN **Managing Human Resources**

CASE   THE FOREIGN EMPLOYEE

Martin was a management professor from New Zealand. He was offered a job in a privately owned college in Indonesia. He asked for and accepted (and was given) a written contract. Among other conditions, this stipulated the standard bureaucratic condition for giving up employment – that he should give three months' notice. He and the college president signed.

Martin was a skilled teacher, and he played an increasingly important role in the professional and social life of the college. But after 10 years, his family circumstances changed, and he decided to return to New Zealand. Six months before the end of the academic year, he gave in his notice.

This was greeted with disbelief by his Indonesian colleagues:

> "We thought we could trust you. Why are you unhappy here?"
> "I'm not unhappy. But I have to go home."
> "This is your home."
> "My parents are in New Zealand, and they are getting old."
> "The president has done his best for you, and he needs you here. You owe him too much and you can't leave now."

Martin returned to New Zealand. Three years later, he returned to Indonesia for a holiday and visited the college. He looked through the window of his old office, and discovered it was just as he had left it.

When he asked why nobody had taken over his office, he was told "Because we know that you're going to come back. You've made a mistake, and when you understand, you'll change your mind."

QUESTIONS

1 What does this show about different expectations of the labor contract?

2 What factors led to this misunderstanding arising?

DECISION

3 *What, if anything, can the president do to prevent this situation arising again?*

CHAPTER TWENTY **Controlling by Staffing**

CASE   GLOBAL PAPER (2)

Following your meeting with the top management team (see the case for Chapter 18) you review your conclusions – recorded in your answers to the case.

It is imperative that a new managing director is appointed in order to oversee the implementation of the controls you want in place. You have three options:

(a)   Press Gavin to remain at post for a further two years.
(b)   Expatriate a headquarters manager to replace Gavin.
(c)   Appoint one of the local management team.

So far as option (a) is concerned, Gavin knows the team, understands the local business environment, and speaks adequate Spanish. You think that a pay rise and bonus would persuade him to stay.

For option (b) any one of three possible candidates in headquarters would benefit from the posting and would be very interested in taking the job. They are all technically proficient and have good experience. Any one of them would maintain strong headquarters control. However, none have worked in this country before, and none speak good Spanish.

For option (c) you examine your notes you have written for the five, and then add these further notes on their personalities.

Juan Pablo Ortelli   ENGINEERING
The youngest. Lacks experience. But brilliant - the others respect his undoubted technical expertise. Enthusiastic. A good sense of humor and obviously well liked.

Ulises Bryant   PRODUCTION
Efficient. A natural politician. Good with guests – he has the reputation for being an effective negotiator. He tries to project himself as the informal leader and spokesman. But you are unsure how far the others trust him in this situation.

Hector Marcos Cima   FINANCE
Quiet and withdrawn, but very competent. You absolutely trust his judgment in his area of expertise. But he shows little interest in other functions.

Silvia Telermann   MARKETING
Sophisticated. An excellent English speaker. She has vision, and can see possible futures for the company. Sometimes prickly – she does not hesitate to criticize her colleagues, which they resent – but often her criticisms are merited.

Marla Luisa Borge   SALES
At present, obsessed by the relationship between sales and marketing. But possibly when she is removed from specific responsibilities for one function to overall control she might adopt a more conciliatory approach. A fighter, greatly respected by her staff. Not a good English speaker.

You were about to retire to bed when you got a phone call from Ulises. He was waiting downstairs at the hotel bar. In a short, friendly chat he made clear his disagreement with Juan Pablo's call for empowerment. He had guessed that you might wish to replace Gavin with a local managing director, and assured you if he were appointed, he would loyally implement all policies made by headquarters - but he couldn't say the same for all of his colleagues.

DECISIONS

1   Given your priorities summarized in your answer to the Chapter 18 case, and your further consideration, which of the options will you take?

(a) Press Gavin to remain at post for a further two years.	2 If you choose (c) (a local appointment), who? And why this person?
(b) Expatriate a headquarters manager to replace Gavin.	3 Are there any conditions that you wish to impose on the appointment?
(c) Appoint one of the local management team.	

CHAPTER TWENTY ONE **Managing Expatriate Assignments**

CASE **APPOINTING A HEADQUARTERS MANAGER TO THE SWISS SUBSIDIARY**

You had recently been appointed director of HRM at ZZ Pharmaceuticals, based in Geneva. You have been asked to recommend a headquarters manager to be assigned to manage the sales department of your subsidiary in Turkey. The final decision will be taken by your CEO, but she is unlikely to go against your recommendation.

The Turkish subsidiary has recently been troubled, and this backstory is significant. As a result of poor maintenance, the risk of contamination in one of your plants was judged unacceptably high. A batch of your most successful anti-depressants was withdrawn from sales outlets across Europe – although there is no evidence of any being used with bad effects. The subsidiary managing director resigned on very short notice, and his replacement had only been in post for two months when the then sales manager fell sick and was repatriated. Added to these calamities, a Chinese company has acquired your leading Turkish competitor and seems set to start investing heavily. The new sales manager will be taking on a tough assignment.

You have reduced the short-list to two candidates; Jordan and Serene.

Jordan is 42 years old. He was a research chemist before entering the private sector, and had an excellent record across a number of functions in headquarters (10 years) before being posted to the Lebanon on a two-year posting to manage the sales department. There, his record was less impressive. However, this was in a time of economic downturn. You also keep in mind that while his job description was written in headquarters, he was evaluated by his local manager, with whom he had a difficult relationship.

He does not speak Turkish, but has a good record dealing with his sales teams and negotiating with customers.

You have heard rumors that if he is not appointed, he will resign – his wife is Turkish and she wants to spend time with the family in Istanbul. His departure would be a loss to the company, where his detailed knowledge of the industry and the competition is an important asset.

Serene is 36 years old, and training as a project manager. When she joined the company she spent five years as a start-up manager, establishing R&D and sales joint ventures across your Latin American division. These seven assignments were all short – on average six months – and her enthusiasm, energy, and talent for organization was much appreciated by the staffs. However, within a year of her departing them, three of these projects had collapsed as a result of irreconcilable conflicts between project staff, and only two were unquestioned successes. Since then she has worked in headquarters in the sales department, where she has a good record. However, she is disliked by some of her peers who resent her tendency to advertise her own accomplishments.

She is half-Turkish and speaks the language well. She is skillful at adapting to different cultures, and has a proven record of motivating her subordinates.

DECISIONS

1 You are preparing to interview the two candidates. Decide on four questions that you will ask Jordan, and four you will ask Serena.

CHAPTER TWENTY TWO **The Expatriate Brand Manager**

CASE TELDASWIFT

The marketing and sales team at the Korean subsidiary of the US automotive corporation Teldaswift (*) have presented you with a draft brief of next year's promotional activities. Included are a new product launch evening at a plush downtown hotel in Seoul and a trade stand for the upcoming national motor show. For both events the local team wishes to use the services of a model to appear as "Miss Teldaswift Korea." Selecting the appropriate model would involve a competition to be advertised at both local universities and in the Thai national press. The major criteria would be personality, education and looks. Once a shortlist had been decided on the girls would then be interviewed at the Teldaswift Korean headquarters.

The successful applicant would be attired for both functions in a "superwoman"-type lycra bodysuit in the corporate brand colors. Her role would be two-fold: (i) at the motorshow stand – attracting local publicity and Thai press photographers and (ii) at the product launch dinner – joining key account representatives (e.g. franchise directors) as a "hostess".

Your direct reports at the Korean subsidiary are strongly in favor of the Miss Teldaswift Korea idea, not least because many of your key competitors in the host country do the same. They are also keen to ensure that (a) the Teldaswift stand is not unduly neglected because of the absence of such a model and (b) that the key account representatives are shown an evening to remember in the way they are accustomed at such events, as a mark of respect and appreciation for their continuing loyalty.

As the expatriate brand manager you have been asked to approve the brief. You are aware that, with the limited budget for local promotional activities and with decreasing flexibility to adapt corporate advertisements your team will be demotivated if corporate control is perceived as overbearing and excessive on this issue. Nonetheless you must adhere to corporate brand values.

DECISIONS

Do you:

1 *Reject outright the use of a Miss Teldaswift Korea?*
2 *Accept the above proposals as they are?*
3 *Accept the above proposals with specific modification requirements?*

*a pseudonym

PART FOUR
Conclusions

The Culture of the Subsidiary: Convergence and Divergence

CHAPTER OUTLINE

Introduction

Corporate Cohesion and Cultural
   Shift

Convergence and Divergence

The Dual-pressure Perspective

Cross-vergence

Implications for the Manager

Summary

Exercise

Notes

23.1   Introduction

An expatriate manager working for an Anglo–American company (disguised here as "Cesarix") made this comment on the difference between the expatriate and local workforces:

> It was during the Asian financial crisis [in 1997] that I began to see how much of a difference there was between the way we expatriates viewed what *we* were doing, and how the Thais saw the company. We'd always assumed that every Thai working here was a Cesarix* employee, albeit a Cesarix (Thailand) Ltd employee. But when the crisis hit, when the audits were being done, that's when our people started thinking "these guys are *Thais*, they're not Cesarix". Or rather they're Thais first and foremost, they're just Cesarix from nine to five . . . and we're here as Cesarix and suddenly we're foreigners. Maybe that was always true, but only when the crisis arrived was the message hammered home to us . . . .
>
>   We'd be sitting in a meeting and all of a sudden I'd hear Nick saying "this is an *international* company!" on the back of something the Thai sales director was saying. And then the sales director would say "yes but this is *Thailand*". And that difference in outlook, that feeling, that

we were split in two as an organization, went on for a good while... the crisis was what opened my eyes to it, but it was plainly the way it had been all the time, it was hidden.

This concluding chapter deals with cultural cohesion within an MNC, and asks how the company can develop it. It builds on the discussion in Chapter 20 which examined different approaches by which an MNC can control its global subsidiaries. These include control of the organizational structure, controlling headquarters–subsidiary relationships, budgeting and financial control, control of technology (Chapter 16) and control by staffing (Chapters 19–21).

23.2   Corporate Cohesion and Cultural Shift

Controlling the culture of a foreign subsidiary involves

- identifying those practices, norms and values of the headquarters that can promote cohesion within the local subsidiary;
- helping managers and employees in the local subsidiary assimilate these practices, etc.

23.2.1   *The multi-domestic approach*

The MULTI-DOMESTIC approach emphasizes the assimilation of practices and behaviors – but NOT necessarily the values that underpin them. This gives each subsidiary a relatively high degree of autonomy with which to manage its operations. It typically chooses a model that fits the social context in which it is embedded. Hence each subsidiary may adopt a different model.

Many successful companies pride themselves on their multi-domestic traditions. Unilever, the Anglo-Dutch consumer goods giant, is a good example. The company has always publicized how the company's operations are rooted in the communities they serve.

Good commercial reasons support the multi-domestic option. The host-context emphasis means that such companies are often pioneers in their respective target markets, securing good governmental contacts and solid distribution networks before the competition can move in. The alignment of subsidiary methods and goals with the working norms of the host environment is also considered integral to gaining local worker satisfaction, motivation and high productivity levels (Giacobbe-Miller et al., 2003; Newman and Nollen, 1996).

However, successive waves of deregulation, advances in communications technology and competitive pressures to standardize operations has meant that the multi-domestic approach has become increasingly untenable. Local differentiation is now being seen as an unnecessary cost hindrance as the traditional multi-domestic structure has given way to the globalization of operational procedures (Kim et al. 2003).

In the quest for seamless integration, global companies increasingly view their corporate cultures as a primary asset, as the glue that unites disparate subsidiaries into an international body of headquarters replicas. Strong corporate cultures are viewed as a factor of resilience, a key plank in the ability to weather turbulent environments over time. Countless studies of enduring organization – those not have survived a century and more – clearly point to the strong sense of shared identity and values (the "Shell way", the "HSBC way" and so forth) as being essential for continuing long-term success.

The remainder of this chapter will concentrate on aspiring global corporations seeking to homogenize their corporate cultures.

23.2.2   *Assessing subsidiary cultures*

Whatever the long-term advantages of global corporate integration, control costs money in the short term. It is not only wasteful but counterproductive to enforce micro-level corporate procedures where local managers become resentful of what they perceive as heavy-handed headquarters interference and so can become demotivated. Similarly, too little investment in control mechanisms – for example, in utilizing the "arm's length" method of bureaucratic control – can be ineffective where prevailing business norms and values are substantially different.

In order to assess the subsidiary culture accurately, the company needs to gauge *accurately* the work values of

- headquarters employees;
- subsidiary employees;
- how the values of headquarters and subsidiary employees differ.

However, this is no easy task. Scholars have tried to apply Hofstede's quantitative mappings to mapping cultural distances between headquarters and subsidiary. Problems arose; Hofstede's findings show distances between cultures on different dimensions but NOT in terms of the total culture.

Questions now arise over how far Hofstede's model can be applied to measuring differences in an era of environmental turbulence. Instantaneous global communication and unprecedented population migration mean that the work values underpinning headquarters and subsidiaries are continually shifting.

23.2.3   *Studying shifting values*

Ralston and his associates have made a study of shifting work values (see Ralston, 2008, Ralston et al., 1993, 1997). This work has led to a rethinking of Hofstede's position.

In 1.3.3 we saw that Hofstede defined culture as the collective programming of the mind which distinguishes the members of one human group from another.

However the definition made by Ralston and his associates is that culture consists of those beliefs and values that are widely shared in a specific society at a particular point in time.

This latter definition enables us to deal with changes and shifting differences from a much more fluid perspective. Global corporations seeking to homogenize their subsidiary cultures must gauge not just the extent to which indigenous work practices and values are converging but also the *pace* to which they are doing so.

Accurately assessing both these factors is invaluable for global MNCs because it allows them to

- predict the ease with which the subsidiary units will assimilate corporate-level strategic change;
- highlight key cultural variables that may impede the process of change;
- examine with greater accuracy the necessity for management expatriation, and specify the optimal number of expatriates needed the optimal length of tenure of each individual assignment;
- encourage greater levels of trust and understanding across the subsidiary network – and as a consequence, a more motivated, committed workforce.

23.3   Convergence and Divergence

As MNCs struggle to understand the diverse value systems of their international management teams, the focus is increasingly directed at

- the convergence, and
- the divergence of work values.

23.3.1   Convergence

Convergence theorists assume that all organizations are increasingly driven by the same desire for efficiency regardless of the society in which they operate (Ralston, 1997; Schneider and Barsoux, 1997). As a result they emphasize the importance of macro-level variables such as structure, systems and technology in the convergence or "coming together" of worldwide business practices and procedures (Andrews and Chompusri, 2001).

For example, the deregulation of economies around the world has led to significant changes in observed workplace behavior towards individual achievement and free-market capitalism. Technological innovation – such as e-communication – has also promoted the adoption of homogeneous internal structures, prompting managers to develop behaviors more consistent with the technology of their work environment than with their traditional societal backgrounds.

Finally, supporting these essentially supply-side factors is the demand-side convergence of consumer needs and wants around globally recognized product brands and services. This also seems to have prompted an apparent emulation of the wider norms and values of the societal contexts from which these brands originate.

The gravitational pull for business-level convergence is strongly Anglo-US oriented, prompting the adoption of the workplace methods which characterize *Western capitalistic societies*. There is little doubt that MNC branch operations have converged towards similar sets of commercial behaviors. But to what extent does such a shift also mean the assimilation of the assumptions and values which underpin them? In other words to what extent does business *modernization* equate to cultural *Westernization*?

23.3.2   *Divergence*

Proponents of divergence generally concede that, albeit to a lesser extent, the structural forces outlined above comprise important forces which lead to similar developments in different societies. However, it is in the *depth* to which such convergence occurs that culture theorists differ. They argue that despite the tendency to globalization, values in the national culture drive values in the organization. And this means that managers will preserve their national value systems in spite of external, macro-level influences (Robertson et al., 2001; Khiliji, 2002; Laurent, 1986).

In most cases this amounts to common sense. The cultural conditioning within a given society occurs from a very early age, and profoundly colors the way in which an individual construes the world outside. Spending one's working day in a US-headquartered local organization is unlikely, as one US expatriate put it, "to make our local guys here Americans with suntans – at most they'll be Asians in blue jeans".

Even with an emphasis on management expatriation the on-the-ground proportion of expatriates to locals will be fractional. In this context the daily interactions between subsidiary employees will be communicated almost entirely in the indigenous tongue. Moreover, when the working day is complete local managers will return home to be immersed once again in the local norms and values which have evolved over thousands of years.

Strictly speaking our labeling of the above perspective as "divergence", is misleading, however. Divergence implies becoming *more dissimilar* whereas the position adopted by culture theorists is that whereas business practices are converging in *some* respects and to *some* degree, the core values and assumptions of a given culture will converge, if at all, much more slowly.

Against this backdrop it is the *temporal* facets of the convergence–divergence debate that move to the fore. The general belief is that business ideology influences – whether structural, systems-based or technological – evolve more rapidly than the cultural influences that are most fundamental to the society's core. Just *how* quickly – and how far this can be internally moderated – is still open to debate. Within the context of "normal", evolutionary change cultural shift may be measured in terms of decades, generations, centuries or even millennia (e.g. Ralston et al. 1997). However, within the context of *revolutionary* change – for example, on the back of a fundamental economic and/or national crisis – one might expect the timeframe to be substantially reduced.

23.4   The Dual-pressure Perspective

Determining how far business ideology on the one hand and cultural values on the other can influence the values held by subsidiary managers is not simple. The main reason is that a subsidiary organization can be a cultural melting pot of complementary and sometimes conflicting pressures.

23.4.1   *Illustrating the dual-pressure perspective*

Here is an illustration. Let's assume the hypothetical case of Alphatec (Vietnam) Ltd, a wholly-owned subsidiary of a US-headquartered global automotive manufacturer. As an organization in its own right Alphatec (Vietnam) Ltd is subject to *two* main sets of cultural forces. The first stems from the *corporation*, from Alphatec Inc. The "Alphatec way" of doing business and the business principles, the brand values, the code of ethics that comprise the "Alphatec way" are all facets of the Alphatec corporate culture. Wherever Alphatec invests in the world there will be this continuous internal pressure based on the assumption that "Alphatec must be Alphatec" irrespective of contextual variation.

The second set of cultural forces emanate from the *host environment* in which the subsidiary is embedded – in this case Vietnam. Vietnamese cultural norms, values and assumptions concerning workplace communication and relationships, teamwork and accountability will directly impact on the workings of the Alphatec subsidiary organization. This can be diagramaticized in Figure 23.1

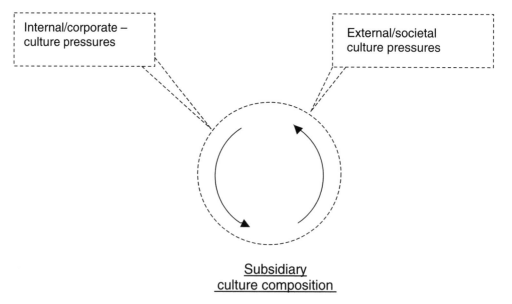

Figure 23.1   The corporate subsidiary: dual culture pressures

The organizational culture of Alphatec (Vietnam) Ltd is therefore a *composite* formed from the Alphatec corporate culture on the one hand and the Vietnamese societal culture on the other. In this way the terms "corporate culture" and "organizational culture", while interrelated, are by no means interchangeable and should not be treated as such. A *corporate* culture is essentially monolithic, a headquarters-derived channel of business customs and assumptions. An *organizational* culture is, in contrast, an amalgam, a blend of cultural forces.

Gaining optimal control over the subsidiary network requires that corporate headquarters learns to understand how the above pressures interact. Within the context of the organizational subsidiary culture theorists have portrayed this debate as between "corporate versus national culture" in identifying the relative influences of the two workforces in question. Where the cultural distance separating headquarters and subsidiary is relatively close (e.g. the French subsidiary of a Swiss corporation) this distinction may be of minor importance. In this case the corporation may choose to rely solely on formal, regulatory "arms' length" coordination mechanisms. However, where the distance is viewed as prohibitive the company may decide to invest in the closer control of local operations through the expatriation of key functional personnel.

23.4.2 Institutional pressures

In recent years a number of frameworks have been developed to better understand the varied forces for convergence and divergence which influence the culture of the subsidiary.

Any institution is subject to three sorts of forces. These are

- *regulatory forces*; the existing laws and rules. These promote certain types of behaviors and restrict others (Kostova, 1999, p. 314);
- *values, beliefs, norms and assumptions* about human nature and human behavior held by the individuals in a given country;
- *cognitive forces*. These reflect the widely shared social knowledge and cognitive categories (e.g. schemata, stereotypes) used by the people in a given country that influence the way a particular phenomenon is categorized and interpreted (Kostova and Roth, 2002, p. 217).

These three forces pressurize the subsidiary on both an internal and external basis (Kostova, 1999, 2002):

- INTERNAL pressures emanate from within the corporation – typically from global/regional headquarters – and stem from the institutional context of the home country environment;
- EXTERNAL pressures emanate from the institutional environment of the national territory within which the subsidiary is embedded.

23.4.3   Using the models

These models of different forces and the pressure sources are useful because they enable us to make more detailed analysis than does the traditional distinction between organizational culture and national culture (see 5.3). It helps us examine both the subsidiary's current cultural composition and what this cultural composition may be like in the future.

The problem is to estimate which of the various parameters is increasing in importance and which is declining at any one point in time. The balance can be estimated by monitoring a range of key environmental factors. These factors are examined in 23.4.4–23.4.9, and include:

- regulatory shift (see 23.4.4);
- political shift (23.4.5);
- diplomatic shift (23,4,6);
- economic shift (23.4.7);
- educational and developmental shift (23.4.8);
- internal pressures (23.4.9).

23.4.4   Regulatory shift

Converging regulatory pressures between the home and host contexts is often viewed as a first step towards the longer-term convergence of business practices and values. Accordingly, when a nation – e.g. Vietnam – signs and adheres to the strictures of a regional trade organization such as ASEAN, or even a global body such as the WTO, this can be taken as a positive indication of a willingness to accept a certain convergence towards global – typically US-oriented – business regulations.

This may be as simple as adhering to tariff reductions within a certain timeframe, but usually over time this will also involve a relaxation of local ownership restrictions and deregulation of a range of industry sectors. The rapidity – and in many cases the uniformity of rule implementation – is, however, another matter. Within China, for example, the imposition of WTO regulations by no means denotes the "level playing field" for foreign corporations often wished for. Among other reasons, implementation varies due to the autonomy of local municipal governments.

23.4.5   Political shift

A party coming to power with a nationalist manifesto might be trying to restrict any moves towards convergence in the local subsidiaries of foreign-owned companies, or at least slow them down. The new government might enact nationalist laws that directly affect the regulatory environment, and indirectly influence how local employees perceive the involvement of expatriates.

23.4.6 Diplomatic shift

Religious or nationalist sensitivities are difficult to predict but when they are aggravated, they can decisively inhibit cultural convergence in the subsidiary. Many companies were surprised by the strength of resentment caused by the publication of the anti-Islamic cartoons in Denmark in 2006. In 2008, French crowds protested against Chinese treatment of Tibet, and took the opportunity to demonstrate against the Beijing Olympic torch when it was carried through Paris; the rise of anti-French sentiment in China was also unexpected. These incidents triggered local hostility aimed, respectively, at Danish-headquartered subsidiaries across the Moslem world and French-headquartered subsidiaries based in China.

23.4.7 Economic shift

Economic downturns in subsidiary contexts can cause local resentment against foreign business interests, particularly when a downturn is severe and prolonged. The Asian financial crisis (1997–2000) provides a well-documented example. The region's worst economic crisis in 40 years started with devaluation that wreaked havoc on both foreign and Thai corporate balance sheets, and obliterated short-term business confidence (Andrews and Chompusri, 2001)

The International Monetary Fund administered its financial medicine, but the crisis continued. Local sentiment became markedly more "anti-Western", particularly when foreign companies were allowed to purchase Thai assets at cheap "fire-sale" prices. This "vulture capitalism" – as it was called – had very negative effects on the motivation and willingness of local subsidiary employees to practice Western business styles (see Legewie and Meyor-Ohle, 2000, and Yeung, 2000).

23.4.8 Educational and developmental shift

The educational customs of a given country are typically too broad and embedded within the wider national culture to be identified with any degree of exactitude. However, the initiation of a nation-wide program of English language development as an economic priority may be taken as an indication of medium- to longer-term convergence – particularly as the shift may be greater than initially anticipated. The new generation of English-competent managers would not just be speaking but also possibly thinking in English – imbuing the local population with a more receptive attitude to Anglo business practices, reasoning and hence values.

23.4.9 Internal pressures

Convergence may also be prompted by pressures internal to the MNC seeking to (re-) inject its norms, values and practices into the subsidiary work–value mix. The most obvious, visible way for this to be done is through the expatriation of management personnel, though it may also be achieved through extrapolating corporate systems, structures (as discussed above) and the strategic objectives for a given host environment.

Shifting the strategic goals provides an apt illustration. If a company produces mass-market consumer goods with share-of-market as the overriding medium-term objective then the subsidiary unit may well be left to operate with a high degree of autonomy. Local knowledge and understanding of local consumers, key account holders and regulatory officials may be viewed as the critical success factors best left under indigenous management direction. However, if the strategy should shift towards profitability and/or brand-driven focus then market share may take a backseat. Subsequent needs to maintain quality, positioning objectives and ultimately brand consistency across markets at the expense of short-term volume concerns may well lead to corporate control as being seen as a higher priority. This would generally then act as a force for local-level convergence towards headquarters-oriented procedures and values.

A major component of this shift would typically be through the medium-term reconfiguration of the host-context customer base. Taking the example of a Western communications infrastructure provider, in their home market context the company may deal exclusively with a technologically advanced consumer base. In the diverse contexts of emerging Asia, however, it may find that a relatively high proportion of its customer cohort (e.g. family businesses and state-owned enterprises) will be relatively traditional in terms of business norms and values. The latter cohort, in demanding an indigenous/national approach would have provided a strong indigenous impetus towards retaining traditional working norms and values. The strategic shift sketched above typically leads to a corollary stress on a narrower, premium-positioned international product range that will see local customers going elsewhere with tacit corporate-level acceptance (i.e. as a short-term sacrifice towards a longer-term aim).

23.5   Cross-vergence

In a rapidly changing global business environment the concepts of convergence and divergence may be inadequate to explain the dynamic interactions between organizations and their environment. Contemporary subsidiary organizations may experience convergence and divergence *simultaneously* becoming *more similar* in terms of structure and technology and yet *retaining* their culturally based dissimilarities.

In a series of studies through the 1990s Ralston found evidence of this phenomenon occurring among managers in China – the paradox being their simultaneous embracement of capitalistic, individualist values without forsaking the Confucian, collectivist values of their cultural heritage (Ralston et al., 1997). In reconciling this apparent contradiction Ralston developed the notion of CROSS-VERGENCE where a melting pot of work values is formed as a result of this confluence of cultural forces.

Although originally conceived as something "in between", as a transitional state during which values move over time from divergence to convergence, Ralston's later work emphasized cross-vergence as a unique value system formed from the synergistic incorporation of specific business ideology and socio-cultural influences in each host country context (Ralston, 2008).

The notion of cross-vergence has important implications for understanding the work behaviors in many developing economies. For one thing is cross-vergence a transitional phase between convergence and divergence and how long is the transition process? To date such questions remain largely unanswered, principally because this would necessitate dynamic, longitudinal explorations of evolving work values (McGaughey and de Cieri, 1999). Almost without exception studies on convergence – divergence – cross-vergence as an evolutionary process have been mere "snapshots", point-in-time examinations that are patently unreliable.

However, where change within a society's business context is revolutionary – i.e. abrupt and severe – it may be possible to capture some or all of these forces *in flight* – thereby acquiring a more robust insight into how subsidiary work values interact and mutate. In essence this was the basis of the argument presented by Andrews and Chompusri (2001, 2005) in the context of the Asian financial crisis. These scholars drew on Benson (1977) and Fombrun (1986) and described the pressures for convergence, divergence and finally cross-vergence as stages in a process. This process was to occur sequentially as a dialectic of pressures, namely force (convergence), counterforce (divergence) and then resolution (cross-vergence) before presumably recommencing at some future point-in-time.

The initial push for convergence stemmed from centrally imposed operational audits in the initial crisis period of 1997–98. Global – particularly Western – corporations sought to "rein in" their relatively autonomous Asian units, reinjecting doses of corporate culture to try to impose greater conformity. To the surprise of local commentators and business practitioners, however, the indigenous response was one of unprecedented resistance and circumvention. Moreover such behavior seemed to reflect the prevailing attitude of the political and industrial elites within the region who sought to enhance the notion of an Asian cultural identity as a cohesive counterforce for divergence in the face of alien Western agendas and values (Bhopal and Hitchcock, 2001).

In resolving this stand-off compromises were generally reached at the headquarters–subsidiary interface, described by Andrews and Chompusri (2001, 2005) as a "working cross-vergence" of relevant practices and values. In this way convergence and divergence express the ebb and flow of contrasting pressures on emerging subsidiary work values, with cross-vergence as a temporary calming of the waters (albeit at a point relatively closer to globally accepted norms).

23.6   Implications for the Manager

The MNC that hopes to build an integrated organizational culture across the global organization needs to

- analyze the work values of different subsidiaries. This helps insure that the money spent on control mechanisms is efficiently dispensed.
- Based on this analysis, develop a model of cultural distances between the subsidiaries. Underestimating cultural distance is risky. It can lead to miscalculating investments needed to make changes in corporate practice and transfer best practice. If changes are resisted, relations between headquarters and subsidiary are soured and trust breaks down. Changes adopted under headquarters pressure may be practiced but not believed in. This leads to a breakdown in trust, demoralization, and declining profitability.
- Continuously monitor work values, in order to understand the shifting values held by subsidiary managers. This is more likely to create positive attitudes than trying to force-fit them into a single, standardized organizational culture.
- This means: identify, understand and accept differences where they occur – and decide how to use them positively.

23.7 SUMMARY

This chapter begins from the fact that competitive pressures in the contemporary business environment lead to an increasing corporate emphasis on global integration and control. Minimizing cultural distances that divide the subsidiary network is now a strategic priority.

Section 23.2 examined problems of ensuring CORPORATE COHESION when CULTURES are SHIFTING. Ensuring that expensive cultural control mechanisms are utilized effectively means ensuring that cultural distance is accurately gauged. In today's volatile global environment this means a focus on the current work values will change over time. To this end the fundamental stasis inherent in traditional models of cultural comparison renders them increasingly obsolete in an era of relentless dynamism. Attending to shifting managerial values emerged as a central concern, although the dual pressures of convergence on the one hand and divergence on the other do not capture adequately the complexity of values change.

Section 23.3 examined the effect of CONVERGENCE AND DIVERGENCE in corporate subsidiaries. These forces may occur simultaneously, and Section 23.4 examined the DUAL PERSPECTIVES that subsidiary managers might develop when they apparently adapt to headquarters ideologies while retaining the core values of their local culture. Section 23.5 examined the phenomenon of CROSS-VERGENCE, and emphasized the need to continuously monitor the work-values balance of each subsidiary at any one point in time. In order to assimilate changes at the corporate level, the manager must predict *future* shifts, so that the pace and depth of adopting these changes can be optimized.

23.8   E X E R C I S E

Using your MNC or one with which you are familiar, compare the type and extent of corporate control exercised across the international subsidiary network. Think of three subsidiary organizations and rank them in terms of cultural distance – beginning with low (e.g. Belgian subsidiary of a French MNC), medium (e.g. Brazilian subsidiary of a Spanish MNC) and high (e.g. Thai subsidiary of a UK MNC).

Using your three examples consider the following:

- How is each type of subsidiary controlled differently in terms of staffing (i.e. expatriates versus local managers)?
- How has the preferred method and extent of control changed during the life of the subsidiary operation?

- Is there or has there been significant evidence of converging cultural norms and values (i.e. internal pressures overcoming external customs) to make the subsidiary culturally more proximate?
- What are the underlying reasons for convergence/divergence in order of priority? (These might include consumer behavior, trade bloc affiliation, shift in corporate strategy, etc.)
- What has been the role of cultural shift in these changes?
- To what extent do you think the current portfolio of control mechanisms is effective in integrating subsidiary operations? Should it be changed to meet future circumstances? How can any changes be made?
- Give examples of cross-vergence among your subsidiaries abroad.

CHAPTER TWENTY FOUR

Ethics and Corporate Responsibility

24.1   Introduction

Paul Wolfowitz, the one-time US Deputy Defense Secretary, became head of the World Bank in 2005. He proclaimed that his mission included rooting out corruption in the institution.

In 2007, he arranged for his girlfriend, a World Bank official, to be promoted from a relatively junior grade to the position of vice-president. Shaha Ali Riza was awarded a massive pay rise which brought her tax-free income up to $244,960 – more than the salary paid to the then Secretary of State, Condoleeza Rice.

By authorizing the rise, Wolfowitz was technically guilty of "girl-friend nepotism", a fatal act for a man who claimed to oppose World Bank corruption. Worse, he claimed to have followed the correct ethics procedures in making the appointment. But it was later discovered that he had drawn up Riza's contract personally, and by thus misleading the bank's executive he sealed his fate. His enemies within the World Bank, in European governments, and elsewhere, used this to force his resignation.

This example shows a senior bureaucrat being punished for breaking his or-ganization's code of practice – in one particular culture. This does not mean that a similar incident would be censored elsewhere or have the same outcome elsewhere.

This short chapter deals with the conditions under which ethical considerations are significant in the workplace and the marketplace. This concludes the book because it draws together several of the themes discussed in previous chapters:

- values in the national culture;
- organizational culture;
- multinational strategy;
- the importance of brand management.

In many circumstances a company that demonstrates adherence to an ethical code profits in the marketplace. And so, in the long term, good ethics translates into good business. Finally the chapter deals with the wider application of ethical standards in the principles of corporate social responsibility.

24.2 Ethics

The concept of ethics includes two related ideas:

- the conduct of behavior according to moral principles;
- the evaluation of behavior according to moral principles.

In many societies, the ethical code is based on the predominant religious system. Elsewhere there may be no obvious religious influence, and instead it is derived from a sense of how people ought to behave, which may closely correspond to values in the culture.

Some experts argue that ethics has no place in business. They claim that a firm's only responsibility is to make profits for its stockholders and that business is morally neutral. Thus, the only factor inhibiting the firm from making profits is the need to stay within the law of the country – because if it breaks the law, the company and thus the stockholders may be punished.

But customers regularly show that they prefer to deal with companies that have a strong ethical profile, and that these companies can increase their profits. So the paradox arises that ethics *does* have a place because it earns revenue – on one condition. The condition is that the company continues to abide by its ethical code at all times, and in particular in adverse conditions. If a company purporting to be ethical is seen to betray its code, the damage may be greater than for a company that had never claimed ethical standards in the first place. The disappointed customers do not easily forgive; they transfer their loyalties to a competitor, and business falls. Section 24.4.3 gives an example.

24.2.1   The significance of ethics

Until recently, little was said about ethics in the workplace. This did not mean that business was any less ethical than it is now, but rather that people did not feel the need to make the ethical underpinning explicit. This was particularly the case in cultures united by a strong, shared religious faith.

But the situation has changed in our globalizing world, and certainly in societies that have seen large inflows of migrant workers from other cultures, because a shared religious or ethical basis cannot be taken for granted. A lack of conformity is often perceived as ethical collapse, and this causes concern. This concern is reflected by the increased attention that unethical behavior receives in the media. Whereas once, politicians were under little danger of having their private lives exposed, now every instance of straying from the path of moral rectitude may be used by enemies, or those genuinely concerned by the effects of moral corruption. The case above gives an example.

Why have public sensitivities to unethical behavior and moral corruption become newsworthy? Here are some reasons:

- the information revolution has led to greater ease in investigating and reporting unethical and corrupt behavior;
- there is a growing awareness of the political, economic and social costs of corruption;
- the swelling middle classes increasingly demand higher standards of behavior by government and company officials;
- workforces are increasingly heterogeneous – particularly in MNCs;
- members come from a range of cultures. The corporate headquarters can no longer take for granted a shared experience of a particular religious code or a shared notion of ethical values;
- changes in the marketplace mean that suppliers and customers increasingly prefer to deal with companies that have a good record on ethical issues.

24.2.2   What it means to be ethical

Supposing that you are doing business with a business partner who offers you a gift on condition that you sign a contract. In other words, the gift is a bribe. This faces you with a range of practical and abstract questions. The practical questions include:

- will any one else – superiors, colleagues, subordinates, other authorities – find out the truth if you take this bribe?
- if the truth is discovered, what punishment might you incur?
- is the bribe large enough to justify the risk of discovery and punishment?

On a more abstract level, you are faced ethical issues:

- is it right to take this bribe;
- what is the right action that should I take?

This might lead you to consider broader issues, which touch on your entire existence:

- how should I live my life?
- what kind of person do I want to be?

And if you are responsible for the decisions taken by an organization:

- what kind of an organization do I want this to be?

These questions are further complicated in circumstances when it is uncertain whether there is an ethical problem at all – for example, when

- the bribe takes the form of a restaurant meal;
- the person offering the bribe is a member of your family;
- the bribe is offered during a religious festival, when gifts are normally exchanged;
- non-acceptance will be construed as a serious insult, and mean that your firm will lose the contract. This loss of work will mean that your colleagues lose their jobs;
- your agent offers to accept the bribe on your behalf, and to deduce the proceeds from his expense account.

The organization protects its members against such ambiguities by an ethical code, to which all members are expected to subscribe.

In more collectivist cultures where members can be expected to share the same beliefs, this code may be implicit, and perhaps not even articulated. But in contexts where a sharing of values cannot be taken for granted and top management feels itself threatened by illegal or unorthodox behavior, considerable investments may be made in formulating and publicizing the code, and ensuring that all members subscribe to it.

24.2.3   The ethical code

The ethical code makes clear how members of the organization are expected to behave. To take the example above, and assuming a legalistic context in which management makes the code explicit, it might specify that

- no gifts are to be accepted, in any circumstances, whether in the country of headquarters or elsewhere;
- gifts may be accepted up to a specified cost, and not above this;
- all gifts offered and/or accepted are to be reported to the compliance manager;
- entertainment may be accepted up to a specified cost and must be reciprocated;
- gifts or entertainment may be accepted up to a specified cost in the country of the headquarters, to some other cost in Country X, and to some other cost in Country Y;
- and so on.

A shared code has the advantage of protecting their employees against uncertainty. It also creates ethical uniformity, which reduces the likelihood of conflict between members following different ethical priorities. In this respect the ethical code contributes to building a strong organizational culture. It also projects a coherent message to the wider environment – suppliers, customers, competitors, and so on. The message says "this is how our members behave". Thus the code acts as a mission statement, and also reduces the uncertainty for a member of some other organization or culture doing business with you.

The examples above have dealt with a single type of ethical question, the acceptance of a bribe. Of course, a full code covers a range of other issues, including bans on offering bribes, dishonest reporting, sexual harassment, relationships judged inappropriate, and any behavior judged likely to draw the organization into disrepute.

The code can specify rights and duties which are – so far as possible – complementary. For example, employees have rights to work quality (or job satisfaction), and duties to comply with the labor contract and to give loyalty to the firm. Correspondingly, employers have duties to improve the quality of work, and rights to demand certain specified levels of productivity and cooperation.

But this specification of rights and duties is formal and legalistic, and typical of Anglo and European cultures. In cultures with other priorities, a bureaucratic approach may not be appropriate. For example, Section 10.5 described the operation of *guanxi* in Chinese cultures. The social values of developing and maintaining relationships are developed through the exchange of gifts. The business person who is not willing to participate loses influence, and hence endangers the interests of his/her organization. How can the individual and the company overcome this contradiction between the code and the practice?

In non-Western cultures, the tendency to formalize rights and duties may appear to detract from the individual's capacity to decide for him/herself how to behave in different situations. This denial of maturity may indicate moral weakness rather than strength. For example, in 2007 Japan's education minister made a speech in which

> he claimed that too much emphasis has been put on human rights. Bunmei Ibuki, 69, also said that Western style individualism was damaging Japan. . . . In his speech in Nagasaki he said that while human rights were important, a society that gorged itself on human rights was like a person with obesity-related illness.[1]

The questions that arise are how far ethical norms are determined by culture, and how far they transcend culture.

24.3   Ethics Across Culture and Time

Some geneticists think that they are close to linking a receptor gene to basic human personality traits such as "loyalty". This raises a number of ethical questions. Should genetic fingerprinting be made available without – or even with – the employee's permission? Should employees have a "right" to reciprocal access to their employer's genetic coding and to evidence of his loyalty to them, particularly in a business context where they fear for their jobs? How widely should this information be published? Should it be admissible in a court of law? And a practical question; how can it be adequately protected?

Further practical questions arise in interpreting this information across cultures.

First, to whom should loyalty be owed? In individualist cultures, this question revolves around relations between the individual and his/her employing organization, but a member of a collectivist culture is more likely to pay loyalty to the manager responsible for employing him/her. For example, say that an Indonesian manager gets into conflict with his expatriate top management. He quits and joins a competitor, taking his subordinates with him. Should *their* behavior be interpreted as disloyalty (because they leave their company and join a competitor), or loyalty (because they stand with their boss)?

Second, does loyalty in, say, the cultural context of headquarters predict loyalty in another context? To a manager from your culture? To a manager from the local culture? In the more collectivist cultures where power distances are high, loyalty to an organization or individual may be regarded as an ethical imperative. In individualist cultures this is far less likely to be the case.

Problems arise when these ethical loyalties come into conflict; for example, when headquarters allows one type of behavior, and the subsidiary condemns it as unethical. Which code does the expatriate follow?

24.3.1 *Identifying the ethics of an organization in the other culture*

In practice, the expatriate resolves the contradiction above by consulting his/her own personal values, or deciding where his/her interests lie. This may not be a major problem.

A more difficult problem arises when the expatriate is

- unable to discover the code formulated in one or both contexts;
- unsure how the code is implemented in one or both contexts;
- unaware that the codes differ.

The third of these may be crucial. Particularly when the subsidiary does not make its code explicit, it is too easy to assume that there are no major differences between the ethical systems applied in the two organizations – or the two national cultures.

The expatriate is forced to do his/her own research in order to discover the ethical code. He does this research by

- asking questions. Evanoff (2006) argues that cross-cultural dialog on ethical differences can lead to the creation of a synergistic "third culture", incorporating positive aspects of both systems;
- observation, and deducing what behavior is allowed;
- observation, and deducing what behavior is NOT allowed.

The last may give a clear indication of the ethical code. For example, when representatives of different companies prefer to hide the details of a deal, this can often mean that a bribe has been offered and accepted. However, even this deduction is not infallible; it might simply mean that they have legitimate business reasons for not informing competitors.

24.3.2   Do ethical values change over time?

Some ethical values are unchanging over time. All the major religions condemn murder, for instance – although even this is variable. In time of war, some forms of murder are legitimated. Other values change radically in time. In the US 40 years ago, few people thought of cigarette smoking as an ethical problem. But that laissez-faire attitude has disappeared; smoking is generally condemned as harmful to the smoker and to other people in the vicinity.

People may be tolerant of antisocial behavior until

- it affects their own interests;
- they perceive that the perpetrators of this behavior are benefiting at their expense. For example, in an economic boom, when everyone is getting rich, patronage relations between politicians and business people may be accepted, even if they are disliked. But when the economy changes from boom to bust and the new middle classes perceive that those in corrupt relationships are profiting unfairly, they are no longer so tolerant;
- increased understanding of the behavior leads to a reassessment of its effects on the community. Until recently, zoos were generally accepted. But as society has become more understanding of the effects of mistreating animals, birds, fish and other living creatures, and the dangers of many species becoming extinct, attitudes have changed. Mistreatment is now an ethical issue, and owners of zoos have to be scrupulous about how they treat the creatures in their care.

In the growth years of the Japanese economy, in the 1960s-1980s, the Japanese public had become wearily used to cases of corrupt patronage relations between politicians and business people, and these received little attention. But in the late 1980s and 1990s, the mood changed, and when the Recruit scandal came to light, the Japanese public erupted in disgust and shame. Here are some possible explanations for this change in attitude:

- the Japanese public had grown more ethical;
- Japanese politicians and business people had grown less ethical;
- the Japanese public had grown less tolerant of such corruption in a time of economic restraint.

The third provides the most likely explanation. The Japanese economy was in recession. The middle classes were feeling increasingly impoverished, and they resented seeing others making illicit profits and were heedless to the plight of everyone else.

At the time of writing in 2009, the global economy has plunged into a recession. This is leading to new concerns about ethical standards. For example, in many rich countries new questions are being raised about the ethics of traditional banking practices.

24.4   Ethics in Branding

Today's consumers are increasingly attracted by brands that are marketed according to ethical codes. In 2006, *The Business* tested this proposition by tracking the sales of five pairs of competing brands; one of each pair was overtly marketed as "green" or "socially responsible" against the other which was not.[2] For example, they paired: Range Rover with Toyota which produced environmentally friendly cars such as Prius; Green and Blacks – makers of organic chocolate – with Nestlé; Ecover, environmentally-friendly detergent, with Fairy. In mid-2007, the magazine published a graph demonstrating that on average the ethical-image brands had significantly pulled away from their competitors.

"Non-ethically marketed" brands are now flat, while the other group is actually continuing to climb.

Customers choose brands that represent values they find attractive. It was once unusual for marketers to focus on ethical or charitable causes, but now this is increasingly usual. Thus it makes good business sense for a producer to follow this route. Tim Mason, the marketing director of Tesco PLC, observed that cause-related marketing makes commercial sense. 'It can deliver greater benefits per pound spent than almost anything else a company can do.'[3]

Of course, whether or not the company or the brand manager genuinely cares about the causes with which they seek association may be open to question.

The major questions arise about ethical branding:

- how can ethical branding be enforced across the different societies in which MNCs operate, particularly in emerging economies where ethical considerations are often paid less attention? And
- how far do global companies seek to project an ethical image, and to position themselves as the *ethical* choice within their industries?

The importance of building and maintaining an ethical image is demonstrated by two global industries:

- oil – see 24.4.1;
- coffee – see 24.4.2.

24.4.1   Building an ethical image: oil

In the case of oil, the recent print-media advertisements used by Shell, BP and Esso express a closely matched fight to dominate in consumers' minds as the environmentally conscious energy brand for the twenty-first century. In real terms sustainable energy production makes little or no money (at the time of writing) for the MNCs concerned. These companies are planning for the future.

In years past BP was known as British Petroleum and its corporate brand logo was a shield. It now brands itself as "Beyond Petroleum" and its logo is a sunflower. The rejuvenation of the Caltex brand logo in the 1990s provides a similar illustration. Aiming to be perceived as "leading edge" among the new generation of drivers, the traditional brand logo colors – red background/white star – came under scrutiny, with the red – symbol of blood, anger and danger – deemed as being too harsh. Accordingly the company – through its agency – softened the image with a soothing deep-sea ocean green, the color of choice for the environmentally conscious.

In short, ethical, cause-related marketing helps build a brand and bring to life the core values that surround it. In this way, perhaps more than anything else, it can help build relationships with customers that are emotional and *enduring*.

24.4.2   *Problems in communicating an ethical image: coffee*

Many brands are sold successfully in the West on the basis of ethical values associated with them. But other markets may be far less enthusiastic. For example, the Bodyshop company expresses its conservation-oriented brand image in part by recycling its packaging, and this gains positive associations in the minds of Western consumers. Thus the ethical code also serves as a successful business tool – in the West. Elsewhere this "green" emphasis is less attractive, and it fails in markets such as Thailand where the practice of recycling its product packaging is dismissed as "unhygienic".

In working in contexts that do not share the cultural and economic values of the headquarters country, the MNC must aim for a gradual, "softly-softly" approach. It must try to ensure that practice and communications in the local context do not contradict the ethical core of the brand. A recent case illustrating the dangers of contradicting the brand message concerns the Starbucks corporation, another company that has worked hard to develop an ethical profile. But the scramble for profit had serious consequences when they induced management to overlook the interests of its Ethiopian suppliers.

Ethiopian coffee is widely recognized as one of the world's finest crops, and the coffee plantations are hugely important for the future development of this impoverished African nation. Since 2005 the government has tried to support the country's farmers by trademarking their coffee in the US market. This is intended to protect the product and to earn up to £50 million annually to the national economy. To the surprise of media commentators the major opponent has not been a bulk-buyer with a purely economic interest in Ethiopian coffee, but the world's largest premium coffee franchise, Starbucks. And this is surprising because Starbucks has a policy of helping local farming communities.

The trademark campaign would have had the effect of raising the price of coffee to Starbucks, which would certainly have caused some damage to the company's bottom line. But at this time the company was buying beans from Ethiopian farmers at between 75¢ and $1.60 a pound and then selling to the end-user across its counters for maybe $26 a pound. And even if local farm prices had doubled, the company did not have a compelling case for opposition.

24.4.3   The damage

But once this position became public knowledge, the company was seriously damaged. The news of the company's stance was fed across global internet sites such as YouTube, where the ethically minded Starbucks corporation was portrayed as a modern-day colonialist exploiting one of the world's poorest countries.[4]

The extent of the damage was massive, perhaps incalculable. The company had allowed local considerations to dilute its core brand tenet of social responsibility. A stroll inside any of the major coffee chains across Europe's capital cities makes it clear just how important the ethical treatment of African farmer's is to the public's perception of the corporate coffee franchise, specifically in its incessant promotion of "strong farmer relationships" and "helping farming communities grow". Starbucks had taken a risk, and failed. As the company's founder, Howard Schultz, observed, a focus on chasing revenue through expansion may result in a serious loss of identity if the core brand values are compromised in the process.

24.4.4   Ethical problems for the expatriate brand manager

The EBM can find himself in a thankless role, continuously pulled in opposite directions while trying to achieve the seemingly impossible. General descriptions of the role – such as the one offered here – can only hint at the practical challenges and problems that arise in a real assignment. Quite apart from the skills, knowledge and intellectual capability needed to survive and prosper at the cutting edge between headquarters and subsidiary, the EBM also needs personal characteristics; strength of character, tenacity, an ability to deal with day-to-day pressures, and an intuitive feel for the soul of the brand.

The EBM may find himself caught between different ethical codes, between that of headquarters and that expressed within the host environment. Without exception the world's top MNCs do not countenance racial or sexual discrimination of any kind – and this will be made clear in the ethical code. On the ground, however, the EBM may find his role more difficult than expected when long-standing members of the subsidiary are prejudiced in ways that are out of step with corporate headquarters policy – and perhaps do not even realize that they are prejudiced. These may show themselves in the initial days and weeks of the assignment when the EBM is being introduced to the various stakeholders involved – including customers, distributors, trade body and government officials and so forth.

24.5   Corporate Social Responsibility

Corporate Social Responsibility (CSR) is defined by Hennigfeld et al. (2007) as

> Undertaking business in an ethical way in order to achieve sustainable development, not only in economic terms, but also in the social and environmental sphere.   *(p. xxix)*

CSR is a rapidly expanding field. This section indicates its scope.

24.5.1 *Sustainibility and profit*

Any company that aims at good corporate citizenship adopts strategies that sustain natural resources and the environment for the good of all society. This has long-term implications for future activity. But the company is in business to make profits and to protect the interests of its stockholders and employers.

The need to earn revenue might appear to have short-term implications only. But in practice the company is concerned about sustaining its capacity to conduct profitable operations. That is, the notions of sustainability and profitability are not in opposition. The company continually revisits the balance between the two in order that both may be achieved.

24.5.2 *CSR and globalization*

CSR has developed as an informal system that bypasses institutions of state, and may differ from or even exceed the formal demands of national legal systems.

In this respect, it is an expression of globalization (see 13.2) and is primarily associated with the activities of MNCs, first in how each applies its own ethical codes (see Dilling et al. 2008). Second, networks of MNCs sharing interests and values join forces to influence business norms in their industry or area of activity. This amounts to recognition that these companies may cause problems but they also have the capacity to unite in resolving them. Third, the development of practical norms is influenced by the intervention of non-governmental organizations (NGOs).

The NGO movement is varied, but in general organizations within the movement deal with

*   their funders;
*   their clients;
*   the corporate world.

Relations with the corporate world include fundraising. But more to the point here, the NGO campaigns for transparency in business operations. It collects information on business activities, and when appropriate, publicizes these activities. For example, if an MNC pollutes the environment, or abuses the rights and persons of employees and others, the NGO may brief the international media. On occasion an NGO stages events that draw attention to abuses; Greenpeace claims that it "exposes threats to the environment and finds creative positive solutions".

Other NGOs go even further in opposing authority, so that rogue extremist groups have been labeled "terrorists – NGOs with bombs".

On occasion, the NGO movement works in tandem with national governments, particularly in situations where it has access and expertise denied to government. For example, a government may hire an NGO to deliver aid to a disaster area. However, NGOs also work independently of government and even contrary to government interests. Because they have influence around the world that is not checked by national boundaries, the NGOs express globalization.

24.5.3   The range of CSR

Just as the theory of CSR is broad, so are the practical implications, and the fields of relevance in which it operates. Notions of CSR have been expressed in a range of fields – for example:

- corporate governance, which is generally concerned with the strategic decisions made by senior executives, and with how decisions made by their companies influence their employees, other persons, and the environment;
- exposing artificial compliance with regulations, in order to protect shareholders' interests;
- protecting the environment against exploitation and pollution;
- waste management;
- protecting the interests of company employees;
- data protection and safeguarding privacy;
- consumer contracts;
- and in other activities.

24.6   Implications for the Manager

Compare an organization that you know well in *your own culture* with a similar organization in *some other culture.*

1 In each of the two organizations, what ethical code is used to regulate members' activities when working and when at leisure?
   (a)   Within each organization, who is responsible for planning the code?
   (b)   How is the code communicated to members?
   (c)   How is ethical behavior taught to members?
   (d)   How is ethical behavior rewarded?
   (e)   How is unethical behavior punished?
   (f)   How clear or how ambiguous is the code?
   (g)   How consistently is the code applied to different ranks in each of the two organizations?
2 Compare the answers that you have given above for each of the two organizations. How do you explain the differences?

3   What problems might arise for managers from the two organizations when working together?
    (a) What ethical differences could a manager from the organization in *your culture* expect to find when working in the other?
    (b) What ethical differences could a manager from the organization in the *other culture* expect to find when working in yours?
    (c) What ethical disagreements might arise for managers from these two organizations when negotiating together?

24.7 SUMMARY

This chapter has examined the theory and practice of ethical business, and has revisited a number of topics developed in previous parts and chapters.

Section 24.2 examined the problems of defining ETHICS, and the significance of ethical behavior in business. Particularly in the Western companies, ethical codes are enforced to give guidance to employees and position the organization in the market. But there may be less need for them in homogeneous cultures elsewhere in the world. Section 24.3 looked at ethics in CULTURE AND TIME. Contradictions arise when different cultures have different ethical values, and these may be costly. Also, ethical values change over time and what was unethical once may be ethical today – and vice versa. Section 24.4 discussed the implications of the ethical code for the BRAND and the EBM. This develops the discussion of the problems facing the EBM in 22.3. Section 24.5 saw how ethics have influenced the principle of CORPORATE SOCIAL RESPONSIBILITY.

24.8 EXERCISE

Debate with other members of your group.

-   Is it desirable that all companies within an industry should follow the same ethical code of practice?
-   Is it desirable that all companies within a culture should follow the same ethical code of practice?

-   Is it desirable that a global code of practice should be published, to which all companies everywhere should subscribe?
-   Is the implementation of a global code of practice possible?

Report your decisions to the full class.

Notes

1 Colin Joyce. "Too many" human rights. *Daily Telegraph*, 27 February, 2007.

2 Stephan Shakespeare. Brandindex. *The Business*, May 5, 2007.

3 www.samaritans.org: accessed June 6, 2008.

4 D. Rushe. Starbucks stirs up storm in a coffee cup. *Sunday Times*, March 4, 2007.

CASES FOR PART FOUR
Conclusions

CHAPTER TWENTY THREE   **The Culture of the Subsidiary: Convergence and Divergence**

CASE — CAS

CAS SA is a facilities maintenance company. It is based in France and has subsidiaries throughout the world. [Now, the French-headquartered facilities maintenance MNC is looking to add to its portfolio of subsidiary organizations in the ASEAN (Association of Southeast Asian Nations) trading bloc.] The company has already developed a number of joint venture partnerships with local partners in Hong Kong, Malaysia, Vietnam and Singapore. Generally these have worked successfully although there have been challenges in all units concerning the day-to-day operation of the business – mostly in the form of disputes over price positioning strategy.

Given the years of experience in the region the regional director for Asia feels that the company should now opt for a wholly-owned subsidiary (WOS) to avoid such problems in future, this time in the developing economy of Thailand. Desk research has shown that a WOS is now legally acceptable in the wake of a relaxation on foreign ownership restrictions.

At the recent Asian regional conference, however, a number of senior corporate executives – in addition to the majority of existing country managers – have voiced their opposition to the WOS option on the following grounds:

(a)   Thailand is culturally distinct from the markets where CAS is already present, rendering the company's knowledge and experience of limited relevance.

(b)   Unlike Hong Kong, Singapore, Malaysia or Vietnam, Thailand has never been colonized by a foreign Western power. The foreign language skills of its people are relatively weak.

(c) CSA cannot depend on using French or English in Thailand. In order to succeed in this market, it needs a local partner who can provide not only the technical "know-who" but also a deep understanding of the local culture and language – Thai.

(d) Prospective partners have been recommended by several of the company's existing affiliates in its other ASEAN markets as an alternative to "going it alone" and developing a subsidiary.

QUESTIONS

1 What are the advantages and disadvantages to be gained in both the short term and the long term from
   (a) forming an IJV with a local partner;
   (b) establishing a wholly-owned subsidiary?

2 Assume that you are the prospective country manager for Thailand. On the basis of the information given, which of the options (a) and (b) above would you recommend?

3 What additional information would you need before making a final decision?

CHAPTER TWENTY FOUR   **Ethics and Corporate Responsibility**

CASE   A DONATION TO THE PRESIDENT'S CAMPAIGN FUND

You are chairman of a multinational oil company called ABC Ltd, which is headquartered in London.

For many years ABC Ltd has been trying to gain access to the large oil and gas fields in a north Asian country called Energyland. Last year you appointed Joe Smith to be managing director of your 100 percent subsidiary in Energyland called XYZ Co. XYZ Co. formed a 50/50 joint venture with an Energyland oil company called Local Inc. and this joint venture has been negotiating with the Energyland government on a concession agreement to exploit the oil and gas reserves of Energyland.

Negotiations have been going well and preliminary agreement has been reached between the JV and the Energyland government. The main terms of this preliminary agreement have been captured in a non-binding Memorandum of Understanding (MOU) which Joe Smith signed on behalf of XYZ Co. a week ago. You have just arrived in Energyland on your first visit in order to meet with the president of Energyland, to express your thanks for the positive attitude shown by his negotiators and explore with the president some ideas for further cooperation. You are in high spirits since this deal could be worth up to $10 billion over the next 10 years and the stock market has reacted favorably to the news.

You will meet with the president tomorrow and you are having a quiet dinner with Joe Smith to go over the details of the progress made to date. During dinner you are shocked to learn that as part of the deal and before the legally binding contract is signed, the JV will have to pay $5 million towards the president's campaign fund for the forthcoming presidential elections. Joe explains that during the earlier negotiations a competitor

had already agreed to make this payment. Without a similar undertaking the government would not have agreed the MOU with the JV.

At this point you remind yourself of the relevant parts of ABC Ltd's Corporate Brand/Business Principles.

ABC companies insist on honesty, integrity and fairness in all aspects of our business and expect the same in our relationships with all those with whom we do business. The direct or indirect offer, payment, soliciting or acceptance of bribes in any form is unacceptable. Facilitation payments are also bribes and should not be made. Employees must avoid conflicts of interest between their private activities and their part in the conduct of company business.

ABC companies do not make payments to political parties, organizations or their representatives. ABC companies do not take part in party politics. However, when dealing with governments, ABC companies have the right and the responsibility to make our position known on any matters which affect us, our employees, our customers, our shareholders or local communities in a manner which is in accordance with our values and the business principles.

Joe further explains that the payment will be made through a company owned by the brother of the president which will invoice the JV for $5 million for services provided to the JV. However, in reality, no such services will be provided. Joe believes that this will effectively hide the donation.

After dinner you are joined at the bar by the MD of Local Inc. who is from a well-known family in

Energyland and whose father is a personal friend of the president. You explain your concerns to him. He explains that in Energyland such a payment is not regarded as a bribe but more as a business necessity. However, he understands your concerns and makes two suggestions.

The JV currently obtains genuine services from another local company Personnel Services (Energyland) Co. Why not ask this company to make the payment to the president and it will then send slightly inflated invoices to the JV to cover the $5 million?

The MD of Local Inc. offers to make the payment personally (he is from a wealthy family). This will be very safe since he and his family make regular payments to the president and there is no way the $5 million payment will be traced back to ABC Ltd or XYZ Co. All he asks in return is that Local Inc. will be the JV partner for any future contracts won by ABC Ltd in Energyland.

As the chairman of ABC Ltd the final decision is yours. You see the president tomorrow morning. The following thoughts are in your mind.

The payment of a bribe is strictly against ABC Ltd's business principles. However, in Energyland such payments are accepted as an everyday part of business. Does that make a difference?

The size of the bribe, $5 million, is small relative to the potential gain of $10 billion. Under these circumstances, is it acceptable to pay this bribe?

Is the fact that the competitor had been prepared to pay the bribe a good enough reason for you to agree to go ahead and pay the bribe?

The stock market has already reacted favorably to the signing of the MOU. Joe warns that if the bribe is not paid, the government will not sign the final contract and it is unlikely that ABC Ltd will get any other business in Energyland in the future. This could damage ABC Ltd's share price. Does this change the situation?

Option 1 suggested by the MD of Local Inc. effectively uses an intermediary to pay the bribe on behalf of the JV. Does that make a difference?

Option 2 appears to remove all links between the JV and the bribe. But there is a residual commitment to the MD of Local Inc. Local Inc. might well be chosen as the JV partner anyway, so does such a residual link matter?

The business principles of Local Inc. seem far removed from those of ABC Ltd. Is this the kind of company the ABC Ltd should be doing business with?

Joe Smith is one of your brightest young executives and the secondment to XYZ Co. was meant to expand his experience and prepare him for a more senior post in ABC Ltd. But he has signed an MOU knowing that it contained conditions which were against ABC Ltd's business principles. What should you do with him now?

The UK has been trying to improve political relations with Energyland and the Prime Minister will visit Energyland in two weeks. The PM phoned you before you left to wish you luck on your visit and to say that he was relying on you to use your business contacts with the president to help smooth UK/Energyland relationships prior to his visit. Does this political dimension make a difference to your actions?

DECISION

1 *You meet Joe for breakfast at 8 a.m. the following morning prior to your visit to the president. What have you decided to do?*

APPENDIX

Planning a Dissertation

MBA and other management degree programmes often require students to write short dissertations and project reports. This APPENDIX shows one way of planning the dissertation or report, from the first stages of deciding on a theme. It focuses on the management problems associated with planning a dissertation. It does not deal with technical questions – for example, how to negotiate access to informants, how to write a questionnaire, how to analyze qualitative and quantitative data.

Dissertation Planning Model

The model consists of questions asked on 12 levels.

Level 1.   What is your research FIELD, or general topic area?
           (For example, Chinese family companies.)
Level 2.   What is your research QUESTION? What are you trying to find out or to prove?
           (For example, how are non-family members employed by Chinese family companies?)
Level 3.   What is your dissertation TITLE?
           (For example, "The employment of non-family members in Chinese family companies: the case in Taiwan.")
Level 4.   What research DATA do you need in order to answer your research question?
           SECONDARY data (print and electronic):
           (a) What academic literature?
                • books;
                • academic journal articles;
                • academic conference reports.
           (b) What official reports?
                • government reports;
                • reports by international agencies.

    (c) What journalism?
- material on the web, etc.;
- newspaper and non-academic journal articles;
- television;
- film;
- transcriptions of television, film.

    (d) What other secondary data?
- company reports;
- advertising;
- trade publications;
- financial data;
- other.

    PRIMARY data:

    (e) What interview surveys?

    (f) What questionnaire surveys?

    (g) What observations?

    (h) What other primary data?

Level 5. Where will data be collected and analyzed?

Level 6. From whom will data be collected? In the case of primary data, who are your target informants?

Level 7. Who will collect the data?

Level 8. How will the data be analyzed? What qualitative and quantitative methodologies will be applied?

Level 9. When will the data be collected and analyzed?

Level 10. How will the dissertation be STRUCTURED? What chapters, sections, subsections do you need? How will they be titled?

Level 11. By when must you SUBMIT the completed dissertation?

Level 12. What is your TIMETABLE for writing the dissertation?

    (a) If you are using interview surveys, by when will you have completed the interviews?

    (b) If you are using an original questionnaire,
- by when will you have piloted it?
- by when will you have revised the questionnaire?
- by when will you run the final version of the questionnaire?

    (c) If you are using observations, by when will you have completed making these?

    (d) By when will you have collected all secondary and primary data?

    (e) By when will you have analyzed all secondary and primary data?

    (f) By when will you have completed a first draft?

    (g) By when will you have completed further drafts?

    (h) When do you need to consult with your supervisor?

How to Use the Model

When you have answered the question on Level 1, proceed to the question on Level 2; and so on.

Levels 1–3 focus attention on the research question to be tested. You start by deciding what general FIELD interests you, and then narrow it down so that it is sufficiently focused to research. The example is given of a very broad research field; "family companies", from which a wide range of research questions can be derived. Levels 2 and 3 may coincide, but not necessarily.

Only when a precise QUESTION and TITLE have been formulated can specific research priorities be decided. Answers at Level 4 make decisions about what DATA are needed to answer the research QUESTION. Answers at Levels 5–9 deal with the practicalities of collecting the DATA and analyzing it. Your QUESTION determines what DATA you need. Some QUESTIONS can be satisfactorily answered using SECONDARY DATA, collected and possibly analyzed by other persons. Secondary data are available in libraries, the media and the web, and a dissertation using these data can sometimes be planned and written at a distance from the events discussed. In general, all dissertations need to be grounded in secondary data; these show the reader how your work relates to and is built upon existing research in the FIELD. A dissertation based entirely on secondary data develops new interpretations of existing materials.

Your choice of FIELD and QUESTION may mean that you have to develop and analyze a body of original PRIMARY data – for example, when the secondary data are out of date, or deals only generally with an industry and is not specific to the country that interests you.

SECONDARY DATA sources are listed in the model before PRIMARY DATA sources because many dissertations use SECONDARY DATA in a Chapter 2 literature survey as a means of reviewing past studies in the FIELD and introducing the PRIMARY DATA, presented and analyzed in subsequent chapters.

Tools for developing primary data include those listed here in Level 4 – structured interviews, structured observations, and questionnaires. The time used in identifying a pool of informants who are prepared to take part in these activities has to be added to that spent in developing the research tools.

An original questionnaire usually has to be piloted. That is, the first draft of the questionnaire is tested on a small group of the informant pool that you hope to use when you conduct the revised and final draft. This piloting gives you feedback needed to

- eliminate questionnaire items that prove irrelevant to your QUESTION;
- eliminate items that are excessive to your research needs. (A short focused questionnaire is usually preferable to a long, repetitive questionnaire that takes a long time to answer.)
- revise items that are ambiguous;
- add new items that fill gaps in your research agenda.

Some new questionnaires benefit from being piloted more than once. Informants used in piloting should not be used again to complete the final version.

Answers at Levels 10–12 deal with the practicalities of STUCTURING the dissertation and TIMETABLING the DATA collection and writing-up phases. If you decide to pilot a new questionnaire to collect DATA, the time involved in this, and rewriting, has to be planned.

The Model is Recursive

The model is RECURSIVE, which means that you can move up levels as well as down. If you can't decide on an answer at one level, try returning to the level immediately before and reconsider your answer to that. If that doesn't help you solve the problem, go back up two levels. For example; if (at Level 2) you have problems deciding on a research QUESTION that interests you, check your FIELD at Level 1. You may decide that you would prefer to work in some other FIELD. If (at Level 3) you cannot formulate a precise TITLE, revise your QUESTION, and then, if necessary, check the FIELD again.

This process of revision can be crucial when deciding on the practical issues of collecting and analyzing DATA at Levels 4–9. If you cannot collect the DATA you need for a particular TITLE and QUESTION, you may need a new TITLE and ask a new QUESTION, or even rethink the FIELD.

For example, two London-based students planned to research patronage networks in Indonesia. Reliable data on patronage is difficult to find; the media seldom report it with sensitivity and most people are cautious of discussing their own experiences unless they fully trust the researcher. The first student found the resources of time and money to make the trip, and thanks to personal contacts prepared in advance was able to conduct useful face-to-face interviews. The second did not have these resources and at a distance could not create the confidence needed. Eventually he was forced to consider two options; either change his question and data sources and write on patronage from a text-based point of view, reviewing the existing literature; or, change to a new field. In fact, he chose the second route, and chose a new field and question asking how American multinational headquarters controlled the organizational cultures of their Indonesian subsidiaries. The written literature was more extensive, and the topic was less contentious. Using his contacts in American industry he contacted a range of American multinational managers on the internet, and conducted an internet survey, which generated some excellent data.

What Writing Style Suits You?

Dissertation planning and writing are creative activities and different people develop individual strategies. Some people prefer to complete all reading and researching before starting to write. At the opposite extreme, others prefer to write as soon as possible and to tailor data collection and analysis to the needs of their writing. Most students find solutions between these two extremes.

Some prefer to start by writing the first chapter, then write the second, and so on, developing the dissertation in strict sequential order. Others start at a midpoint, then move backwards and forwards, filling in different sections as their knowledge and understanding develop. Some try to complete all writing in one or two drafts whereas others continually draft and redraft.

The factors that influence how you write include the type of project, the topic, availability and type of data, time factors, and your psychological make-up. This last may be the most important. There is no one way to research and write an extended project, and different people may follow very different strategies to write about the same topic.

Be prepared for problems to arise – they undoubtedly will. How will you resolve them?

BIBLIOGRAPHY

Abdul-Gaber, A.H. 1996: Usage pattern and productivity impact of computer-mediated communication in a developing country: an exploratory study, *International Journal of Information Management*, **16** (1), 39–49.

Abu-Doleh, J. and Weir, D. 2007: Dimensions of performance appraisal systems in Jordanian private and public organizations. *International Journal of Human Resource Management*, **18.1**, 75–84.

Adedaji, A. 1995: The challenge of pluralism, democracy, governance and development. *The Courier*, March–April. Brussels: European Union, 93–5.

Adler, N.J., Campbell, N.C. and Laurent, A. 1989: In search of appropriate methodology: from outside the People's Republic of China looking in. *Journal of International Business Studies*, **Spring**, 61–74.

Allee, V. 2003. *The Future of Knowledge*. London: Butterworth-Heinemann.

Al-Rasheed, A. 2001: Features of traditional Arab management and organization in the Jordan business environment. *Journal of Transnational Management Development*, **6** (1–2), 27–53.

Al-Tamini, S. 2004: The Ties that Bind: The Development of a Saudi Family Business. School of Oriental and African Studies, University of London: unpublished MSc dissertation.

Anderson, Peter. 2000: Cues of culture: The basis of intercultural differences in nonverbal communication. In: Larry A. Samovar and E. Porter Richard, Editors, *Intercultural communications. A reader*, Wadsworth Publishing Co., Belmont, CA, 258–69.

Andrews, T.G. and Chompusri, N. 2001: Lessons in "cross-vergence": restructuring the Thai subsidiary corporation. *Journal of International Business Studies*, **32** (1), 77–93.

Andrews, T.G. and Chompusri, N. 2005: Temporal dynamics of crossvergence: institutionalizing MNC integration strategies in post-crisis ASEAN. *Asia Pacific Journal of Management*, **22**: 5–22.

Andrews, T.G., Chompusri, N. and Baldwin, B.J. 2003: *The Changing Face of Multinationals in Southeast Asia*. London: Routledge.

Andrews, T.G. and Mead, R. (eds). 2008: *Cross Cultural Management: Critical Perspectives in Business and Management*, vols **1–4**). London: Routledge.

Baba, S. 2004: Remodelling employment for competitive advantage: what will follow Japan's "lifetime employment"? *Asia Business Management*, **3**, 221–40.

Barber, B. 2001: 1995: *Jihad vs. McWorld*. New York: Ballantine Books.

Bargiela-Chiappini, F. and Nickerson, C. 2003: Intercultural business communication: a rich field of studies. *Journal of Intercultural Studies*, **24** (1), 3–15.

Bartlett, C.A. and Goshal, S. 1989, 1998: *Managing Across Borders: The Transnational Solution*. Boston, MA: Harvard Business School Press.

Baudrillard, J. 1994: 2006: *Sumulcra and Simulation.* ·······: University of Michigan.

Benson, J.K. 1977: Organizations: a dialectic view. *Administrative Science Quarterly,* **22,** 1–21.

Bhawuk, D. 2001. Evolution of culture assimilators: toward theory-based assimilators. *International Journal of Intercultural Relations,* **25** (2), 141–63.

Bhopal, M. and Hitchcock, M. 2001: The culture and context of the ASEAN business crisis. *Asia Pacific Business Review,* **8** (2), 1–19.

Birley, S. and Niktari, N. 1995: *The failure of owner-managed businesses: the diagnosis of accountants and accountants.* London: The Institute of Chartered Accountants.

Birkinshaw J., Braunerhjelm, P., Holm, U. and Terjesen, S. 2006: Why do some multinational corporations relocate their headquarters overseas? *Strategic Management Journal,* **27,** 681–700.

Bjerke, B. 2000: A typified, culture-based interpretation of management of SMEs in Southeast Asia. *Asia Pacific Journal of Management,* **17,** 103–32.

Blair, L. 2008: *Straight Talking.* ·······: Piatkus.

Blau, P.M. 1968: The hierarchy of authority in organizations. *American Journal of Sociology,* **73,** 453–67.

Blumen, J.L. 2002: The age of connective leadership. In Hesselbein, F. and Johnston, R. (eds), *On Leading Change.* San Francisco, CA: Jossey Bass, 89–101.

Boston Consulting Group, 1970: *The product portfolio.* Perspectives 66. Boston MA.

Bourantas, D. and Papalexandris, N. 1999: Personality traits and discriminating between employees in public- and in private-sector organizations. *International Journal of Human Resource Management* **10** (5), 858–69.

Boyacigiller, N.A., Kleinberg, M.J., Phillips, M.E. and Sackmann, S.A. 2003: Conceptualizing culture: elucidating the streams of research in cross-cultural management. In Punnett, B.J. and Shenkar, O. (eds), *Handbook for International Management Research.* Ann Arbor, MI: ·····, 99–167.

Bozionelos, N. and Wang, L. 2007: An investigation in the attitudes of Chinese workers towards individually based performance-related reward systems. *International Journal of Human Resource Management,* **18.**2, 284–302.

Braudel, F. 1984: *The Perspective of the World: vol. 3, Civilization and Capitalism.* London: Collins.

Brummelhuis, H.T. 1984: Abundance and avoidance: an interpretation of Thai individualism. In Brummelhuis H.T. and Kemp, J. (eds), *Strategies and Structures in Thai Society.* Antropologisch–Sociologisch Centrum, Universiteit van Amsterdam, 39–54.

Budhwar, P. and Mellahi, K. (eds) 2006: *Managing Human Resources in the Middle East.* London: Routledge.

Burns, P. 2001: *Entrepreneurship and Small Business.* London: Palgrave.

Bush, J.B. Jr and Frohman, A.L. 1991: Communication in a "network" organization. *Organizational Dynamics,* **Autumn,** 23–35.

Byron, K. 2008: Carrying too heavy a load? The communication and miscommunication of emotion by email. *Academy of Management Review,* **33** (2), 309–27.

Caligiuri, P., Phillips, J., Lazarova, M., Tarique, I. and Bu'rgi, P. 2001: The theory of met expectations applied to expatriate adjustment: the role of cross-cultural training. *International Journal of Human Resource Management,* **12** (3), 357–72.

Carter, M. 2001: *Anthony Blunt: His Lives.* London: Macmillan.

Cartwright, R. 2000: *Mastering the Business Environment.* London: Palgrave.

CHA Workplace Communications Consultancy. May 2007: *Talking in the Dark.* London.

Chakravarthy, B. and Lorange, P. 2007: *Profit or Growth: Why You Don't Have to Choose.* ·····: Wharton School Publishing.

Chan, A. and Lui, S. 2004: HRM in Hong Kong. In Budhwar, P., *Managing Human Resources in Asia-Pacific.* London: Routledge, 76.

Chen, C.C., Ford, C.M. and Farris, G.F. 1999: Do rewards benefit the organization? The effects of reward type and the perceptions of diverse R&D professionals. *IEEE Transactions on Engineering and Management,* **46** (1), 47–55.

Child, J. 1981: Culture, contingency and capitalism in the cross-national study of organizations. In

Cummings, L. and Straw, B. (eds), *Research in Organizational Behavior*. Stamford, CT: JAI Press.

Chow, I.H.-S. 1988: Work-related values of middle managers in the public and private sectors. *Proceedings of the 1988 Academy of International Business Southeast Asia Regional Conference, Bangkok*, A14–A25.

Coulter, M. 2008: *Strategic Management in Action*, 4th edn (Pearson International Edn). ·····: Pearson/Prentice Hall.

David, F.R. 1993: *Concepts of Strategic Management*. New York: Macmillan.

Davies, H. 1995: Interpreting guanxi: the role of personal connectedness in a high-context transitional economy. In Davies, H. (ed.), *China Business Context and Issues*. Hong Kong: Longman Asia.

Day, J.D., Mang, P.Y., Richter, A. and Roberts, J. 2002: Has pay for performance had its day? *McKinsey Quarterly*, 4, 46–56.

Delios, A. and Björkman, I. 2000: Expatriate staffing in foreign subsidiaries of Japanese multinational corporations in the PRC and the United States. *International Journal of Human Resource Management*, 1 (2), 278–93.

Dilling, O., Herburg, M., Winter, G. (eds). 2008: Introduction. In *Responsible Business*. Oxford and Portland, OR: Hart Publishing, 1–14.

Elsom, J. 2007: *Missing the Point*. Cambridge, UK: Lutterworth Press.

Eschbach, D.M., Parker, G.E. and Stoeberl, P.A. 2001: American repatriate employees' retrospective assessments of the effects of cross-cultural training on their adaptation to international assignments. *International Journal of Human Resource Management* 12 (2), 270–87.

Evanoff, R. 2006: Integration in intercultural ethics. *International Journal of Intercultural Relations*, 30 (4), 421–37.

Fang, T. 2006: From "onion" to "ocean": paradox and change in national cultures. *International Studies of Management and Organization*, 35 (4), 71–90.

Fedor, K.J. and Werther, W.B. Jr. 1996: The fourth dimension: creating culturally responsive international alliances. *Organizational Dynamics*, Autumn, 39–51.

Finlayson, I. 1993: *Tangier: City of the Dream*. ·····: Flamingo.

Flood, P., Dromgoole, T., Carroll, S. and Gorman, L. 2000: *Managing Strategy Implementation*. Oxford: Blackwell.

Fombrun, C.J. 1986: Structural dynamics within and between organizations. *Administrative Science Quarterly*, 31, 403–31.

Forster, N. 2000: The myth of the "international manager". *International Journal of Human Resource Management*, 11 (1), 126–42.

Forte, M., Hoffmen, J.J., Lamont, B.T. and Brockmann, E.N. 2000: Organizational form and environment: an analysis of between-form and within-form responses to environmental change. *Strategic Management Journal*, 21, 753–73.

Franklin, D. 2004: Changing the climate. *IEEE Manufacturing and Engineering*, April–May, 45–7.

Furuholt, B. and Orvik, T.U. 2006: Implementation of information technology in Africa: understanding and explaining the results of ten years of implementation in a Tanzanian organization. *Information Technology for Development*, 12 (1), 45–62.

Garz, H. and Gerdes, T. June 2007: Corporate Ageing. FAIRE conference: www.Frenchsif.org/Fr/documents/Faire2007/Corporate_Ageing/FAIRE0

Gavetti, G. and Rivkin, J.W. 2005: How strategists really think. *Harvard Business Review*, April, 54–63.

Geppert, M. and Williams, K. 2006: Global, national and local practices in multinational corporations: towards a socio-political framework. *International Journal of Human Resource Management*, 17 (1), 49–69.

Giacobbe-Miller, J.K., Miller, D.J., Zhang, W. and Victorov, V.I. 2003: Country and organizational-level adaptation to foreign workplace ideologies: a comparative study of distributive justice values in China, Russia and the United States. *Journal of International Business Studies*, 34 (4), 389–406.

Gooderham, P.N. and Nordhaug, O. (eds). 2004: *International Management*. Oxford: Blackwell.

Gowan, P. 1999: *The Global Gamble: Washington's Faustian Bid for World Dominance.* London: Verso.

Grant, R.M. 2002: *Contemporary Strategy Analysis: Concepts, Techniques, Applications*, 4th edn. Oxford: Blackwell.

Grey, J. 1990: *False Dawn: The Delusions of Global Capitalism.* London: Granta Books.

Gray, J. 2000: *Two Faces of Liberalism.* London: Polity Press.

Griffin, W. and Pustay, W. 1999: *International Business: A Managerial Perspective.* ⋯⋯: Addison-Wesley.

Griffith, T.L. 1996: Cross-cultural and cognitive issues in the implementation of new technology: focus on group support systems in Bulgaria. Working Paper, Washington University, St. Louis, MO.

Grosse, C.U. 2002: Managing communication within virtual intercultural teams. *Business Communication Quarterly*, **65** (4), 22–38.

Hagedoorn, J. 2006: Understanding the cross-level embeddedness of interfirm partnership formation. *Academy of Management Review*, **31** (3), 670–80.

Hall, E.T. 1976: *Beyond Culture.* ⋯⋯: Anchor Press/Doubleday.

Hall, E.T. 1983: *The Dance of Life.* Anchor Press/Doubleday.

Hall, E.T. and Whyte, W.F. 1961: Intercultural communication: a guide to men of action. *Human Organization*, **19** (1), 5–12.

Hamill, J. 1989: Expatriate policies in British multinationals. *Journal of General Management*, **14** (4), 18–33.

Hammer, M. and Champy, J. 1993: *Re-engineering the Corporation: A Manifesto for Business Revolution.* New York: Harper Business.

Hampden-Turner, C. and Trompenaars, F. 1997a: *The Seven Cultures of Capitalism.* New York: Doubleday.

Hampden-Turner, C. and Trompenaars, F. 1997b: *Mastering the Infinite Game: How East Asian Values are Transforming Business Practice.* ⋯⋯: Capstone.

Harris, J. 2007: Why home doesn't matter. *Prospect*, May.

Harvie, C. and Lee, B.-C. (eds). 2002: Editorial. In *The Role of S. M. Es in National Economies in East Asia.* Cheltenham, UK: Edward Elgar, 1–20.

Harzing, A.-W. 1999: *Managing the Multinationals – An International Study of Control Mechanisms.* Cheltenham, UK: Edward Elgar.

Harzing, A.-W. 2001: Who's in charge? An empirical study of executive staffing practices in foreign subsidiaries. *International Journal of Human Resource Management*, **40** (2), 139–58.

Harzing, A.-W. and Noorderhaven, N. 2006: Geographical distance and the role and management of subsidiaries: the case of subsidiaries down-under. *Asia Pacific Journal of Management*, **23**, 167–85.

Held, D., McGrew, A., Goldblatt, D., Perraton, J. 2000: *Global Transformations: Politics, Economics, and Culture.* London: Polity Press.

Hennigfeld, J., Pohl, M. and Tolhurst, N. (eds). 2007: *The ICCA Handbook on Corporate Social Responsibility.* New York: Wiley.

Henshall, K. 2005: *A History of Japan from Stonehenge to Superpower*, 2nd edn. London: Palgrave Macmillan.

Herzberg, F., Mausner, B. and Snyderman, B. 1959: *The Motivation to Work.* New York: Wiley.

Herzberg, F. 1968: One more time: how do you motivate employees? *Harvard Business Review*, **46**, 53–62.

Hesselbein, F. 2002: The key to cultural transformation. In Hesselbein, F. and Johnston, R. (eds), *On Leading Change.* San Francisco, CA: Jossey Bass, 89–101.

Hills, M. 2002: Kluckhohn and Strodtbeck's values orientation theory. In Lonner, W., Dinnel, D., Hayes, S. and Sattler, D. (eds), *Online Readings In Psychology and Culture*, Unit 6, Chapter 3. Center for Cross-Cultural Research, Western Washington University, Bellingham, Washington USA: http://www.wwu.edu/~culture.

Hofstede, G. 1980: *Culture's Consequences: International Differences in Work-related Values.* Beverly Hills, CA: Sage.

Hofstede, G. 1983: National cultures in four dimensions. *International Studies of Management and Organizations*, **13** (1–2), 46–74.

Hofstede, G. 1984: *Cultures Consequences: International Differences in Work-related Values*, abridged edn. Beverly Hills, CA: Sage.

Hofstede, G. 1985: The interaction between national and organizational value systems. *Journal of Management Studies*, 22 (4), 347–57.

Hofstede, G. 1991: *Cultures and Organizations: Software of the Mind*, 1st edn. ·····: McGraw-Hill.

Hofstede, G. 1997: *Cultures and Organizations: Software of the Mind*, 2nd edn. ·····: McGraw-Hill.

Hofstede, G. 2001: *Culture's Consequences*, 2nd edn. London: Sage.

Hofstede, G. and Bond, M. 1988: The Confucius connection: from cultural roots to economic growth. *Organizational Dynamics*, 16 (4), 5–21.

Holzhausen, A. 2000: Japanese employment practices in transition: promotion policy and compensation systems in the 1990s. *Social Science Japan Journal*, 3 (2), 221–35.

House, R., Hanges, P., Ruiz-Quintanilla, S., Dorfman, P., Javidan, M., Dickson, M. and Gupta, V. 1999: Cultural influences on leadership and organizations: project globe. In *Advances in Global Leadership*. Greenwich, CT: JAI Press, 171–233.

House, R., Hanges, P., Javidan, M., Dorfman, P. and Gupta, V. 2004: *iCulture, Leadership and Organizations: The GLOBE Study of 62 Societies*. Beverly Hills, CA: Sage.

Huang, T.-C. 1999: Who shall follow? Factors affecting the adoption of succession plans in Taiwan. *Long Range Planning*, 32 (6).

Ishizumi, K. 1990: *Acquiring Japanese Companies*. Blackwell.

Jackson, K. 2003: The emerging structure of trust in international HRM: case studies from the Japanese pharmaceuticals industry. Manuscript: kgj824@aol.com

Jackson, K. and Tomioka, M. 2004: *The Changing Face of Japanese Management*. London: Routledge.

Jaeger, A.M. 1983: The transfer of organizational culture overseas: an approach to control in the multinational corporation. *Journal of International Business Studies*, Fall, 91–114.

Johnson, P. 2007: *The Economics of Small Firms: An Introduction*. London: Routledge.

Jolly, D. 2002: Sharing knowledge and decision power in Sino-foreign joint ventures. *Asia Pacific Business Review*, 9 (2), 81–100.

Judt, T. 2008: *Reappraisals*. London: William Heinemann.

Kabasakal, H., Asugman, G. and Develioğlu, K. 2006: The role of employee preferences and organizational culture in explaining E-commerce orientations. *International Journal of Human Resource Management*, 17 (3), 464–83.

Kambayashi, N. 2003: *Cultural Influences on IT Use*. Houndmills, UK: Palgrave-Macmillan.

Kay, D. and Hinds, R. 2002: *A Practical Guide to Mentoring*. Oxford: Howtobooks.

Kaynak, E. 1986: *International Business in the Middle East*. Berlin: De Gruyter.

Kelly, M.J., Schaan, J.L. and Joncas, H. 2002: Managing alliance relationships: key challenges in the early stages of collaboration. *R&D Management*, 32 (1), 11–23.

Khiliji, S.E. 2002: Modes of convergence and divergence: an integrative view of multinational practices in Pakistan. *International Journal of Human Resource Management*, 13 (2).

Kim, K., Park, J.-H. and Prescott, J.E. 2003: The global integration of business functions: a study of multinational businesses in integrated global industries. *Journal of International Business Studies*, 34 (4), 327–344.

Klingel, F. 2002: Comparison of Asian and German Family Firms on the Basis of Corporate Governance and Corporate Finance. Unpublished MSc dissertation, School of Oriental and African Studies, University of London.

Kluckhohn, F.R. and Strodtbeck, F.L. 1961: *Variations in Value Orientations*. New York: Peterson.

Knight, R. and Pretty, D. 2003: Risks that matter. In Jolly, A. (ed.), *Managing Business Risk*. London: Kogan Page, 6–16.

Kopp, R. 2001: Why it is so difficult to tell what a Japanese person is thinking? *Japan Close-Up*, **November**.

Kostova, T. 1999: Transnational transfer of strategic organizational practices: a contextual perspective. *Academy of Management Review*, 24 (2), 306–24.

Kostova, T. and Roth, K. 2002: Adoption of an organizational practice by subsidiaries of multinational corporations: institutional and relational effects. *Academy of Management Journal*, **45** (1), 215–33.

Kovach, K.A. 1987: What motivates employees? Workers and supervisors give different answers. *Business Horizons*, **September–October**, 58–65.

Kumar, S. and Seth, A. 1998: The design of coordination and control mechanisms for managing joint venture–parent relationships. *Strategic Management Journal*, **19**, 579–99.

Kwok, C.C.Y. and Tadesse, S. 2006: National culture and financial systems. *Journal of International Business Studies*, **37**, 227–47.

Lall, S. and Ghosh, S. 2002: Learning by dining: informal networks and productivity in Mexican industry. World Bank, Washington, DC, 20433.

Laurent, A. 1981: Matrix organizations and Latin cultures. *International Studies of Management and Organization*, **11**, 101–14.

Laurent, A. 1983: The cultural diversity of Western conceptions of management. *International Studies of Management and Organization*, **13** (1–2), 75–96.

Laurent, A. 1986: The cross-cultural puzzle of international human resource management. *HR Management*, **25**, 91–102.

Leach, P. 2007: *Family Businesses: The Essentials*. London: Profile Books.

Leamer, E.E. and Storper, M. 2001: The economic geography of the internet age. *Journal of International Business Studies*, **32** (4), 641–65.

Lee, C. 2003: *Cowboys and Dragons: Shattering Cultural Myths to Advance Chinese–American Business*. Chicago, OH: Dearborn Trade Publishing.

Legewie, J. and Meyer-Ohle, H. 2000: Economic crisis and transformation in southeast Asia: the role of multinational companies. In Legewie, J. and Meyer-Ohle, H. (eds). 2000: *Corporate Strategies for Southeast Asia after the Crisis*. London: Palgrave.

Lenartowicz, T. and Roth, K. 1999: A framework for culture assessment. *Journal of International Business Studies*, **30** (4), 781–99.

Leong, S. and Tan, C. 1993: Managing across borders: an empirical test of the Bartlett and Ghoshal (1989) organizational typology. *Journal of International Business Studies*, **24** (3), 449–64.

Lessassy, L. and Jolibert, A. 2007: Internationalization of retail strategies. *Journal of Euromarketing*, **16** (3).

Lewis, P. 2007: *Growing Apart: Oil, Politics and Economic Change in Indonesia and Nigeria*. Ann Arbor, MI: University of Michigan Press.

Liang, Y. 2007: *Comparisons of Industrial Family Businesses in Canton and Shanghai, China*. FDPS Independent Study Project, School of Oriental and African Studies, University of London.

Lindgren, M. and Bandhold, H. 2003: *Scenario Planning: The Link between Future and Strategy*. New York: Palgrave Macmillan.

Littrell, R. 2002: Desirable leadership behaviours of multi-cultural managers in China. *Journal of Management Development*, **21** (1), 5–74.

Lowe, S. 2002: The cultural shadows of cross cultural research: images of culture. *Culture and Organization*, **8** (1), 21–34.

Luo, Y. and Shenkar, O. 2006: The multinational corporation as a multilingual community: language and organization in a global context. *Journal of International Business Studies*, **37**, 321–39.

Ma, R. 1996: Computer-mediated conversations as a new dimension of intercultural communication between East Asian and North American college students. In S. C. Herring (Ed.), *Computer-mediated communication: Linguistic, social and cross-cultural perspectives*, 173–185. Amsterdam/Philadelphia: John Benjamins Company.

Madhok, A. 2005: 1995: Revisiting multinational firms' tolerance for joint ventures: a trust based approach. *Journal of International Business Studies*, **26** (1), 117–37.

Malik, M. 2004: The role of the private sector. In Wilson, R. (ed.), *Economic Development in Saudi Arabia*. London: Routledge Curzon.

Malone, T.W. 1997: Is empowerment just a fad? Control, decision making and IT. *Sloan Management Review*, **Winter**, 23–35.

Manolopoulos, S. 2006: What motivates R&D professionals? Evidence from decentralized laboratories in Greece. *International Journal of Human Resource Management*, **17** (4), 616–47.

Martinsons, M.G. and Westwood, R.I. 1997: Management information systems in the Chinese business culture: an explanatory theory. *Information and Management*, **32**, 215–28.

Maslow, A.H. 1954: *Motivation and Personality*. New York: Harper and Bros.

McClelland, D.C. 1976: *The Achieving Society*. New York: Irvington.

McGaughey, S.L. and de Cieri, H. 1999: Reassessment of convergence and divergence dynamics: implications for international HRM. *International Journal of Human Resource Management*, **10** (2), 235–50.

McSweeney, B. 2002: Hofstede's model of national cultural differences and their consequences: a triumph of faith – a failure of analysis. *Human Relations*, **55** (1), 89–118.

Mead, R. and Jones, C.J. 2000: Cross-Cultural Communication: Style and Task. In (eds) Gannon, M and Newman, K. 2000. *Handbook of Cross-Cultural Management*. Georgetown University Press.

Mead, R., Jones, C.J. and Chansarkar, B. 1997: The management elite in Thailand: their long- and short-term career aspirations. *International Journal of Management*, **14**.

Megginson, L., Byrd, J. and Megginson, W. 2003: *Small Business: An Entrepreneur's Guidebook*. New York: McGraw-Hill Higher Education.

Mellahi, K., Frynas, J. and Finlay, P. 2005: *Global Strategic Management*. Oxford: Oxford University Press.

Mennecke, B.E., Valacich, J.S. and Wheeler, B.C. 2000: The effects of media and task on user performance: a test of the task–media fit hypothesis. *Group Decision and Negotiation*, **9** (6), 507–29.

Michaud, C. and Thoenig, J.-C. 2003: *Making Strategy and Organization Compatible*. London: Palgrave.

Ministry of Economic Affairs, Taiwan. 2003: *Small and Medium Enterprises: Standard Definitions*. Ministry of Economic Affairs, Taipei, Taiwan.

Mintzberg, H. 1975. The manager's job: folklore and fact. *Harvard Business Review*, July–August, 4–16.

Mintzberg, H. 1994: *The Rise and Fall of Strategic Planning*. ⋯⋯: Prentice-Hall.

Mittelman, J. 2000: *The Globalization Syndrome: Transformation and Resistance*. ⋯⋯, NJ: Princeton University Press.

Morgan, G., Kelly, B., Sharpe, D. and Whitley, R. 2003: Global managers and Japanese multinationals: internationalization and management in Japanese financial institutions. *International Journal of Human Resource Management*, **14** (3), 389–407.

Neghandi, A.R. 1979: Convergence in organizational practices: an empirical study of industrial enterprises in developing countries. In Lammers, C.J. and Hickson, D.J. (eds), *Organizations Alike and Unlike: International and Institutional Studies of the Sociology of Organizations*. London: Routledge and Kegan Paul, 323–45.

Newman, K.L. and Nollen, S.D. 1996: Culture and congruence: the fit between management practices and national culture. *Journal of International Business Studies*, **27** (4), 753–79.

O'Connell, J. 1998: International management. In Cooper, G.L. and Argyris, C. (eds), *The Concise Blackwell Encyclopedia of Management*. Oxford: Blackwell.

Onedo, A.E.O. 1991: The motivation and need satisfaction of Papua New Guinea managers. *Asia Pacific Journal of Management*, **8** (1), 121–9.

Owens, D.A., Neale, M.A. and Sutton, R.I. 2001: Technologies of status management: status dynamics in e-mail communications. In *Research on Managing Groups and Teams*, **3**. Stamford, CT: JAI Press, 203–230.

Parkhe, A., Wasserman, S. and Ralston, D. 2006: New frontiers in network theory development. *Academy of Management Review*, **31** (3), 560–68.

Pavida, Pananond. 2001: The making of Thai multinationals: A comparative study of Thailand's CP and Siam Cement groups, *Journal of Asian Business*, **17** (3), 41–70.

Petersen, M. 2004: Culture, leadership and organizations: the GLOBE study of 62 societies. Book review. *Administrative Science Quarterly*, **49** (4), 641–7.

Pettinger, R. 2001: *Mastering Management Skills*. London: Palgrave.

Raelin, I. 2006: Finding meaning in the organization. *MIT Sloan Management Review*, **Spring**, 64–68.

Ralston, D.A. 2008: The crossvergence perspective: reflections and projections. *Journal of International Business Studies*, **39** (1), 27–40.

Ralston, D.A., Holt, D.H., Terpstra, R.H. and Kai-Cheng, Y. 1997: The impact of national culture and economic ideology on managerial works: a study of the United States, Russia, Japan and China. *Journal of International Business Studies*, **28** (1), 177–207.

Ralston, D.A., Gustafson, D.J., Cheung, F.M. and Terpstra, R.H. 1993: Differences in managerial values: a study of US, Hong Kong and PRC managers. *Journal of International Business Studies*, **24** (2), 249–75.

Raman, K.S. and Watson, R.T. 1994. National culture, IS and organizational implications. In Deans, P.C. and Karwan, K.R. (eds), *Global Information Systems and Technology: Focus on the Organization and Its Functional Areas*. Harrisburg, PA: Idea Group.

Ravasi, D. and Schultz, M. 2006: Responding to organizational identity threats: exploring the role of organizational culture. *Academy of Management Journal*, **49** (3), 433–58.

Robertson, C.J., Al-Habib, M., Al-Khatib, J.A. and Lanoue, D. 2001: Beliefs about work in the Middle East and the convergence vs. divergence of values. *Journal of World Business*, **36** (3), 223–44.

Robson, J. 2002: Applying the Model of Scenario Planning: The Case of China. Unpublished MSc dissertation, School of Oriental and African Studies, University of London.

Rosenzweig, P.M. and Singh, J.V. 1991: Organizational environments and the multinational enterprise. *Academy of Management Review*, **16** (2), 340–62.

Russo, W.K. 2000: *Finding the Middle Ground: Insights and Applications of the Value Orientations Method*, Yarmouth, ME: Intercultural Press.

Rutten, M. 2000. Commercialism and productive forms of business behaviour: rural entrepreneurs in India, Malaysia, and Indonesia. *Journal of Asian Management*, **16** (3), 1–25.

Samovar, L.A. and Porter, R.E. 1995: *Communication Between Cultures*. ·····: Wadsworth.

Saxton, K. 2004: Comparing Views in Strategy: Exploring Japanese and Western Minds. Unpublished MSc dissertation, School of Oriental and African Studies, University of London.

Scarborough, J. 1998: Comparing Chinese and Western cultural roots: why "east is east and …". *Business Horizons*, **November–December**, 15–24.

Schein, E.H. 1981: Does Japanese management style have a message for American managers? *Sloan Management Review*, **Fall**, 55–68.

Schneider, S.C. and Barsoux, J.-L. 1997: *Managing Across Cultures*, Prentice Hall.

Schwartz, S. 1994: Are there universal aspects of the structure and contents of human values? *Journal of Social Issues*, **50** (4), 19–45.

Schwartz, S. 1999: A theory of cultural values and some implications for work. *Applied Psychology: An International Review*, **48** (1), 23–47.

Schwartz, S. and Sagiv, L. 1995: Identifying culture-specifics in the content and structure of values. *Journal of Cross-Cultural Psychology*, **26** (1), 92–116.

Shane, S. 1993: The effect of cultural differences in perceptions of transaction costs on national differences in preferences for international joint ventures. *International Journal of Human Resource Management*, **10** (1), 58–69.

Shenkar, O. 2001: Cultural Distance Revisited: Towards a More Rigorous Conceptualization and Measurement of Cultural Differences. *Journal of International Business Studies*, **32**: 519–35.

Shenkar, O. and Zeira, Y. 1987: Human resources management in international joint ventures: directions for research. *Academy of Management Review*, **12** (3), 546–57.

Sivakumar, K. and Nakata, C. 2001: The stampede towards Hofstede's framework: avoiding the sample design pit in cross-cultural research. *Journal of International Business Studies*, **32** (3), 555–74.

Small Firms Statistics Unit. August 2000: *Small and Medium-sized Enterprise Statistics for the UK, 1999*. London: Department of Trade and Industry.

Smith, P.B. 2002: *Culture's Consequences*: something old and something new [review article and response to McSweeney, 2002]. *Human Relations*, **55** (1). 119–35.

Sproull, L. and Kiesler, S. 1986: Reducing social context cues: electronic mail in organizational communication. *Management Science*, **32** (11), 1492–512.

Stern, J. 2003: The protean enemy. *Foreign Affairs*, **82** (4), 27–40.

Stewart, J.M. 1995: Empowering multinational subsidiaries. *Long Range Planning*, **28** (4), 63–73.

Sugarman, B. 2001: A learning-based approach to organizational change: some results and guidelines. *Organizational Dynamics*, **30** (1), 62–76.

Svejenova, S. 2006. How much does trust really matter? Some reflections on the significance and implications of Madhok's trust-based approach. *Journal of International Business Studies*, **37**, 12–20.

Taleb, N. 2007. *The Black Swan: The Impact of the Highly Improbable*. New York: Allen Lane.

Taylor, S., Beechler, S. and Napier, N. 1996: Towards an integrative model of strategic international human resource management. *Academy of Management Review*, **21** (4), 959–85.

Tharenou, P. and Harvey, M. 2006: Examining the overseas staffing options utilized by Australian headquartered multinational corporations. *International Journal of Human Resource Management*, **17** (6), 1095–114.

Torrington, D., Hall, L. and Taylor, S. 2004: *Human Resource Management*. FT/Prentice-Hall.

Triandis, H., Bontempo, R., Villareal, M., Asai, M. and Lucca, N. 1988: Individualism and collectivism: cross-cultural perspectives on self-ingroup relationships. *Journal of Personality and Social Psychology*, **54** (2), 323–38.

Trompenaars, F. 1993: *Riding the Waves of Culture*. London: Nicholas Brealey.

Trompenaars, F. and Hampden-Turner, C. 1997: *Riding the Waves of Culture*, 2nd edn. McGraw-Hill.

Tung, R.L. 1987: Expatriate assignments: enhancing success and minimizing failure. *Academy of Management Executive*, **1** (2), 117–26.

Vohs, K.D., Mead, N.L. and Goode, M.R. 2006: The psychological consequences of money. *Science*, **314**, 1154–6.

Wang, S.-Y. 1998: Recruiting to the Chinese Family Company. Unpublished MA dissertation, School of Oriental and African Studies, University of London.

Wang, Y.C. 2004. Managing Start-up Companies in Taiwan. How Far the Opportunities and Problems Correspond to those Common in the United Kingdom. Unpublished MBA dissertation, Oxford-Brookes University.

Watson, F., Corry, S. and Pearce, C. 2000: *Disinherited: Indians in Brazil*. Survival International.

Wybrew-Bond, I. and Stern, J. 2002: *Natural Gas in Asia: The Challenges of Growth in China, India, Japan and Korea*. Oxford: Oxford University Press.

Yoshimori, M. 1995: Whose company is it? The concept of the corporation in Japan and the West. *Long Range Planning*, **28** (4), 33–4.

Zaheer, S. and Zaheer, A. 2006: Trust across borders. *Journal of International Business Studies*, **37**, 21–9.

INDEX